Taking STOCK

Make money in microstock creating photos that sell

Rob Sylvan

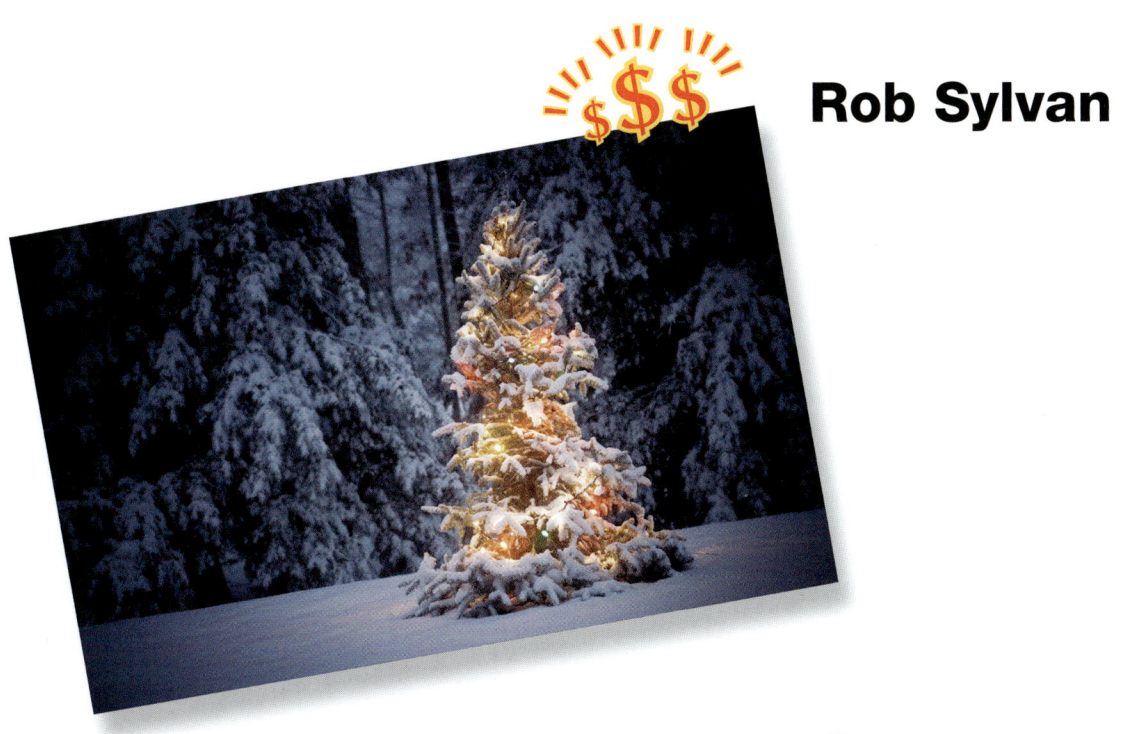

Peachpit Press

Taking Stock: Make money in microstock creating photos that sell
Rob Sylvan

Peachpit Press
1249 Eighth Street
Berkeley, CA 94710
510/524-2178
510/524-2221 (fax)

Find us on the Web at: www.peachpit.com
To report errors, please send a note to errata@peachpit.com

Peachpit Press is a division of Pearson Education.

Copyright © 2011 by Rob Sylvan

Project Editor: Nikki Echler McDonald
Production Editor: Becky Winter
Development and Copy Editor: Cathy Fishel Lane
Technical Editor: Ethan Myerson
Proofreader: Liz Welch
Compositor: Danielle Foster
Indexer: FireCrystal Communications
Cover and interior design: Mimi Heft
Cover production: Andreas deDanaan

Notice of Rights
All rights reserved. No part of this book may be reproduced or transmitted in any form by any means, electronic, mechanical, photocopying, recording, or otherwise, without the prior written permission of the publisher. For information on getting permission for reprints and excerpts, contact permissions@peachpit.com.

Notice of Liability
The information in this book is distributed on an "As Is" basis without warranty. While every precaution has been taken in the preparation of the book, neither the author nor Peachpit shall have any liability to any person or entity with respect to any loss or damage caused or alleged to be caused directly or indirectly by the instructions contained in this book or by the computer software and hardware products described in it.

Trademarks
Many of the designations used by manufacturers and sellers to distinguish their products are claimed as trademarks. Where those designations appear in this book, and Peachpit was aware of a trademark claim, the designations appear as requested by the owner of the trademark. All other product names and services identified throughout this book are used in editorial fashion only and for the benefit of such companies with no intention of infringement of the trademark. No such use, or the use of any trade name, is intended to convey endorsement or other affiliation with this book.

ISBN 13: 978-0-321-71307-0
ISBN 10: 0-321-71307-9

9 8 7 6 5 4 3 2 1

Printed and bound in the United States of America

Dedication

For my Mom and Dad. I love you.

Acknowledgments

This book would not exist if it weren't for the help, support, opportunities, and encouragement from so many people over the last eight years. It is my great pleasure to be able to thank so many of them in such a public way.

My deepest thanks go to Nikki McDonald, who provided the original spark of an idea for this book, somehow nudged all the stars into alignment to make it come to pass, and provided fantastic feedback and encouragement along the way. You rock! I owe a special debt of gratitude to the awesome team of folks who were down in the trenches with me every step of the way; Cathy Lane, my development editor, who kept me on track, asked all the right questions, made sure I wrote in complete sentences, and remained as steady as a rock throughout; Ethan Myerson, my technical editor, who watched my back and kept me honest; and Becky Winter, Mimi Heft, and Danielle Foster, who made the book look so awesome on the inside and out. Thank you all so much!

Thanks to everyone at Peachpit, but especially Ted Waitt, Scott Cowlin, Sara Jane Todd, and Nancy Aldrich-Ruenzel for believing in this book and in me.

My heartfelt thanks go to all my friends at iStockphoto for all that you have taught me, and all the laughs and memories we've shared over the years. I want to specifically thank Bruce Livingstone for getting this party started, and Kelly Thompson for keeping it going strong. Special thanks goes to Lobo, Andrew Wedderburn, Donald Gruener, Michael Zwahlen, Ethan Myerson, and Joy Griffith for picking up my slack every time I was up against a deadline. A deep bow of respect must to JJRD, and all the members of the iStockphoto content team, whose passion for kick-ass imagery knows no bounds. I am eternally grateful to all of my fellow contributors who willingly shared their hard-earned tips and tricks that have enriched this book beyond measure. I wish I could have packed more of you in! I also want to give a shout out to everyone in the forums, who really are the lifeblood of this place as far as I am concerned. Cheers to you all!

In addition, I'd like to thank Scott and Kalebra Kelby, Jeff Kelby, Jim Workman, Jean Kendra, Dave Moser, Larry Becker, Pete Bauer, Mike Mackenzie, Julie Stephenson, Jeanne Rubbo, and all the staff at the National Association of Photoshop Professionals for creating and nurturing an organization that is such a vital resource to so many, and that has given me so much.

My deep gratitude goes to Crackskull's Coffee & Books for keeping me well caffeinated; otherwise, this book would have been six chapters instead of 12.

I am grateful most of all for my wife, Paloma, and my son, Quinn, for providing all the love, encouragement, and patience this project required. We did it!

Contents

Foreword viii

CHAPTER 1   Is This Book for You? 2
- How I Got Started 4
- *Boy Looking at Math Problem* 7
- The $13,000 Christmas Tree 8
- What's in It for You? 10
- Quality vs. Quantity 11
- *Man Resting in the Alps* 12

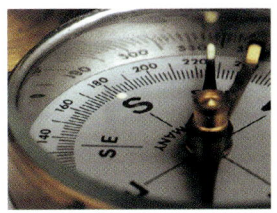

CHAPTER 2   What Is Stock Photography? 14
- Who Uses Stock? 14
- When Is a Photo a Stock Photo? 16
- Understanding the Licensing Models 17
- *Better Be Prompt* 19
- The Ways That Money Changes Hands 21
- *Gentle Surf* 22
- The History of Microstock 23

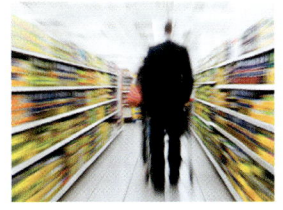

CHAPTER 3   Getting into a Stock Frame of Mind 26
- Knowing Your Customers 26
- *New Development* 33
- *Searching* 35
- Ingredients of a Stock Photo 36
- Assignment 41

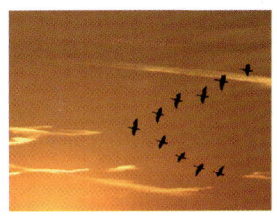

CHAPTER 4   Of Rights and Wrongs 42
- Reading the Fine Print 44
- The Role of the Model Release 47
- A Healthy Respect for Property 49
- *Mr. Muscle, Looking for Date* 51
- Being Inspired by Others (But Not Too Much) 52
- *Real Estate* 54
- Assignment 55

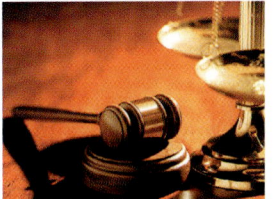

CHAPTER 5 — Tools of the Trade 56
Gear Crazy 56
Camera Choices 59
Busy Warehouse 61
Raw vs. JPEG 62
Key Camera Settings 64
Chef 66
Beyond the Camera 67

CHAPTER 6 — Shooting Tips from the Pros 70
Nancy Louie 72
The Importance of Good Exposure 74
Joshua Blake 78
Sean Locke 80
Top Tips for Your Next Photo Shoot 82
Katja Govorushchenko 84
Roberto A. Sanchez 86
Kelly Cline 90
Anna Bryukhanova 92

CHAPTER 7 — Setting Up Your Digital Darkroom 96
Hardware Choices 96
Ocean Fury 102
Software Choices 104
Hardy Waterlily 105
Choosing a Color Space 106
Assignment 111

CHAPTER 8 — Digital Editing Basics 113
Focus on Quality 113
Setting Defaults and Creating Presets 116
Two Generations 117
Adjusting White Balance 121
Making Exposure Adjustments 126
Sharpening for Stock 130
Young People in a Movie Theater 131
Dealing with Noise 135
Assignment 138

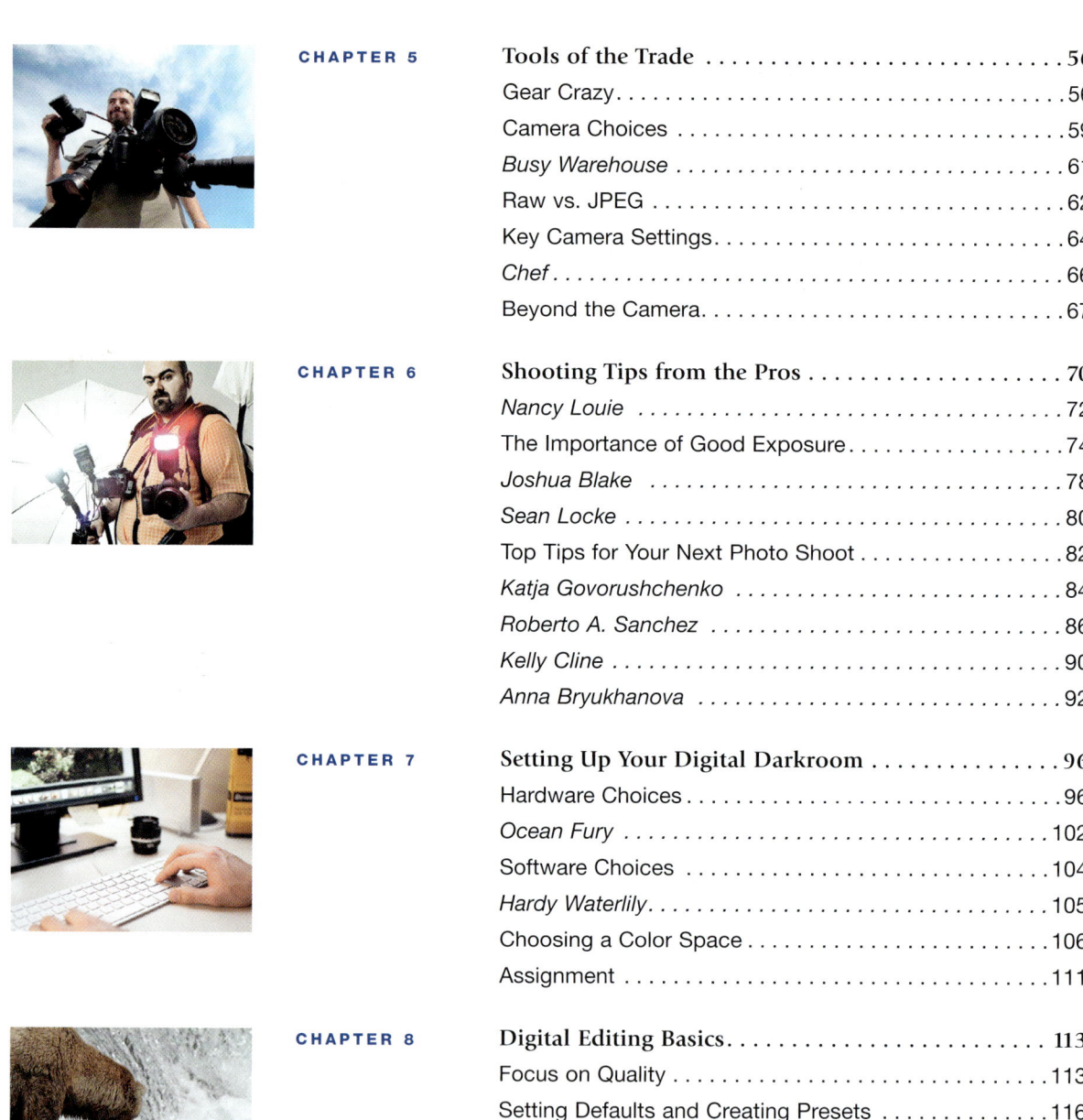

CHAPTER 9	**Avoiding Rejection** 140	
	Digital House Cleaning 140	
	Healthy Eating 149	
	Avoid Overprocessing 157	
	Wintery Decorations 159	
	Assignment 162	
CHAPTER 10	**Seeing Like an Inspector** 165	
	Being Your Worst Critic 166	
	One Minute to Midnight. 169	
	Developing an Inspection Workflow 170	
	Dealing with Rejection. 173	
	Group of Kids Running with Balloons 176	
	Assignment 177	
CHAPTER 11	**Putting It All Together** 179	
	First Things First 180	
	Container Terminal, Harbor 182	
	Importing into Lightroom. 183	
	Wheat from the Chaff: Reviewing 189	
	The Wonderful World of Metadata. 193	
	Sticky Situation 202	
CHAPTER 12	**Moving Out into the World**. 205	
	Save Your Final Versions. 205	
	Establish a Name for Yourself 210	
	Protection 212	
	Find Your Photos in Use 213	
	Move to the Next Level 215	
	Planning a Trip. 217	
	Parting Words 218	
	Afterword 220	
	Index. 222	

Foreword

I met Rob Sylvan at Photoshop World in 2008. Until then, I'd only known him through the forums on iStockphoto as the well-known admin sylvanworks. I was surprised to find out that he was not only an iStock photographer, but also a fellow Navy veteran (we squids have to stick together). All joking aside, he is, without a doubt, the best person I know of to write this book, and if you're itching to get into the world of microstock, you will not be disappointed.

I'm just a small piece of the pie, but I somehow managed to make my way up the microstock ladder, when all I started with was a camera and a passion for photography. You might just find that you're not all that different from me. We all have to start somewhere and I, like many other microstock contributors, started off as a noob with a camera. It was my determination and persistence that kept me going and got me where I am today.

When I was in high school I dreamed of being a professional photographer. Photography was my passion; I was good at it, and never wanted to stop. But for some reason I told myself that the industry was too competitive, so I pushed that dream aside, and settled on photography just being a hobby.

After high school I joined the U.S. Navy and worked as a linguist for more than eight years, but I never forgot about my passion. In 2005, I got my first digital SLR, a Nikon D2H, and fumbled around with it until I grasped the concept of raw files, and furthered my very minimal (at the time) understanding of digital editing.

About a year later I was having fun, but I wanted more. I wanted to be challenged photographically. I looked into taking local photography classes, but everything I found wasn't at the skill level I was hoping for. One day while reading a photography magazine, I came across an article on microstock and thought to myself, "I can do this!" I knew that people made money from it, but I was only hoping to pay for my expensive hobby.

I started my entry into microstock by signing up for about five different agencies. After being with them all for a few months, one site in particular was on my radar more than the others: iStockphoto. I was making more money there than at the other sites (around $80 in the first five months), and I also started to interact with its community in the forums. After learning about the company's exclusivity program, I decided that it was exactly what I wanted to do, so I pulled my images off the other sites, waited until I made "bronze" (the canister level equaling 500 downloads) and got my shiny crown icon, which indicated that the only website I licensed royalty-free images through was iStockphoto.

That's when I took off, photographically speaking, that is. I was out finding models, taking photos of families, and photographing as many things as I could get my hands on. I read through the forums to learn more about artifacting, chromatic aberration, "overprocessing," and made a conscious effort to learn from my rejections…and I did! Not long after that, I separated from the military, and in just three years time my portfolio had grown to having more than 5,000 files, and I now do this as my full-time job.

Now, my success wasn't overnight. It took a lot of problem solving, research, practice, and self-discipline to get where I am today. I jumped in feet-first and knew this was what I wanted. Pretty much everyone I know who has achieved (at least) this level of success in microstock has done it on his or her own—from figuring out how to process images so they don't get rejected to learning what types of photographs sell. I'm sure that you already realize that microstock isn't a "get rich quick" industry. It can take time to build your portfolio, find your niche, and start to create photos that really sell.

The great thing is that if you are reading this book, then you're already one step ahead and will soon be taking huge leaps in the right direction. I can only imagine how my journey would have been affected if I had had the information in this book when I first started. This book sheds light on the foundations and many other aspects of microstock photography, and should answer most (if not all) of those questions you know you want to ask.

Now, not everyone will make it "big" in microstock. Some of us have somehow pushed our way to the top of the list and are blessed to be able to do this as our job. I can even contribute the success in other areas of my career to being involved with microstock, and I'm often amazed at how far I've come. (Heck, Rob asked me to write the foreword for his book…I must be doing something right!)

One last thing to add, and this is an important one. If you are reading this book, it's not because you're passionate about microstock; it's because you are passionate about photography. Never forget that! As much as I enjoy making a living doing what I love, I'm always reminding myself that yes, it's work, but it's also fun. And it's not just the photography that makes it so great, but the people I've met along the way. My life has drastically changed (for the better) because of the people I've gotten to know ever since signing on to this new life of being a stock photographer, and all I ever expected to do was learn more about photography.

Nicole S. Young, full-time microstock photographer

1
Is This Book for You?

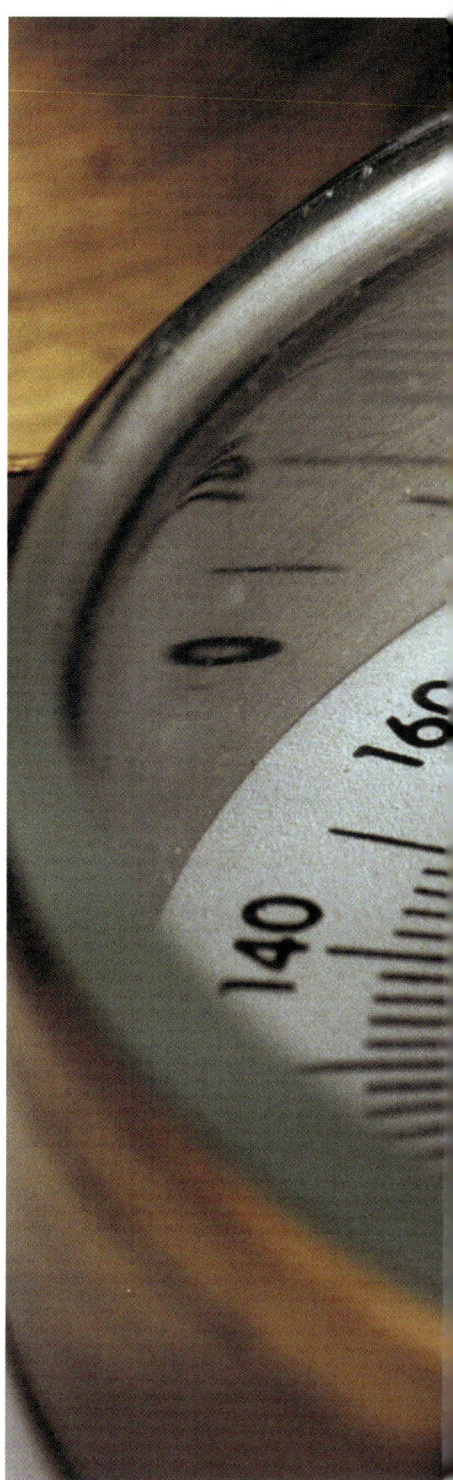

This is a critical question to answer right off the bat. I'd like nothing more than for you to discover that this is the exact book you've been looking for, and it sets you off down the road to creative freedom and financial prosperity. But let's be real, what are the odds? Seriously, I don't mean to knock my own book, but you should have realistic expectations before you go much further.

What this book represents is the sum total of what I have learned over the last eight years from my involvement in what has become known, for better or worse, as *microstock*. I have been involved with this crowdsourced industry from nearly the start as an image consumer, image creator, and industry insider. I have also been deeply involved in the community of artists that has helped shape the landscape that exists today. My story is their story too, and many of them have been generous in their contributions to making this book more valuable to you. But I am getting ahead of myself.

Back to the question at hand, is this book for you? Well, I'll assume since you've picked it up and have read this far that we have a few things in common. I'm willing to bet you love creating images. You are your family's staff photographer. You give books, framed prints, and cards with your photos on them to friends and family. You get asked to photograph weddings. You might already be earning all or part of your living from your photography, but you could just as easily be a teacher or a pilot, a nurse or a graphic designer, a chef or a student. No matter how it is that you earn your keep, you deliberately (and joyfully, I might add) carve time out of your busy life to stand behind a lightproof box and press a small silver button in the hope that you just captured in pixels what you feel in your mind's eye. You are, in its most core definition, a photographer.

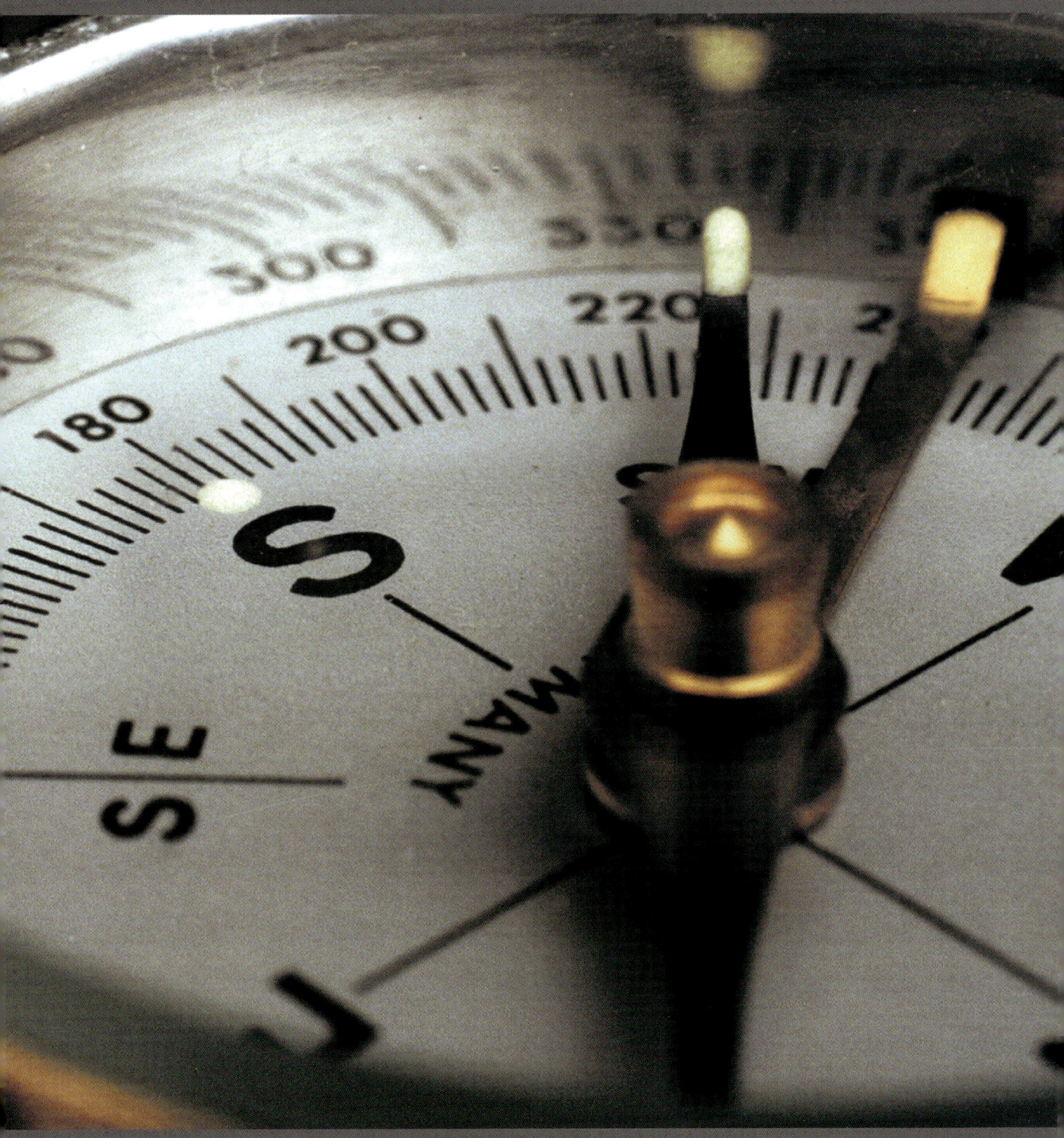

Figure 1.1 Compass, direction.
© Bruce Livingstone (istockphoto.com/bitter)

If you nodded your head at any time during that last paragraph, then chances are good there is something in this book for you. I won't promise that you will make a fortune through licensing your photos as royalty-free stock. I do promise that there is a world of opportunity that exists right now, where you can get feedback on your photography in a way you never experienced; can meet and interact and learn from people walking the same path all over the world; and have the potential to earn a residual stream of income that I have seen range from "mad" money to six figures.

Can you do all of that without this book? Yes, go for it! Tens of thousands of people already have. What this book offers is simply a head start and the wisdom of the cumulative experience of those who have gone before you, all packaged neatly in the pages you are holding right now.

How I Got Started

While I've always had an interest in photography, it really wasn't until digital came along that I fell completely in love. In 2001, while anticipating the arrival our first (and only) son, my wife and I purchased a Kodak DC4800, a whopping 3 megapixel digital camera, to capture all the memories that were to come in nine months. I was working as an instructional designer writing Web-based courses for large corporations on such riveting topics as proper hand washing, forklift operation, and how to safely climb a ladder.

I worked for a small company (nine of us), and the budget for each training project was equally as small. In an effort to make these mind-numbingly boring topics engaging, we included as much visual content as possible. This was a real challenge, since at the time the cheapest source of royalty-free content were CD-ROM collections of clip art. The CDs were hard to search, and what you did find was never quite what you had in mind. The quality of the imagery often left a lot to be desired, but the price was right because we just didn't have the budget to do custom photo shoots or license the much more (relatively) expensive royalty-free content that could be found online at the time.

As a writer, part of my job was describing the type of visuals to accompany the text. As a result, I spent a lot of time looking at images and searching for new sources of (legal) visual content that fit our budget. It was during one of those (often fruitless) searches in 2002 that I stumbled upon iStockphoto. It had a collection of about 20,000 files that you could search, and you could immediately download what you wanted for 25 cents a pop. Yes, you read that right: twenty-five cents for a royalty-free license. Actually, it seemed too good to be true, and I can honestly say I viewed it with more than a bit of suspicion.

From Content Consumer to Content Creator

After spending quite a bit of time searching through the iStockphoto collection and finding content that we could use in our projects, I also discovered that the content was supplied by the site's users. Anyone could apply to become a contributor and, in return, receive five cents every time someone downloaded one of your photos. Yes, five whole cents!

But let's put this in context. It's 2002, consumer digital camera demand is taking off and pushing image quality higher, faster Internet access is becoming more widely available, and demand for Web content is booming: Everybody and every business wanted a website. On iStockphoto, there was a core group of Web designer/developers and associated techno-geeks who were digitally savvy. There was a huge demand for visual content from people who had low-to-no budgets. In other words, it was a perfect storm. How could people not start sharing their visual content with one another over the Internet?

Being a member of the techno-geek tribe, I wasted no time in applying to become a contributor. Looking over my application sample images (**Figure 1.2**), I can safely say the standards for approval were a lot lower back then.

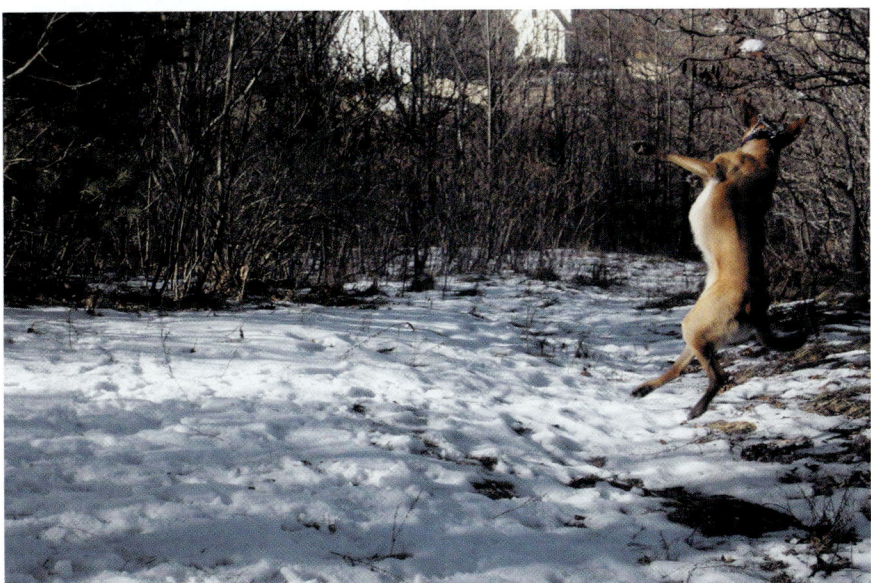

Figure 1.2 Sad but true, this is one of my original application sample photos that got me in the door. The lighting is awful and the subject blends in with the background, but it was downloaded 15 times over 5 years before I took it offline.

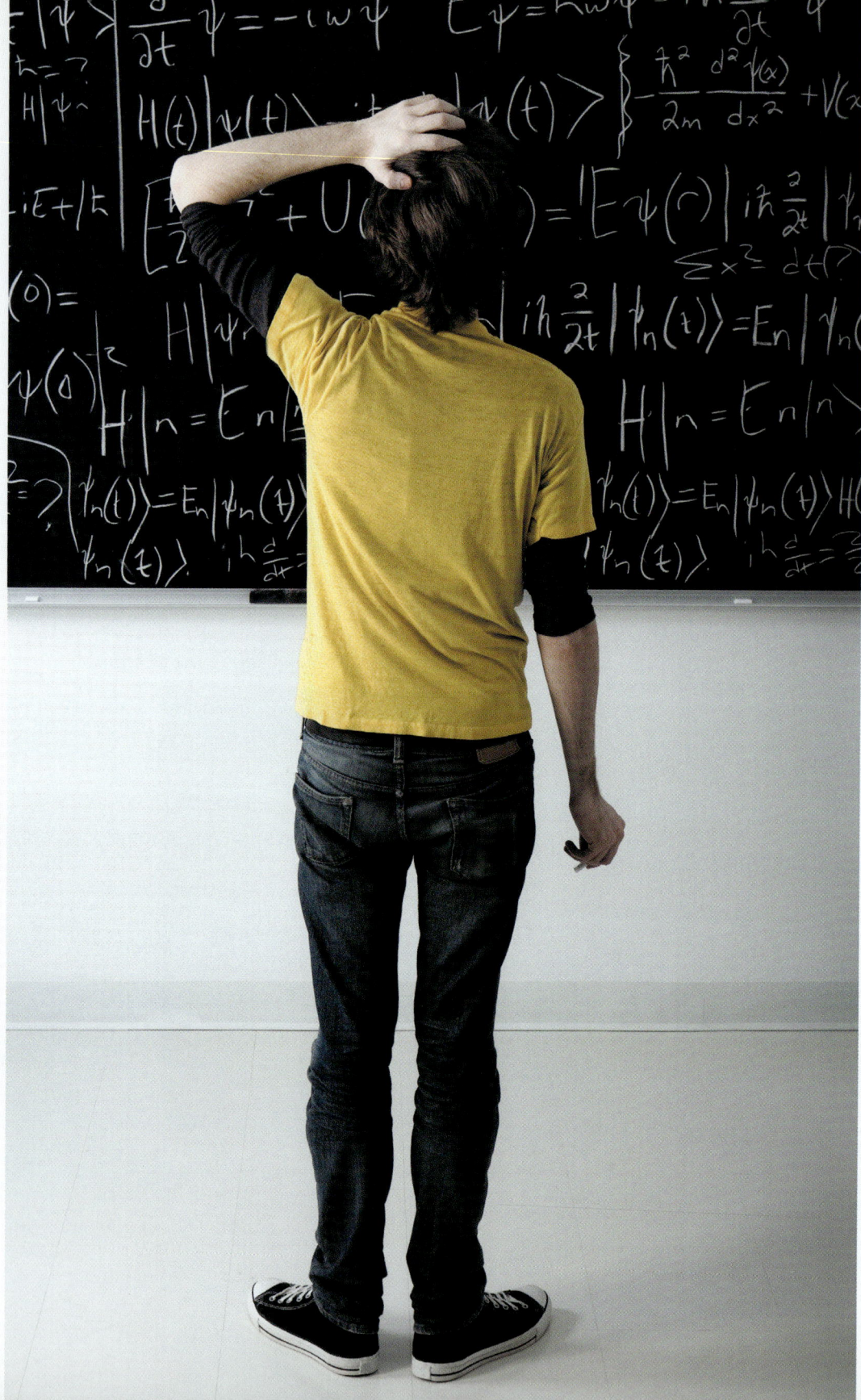

Boy Looking at Math Problem

Creator	Diane Diederich (istockphoto.com/diane39)
Started	2002
Home	USA
Total portfolio	1,985 images
Total downloads	Over 200,000
About this photo	Diane says, "I think this photo has been successful because of its compositional simplicity. The concept looks very simple and straightforward, but it can be interpreted in many different ways. Confusion, overcoming adversity, overwhelming odds, and so on. It also has flexibility for the placement of text and other design elements on top of the image."
Diane's tip	"The time has passed in microstock for shooting everyday objects lying around the house and expecting them to get hundreds of downloads. If you are going to be successful in the current market, you have to work, and work hard for it now. MAKE the picture...don't just take it."

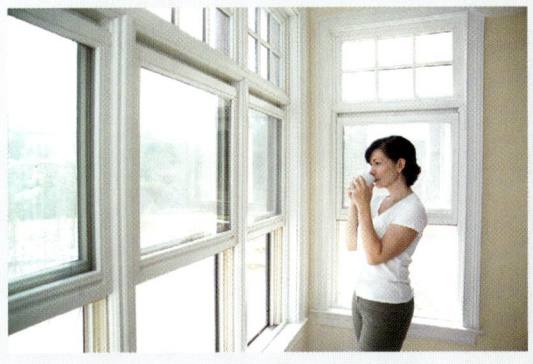

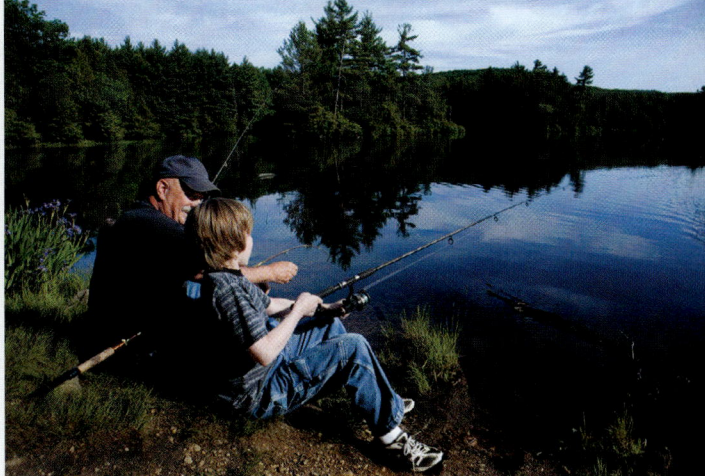

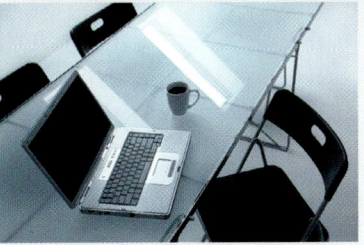

Figure 1.3 Boy looking at math problem on blackboard. Downloaded over 2,400 times.

Figure 1.4 Woman Standing by a Window

Figure 1.5 Grandfather and Grandson Fishing

Figure 1.6 Laptop on a Table

While it was the access to cheap content that led me to microstock (though it was called *micropayment stock photography* back then), it was getting involved with the online community of fellow designers that got me completely hooked on the concept. Don't let anyone tell you that microstock was started simply by hobbyist photographers who just decided to give their work away without realizing its value. Microstock was started by image consumers who needed visual content and knew its value, but balked at the license fees asked by existing suppliers and were dissatisfied by other sources. A tipping point occurred when they realized they had the tools (affordable digital cameras and awareness of demand) to create the content and the distribution platform (the Internet) to exchange it. The people who would identify themselves as photographers first didn't arrive until much later.

Over time, the amount of contributors, buyers, and content continued to grow at a phenomenal rate. Other microstock sites eventually popped up following the same simple model: throw open the doors to anyone and everyone to contribute *and* license content. The rest is history, which I'll cover in the next chapter.

The $13,000 Christmas Tree

Fast-forward to 2007. In a tradition started after my wife's grandfather had given us an extra Christmas tree he'd cut on his property, we started putting up two Christmas trees each year, one inside and one out. The outdoor tree is always a rather simple affair, with a single strand of the classic big-bulb colored lights. We position it so it can be seen easily when looking out the windows, and it is the extent of our outdoor holiday décor.

A benefit from living in a rural part of New Hampshire is that we live practically down the street from a Christmas tree farm. It is a family-run business where you walk through the fields to pick out your tree, cut it yourself, and haul it down to the house where they offer hot chocolate while they shake off the loose needles and stray, wind-blown leaves. Our outdoor tree budget is usually around $15, which buys a pretty decent 6-foot tree.

This particular year found us putting up our tree on the first weekend of December. The first real snow of the season was forecast to arrive Sunday night, and we wanted the tree up before it hit. When the snow started falling that night, I left the tree's lights on and went to bed thinking it could be ideal conditions for taking pictures in the morning. Few things are prettier than freshly fallen snow, and if you throw in a twinkling Christmas tree it could make a perfect picture postcard.

When I awoke the next morning, the scene looked as wonderful as I'd hoped the night before. While waiting for the coffee pot to fill, I grabbed my Nikon D200, 60mm lens, and tripod. I propped open the front door and took eight exposures before closing the door and going back for coffee. It was just before 7 a.m.

With coffee in hand, I downloaded the photos onto my computer and started working on the one I liked best (**Figure 1.7**). In my mind's eye from the night before, I had envisioned something that captured that magical quality of freshly fallen snow, quiet pre-dawn light, and Christmas, which are all very evocative visuals that are perfect for stock.

I shot in raw mode and did all my processing in Lightroom and Photoshop. In an effort to create the image I'd previously imagined, I darkened the background slightly around the edges and left the cool blue cast of the pre-dawn winter light. To make the tree pop a little more (**Figure 1.8**) I brought it into Photoshop and used a simple technique I'll share with you later in Chapter 9.

I uploaded the photo to iStockphoto that same day, and it was approved by the next. It was licensed for the first time within an hour of being approved, and by the time Christmas day rolled around it had put more than $800 in my pocket. I was pretty pleased, to say the least, but not just for the extra cash. I had enjoyed every aspect of the process that went into the creation of that image. From the choosing and cutting of the tree (love that piney-Christmas tree smell!), putting it up on my lawn with my wife and son, going to bed that night imagining what it might look like in the morning, waking up with it on my mind, taking the pre-coffee shots and processing them a few minutes later, to watching the dollar amount in my account jump up and up every day.

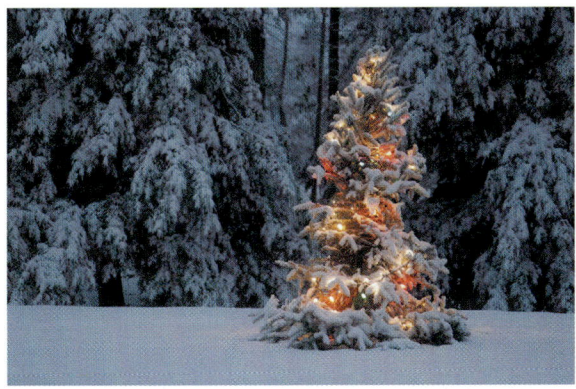

Figure 1.7 Unprocessed photo straight out of the camera. f/2.8 1/10 ISO 400

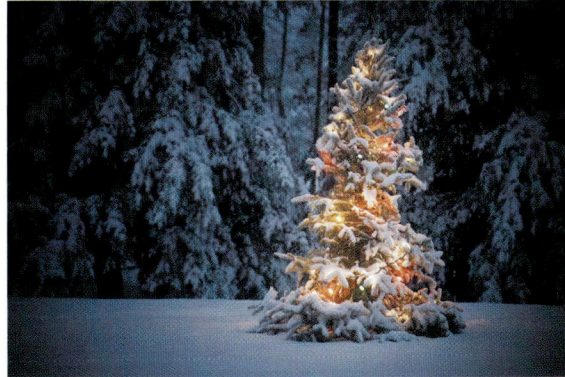

Figure 1.8 The final processed version.

I wasn't sure how the shot would do after that Christmas, but somewhat to my surprise it continued to get downloaded throughout the year and added another $6,283.43 to my bank account that first full year. At the time of this writing, my total net revenue from that single photo has exceeded $13,000. Merry Christmas, indeed! You'll have to check back with me in the future to find out how it fares, but I can safely say it had long ago exceeded my expectations in every possible way.

The image of that tree is my most successful stock photo to date and, for me, it embodies all that is possible in a model that allows you to turn regular moments from your everyday life into evocative images that are useful to others and accessible to the world. What's in your mind's eye?

What's in It for You?

The unique opportunity offered by microstock is that because it is so accessible to image creators and image consumers alike, there is an unprecedented level of feedback at multiple points in the process, which provides you with an unprecedented opportunity for rapid learning and growth. In addition, as license fees have steadily increased over the years, there is greater opportunity to earn a steady stream of income that is largely limited only by your own ability to provide content people want to license.

Due to the accessible price point for licenses (under $1 at the low end) and the low barriers to entry for contributors, the number of people involved in microstock is quite staggering. There are literally millions of people involved in the creation and licensing of microstock files. iStockphoto alone reports that, on average, a file is downloaded somewhere in the world every second of the day.

Before your files make it in front of the buying public, though, they have to pass through a review process where each file is examined by a trained inspector who looks over every pixel for composition, technical, and legal problems. These people look at tens of thousands of files per week and act as a valuable filter on submitted content. While no one, and I mean no one, likes having his or her work rejected, there is much to be learned from the process. Hopefully, by the time you finish this book, you will experience fewer rejections at the hands of inspectors, although likely many more by your own hand.

Once your files have passed inspection, they are immediately available to be licensed by the world. Most agencies will also provide a range of statistics—from number of views to sales and member ratings—to help you measure progress. I think most will agree that the most important statistic is sales, but views—the number of people who actually clicked on your file to look at it a little closer—has its own value, and we'll discuss that more later.

Some people find this level of feedback a little overwhelming at first. If you are used to the approving nods of family members and friends when showing them your latest photo, it can be quite a shock to find that same photo was rejected for too much noise, or that no one leaves any comments, or worse, the sales don't start rolling in. I'll provide some strategies for dealing with these situations later, but let me just say now that this feedback is an opportunity, not a dead end.

I also want to clarify that shooting for stock is just one of many outlets for photographers. It is not the be-all and end-all, and it is not the right outlet for every photo. There are lessons to be learned here that have wide application in all types of photography, but you, as the photographer, need to discover what works best for your particular style.

Quality vs. Quantity

This isn't an either/or question, and there isn't a single one-size-fits-all approach to what leads to success as a stock contributor. My approach has been to focus on quality first and let quantity take care of itself over time. I say this with a meager stock portfolio of fewer than 300 files after nearly eight years of being involved, but over the last three years, those files have put more than $30,000 in my bank account.

Could I have added more? No doubt! However, I have never aspired to be the top-selling creator of stock imagery. Instead, I have aspired to remain an amateur at heart and cling mightily to the joy I feel holding a camera in my hands and looking at the world through that little viewfinder, while creating the types of images that I enjoy creating. That is the same feeling I had in 2001 when I got my first digital camera, and I cherish it. I always wish I was creating more and hope that never changes! I enjoy looking at my stock portfolio and feeling pleased with both the growth it shows and the experiences it represents.

Of course, you may have different aspirations and priorities. This is actually one of the great benefits of the microstock model: You are in complete control of how much content you create and submit over time. There are no minimum requirements to keep your account going, though various sites have different maximum amounts you can submit in a given time period.

An equally valid approach in my view is to create constantly and upload continually. This has the benefit of generating a great deal more feedback in a shorter period of time, and the greater potential of more of that feedback coming in the form of revenue. There is truth to the sentiment that this is largely a numbers game. The more you have in the game, the more your odds increase that your work will be found. I don't dispute that this path has been successful for many

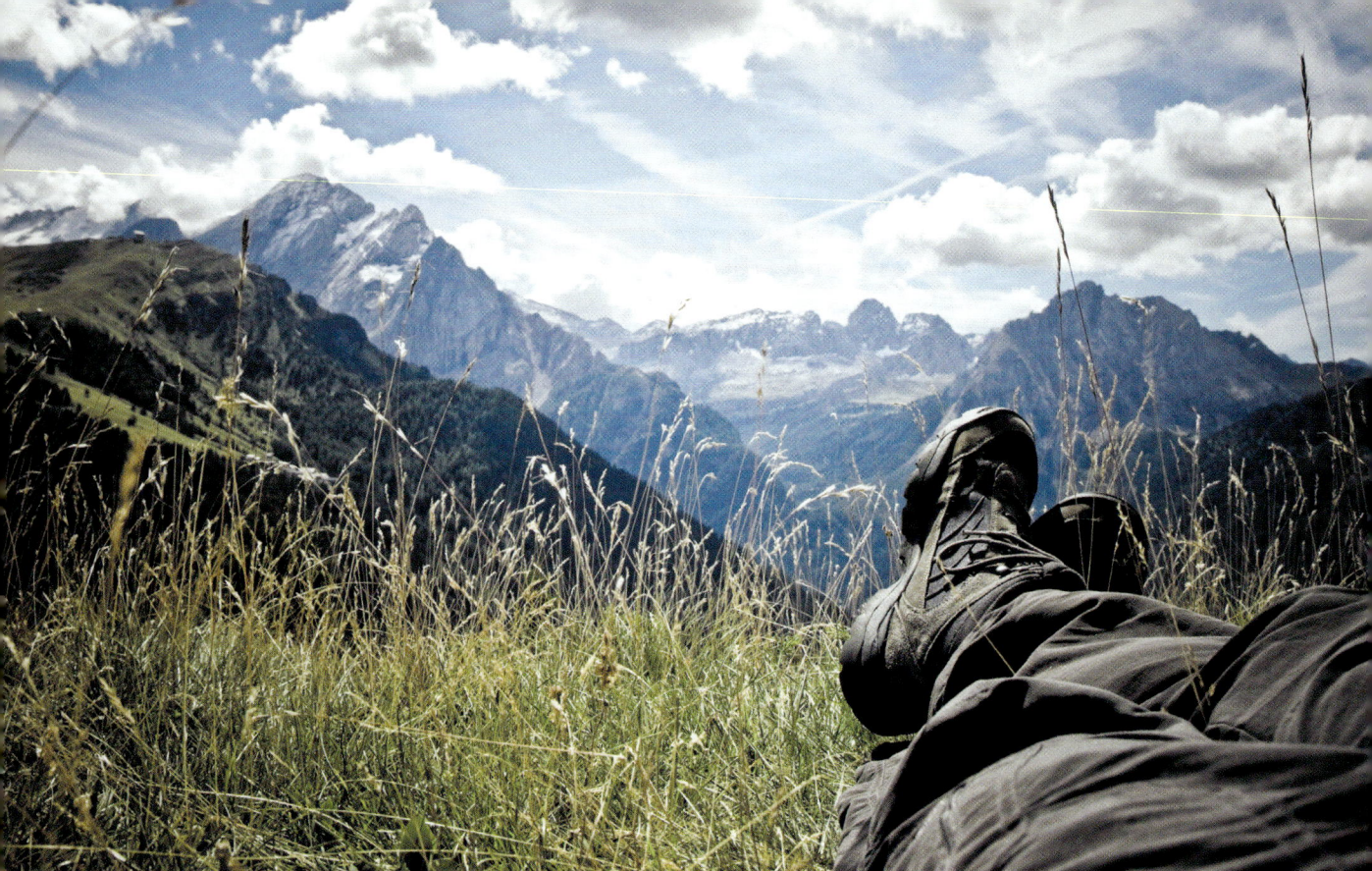

Figure 1.9 Man resting in the Alps. Downloaded over 360 times.

Man Resting in the Alps

Creator	Giorgio "Gio" Fochesato (istockphoto.com/gioadventures)
Started	Oct. 2006
Home	Italy
Total portfolio	3,900 images
Total downloads	Over 41,000
About this photo	Gio says, "The concept and the beauty of the panorama [famous Italian Alps] are the winning points. This image conjures thoughts of holiday, relaxation, imagination, hiking, and freedom. Also, the composition adds value in that the main subject is not in the center, so it is possible to add text or fit into a design." Photo taken with Canon EOS 400D with Sigma 17-70 f2.8/4.5.
Gio's tip	"Don't give up! The first impact with stock is hard. The quality standards are very high, but if you are ready to learn and understand how an image has to be processed you will get a lot of satisfaction."

people. I simply offer my view that it is not the only way to play the game. I firmly believe that high quality and useful imagery that is keyworded effectively can be just as rewarding for those not interested in high-volume output.

Throughout each chapter I feature the work of some of the most generous, talented, and successful microstock contributors I know. Along with one or more photo from their respective portfolios, I've included some information about each photographer along with some of the wisdom they wanted to share with you. I wish I could have included more, but be sure to check the provided links to their stock portfolios to see what else they have to offer, and don't be afraid to drop them a line and say hello. ■

2
What Is Stock Photography?

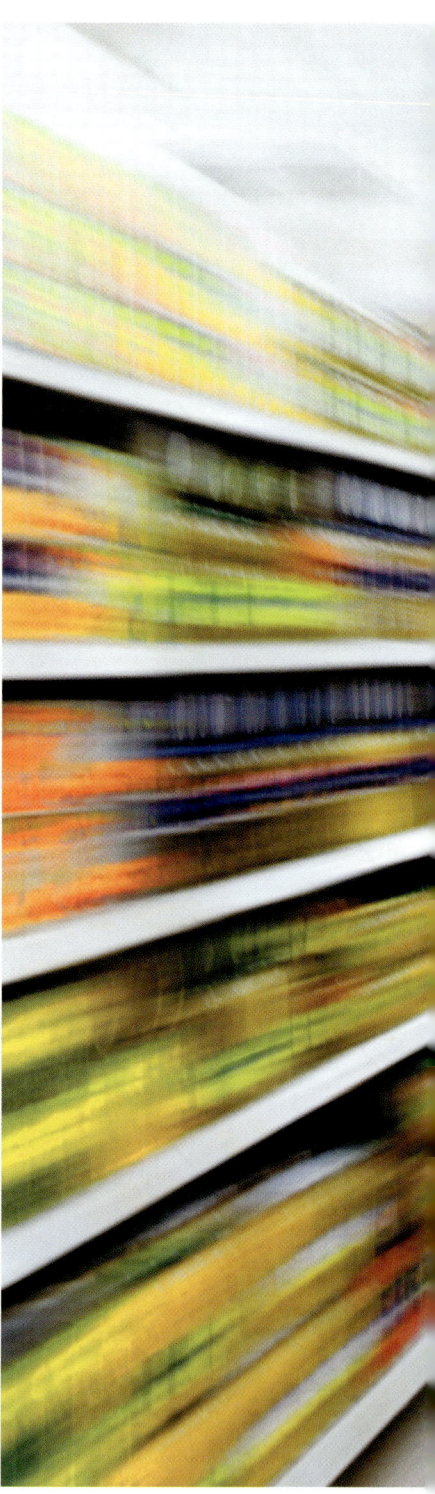

Originally born of outtakes from photographic assignments, the word *stock* referred to images that were part of a photographer's archive (think stock on store shelves as opposed to the stock market). These existing photos could be licensed to interested parties for specific uses, and in return, could provide the photographers with an additional income stream beyond the original assignment. Over time, as photography, media consumption, and technology evolved, the production of stock imagery came into being as an end unto itself. Now there are millions upon millions of stock images sitting on virtual shelves across the Internet being searched, downloaded, and used by people with a variety of needs and uses in mind.

Who Uses Stock?

Whether you realize it or not, you see stock photos in use all the time. From billboards to Web banners, from blogs to magazines, from annual reports to promotional flyers, stock images are used just about anywhere you see images. Advertising makes up one of the most visible uses for stock images, and it is not unusual to start recognizing certain images, models, and contributor styles as you become familiar with the content available on various microstock sites. In time, you'll probably even see some of your own. I once opened my local small-town newspaper to find one of my stock photos of my dog (**Figure** 2.2) used in an advertisement for pet obituaries. Sure, it was nice to see how it was being used, but it was a bit surprising, given the context. (He remains one of my favorite models.)

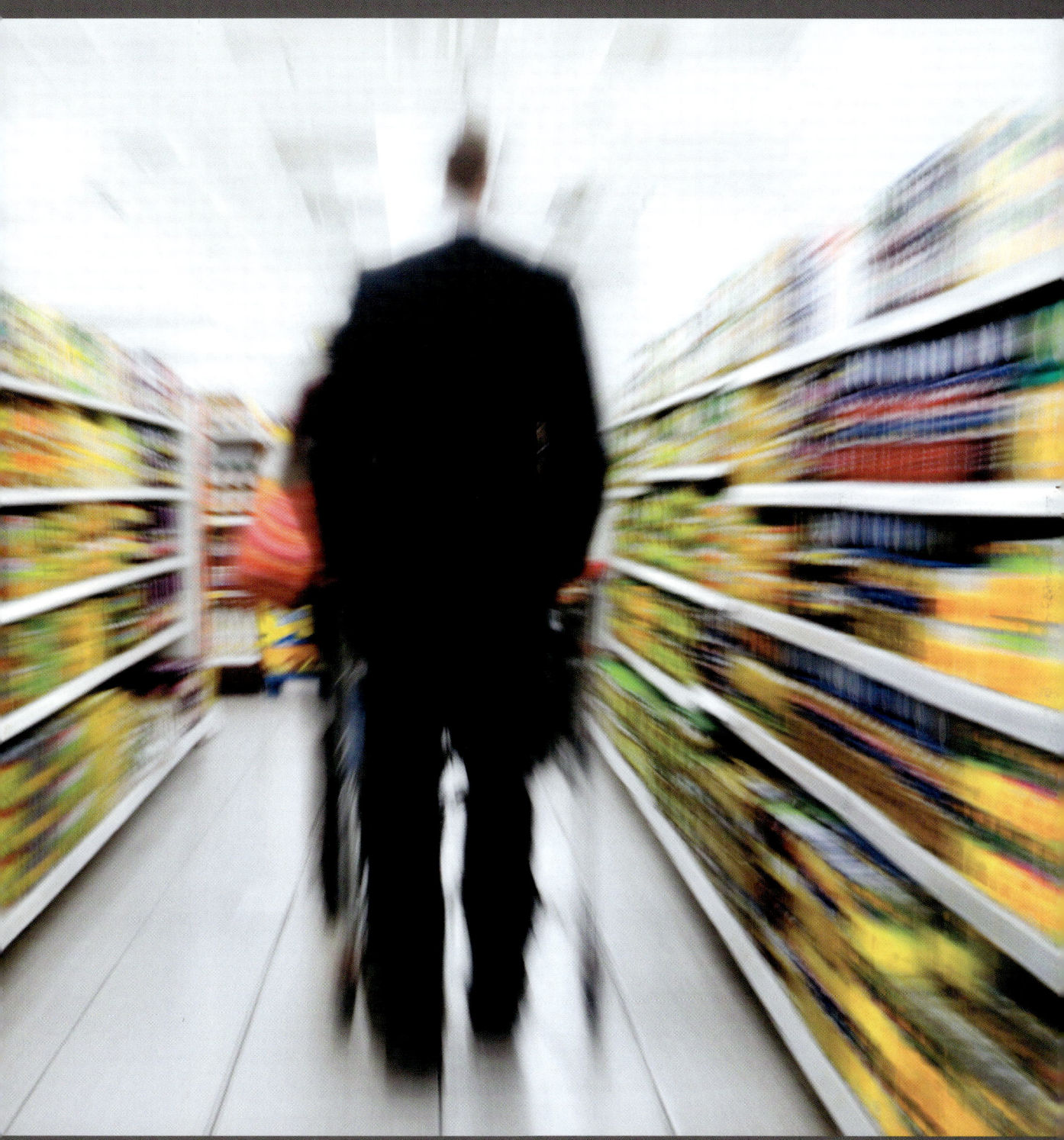

Figure 2.1 Shopping.
© Dane Steffes (istockphoto.com/danesteffes)

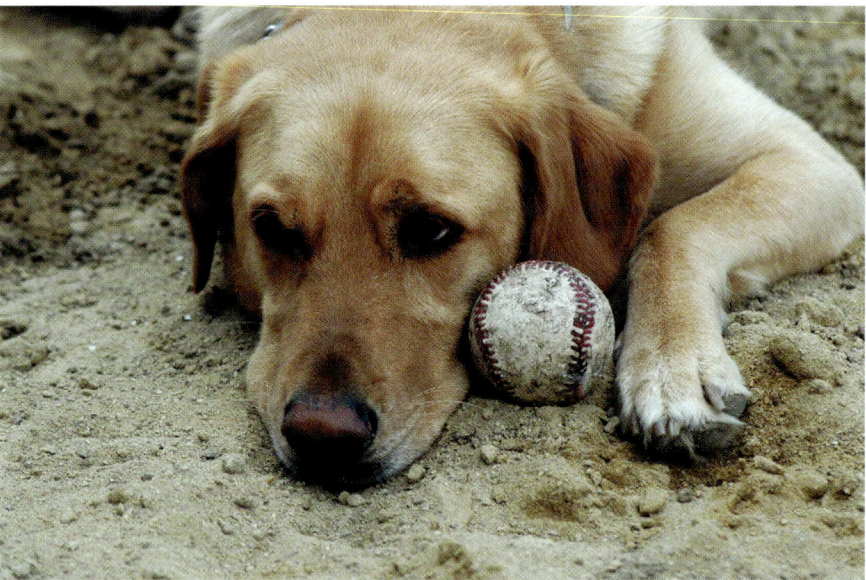

Figure 2.2 Dog and His Ball. © Rob Sylvan (istockphoto.com/sylvanworks)

A key concept that you are wise to embrace as early as possible is that stock images are meant to be the raw materials used in larger projects. Usefulness is a core trait of a successful stock photo.

When Is a Photo a Stock Photo?

The oldest active file in my stock portfolio (**Figure 2.3**) is from my long-retired Kodak DC4800. It has been downloaded slowly but surely every year since 2002. I took that while walking my dog in a neighborhood park. I was just struck by the phrase—Guests Strike Out—created by that particular composition. I converted it to black and white mostly to cover up the digital noise from that camera, but I think it works since it was essentially monochrome already. That photo wouldn't likely pass today's quality acceptance criteria for noise at most stock sites, and it's not particularly clever or pretty, but it garnered my first ever comment from a fellow contributor, Pete Rockwell, back in 2002, who wrote, "Now THAT'S stock photography."

As a new contributor, I was quite curious about this comment, and while I liked the image enough to upload it, I didn't think it particularly worthy of such enthusiastic praise. I sent a message to Pete, and asked if he could tell me more about what struck him about that photo. He wrote back, "My comment on your

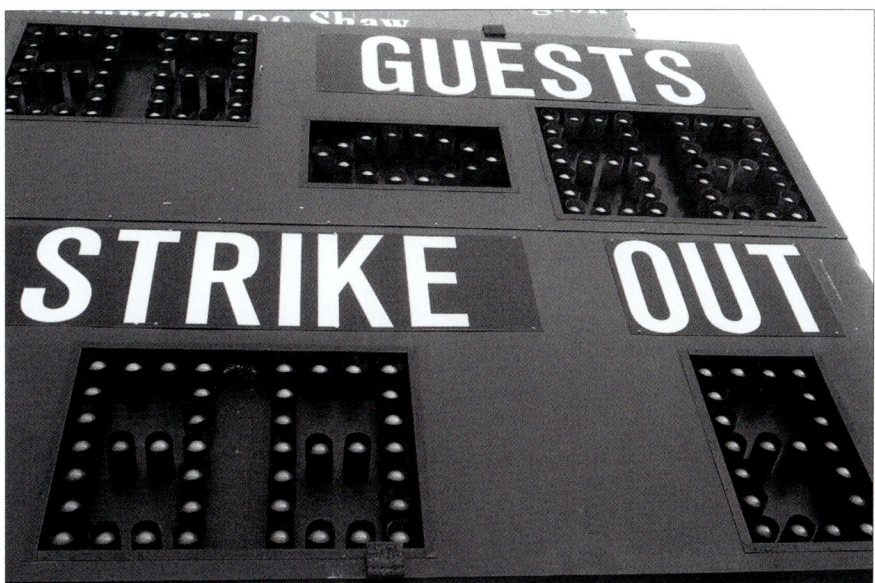

Figure 2.3 Guests Strike Out. © Rob Sylvan (istockphoto.com/sylvanworks)

work, though admittedly somewhat cryptic to a new user, was essentially saying two things: One, that your image, in my opinion, exemplifies stock photography and by extension, two, is exactly the kind of image people come here to find."

The winning ingredient of that photo is that it is very simple and clear in communicating a message. It isn't pretty to look at. It isn't my best work. It is actually a little bit embarrassing to keep around due to its faults, but I keep it in my active portfolio because of the lesson it taught me, and because we should never forget our roots.

Understanding the Licensing Models

Every industry has its vocabulary that every new entrant should learn as quickly as possible in order to participate and succeed. One of the most important concepts to wrap your brain around first is called licensing. In the normal course of business, in a transaction that involves the copyright holder (i.e., you), an image consumer (the person who wants to use your image), and typically, a third-party distributor, an image is never sold. Instead, the copyright holder authorizes the image consumer to use the photo in specific ways, spelled out by a license drawn up by the distributor, in exchange for a fee. Licenses fall under two broad models: rights-managed and royalty-free.

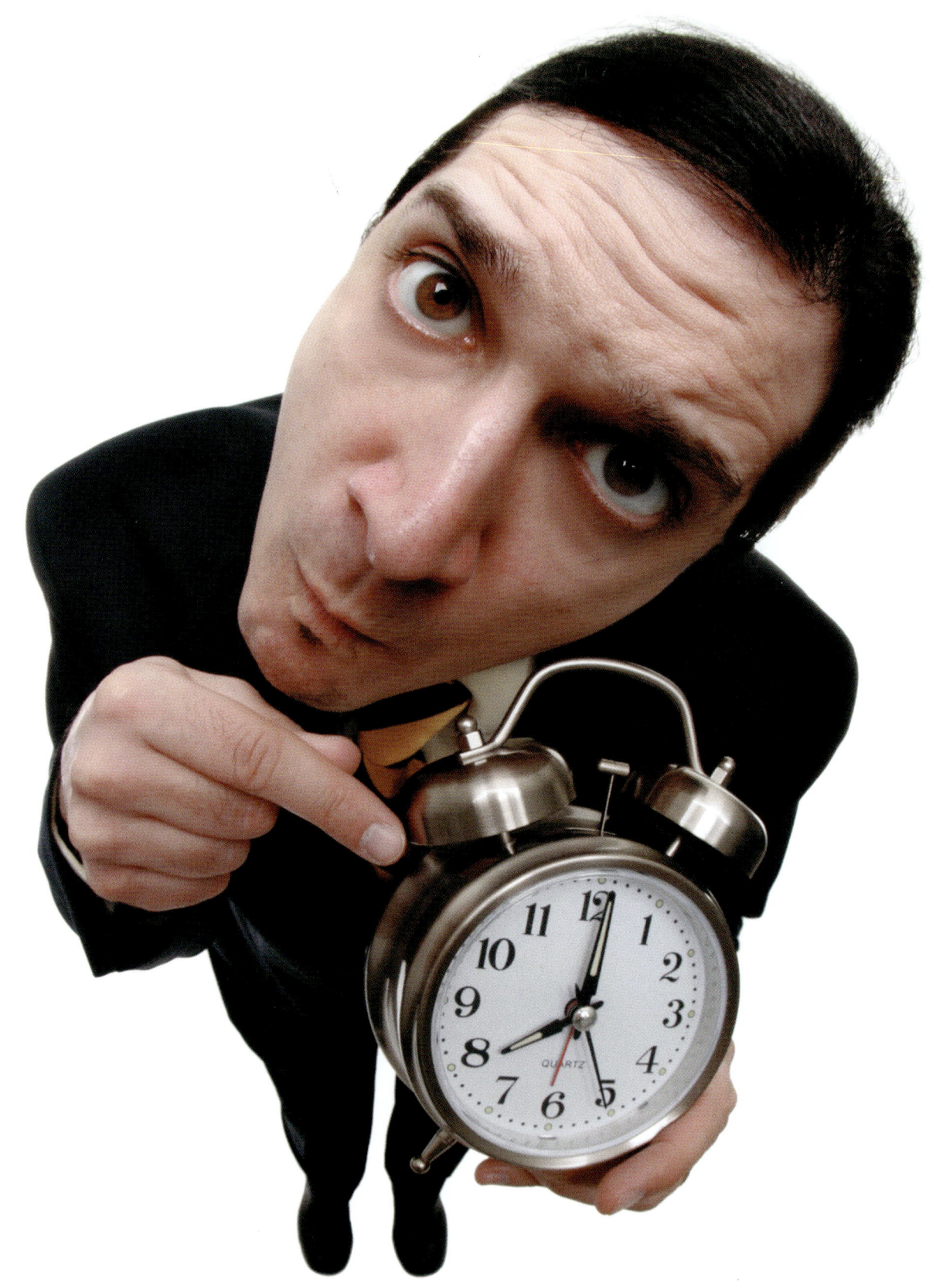

Better Be Prompt

Creator	Sharon Dominick (istockphoto.com/sdominick)
Started	2002
Home	USA
Total portfolio	4,600 images
Total downloads	Over 195,000
About this photo	Sharon says, "People can relate to stress and frustration. Putting a twist on these negative emotions and adding a humorous approach by using a fisheye lens is what I believe makes this images so successful. Taken with Canon 5D, Canon 15mm Fisheye Lens, and 4 Alien Bee Strobes."
Sharon's tip	"Getting started in stock photography can bring a mix of emotions. Patience, persistence, and creativity are the keys to a successful journey in stock photography. Find ways to make yourself stand out from others. Most importantly, enjoy the process!"

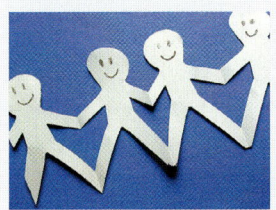

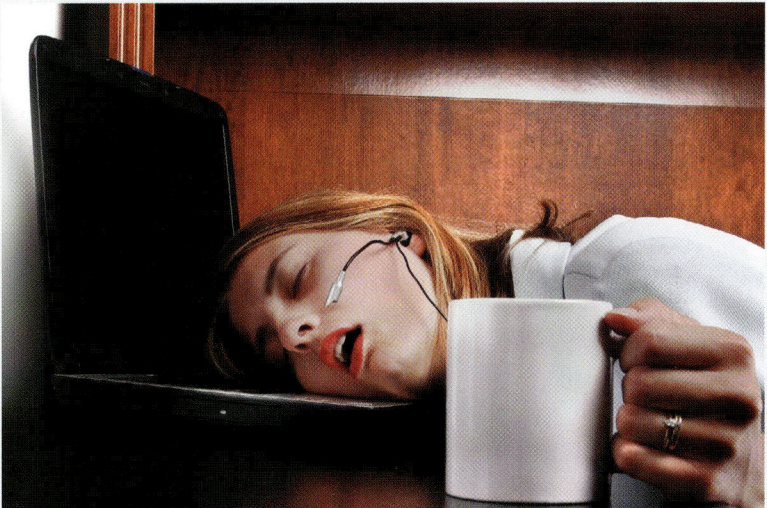

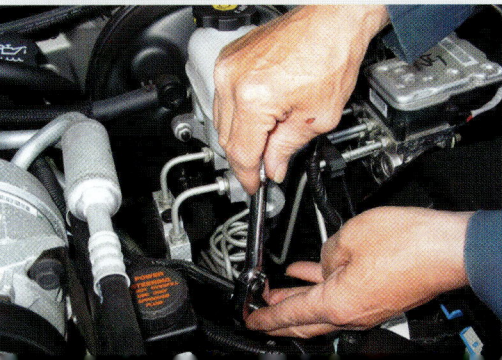

Figure 2.4 Better Be Prompt! Downloaded over 1,700 times.

Figure 2.5 Blank Paper People

Figure 2.6 Who Gave Her Decaf?

Figure 2.7 Mechanic—Under the Hood

Rights-Managed

The rights-managed model goes back to the roots of stock photography, which evolved from photographic assignment work. The core of a rights-managed license is that the use granted is specific and limited to a particular set of mutually agreed upon uses and time period. A rights-managed license may also include a guarantee of exclusive use for that time period, but this is not required. If the image consumer wishes to use that image again in any way not spelled out by the original license, a new license needs to be negotiated and an additional fee is paid. The fee amount is based entirely upon the specific use and time period, and can therefore vary widely.

Royalty-Free

A royalty-free license also spells out a specific set of allowable uses, though much more broadly than a rights-managed license. But what makes it fundamentally different from a rights-managed license is that there is no time limit and only a one-time fee paid at the initial image acquisition. The name *royalty-free* is a source of confusion as some people mistakenly assume no fee is ever paid. But the name means that no additional royalties are required for subsequent uses after the initial purchase of the license.

Royalty-free is the dominant model in the microstock world. Pricing essentially revolves around image size in pixel dimensions: the more pixels, the higher the cost for a license. This size-based pricing is intended to somewhat correspond to potential use: A larger image can be used for high-quality print projects, much smaller-dimension Web projects, and everything in between. But a blogger might just need the smallest sized image available to accompany his next blog post.

Editorial

An editorial license can be found in both rights-managed and royalty-free flavors. The defining aspect of an editorial license is that it says a particular image can be used only in a newsworthy or educational context and not for advertising. The reason for this type of license is that there are many images of newsworthy or educational subjects that do not have the proper model or property releases, which I'll cover more deeply in Chapter 4, to allow them to be used in any other context. Think of images of politicians, celebrities, or just regular people doing newsworthy things being used in newspapers, magazines, blogs, and textbooks as the most common examples of this type.

The Ways That Money Changes Hands

There are two types of payment models used by microstock sites: Pay-As-You-Go and Subscription. It is not uncommon these days for many sites to offer some form of both types. The way these models work have a big impact on how you get paid.

Pay-As-You-Go

The problem iStockphoto faced when it went from free to fee was how to provide a secure method for payment transactions. Credit cards were the obvious solution, but thousands of 25-cent credit card transactions weren't going to work, so they came up with the idea of selling credit packages. Customers could purchase credit packs starting at a minimum dollar amount. Once purchased, these credits would appear in the member's account, and he or she could start downloading.

Over time, as the price for a royalty-free license increased, the purchasing of credit packs turned into an opportunity to provide discount bulk pricing: the more credits purchased, the larger the discount. The attraction to the pay-as-you-go model to customers is that they can get bulk discounts on large credit purchases, and they only pay for what they use.

Every site has its own take on credit pricing in terms of how many credits for how much money, but they all tend to follow the common practice of paying the contributor a percentage of the credit value used to download one of their files. That percentage varies from site to site (typically ranging from 20 to 60 percent of credit value), and some sites also offer bonus percentages for images that are made exclusive to their particular site.

Subscription

The subscription model is sort of analogous to the all-you-can-eat buffet. The customer pays one price to download up to a preset number of images over a set period of time. Subscription packages can vary from weeks to months to a full year. The subscription model appeals to customers who have a steady, recurring need for new images over time. The subscription model also appeals to buyers who prefer a fixed recurring expense over a set period of time.

Sites that use a subscription model tend to pay contributors a fixed amount per file download (ranging from 19 to 40¢ per download). Some sites also add incentives to contributors in the form of bonuses based on performance on top of that set amount. While the amount per download is small, the volume of downloads on a successful subscription site is astoundingly high. Financial success in a subscription model all boils down to volume.

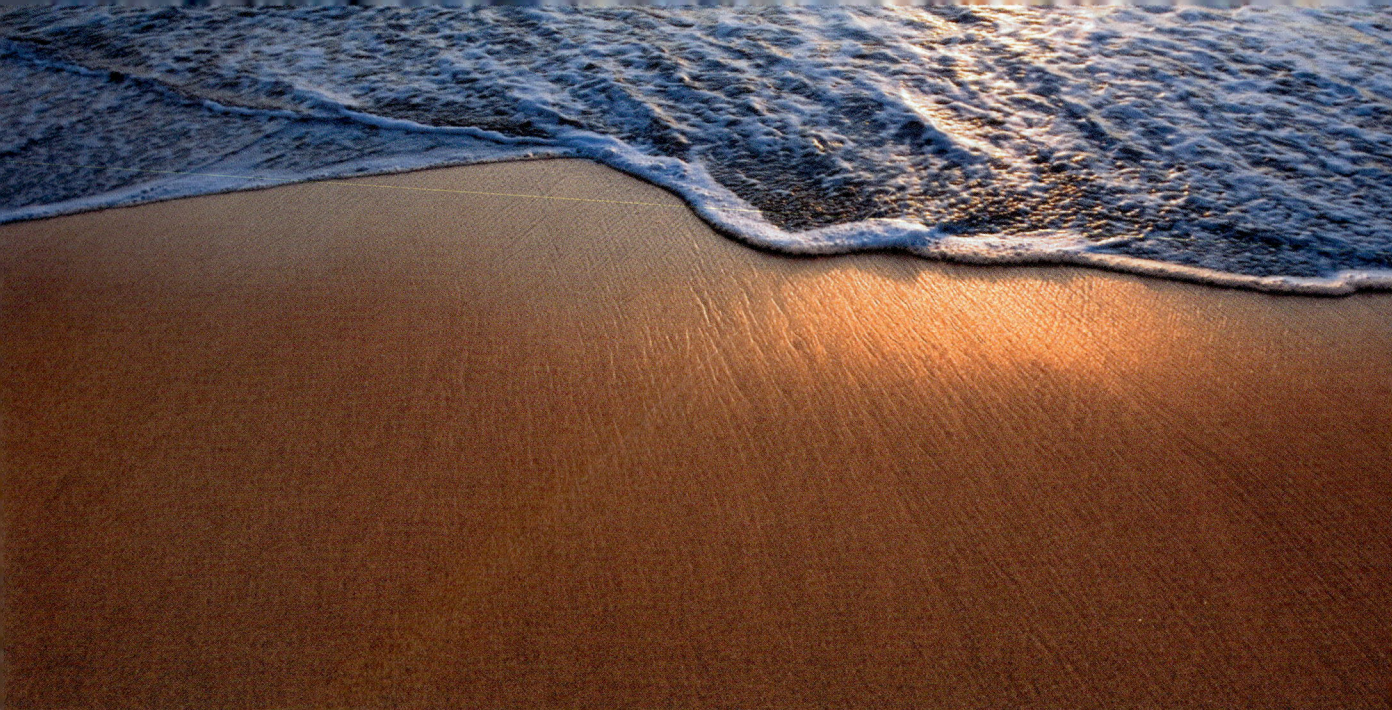

Figure 2.8 Gentle Surf. Downloaded over 2,900 times.

Gentle Surf

Creator	Christine Balderas (istockphoto.com/DNY59)
Started	2005
Home	USA
Total portfolio	6,300 images
Total downloads	Over 690,000
About this photo	Christine says: "What I think is so special about this image is that it is a subject matter that has been done at least a million times. It is so simple. Nothing special or amazing about the surf. But if the camera had been a little higher or lower with respect to the sun's reflection, or a fraction of a second earlier or later with the snap of the shutter, it wouldn't have been so special. Also the negative space, which I think is huge in a stock image, comes in handy. Crop it horizontal or vertical, it doesn't matter. I think it's been successful because it is so versatile. It was taken with Canon Rebel XTi and 24-70mm lens, a camera I rarely use, but I took it with us on a vacation to Hawaii a couple of years ago."
Christine's tip	"Don't get caught up in the technical details. Don't worry so much about megapixels. Worry about concepts and where the buyer might want to overlay some type."

The History of Microstock

As the story goes, back in early 2000, a young entrepreneur by the name of Bruce Livingstone attempted to enter into the royalty-free stock market by producing a series of royalty-free CD collections comprised largely of his own photographs. After deciding he would not find success in selling the CDs, he put the whole collection of several thousand photos online and allowed anyone to sign up to his site, iStockphoto.com, and download them for free. This idea didn't come out of thin air, though: Bruce's stock photography roots go back to the early 1990s when he worked in the mail room at a Calgary-based stock image company, Image Club Graphics, where he first had the idea for selling clip art over the Internet. A few years after leaving Image Club Graphics, Bruce founded his first company, where his interests in stock imagery, Web development, and music would converge.

iStockphoto quickly gained popularity among other Web designers, due in large part through its association with Web design guru Jeffrey Zeldman, who was featured prominently on iStockphoto's home page in the early years. While many fellow Web designers enjoyed access to free content that they could use in their projects, they also wanted to contribute images of their own. So iStockphoto evolved into a photo-sharing model that allowed contributors to download one photo for every five they uploaded.

By the end of 2001, iStockphoto had more than a million registered members and a growing bill for bandwidth as a result of all the uploading and downloading that was taking place. The company actually toyed with the idea of a subscription model, but after polling its members in early 2002, it instead started the first micropayment model of licensing stock photos for 25¢ a download. Twenty cents went to cover operating costs, and 5¢ was given to the contributor of the downloaded file.

Clearly, members weren't signing up with the intention of earning any sort of income, but considering that up until that point in time they were giving it away for free, the 5¢ return allowed members to funnel their earnings back into downloading content for their own projects without opening their wallets, just as they had been doing when it was free. More importantly, it paved the way for new members who just wanted to spend money without uploading their own work to join the party.

iStockphoto saw its first competition enter the microstock arena in 2004 when Bigstockphoto.com, Canstockphoto.com, Dreamstime.com, and Shutterstock.com were launched during the course of the year. Bigstockphoto, Canstockphoto, and Dreamstime all built upon the same open-to-the-public, credit-based micropayment model started by iStockphoto. Shutterstock's founder took a different tack and used 30,000 of his own photos to launch the first subscription-based micropayment offering, and he eventually opened the doors to all interested contributors. One thing the founders of all the competing microstock sites had in common was a background in Web development and Internet businesses.

In the years that followed, many more microstock sites appeared, but few gained serious market share, and some no longer exist. A notable exception is Fotolia.com, which launched in 2005. It has found greater success than many of the newcomers and is considered among the top five highest earners for some contributors.

In 2006, iStockphoto was purchased by Getty Images, the industry's largest stock company, for 50 million dollars. Bruce Livingstone stayed on as the CEO of iStockphoto and as a senior vice president in Getty Images for three years after the acquisition, and has since moved on to new ventures. Acquisitions and mergers are par for the course in the stock image industry, but this was the first merger between an established leader of the pre-microstock industry and a leader of the upstart microstock industry.

The Top Microstock Sites to Start With

From my own experience, and from following the experiences of others over the years, I believe there are five microstock sites that are worth checking out when you are getting started:

- iStockphoto.com
- Shutterstock.com
- Dreamstime.com
- Fotolia.com
- Bigstockphoto.com

Each of these sites has established itself in the industry. They support large (and growing) image libraries, and, based on publicly available data, appear to deliver the largest returns to their contributors. Your mileage may vary, of course, but I think this is the best way to get your feet wet.

There are new sites popping up all the time, and perhaps one of them will be the next big thing, but I would advise to any new contributor to start slow. The microstock industry is constantly evolving, morphing, and merging. The best way to learn the specifics of any one site is to go there yourself and start reading and asking questions. Every one of these sites has its own community forum, help files, and support system.

Check out the industry leaders, read all the fine print, talk to other contributors who are already involved and have years of experience, and get a few months under your belt before you invest a lot of time in the new kids on the block. I do believe there is a law of diminishing returns, but it is up to you to find your own limits.

One of the great things about microstock is the amount of publicly available data and experienced contributors willing to share it. The two most valuable resources you will find, outside of what each individual site may provide, are:

- Microstockgroup.com, which is the most popular site-independent forum for microstock contributors in existence. There is a treasure trove of data to be found there as well as very frank discussion about what is happening in the industry.

- Microstockdiaries.com, which is a blog written by Lee Torrens, who has been a participant and thoughtful observer of the microstock industry for years. He is a trusted voice among contributors and has a lot of valuable information to share.

A further word of advice regarding any Internet forum you decide to get involved with: Don't take what other people say personally, and always use the search function before asking questions.

3
Getting into a Stock Frame of Mind

As photographers, we're all drawn to different types of photography. Certain subjects, locations, techniques, and styles exert a pull on our creative minds more than others and fit better with who we are in the world. I love to be outdoors as much as I love how photography helps me capture and share that love with others. Embrace and nurture whatever it is that pulls the strongest for you. Own it! Leverage those passions as you attune your mind's eye to shooting for stock.

The key concept to keep in mind when you shoot for stock is that you are creating the raw materials for someone else to use for his or her purposes. That is the whole point of stock photography. This may be a paradigm shift from what you are used to doing with your photography, so the sooner you can start seeing in that light, the more satisfying this process will become. One of the best ways to understand this point of view is to put yourself in the shoes of the people you are trying to serve.

Knowing Your Customers

The types of people who license images from microstock sites are impossible to lump into a single category. Due to the combination of a low price point for licensing and the ever-expanding demand for images to be used in print and online projects, you will find microstock customers run the gamut from regular people blogging about their lives to large media outlets and

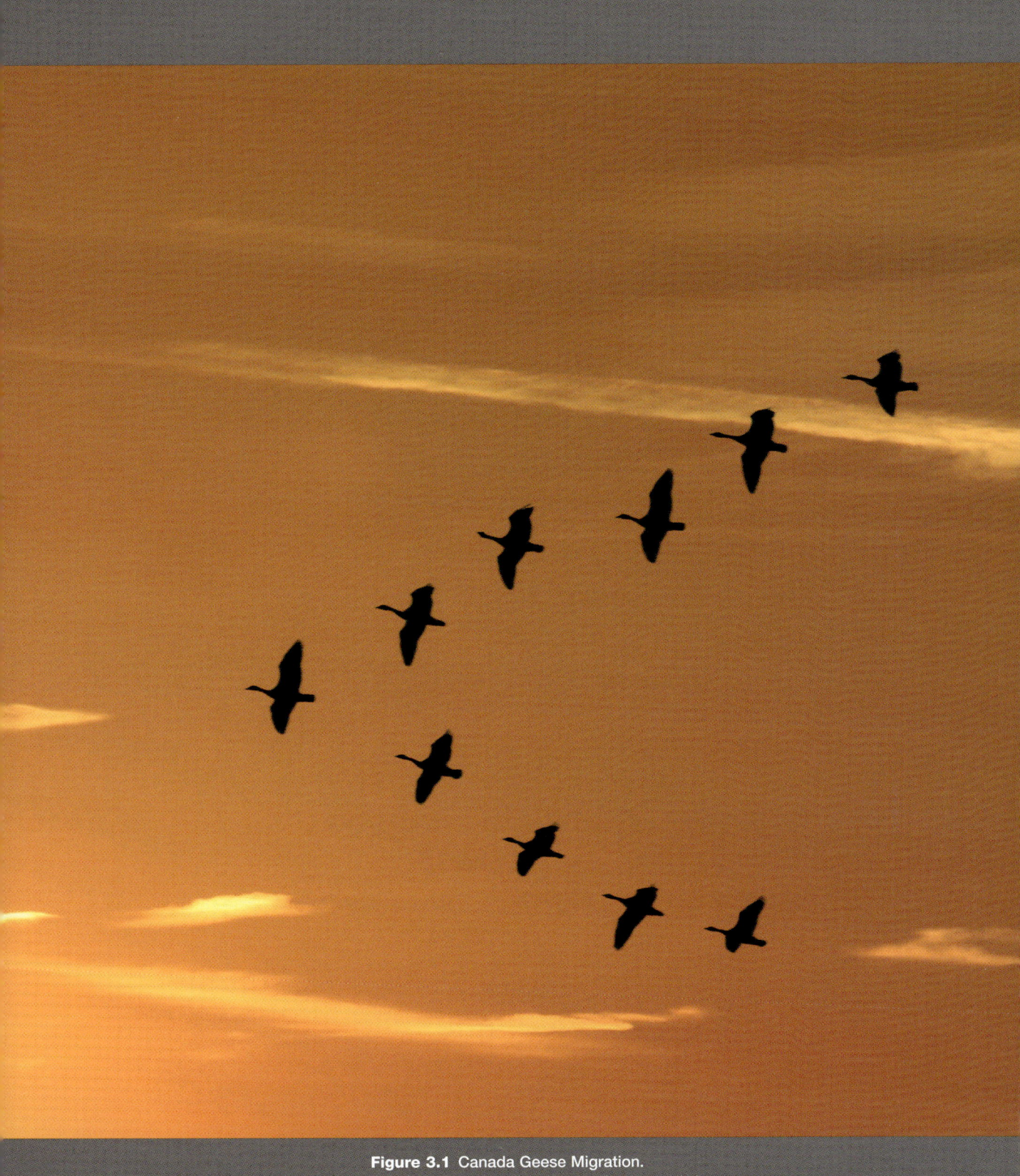
Figure 3.1 Canada Geese Migration.
© Rob Sylvan (istockphoto.com/sylvanworks)

from graphic designers to church groups. What they all have in common is the desire to find a selection of images that fit their specific needs and projects.

You can't know who will find your stock photos useful and you have no control over what projects your shots will wind up in, but you will find more success if you can visualize examples of how a photo could be used before you start shooting. Then you can shoot with those uses in mind. Luckily, there are examples of how stock photos are used all around you. You just have to start looking for them.

Doing Your Research

Magazines are a great place to start looking because each one is designed to appeal to a certain demographic. It is a safe assumption that your magazine subscriptions reflect your taste, politics, interests, and hobbies. Pick up any magazine and just look at the images. Stock images are used on covers (I've seen microstock images on the cover of *Time* magazine), as supporting elements to feature articles, and in the advertisements. All of these uses are targeted to appeal to people just like you—which puts you in a great position to start creating some of those types of images.

I was on a plane recently and spent a few minutes flipping through the in-flight magazine, a treasure trove of stock photos in use. The types of stock photos range from simple objects on plain backgrounds (like cell phones, wine corks, cassette tapes, coat hangers, and so on) to people engaged in all manner of activities (walking, sleeping, talking, and eating, to name a few) to iconic postcard images of locations around the world (the kind that make you want to travel to those locations).

You don't need to book a flight to do your research, though. Hop in your car instead and go billboard hunting. At the time of this writing, the first billboard you'll see when you enter New Hampshire on Interstate 95 is a lovely photo of a senior couple (**Figure 3.2**). As soon as I saw that billboard it brought a smile to my face because I recognized the subjects as the parents of an old friend and fellow microstock contributor. If you live in the city, you need only to step out your door to look at bus wraps, posters, shop windows, and restaurant menus.

Don't get out much? That's OK, too, because you can finally find a purpose for all that junk mail coming to your door every day. Look at the store flyers, pamphlets, coupons, and sale circulars at the holidays. You know the photos you see superimposed on all the TV sets and LCD screens in those ads? Odds are they are stock photos. My wife's grandfather once got a surprise in the mail when he opened the annual report for a school he was affiliated with and found his granddaughter and great-grandson (**Figure 3.3**) on the cover!

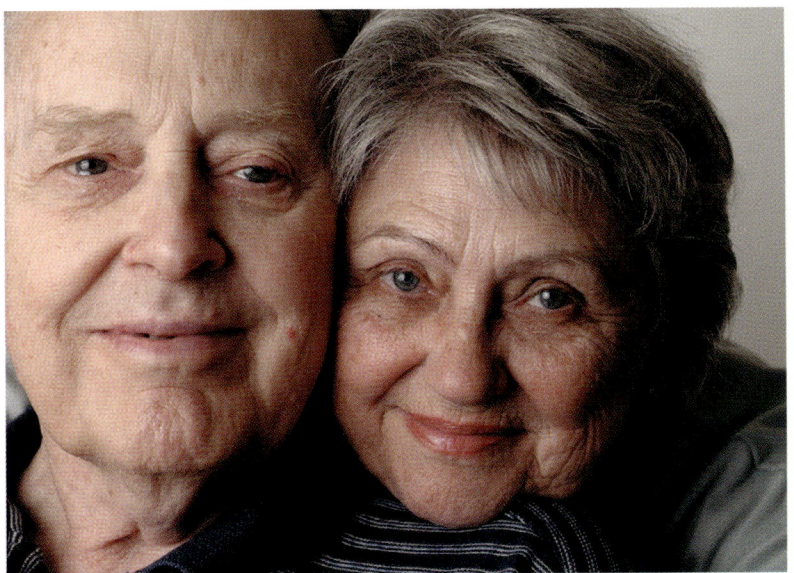

Figure 3.2 My Parents. © Joseph Jean Rolland Dubé (istockphoto.com/JJRD)

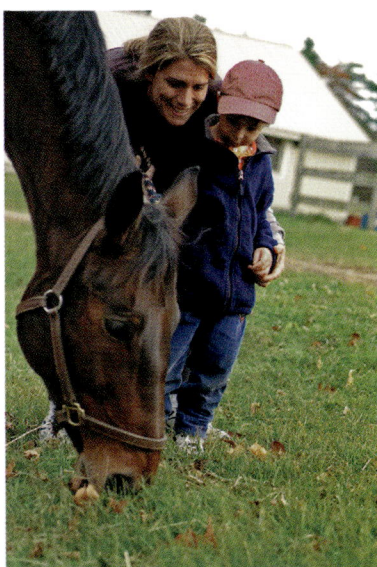

Figure 3.3 Mother and Son. © Rob Sylvan (istockphoto.com/sylvanworks)

Of course, the Web is awash in stock images too. Microstock would not exist without the Internet, and these days the Internet seems to be increasingly hungry for microstock images. In fact, you'll be hard pressed to find any website that doesn't have some stock element being used somewhere.

Clearly, some of the photos you will see in all of these various mediums were shot on assignment for that purpose specifically, but remember that stock photography is an offshoot of assignment photography and filling a specific purpose is still the name of the game. This is your chance to choose and create your own assignments.

Keeping Track

Now that you are seeing all these images being used in all these different places, you need to hone in on the styles and types that speak to you the most. One of the best ways to do that is to keep a file of the ones you like the most. Grab scissors, a file folder, a notebook, and your camera. If you can, cut out the advertisement, article, or design that interests you and put it in the folder. Can't cut it out? Take out your camera and photograph it, or take some notes in your notebook. Build up a collection and keep adding to it over time. Don't be surprised to find yourself starting to think about ideas or concepts of things to shoot, so keep that notebook with you at all times to write those ideas down.

As you are building this collection of images and ideas, take time to stop and analyze what you have. Ask yourself some questions:

- What types of photos could you see yourself creating?
- What is it about those photos that interests you?
- What resources, skills, and knowledge do you bring to the table for creating those types of images?
- What are the predominant colors used in the examples you have collected?
- What themes do you see emerging?

The point of this exercise is twofold: to help attune your eyes to spot how stock photos are used and then to home in on the types of shots you are most interested in creating. As you identify style and subject matter that appeals to you, it can inform the choices you make about what gear to buy (do you need lighting for indoor studio work, or do you need a new macro lens for getting up close and personal with wildlife?), the types of props you will need, and the types of locations you need to access.

You will start out creating a collection of images. But you will find in time that you are learning a lot about yourself, and this I think is incredibly useful. When you are first starting out, I highly encourage you to find ways to create stock within your current means. What do you do for a living? What are your interests and hobbies? Where do you live and what is interesting about it? Who do you know and where can you gain access? What gear do you have and how can you maximize it? You'll be amazed at all the opportunities for creating stock that are all around you. Yes, you will also find that many of these types of stock images—such as flowers, pets, keyboards, and brick walls, to name a few—are incredibly overdone and oversaturated. Don't let that stifle your creativity! You need to crawl before you can walk, so start slow, set goals, and keep moving forward. Besides, if I had succumbed to the notion that the world already has enough photos of Christmas trees, I'd never have created my most successful stock photo to date.

Thinking Like an Image Consumer

When I worked as an instructional designer, I would work with the client to transform whatever training materials the organization had into smaller, easily digestible, and more simply communicated lessons. A big part of the process was finding or creating visuals that could assist in effectively communicating the core messages each lesson was trying to teach. Sometimes a simple visual that just said, "Here is what this thing looks like," fit the bill. Other times a more complex image demonstrating some action was required. One of the most common types of images we looked for (and which were very hard to find) showed the same two people engaged in dialogue with a variety of expressions and gestures that we could use in different sections throughout the training.

In all these cases, the person looking for stock images has a specific need to communicate a specific message, and the role of the stock image is to aid in that communication as simply and effectively as possible. As the photographer, this is where you need to shift your thinking from "How can I best capture a given scene?" to "How can I capture this scene to most effectively communicate a message that will be useful to someone else?"

Many of the most successful microstock contributors started out as graphic designers or still have their design day jobs. These people are successful because they know what is useful. They have a great eye for composition and know how to communicate visually. Take your growing clip file of images and spend time thinking about what messages are being communicated in each one. Try to imagine yourself in the role of the designer for each clipping in your file.

Greater Than the Sum of Its Parts

Let's walk through a real-world example of how a simple object found its way into someone else's project. I have a photo of a frying pan in my portfolio (**Figure 3.4**). The classic cast-iron frying pan is an iconic kitchen staple. It's easily recognized for what it is and what it does. I shot it on a white background (which we'll cover in more detail in Chapter 6) in the simplest way possible.

> **Tip**
>
> As an aside, an issue that you will continually have to grapple with is how to keep your production costs as low as possible while producing high-quality work and not caving in to feeding your gear habit at every possible turn. I would encourage you to always try to live within your photographic means.

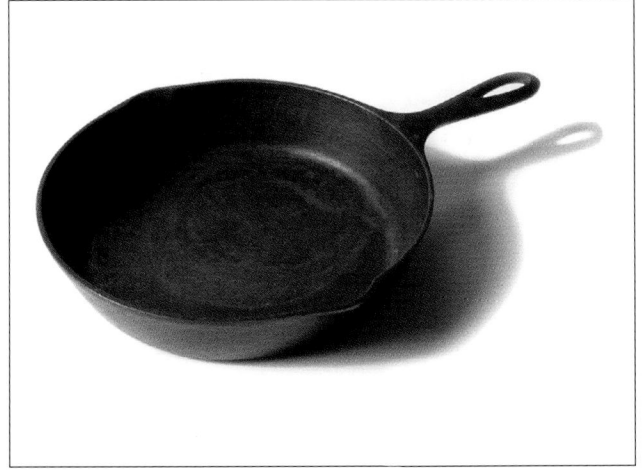

Figure 3.4 Frying pan.

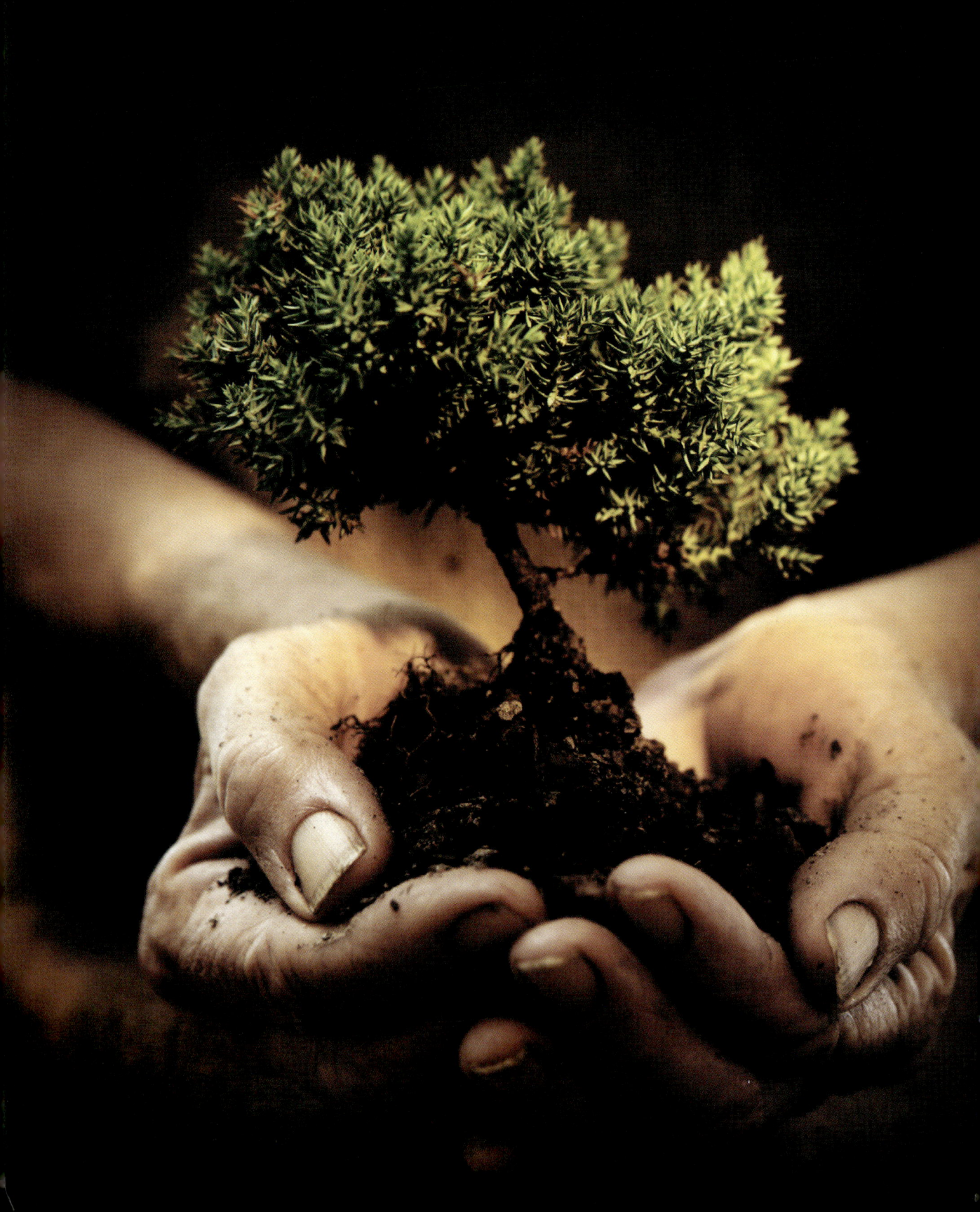

New Development

Creator	Amanda Rohde (istockphoto.com/hidesy)
Started	2003
Home	Australia
Total portfolio	13,000 images
Total downloads	Over 570,000
About this photo	Amanda says, "This was taken on my parents' veranda, with a large piece of hessian as the background, and a torch to add to the natural lighting. My camera was the 1ds Mark II at the time, and my lens was a 24-70 f2.8 Canon. I think it's successful for a number of reasons: The concept is obvious, but reasonably broad; it encompasses growth, protection, development, infancy, and environmental concepts. The colors fit with many of the colors used in these types of designs, and the torchlight adds warmth to the image. The hands are just right for the image. They aren't smooth, well-manicured hands, but are hard-working, older hands, which enhances the earthy tones to the image."
Amanda's tip	"Research what your target audience wants. Think about things that you enjoy photographing, and work out how they should be photographed to provide a useful product to designers. Study advertisements that you see—billboards, magazine ads, television, brochures, reports, church newsletters, junk mail—the list of places stock photography is used is huge. At the beginning of my time on iStockphoto, I spent months cutting up magazines that I bought by the stack from garage sales, and put them in scrapbooks for ideas, inspiration, and composition."

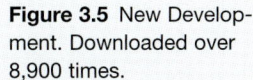

Figure 3.5 New Development. Downloaded over 8,900 times.

Figure 3.6 Delight.

Figure 3.7 Take Flight.

Figure 3.8 Coffee at Cafe.

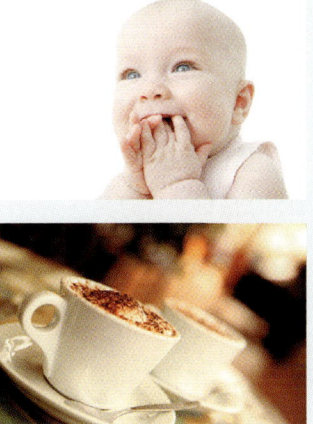

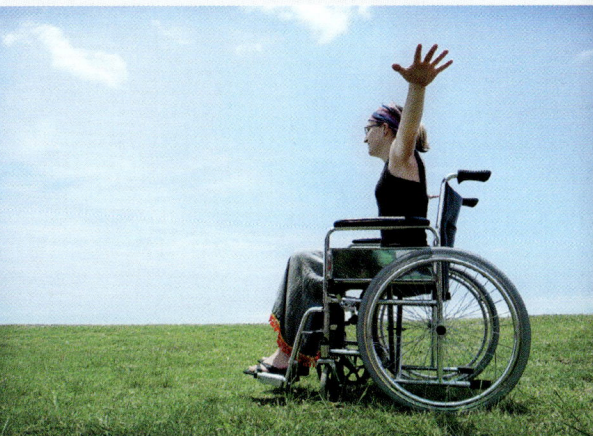

An object on a white background is a perfect example of raw material just waiting to be put to use in a larger project, which is why you will see so many examples of this type of stock everywhere. In this case, an art teacher (and microstock contributor as well), Mark Evans, was putting together a poster (**Figure 3.9**) for an annual student art exhibition at his school in Melbourne, Australia. The exhibition included work from visual arts, food technology, media, woodwork, and metalwork students. He sought out various stock images that were representative of those disciplines and crafted them together to create the figure in the poster. My frying pan never looked so happy.

When I shot that frying pan I did not intend for it to be a work of art, but because of its ability to communicate a simple message, it found a new life in a fun project all the way on the other side of the world from my kitchen. It's been downloaded more than 100 times, and I can only imagine all the other places it has been.

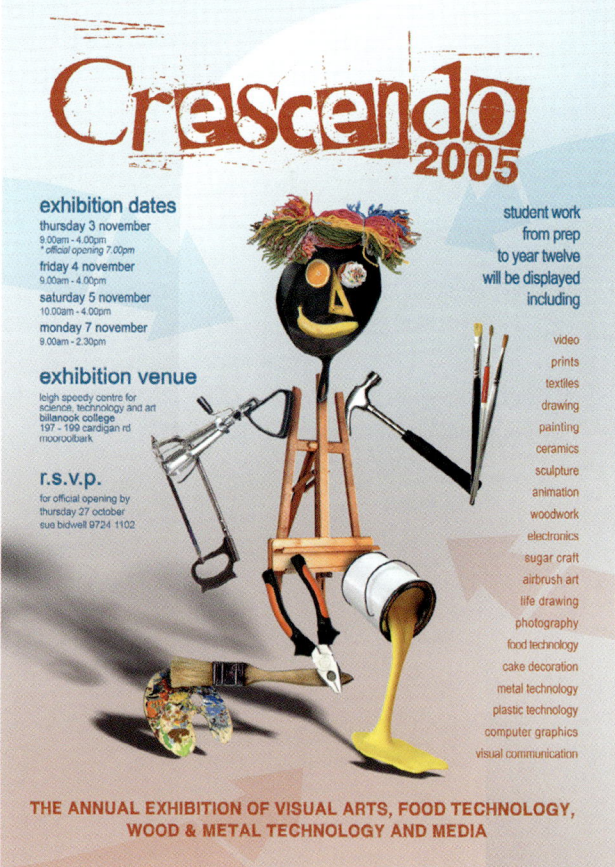

Figure 3.9 Crescendo exhibition poster.

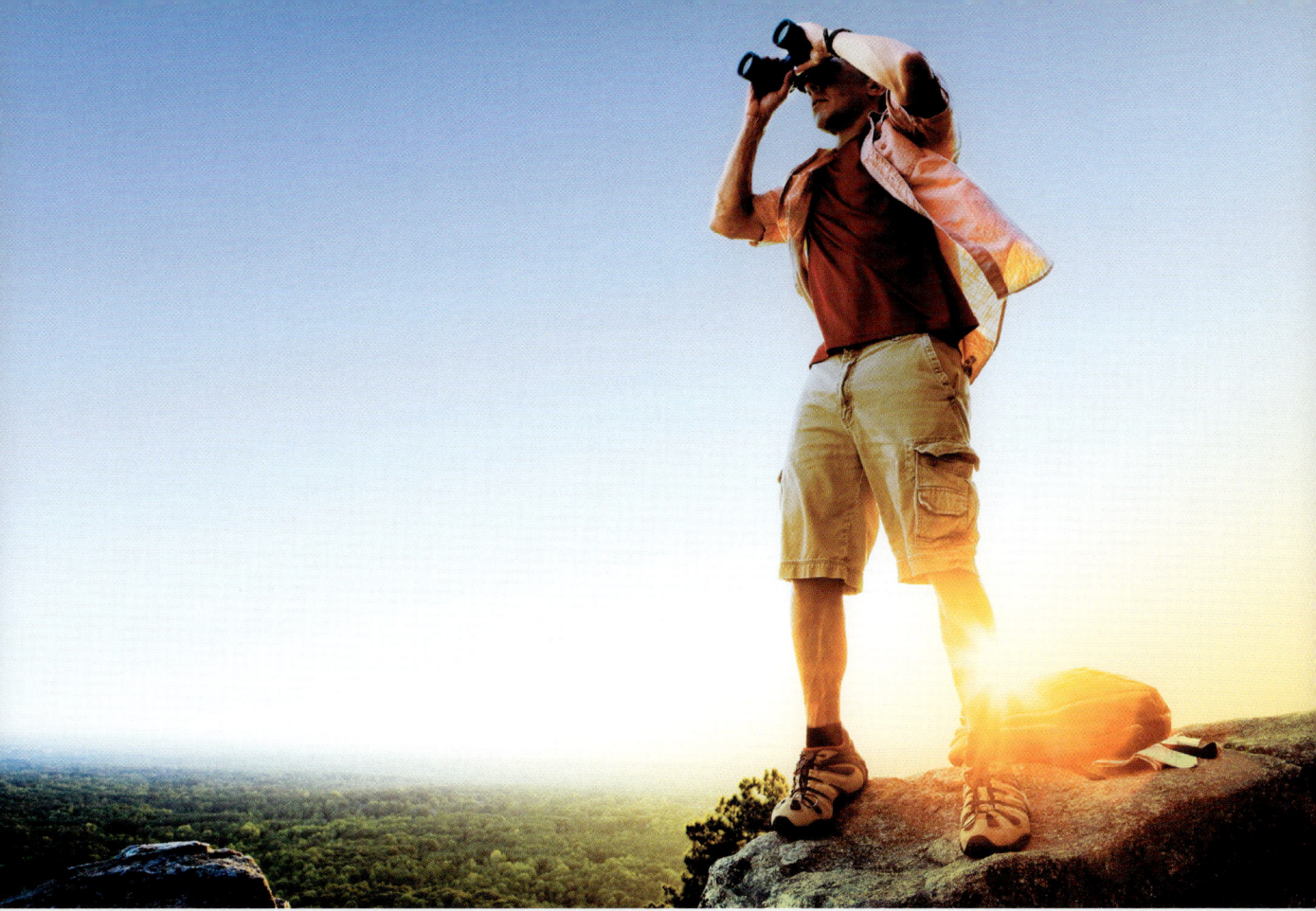

Figure 3.10 Searching. Downloaded over 700 times.

Searching

Creator	Steve Cole (istockphoto.com/stevecoleccs)
Started	2006
Home	USA
Total portfolio	900
Total downloads	Over 72,000
About this photo	Steve says, "All my shoots are carefully planned out days or weeks in advance. We spent a few hours on this mountain shooting different concepts. I asked the model to stand on the rock, and what do you know, the wind started blowing his shirt around in just the right direction, adding more action. Captured with a Canon 1DS MKIII and Elinchrome Ranger 1200WS Power Pak."
Steve's tip	"Shoot loose! Crop later! Quit thinking about the megapixels, f/stops, shutter speed, and so on. Think concept first and technical second. Focus on ideas!"

Spectrum of Stock

If an isolated object on white is on one end of the stock photo spectrum, the conceptual stock photo would be on the other end. My photo of the flock of geese flying in the classic V formation at the beginning of this chapter (Figure 3.1) is actually an image I created in Photoshop by merging a photo of a sunset with geese in flight from another photo. I did actually shoot both images at the same location, but not on the same day. It was in a field I used to pass every day on my commute to and from work (another reason to always have your camera with you). I shot the geese one morning on my way to work and shot the sunset another time on my way home. No one has ever asked if the photo is "real" or not, and I hope I didn't ruin the illusion for you, but that is not really the point of a stock image. The point of a stock image is to communicate.

The sight of a flock of geese in formation is an iconic symbol of the changing seasons. Seasonal changes are rich in metaphor and meaning. Images of spring might conjure thoughts of new life and new beginnings, whereas images of autumn can conjure thoughts of maturing. Migration brings to mind transitions and change. A sunrise is a new beginning, and a sunset is another ending. I've since seen that flock of geese image used in very concrete ways alongside news stories about avian migration; I've also seen it as the cover art on a music CD.

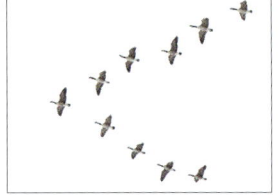
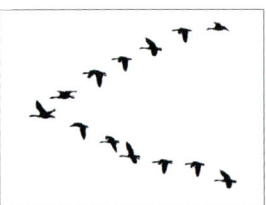

Figure 3.11 Different versions of the same flock of geese images.

Having done the work to isolate the images of the geese to use with the photo of the sunset, I thought those geese images alone would make a useful element all by themselves. I created two versions—one of the geese in silhouette and one just a straight photo—and put both on white backgrounds (**Figure 3.11**). Together, the three images have been downloaded more than 1,400 times.

Ingredients of a Stock Photo

Now that you are seeing stock everywhere and thinking about how different images are used in different projects, I want to focus on some key ingredients that help set stock photos apart from ordinary snapshots. Hopefully, you are starting to keep a list of concepts and ideas that you are excited to create. As you create your list, scout locations and assemble props you'll need to focus in on what exactly it is you want a specific photo to communicate. What will its core message be? Are you trying to evoke a specific feeling, or are you making a photo that is simply representative of a particular item?

Ingredients of a Stock Photo **37**

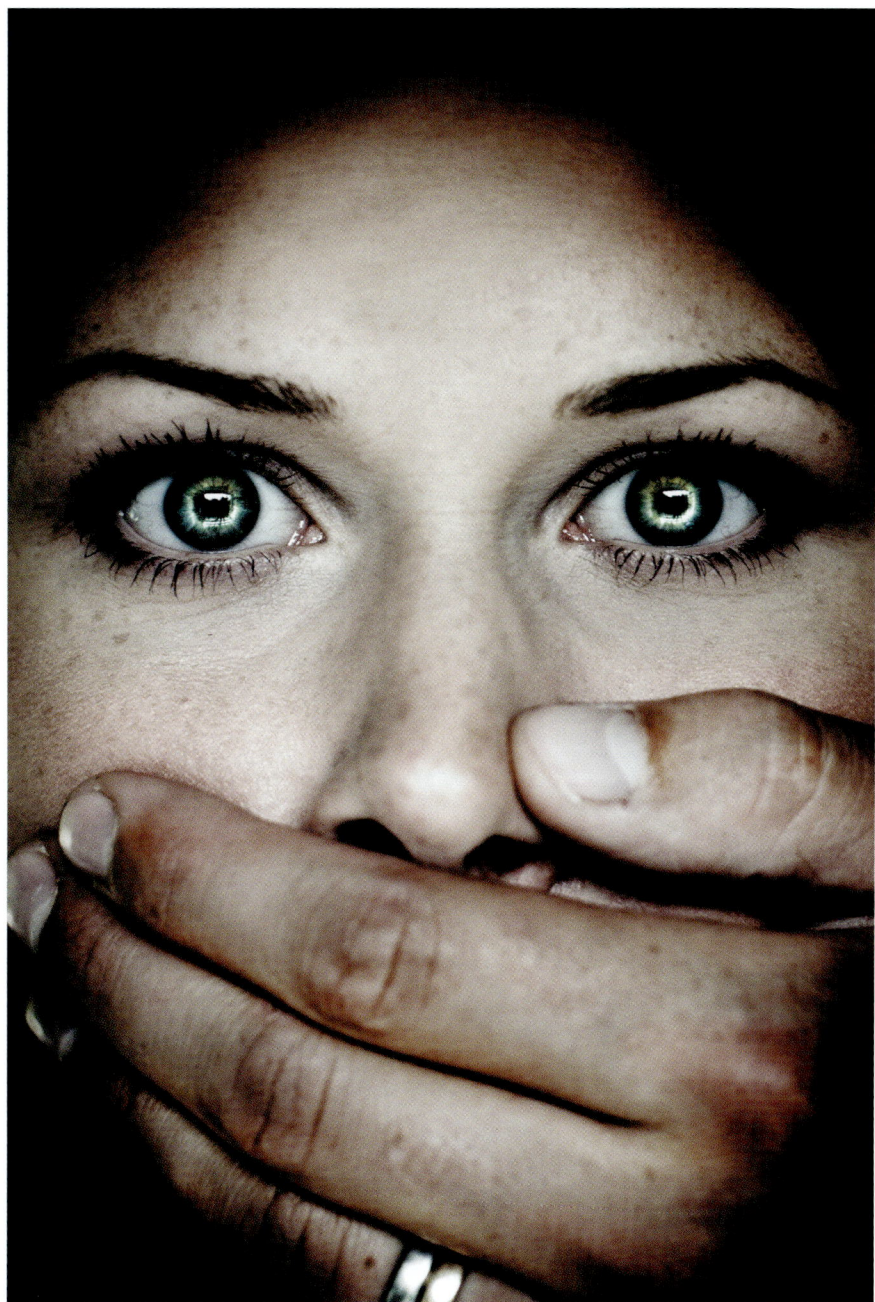

Figure 3.12 Abuse. © istockphoto.com/knape

Communication Is Key

Think about being afraid for a moment. Imagine your eyes widening, your senses on full alert; perhaps the hair on the back of your neck stands up, and your pulse quickens. Tapping into emotion as a means of communication is extremely powerful because it is a message that translates very quickly and bypasses spoken language.

The wide eyes in **Figure 3.12** immediately grab your attention and begin to communicate a message of fear, which is further supported by the enclosing dark vignette around the edges and completely brought home by the large male hand covering the mouth. I've seen that photo used in projects ranging from violence prevention programs to a low-budget horror film poster. It completely succeeds as a communication device.

Contrast that against the sense of fun and adventure in **Figure 3.13**. The clever use of starfish in an anthropomorphic pose, their arms held whimsically in the air while the surf crashes in the background, screams fun vacation getaway. Just because you are intending to communicate an emotion doesn't mean you have to actually use a real person in the shot.

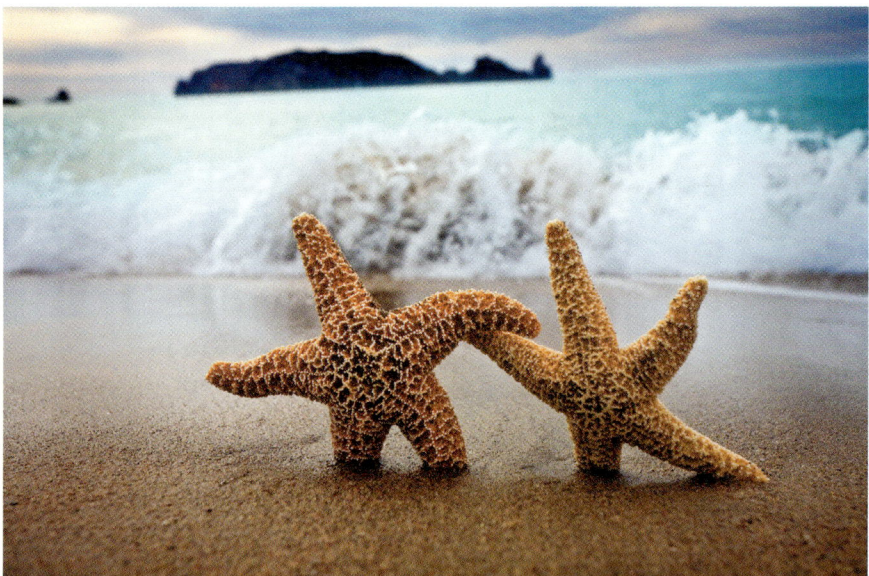

Figure 3.13 In the Mood for Love—Couple of Starfish. © Angel Herrero de Frutos (istockphoto.com/pinopic)

Simplicity of Message

Like a good joke, a good stock image needs to communicate its punch line very simply and clearly. If you have to explain the joke, it probably wasn't very funny or it was too complex. You won't have the opportunity to explain your stock image to anyone, so it has to do that job all on its own.

If you are going to photograph an apple for stock, then strive to shoot the quintessential apple, the personification of applehood, the crispest, healthiest dang apple the world has ever seen. Anyone can drop an apple on a white background and shoot it, so your job is to rise above the rest and create an image that takes *appleness* to a new level. **Figure 3.14** is a great example. The angle it was shot at makes the fruit look like it is standing tall and ready for duty. The bright green leaf jutting off the stem speaks of freshness, as if it were just plucked off the tree. The skin is free of blemish and the reflection of light on the top just makes it shine.

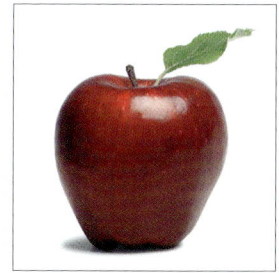

Figure 3.14 Red Apple. © istockphoto.com/DNY59

You don't have to shoot against a white background to be simple, though. Take that same apple (OK, not that same exact apple) and put it in the hand of a lovely young woman lying in the dappled sunlight of a late summer's day, and you can still communicate a message of health or happiness just as simply and clearly (**Figure 3.15**).

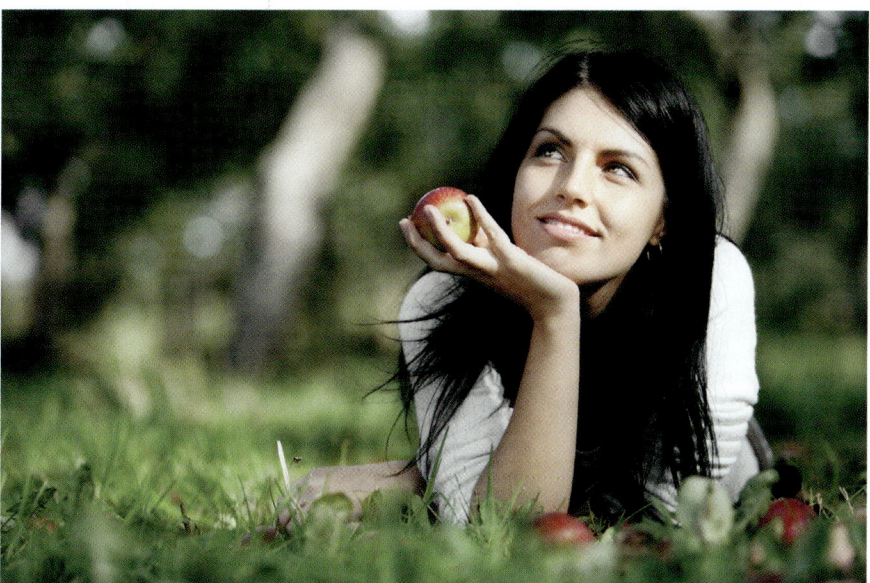

Figure 3.15 Happy Woman. © Lise Gagne (istockphoto.com/lisegagne)

Give Equal Weight to the Background

It is easy to become so focused on the subject of a photo that you forget about the background. This is a critical (and all too common) error when shooting for stock. The background is a key contributor to the usefulness factor of a stock photo. Think back to how you are seeing photos used in advertisements, on magazine covers, alongside articles, on packages, and so on. In many cases, the designer of the project has placed text, logos, or other images on top of the original photo.

Looking back at some of the examples I've shown here, you can see the background lends just as much to the photo as the subject does. In the case of a subject on a white background, like the apple or my frying pan, the background can very easily be removed completely or expanded in any direction, as the final project requires.

However, the background doesn't have to be pure white to be useful. An expanse of solid color or the use of a shallow depth of field that throws the background out of focus is equally successful at supporting the simple message of the subject, while still providing what is called "copy space" within the photo. Copy space is the area of a photo that doesn't contain the subject and provides a natural location for a designer to place text or some other design element (**Figure 3.16**).

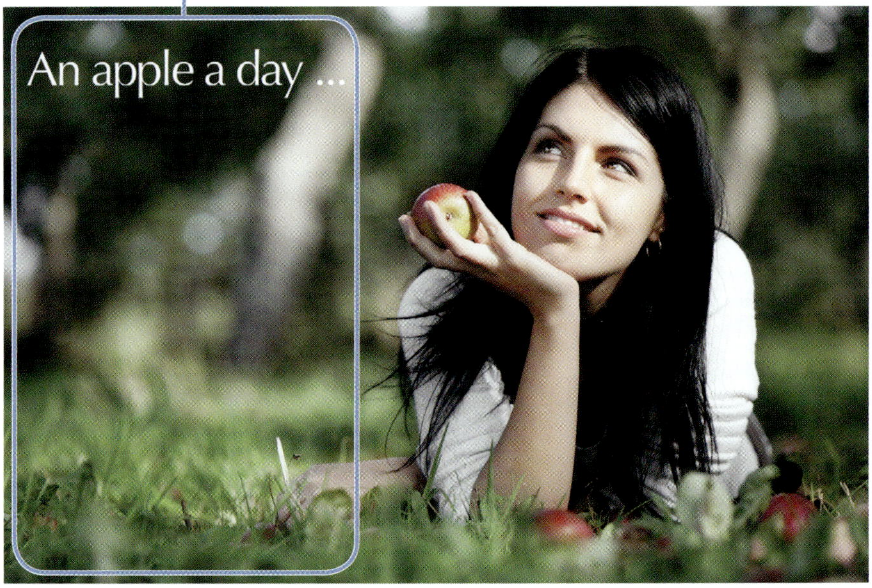

Leaving room for text and other design elements makes a stock photo more useful.

Figure 3.16 Example of how copy space is used.

You have to think about the background when you are composing the shot. We'll talk more about the shooting aspect later, but for now embrace the notion that the background is a key element in your photo's ability to communicate its message. The background needs to support the subject, fit the context, and become an asset to the people who want to use your work in their projects. Remember, when a person licenses your photo for use, he is paying for every pixel, so make them all count.

Assignment

Look through your clip file and take out your favorite three to five pieces. Put yourself in the role of the designer for each piece and visit a few microstock sites to search for images you could use to create a similar project. Take note of the messages you are trying to communicate and the types of images you actually find.

Pick one of the images you found and try to shoot a similar concept (don't just copy what you see; make it your own) that could be used in the same way. Don't focus on the technical quality of your final photo—just focus on the process. ■

4
Of Rights and Wrongs

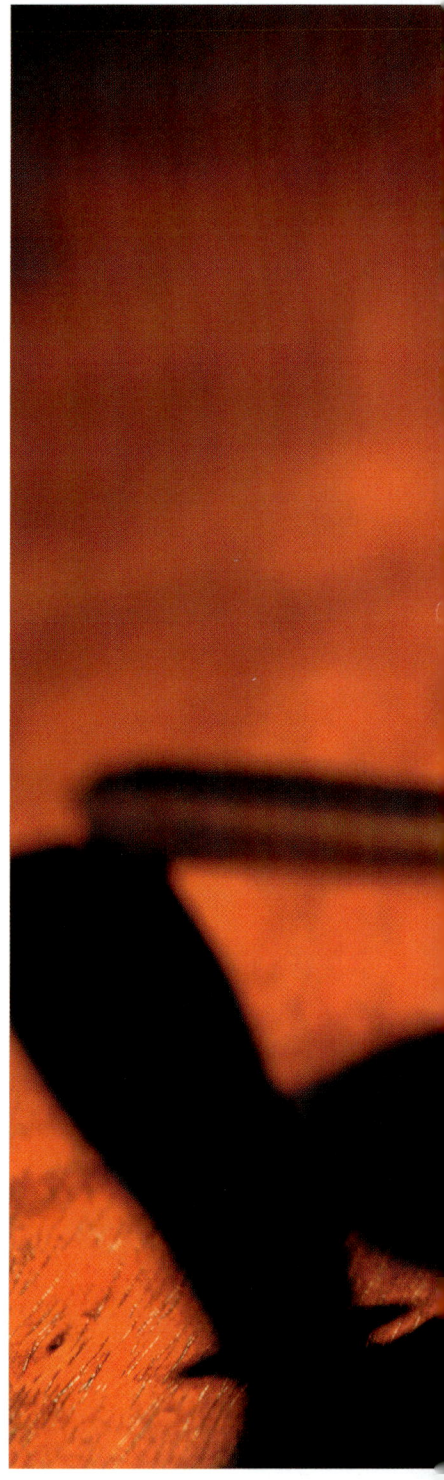

In the United States, as a creator of artistic works—your photos in this case—you have the legal right to control how your photos are used for a limited period of time (your lifetime plus 70 years). This right is what is known as *copyright*, and it is the same right extended to authors, composers, playwrights, and other artists creating new works that are fixed in some tangible form. Assuming you are not working on someone else's time or dime (in a work-for-hire situation), the moment you create a photo you own the copyright to that work. When you make your photos available on a stock site, you are saying that you are willing to let others use your creative work in exchange for a licensing fee. That is the foundation upon which this whole stock concept operates.

When it comes to licensing your photos as royalty-free stock, you also need to be cognizant of the copyrights of other artists, the rights of the people who may be visible in your photos, and the concerns of individuals and companies whose trademarks or other properties may appear in your photos. I'm not a lawyer and do not intend to give legal advice (always seek a trained professional when you want legal advice). This chapter is simply a roadmap for avoiding rejections due to rights problems, so you can focus your energy on the more fun and revenue-generating parts of the process.

The legal issues that relate to what subjects can be used in commercial stock photography can be a source of frustration to many contributors because the clear examples of what you can and cannot use tend to reside at the extreme ends of the spectrum. This leaves a wide area of gray in the middle that is open to interpretation and which can be heavily influenced by the unique context of any given photo. Over the years I have seen microstock

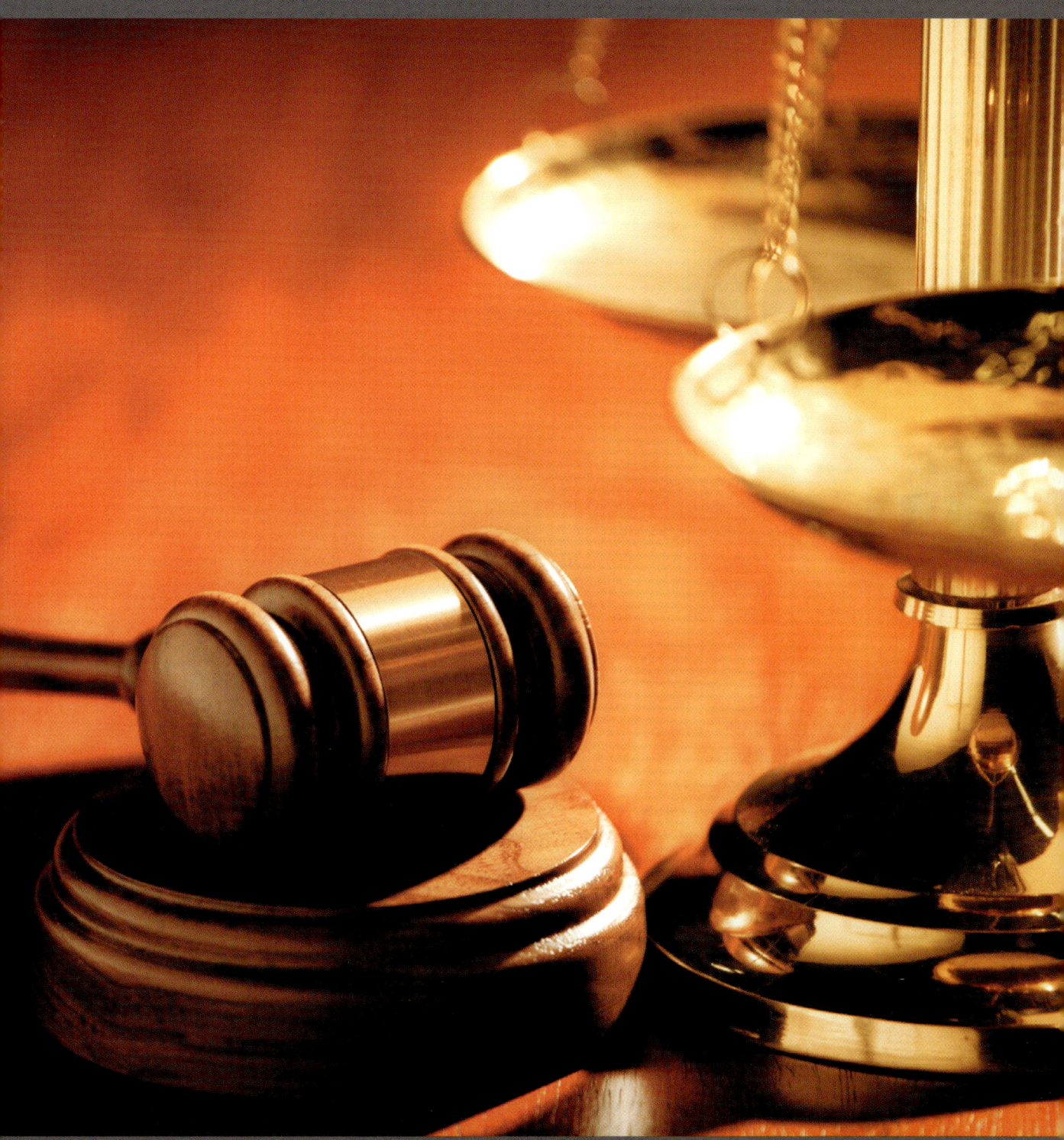
Figure 4.1 Justice Scale and Gavel.
© istockphoto.com/DNY59

agencies steadily become more risk-averse, meaning they are less willing to accept images that are potentially problematic for their customers to use in commercial projects, that is, unless the contributors are able to secure specific permissions in the form of releases of liability from the people or property owners of the items used as subjects in the images.

The key point to keep in mind when creating royalty-free stock is that you are producing images for other people to use in a wide range of projects. The potential uses of the images is what drives the acceptance guidelines at various microstock sites, and it is those guidelines that I want to help you navigate. The best place to start is by understanding exactly what types of uses are granted to the people who buy the licenses.

Reading the Fine Print

As you consider the idea of submitting your work to any stock site, I suggest you start by reading the terms of the site's license that spells out how your photos can be used. Every site will have its content license posted somewhere along the path a customer takes between opening the wallet and downloading a photo. The content license is typically found linked off the same page the photos are displayed, but it may also be in a section of the site devoted to its legal documentation.

No two licenses are worded exactly the same, so take the time to read each site's license carefully. If you find there are uses allowed that you don't agree with, then do not submit your work to that site. For example, perhaps you do not want to see images of your son or daughter used in any advertising, or perhaps you have a person in mind for modeling who doesn't mind advertising uses as long as they can choose the product. If you want more control—and there is nothing wrong with that since this is your intellectual property—then you should pursue other avenues for licensing your work. People who do contribute to microstock sites have decided they have some images they don't mind being used in the ways outlined in the license. The choice is entirely yours to make. Just go in with both eyes open so that you know what you are allowing people to do with your photos before you submit them.

Permitted Uses

Licensing documents can take a little time to read and digest. It is important, though, to read them in full to get the complete picture. I want to highlight the permitted uses sub-section from iStockphoto to give you an idea of the range of uses that are covered (every site has its own version of these uses, so read each carefully). The following are "Permitted Uses" of content:

- Advertising and promotional projects, including printed materials, product packaging, presentations, film and video presentations, commercials, catalogues, brochures, promotional greeting cards and promotional postcards (i.e., not for resale or license);
- Entertainment applications such as books and book covers, magazines, newspapers, editorials, newsletters, and video, broadcast and theatrical presentations;
- On-line or electronic publications, including web pages to a maximum of 800 × 600 pixels for image or illustration content or to a maximum of 640 × 480 for video content;
- Prints, posters (i.e., a hardcopy) and other reproductions for personal use or promotional purposes specified in (1) above, but not for resale, license or other distribution; and… (This is just a portion of the document. You can read the complete document at www.istockphoto.com/license.php.)

These uses are where the rubber meets the road, and this is what drives the creation of each site's rules and guidelines for submission. In a nutshell, because such a wide range of uses are permitted in a standard license, each site is only going to accept content that can safely be used in any of those scenarios without causing legal problems for their customers.

Ultimately, it is the responsibility of the end user—the person paying for the license—to ensure that they have the proper permissions to use the content before they publish. But it doesn't make any sense from the stock site's point of view to provide customers with content that they might not be able to get permission to use. The most effective way for a site to provide useful content to its customers is to enforce relatively conservative submission guidelines so that riskier and potentially more problematic content is kept off the site completely.

In the last few years, an increasing number of microstock sites have begun to offer their customers an editorial-only royalty-free license, which is a more restrictive version of their standard commercial royalty-free license, in an attempt to enter the market for licensing content in specific ways that do not require having releases of liability from the subjects in the images.

Editorial Options

What makes the editorial option different is that it doesn't allow for any advertising or promotional uses of the images. The allowed uses are always the key. There are situations—such as news reporting and academic works—that don't

> **Tip**
>
> I highly recommend attending photography-related trade shows and conferences. They are great for networking with peers, learning from industry leaders, and getting your hands on new products. Imaging USA, PhotoPlus Expo, and Photoshop World are three of my favorites.

require model and property releases for the subjects in the photos. You see these types of uses every day when you watch the evening news, open a newspaper, or check out your favorite news website.

I recently attended the Imaging USA 2010 Convention and Expo. One of the coolest items I saw there was The Polester, a telescoping pole with a camera mount on the top and a built-in remote shutter release. I got a chance to test-drive one, and with my camera about 15 feet off the ground I snapped a few shots for what I hoped could later be stitched into a panorama. I published the resulting photo (**Figure 4.2**) on my blog in a story about my experience at the expo. In this type of editorial use, I did not need to acquire model releases for the people appearing in the scene, nor did I need to remove logos or the many copyrighted photographs you can see on display.

Generally speaking, what might get accepted for editorial is variable because most sites are looking for content that will have a large potential audience. Celebrities, nationally known politicians, and world events are more in demand than your local school board meeting or a random person walking down the street.

The editorial option is worth investigating if you are interested in creating that type of content, but research each site individually to learn what subjects the sites are most interested in so you don't waste your time. The bulk of the business of microstock sites falls under the standard royalty-free license, so let's focus on what you will need to get your photos accepted.

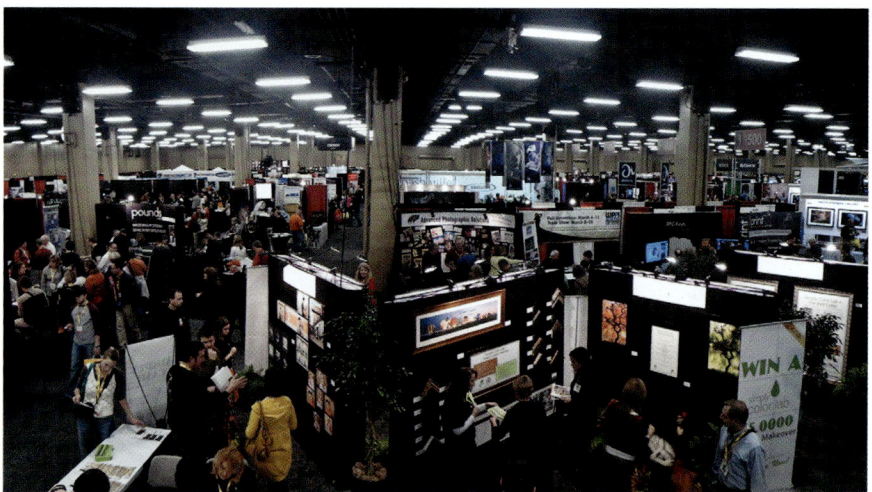

Figure 4.2 The view from 15 feet above the floor of Imaging USA. © Rob Sylvan

The Role of the Model Release

When you ask someone to sign a model release you are asking that person to do two things: to give permission for his or her likeness to be licensed in a multitude of ways, and to agree that all rights to the image belong to the photographer. It doesn't matter if that person is a professional model, your mother-in-law, or even yourself. As people, we are all protected by laws (publicity laws) that give us the right to determine how our *likeness* is used by others for promotional purposes.

The act of getting a signed release opens up many more doors for how you can license a photo that contains a person. If the person is the primary subject in the photo, then you can expect it won't even be accepted at most sites without a signed release. It has become the job of the photographer to acquire the signed release because the photographer has the greatest access to the individual in the photo at the time of the shooting, and the photographer is the one making the decision to license the photo in the first place. Don't waste your time trying to figure out how much of a person has to be in a photo in order for a release to be required. Just ask the person if he or she would be willing to sign a release, and then you will be covered if you need one down the road.

In my experience, most people new to submitting work to microstock sites start by using people who are closest to them: Friends, family, and self-portraits are the norm (some of the most successful contributors use themselves as their primary model). Asking for permission to use someone's likeness is an act of respect for that person, and it creates an opportunity for you to discuss all the possible ways that image might get used. Bring along your folder of clippings to help provide visual examples of potential uses. Believe me, you don't want to get a call from an upset friend/family member/lover (or heaven forbid, ex-lover) wondering how his or her photo ended up in an advertisement or on the package of some product without his or her knowledge. It is a lot more fun and rewarding to involve them right from the start and manage expectations for what could happen. Not everyone is interested in signing a release, and that is perfectly understandable and should be respected.

You will find that each site has electronic copies of its own model release you can download for free. However, you will also find each site might have a nuanced take on what elements make a release acceptable. The best advice I can give is to use the release from the site with the strictest standards (which in my opinion is iStockphoto) to increase your chances of it being accepted at the most places. It is perfectly acceptable to print a release on your own letterhead if you prefer. What is most important is that you do not leave any fields blank.

Tip

Head over to www.istock-photo.com/license.php to find links to versions of releases in 13 languages.

Finding People Willing to Model

If you are not surrounded by people who are willing to sign a release, and you are not interested in stepping in front of the camera, then you might consider looking for models by placing advertisements or contacting local modeling agencies. A common path taken by many microstock contributors is to enter into a trade arrangement with a model that exchanges the model's time (and signature on a release) for a specific number of prints (or electronic copies on CD) that they can use for their own portfolios and promotion. You might hear this referred to as TFP (Time for Prints or Time for Portfolio) or TFCD (Time for CD) or some variation on the theme. Craig's List (www.craigslist.org), One Model Place (www.onemodelplace.com), and Model Mayhem (www.modelmayhem.com) are good resources to check out for finding models in your area.

One other great resource worth exploring is your fellow microstock contributors. Many sites have extremely active communities of members (I'll cover this more in Chapter 12) who arrange events that are equal parts social events and photo shoots. I've been to quite a few, and they are a blast. They are great learning opportunities and an excellent way to share the costs associated with locations, models, props, and equipment.

Can I Get a Witness?

Finding a model is the first step, but it is also in your best interest to have a neutral third party (who is at least 18 years old) on hand to witness the model signing the release. This third party's sole job is to witness the signing of the release. They don't need to be present at the time the photo was taken, and they don't even need to see the photos. All they need to do is see the model signing the release, and then they also sign and date the release right after the fact.

This may seem like overkill, especially if the model is someone you know, but it is a precaution worth taking for your own protection, and most sites require a witness signature on the release. The one instance where a witness is usually not required is in the case of a self-portrait since there is little chance you will sue yourself.

Objects do not have rights like people do, but there are issues you need to be concerned with regarding the objects that appear in your photos intended to be licensed as royalty-free stock.

A Healthy Respect for Property

An object's design can be protected by copyright. However, simply taking a photo of that object does not violate its owner's copyright. Where it can get touchy is how that photo might get used as defined in a typical royalty-free license. Some objects and designs become associated with a company's identity because they are legally trademarked and used precisely for that purpose. For example, a company's logo is a very recognizable symbol of the organization's identity, and a lot of money is spent protecting how that identity is used. So when you produce stock images, you need to be very mindful of the objects you use as props so that you can avoid including problematic content in your photos, such as logos and trade names. There are other things, everyday objects, and you need to seek out the most generic-looking and nondescript versions to use as your stock photo props. Remember, good and useful stock photos are extremely generic so that they can communicate their message simply.

Prevention Pays Off

We'll spend some time going over how to remove problematic elements from your photos after the fact using software solutions in Chapter 9, but the most efficient way to remove problem items is to do it before you trip the shutter. Here are a few tips:

- Survey the scene for logos, trademarks, and copyrighted subjects before you shoot and keep them out of the frame.
- Ask your models ahead of time to wear generic clothing that does not carry logos, and then bring some extra clothing items for backup if needed.
- Use shallow depth of field to blur problem content so that it is unrecognizable.
- Find a camera angle that obscures problem content.
- Cover, move, remove, or otherwise physically obscure logos and problem content.

If you have an object that you want or need to be the primary subject of the photo, find out if it is possible to acquire a property release from the copyright owner. A common scenario is when a painting is used as a prop in the background of a room setting. Some photographers will simply use software later to replace the painting with an image for which they own the copyright, or, if they know a painter, they'll try to get the artist's permission to use a painting in the scene.

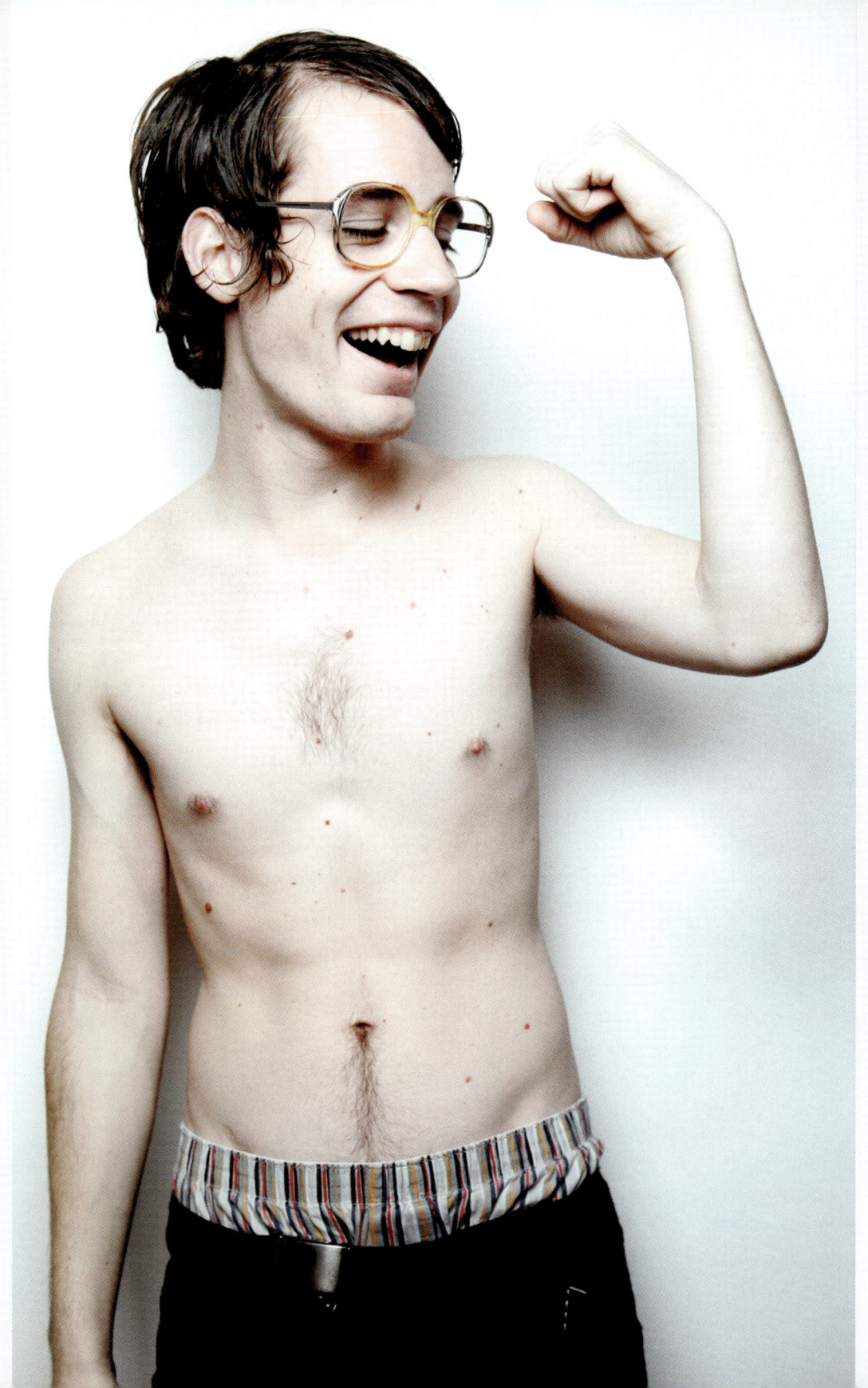

Mr. Muscle, Looking for Date

Creator	Ivar Teunissen (istockphoto.com/ivar)
Started	2003
Home	The Netherlands
Total portfolio	310 images
Total downloads	Over 8,500
About this photo	Ivar says, "Even though this image is really simple, it's been quite popular. I keep getting emails from people spotting it all over the world, and have gotten photos of people posing next to the photo! To me, the strength of the image lies in the fact that it's such an easy image. It was created during a session where we just decided to have some fun. People seem to be able to connect with the level of joy and reality the image seems to emit. I used a Canon 5D, 150ws falcon eyes with 60*60cm softbox, secondhand granny glasses, and loads of cheap hair gel. The image was shot in my living room, against a white wall."
Ivar's tip	"Keep putting love into it, and make sure it's a nice experience. It will show in a photo if you had a good time on the set, and people really seem to feel connected with those kind of photos."

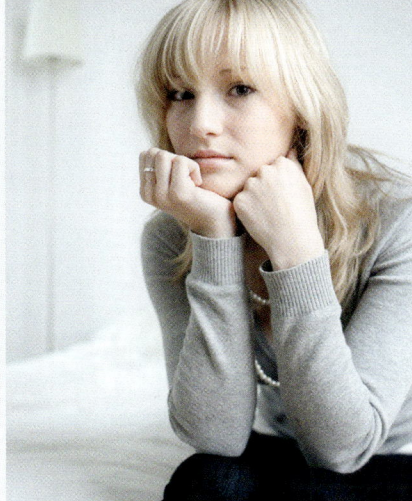
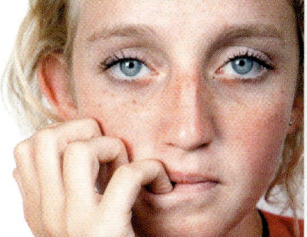
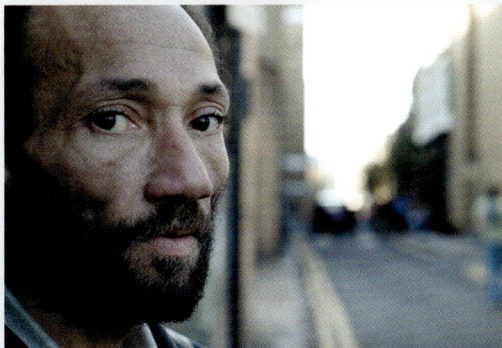

Figure 4.3 Mr. Muscle, looking for a date. Downloaded over 600 times.

Figure 4.4 On the Edge.

Figure 4.5 Been Thinking About You and Me.

Figure 4.6 Other Side of the Street.

A property release does the same job as the model release, which is to grant permission for the use and to agree that the photographer owns all the rights to the photos that are created during the shoot. You can find a sample property release at www.istockphoto.com/license.php.

The context in which the object is used in the photo is a primary factor in determining how problematic it might be. For example, a stuffed Beanie Baby™ teddy bear on a plain white background would be a problem, but that same bear sitting on a shelf in the background of a photo depicting a child doing homework could be just fine. I'm sorry to say there is no easy answer, but keep in mind that most sites tend to err on the side of caution when evaluating submitted content, so you should, too. You'll soon learn the common mantra recited by all experienced microstock contributors, "When in doubt, clone it out."

Being Inspired by Others (But Not Too Much)

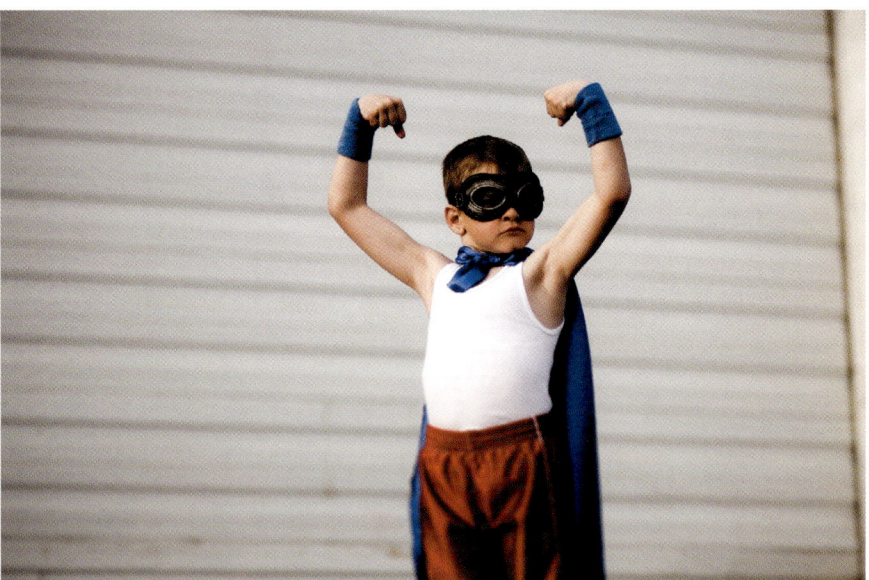

Figure 4.7 Short Superhero. © Andrew Rich (www.istockphoto.com/RichVintage)

There is nothing wrong with being inspired by others to do great things. We all have heroes and role models who we aspire to emulate. When it comes to art, artists have been influenced by other artists since the first drawing went up on the cave wall. These days we are surrounded by images at every turn, and it is impossible to not be influenced by what we see in some way. I've long lost count of how many images have passed before my eyes, but I still find myself awestruck on a regular basis by some new image that makes me think, "Dang! I wish I could do that!" I file those images away in my mind and try to figure out the qualities that caused me to stop in my tracks. Those qualities inspire me to improve my own work in the hope that I may one day have the same effect on someone else.

When you create an image, it is your expression of the subject that is copyrighted, not the idea that served as the inspiration for its creation. It is not possible to copyright a concept or a subject. If you create an image after being inspired by someone else's image, it is your job to respect that artist's copyright by making your image your own unique expression. Think about all the elements of a photo that the photographer can control to express his or her vision, such as:

- Choice of subject
- Arrangement of subjects
- Quality of light (time of day, harsh, soft, intense, diffuse, warm, cool, and so on)
- Camera angle (head on, far away, close up, from below, from above, and so on)
- Choice of colors represented
- Choice of background and negative space

> **Tip**
>
> The US Copyright Office allows you to create a public record connecting you to your work. It's a completely optional process, but something you should be aware of before letting your work go out into the world. The American Society of Media Photographers has an excellent resource and walk-through of the copyright registration process. See http://asmp.org/tutorials/best-practices.html.

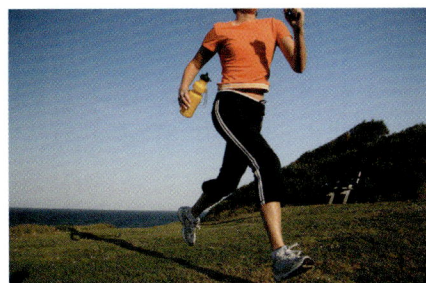

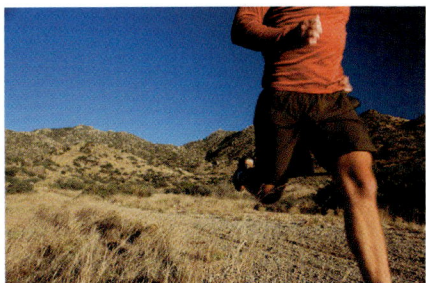

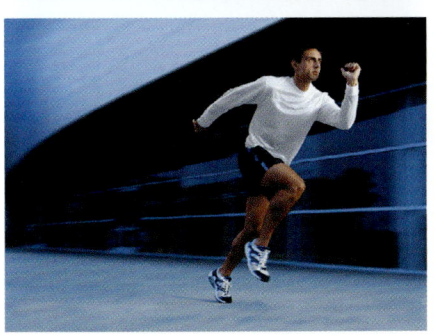

Figure 4.8 Three different takes on jogging. Collectively downloaded over 13,000 times. (www.istockphoto/blublaf, www.istockphoto/amygdala_imagery, www.istockphoto.com/EricHood)

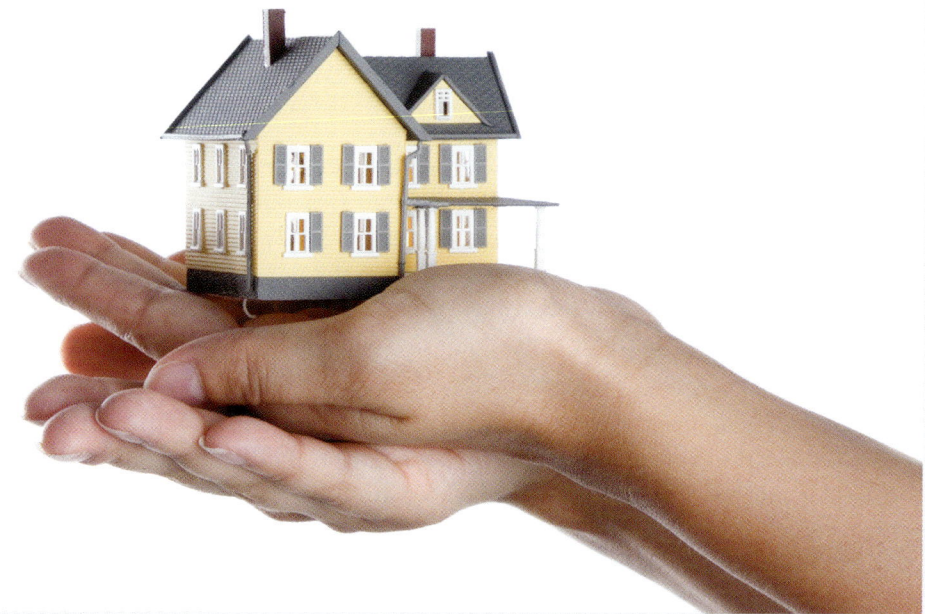

Figure 4.9 Real Estate. Downloaded over 1,400 times.

Real Estate

Creator	Arthur Kwiatkowski (istockphoto.com/arsenik)
Started	2005
Home	Canada
Total portfolio	3,800 images
Total downloads	Over 63,000
About this photo	Arthur says, "This has been a very successful image for me, and that concept led to many other images in my portfolio. It was shot with a Canon 20D, and a Canon EF 24-105 mm f/4L lens. The lighting was 2 Alien Bees 800s with a roll of white background paper. I noticed the toy/model house in a hobby shop and had an idea for a real estate photo. After purchasing the house, I wanted to verify with the manufacturer that there were no copyrights and that I was legally able to use the house as stock photography. I contacted the CEO of the company and received written permission to use the model house for stock. The images from this concept have paid off the initial expense of the model house and made a substantial profit for me."
Arthur's tip	"Don't be afraid to ask for permission to shoot somewhere. If I see a location that I think would be great for a photo shoot, I'll pick up the phone and call, or I'll send an email. You'd be surprised how many positive responses you'll get if you just ask for permission. What's the worst that can happen? If the person says, 'No,' you move on and ask someone else."

There are many more variables, but each deliberate creative choice is part of your unique expression that contributes to the overall look and feel of your photos, and over time, may become the hallmarks of your particular style.

In the world of stock photography it can be a challenge to produce completely unique work because customers like to have a variety of images to choose from on any given subject—jogging, for instance. A search on *jogging* (**Figure 4.8**) would show there is a lot of publicly available data, such as download totals, that might indicate that jogging photos are in high demand. You have the responsibility to respect the copyrights of your peers and not simply copy their jogging photos. But no one owns a particular subject or idea, and the more common the composition, the harder it is to make a case that no one else can create a photo the same way.

For example, consider a pair of horseshoes on a white background (**Figure 4.10**) or pretty much any common object on a plain background, for that matter. There is no judge or jury in the world that would decide that only I can create stock photographs of horseshoes on plain white backgrounds. I may own the copyright to this particular photo, but when it comes to such commonplace subjects and plain compositions, it just isn't fair or reasonable to grant a monopoly to a single person. The less common the objects, and the more creative you are in creating the composition, the more complex the issue becomes.

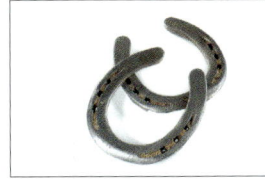

Figure 4.10 Horseshoes.
© Rob Sylvan

This is a complicated issue to do justice to in this small space, but be respectful as you create new works. Take inspiration from what you see around you. Do not become a human copy machine creating reproductions of other artists' works as a shortcut to creativity.

Assignment

Take a close look at the three photos in Figure 4.6. Grab a sheet of paper and draw three columns. Label the first column *similarities*, the second column *differences*, and the third column the *core message* (what you think a photo is trying to communicate).

With that in mind, choose a message you would like to illustrate with a photo of your own. Carefully consider all the elements at your disposal for creating an image that is similar in theme, but different in execution. Then do it! Don't worry about it being good enough to submit for stock. The point of the exercise is that there is so much learning involved in the doing that the thinking alone cannot achieve.

Bonus points: Print out a model release and approach someone you know and ask her to be your model. Show her your clip file and discuss all the possible ways this photo could be used. ■

5
Tools of the Trade

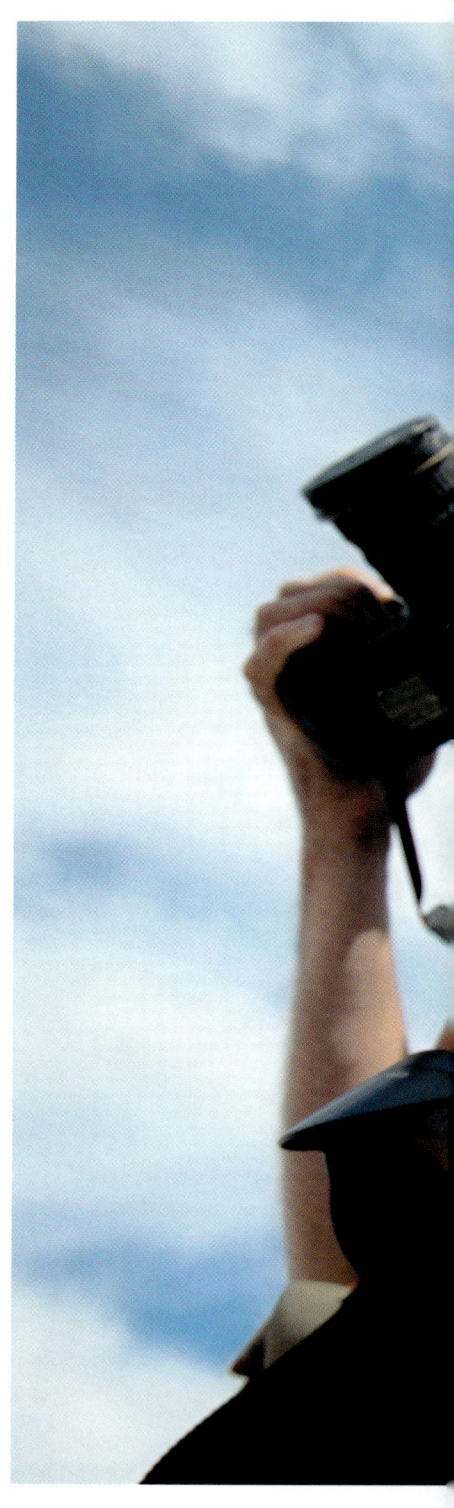

> *It's gotta be the shoes.*
> —Mars Blackmon

There was a series of commercials for Nike's *Air Jordan* sneakers in the late '80s that featured Mars Blackmon, Spike Lee's fictional alter-ego, and legendary basketball player Michael Jordan. The gist of the commercial was that Mars Blackmon attributed Michael Jordan's prowess on the court to his shoes, despite Michael's repeated, patient, yet slightly exasperated, denial that no, it was not the shoes at all.

If you've ever shown someone a photo you are really proud of only to hear, "Wow, you must have a really great camera," you can just politely smile and think of Mars Blackmon.

The flip side, of course, is that there is a wide (and ever-growing) range of camera equipment, in terms of quality, cost, ease of use, and functionality. The challenge we face as photographers (at all levels) is how to navigate through the dizzying array of choices and make the best investments we can on equipment that offers us the best fit, with a little room to grow (and wiggle our creative toes) without breaking the bank.

Gear Crazy

Talking about photo gear with other photographers can be fun and enlightening, but sometimes a little crazy-making, too. You may hear a lot of seemingly conflicting advice about what is the best and why. Some will swear you need this gadget or should never use that brand, and then you'll find people who

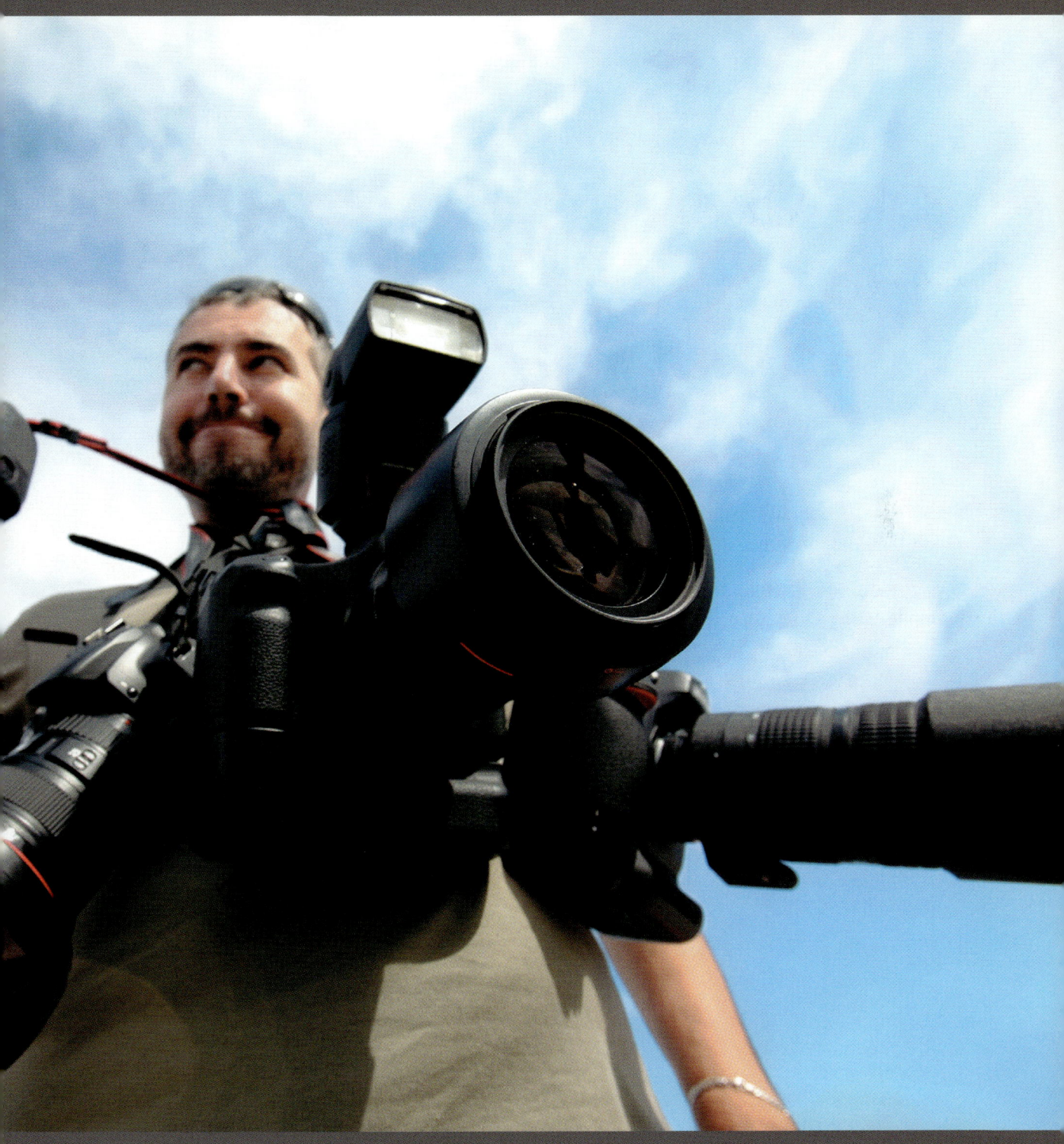
Figure 5.1 Crazy Paparazzi.
© Peeter Viisimaa (istockphoto.com/peeterv)

say the exact opposite. It is easy (and sometimes fun) to get caught up in these often lively gear debates or to get swept away by someone else's glowing review of his latest acquisition. After awhile you may find yourself thinking that if you just had *that* camera or *this* lens, you'd be getting the shots you want. This is a place we all go to at some point.

My advice is to not buy anything … yet. I don't know you. I don't know what experiences you've had, what gear you already own or have access to, or where you want to go in the future. I have to assume that you already have some equipment at your disposal or you wouldn't be holding this book. And there is definitely new gear in your future because there is no way around that simple fact.

However, before you open your wallet I suggest you first seek mastery over what you already have. Sure, you may find out that what you have is not good enough to get you where you want to go, but discovering exactly what limitations your current gear has will be incredibly valuable for honing in on what you want to invest in next.

I can't teach you everything you need to know about photography gear in a single chapter. What I can do is make the case for what equipment choices I think will help you improve your chances at getting your stock photos approved.

The most essential piece of gear (after your brain) is, of course, your camera. Cameras tend to be lumped into two general categories: point-and-shoot or digital single lens reflex (DSLR). Due to advances in digital camera technology, the line between these two rather broad categories has become increasingly blurred, but a DSLR is pretty much defined by the fact that it has interchangeable lenses, while a point-and-shoot does not. Some cameras are designed for the casual shooter who just wants an easy way to capture special moments in life, while

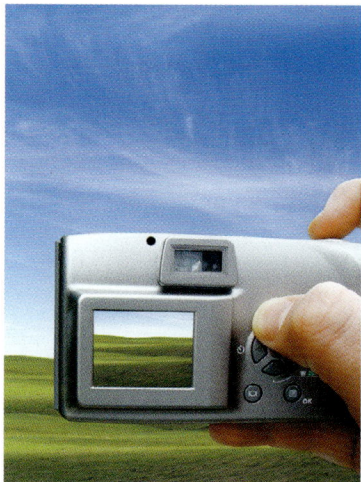 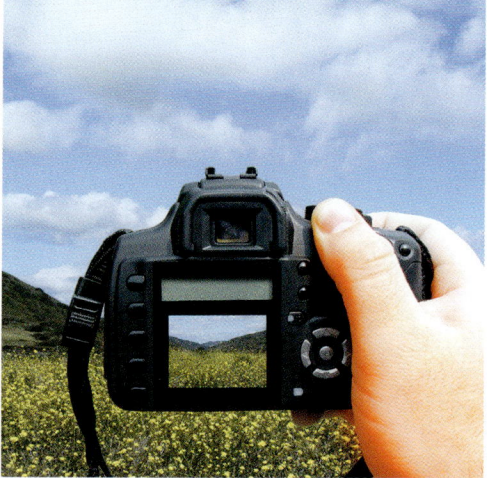

Figure 5.2 Taking a Photo. Both. © Lee Pettet (istockphoto.com/LPETTET)

other cameras offer more features for a higher price and target the *prosumer*, the person who wants to do more and is willing to pay more but who is not earning their living from photography. At the top is the pro gear that typically offers the largest feature set, the best quality, and the highest cost.

It has been my experience that the majority of microstock contributors enter the field at the prosumer level. Over time, as their experience, knowledge, and success grows, so does their equipment budget. There are people who have started with a high-quality point-and-shoot, and have gone on to build complete photographic studios. But as the microstock industry has matured and the opportunity to earn more has increased, I see more people enter at the professional level.

At the end of the day, when people are looking at photos to download for their projects, they care more about the usefulness of the photo than about what camera it was created with. That said, your photos still need to get past the gatekeepers. The right equipment will improve your odds.

Camera Choices

A question I often hear from people who are new to microstock is, "Can I submit photos taken with my point-and-shoot camera?" This is a fair question since it is the type of camera many of us have when we first get bitten by the shutterbug. Back in 2002, I started with a 3 megapixel point-and-shoot camera, but that camera wouldn't cut it today.

However, the technological advances in point-and-shoot cameras have come a long way since 2002. Your cell phone may have a better camera in it than my old Kodak DC4800. So, can you submit point-and-shoot photos? Yes, but the range in circumstances under which you can get images of acceptable quality for stock is going to be significantly smaller than the range of a DSLR.

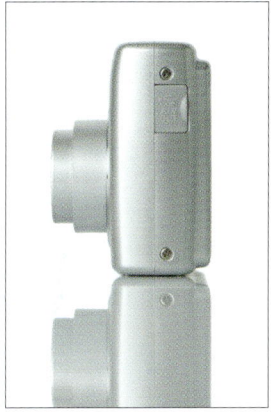

Figure 5.3 Point-and-shoot digital camera. © istockphoto.com/ jsemeniuk

Every camera and lens combination has a sweet spot; a set of conditions that will produce an optimal result. Even the worst camera in the world has its sweet spot. When you make the commitment to purchase any piece of photographic equipment, you should also make the commitment to learn the optimal set of conditions required to get the best result out of that gear.

When I say optimal conditions I mean, what combinations of ISO, f-stop, and exposure produce the most noise-free and tack-sharp results? What is the closest you can stand to your subject and still be able to focus? What is the farthest away you can be and still fill the frame? What is the widest aperture you can use to get the shallowest depth of field? If you are using a zoom lens, what focal length produces the sharpest result with the least edge distortion?

I do want to warn you that some of this may involve a little-used and somewhat scary trick of the trade called "reading the manual." You don't have to read it cover to cover; just keep it handy for emergencies—like the moment you are ready to put all your gear on eBay and take up knitting.

Some of a photo's problems can be fixed later in post-production, but ideally, if you get to know your camera's sweet spots you can save yourself a lot of post-production time by avoiding problems in the first place. You'll also know when you to have to move out of the optimal zone because there just is no other way to get a certain shot.

The most essential difference between a point-and-shoot and a DSLR is the size of the sweet spot. Because a DSLR allows you to change lenses, you have entirely new worlds of possibilities that point-and-shoots just can't enter.

The flip side, of course, is that the compactness of a point-and-shoot camera makes it much more mobile, which means it is much more likely to be within arm's reach. It is also much less "in your face" when you point it at someone, so other people will be more at ease around you. For these reasons, I still keep a point-and-shoot camera in my bag and am quite fond of it, but I wouldn't dream of not having a DSLR that provided much more flexibility.

So, back to the original question: Do people submit photos from a point-and-shoot and get them accepted? Yes. Are those same people on a trajectory that will lead to their first purchase of a DSLR? If they are planning to continue shooting for stock, the answer is "yes" again.

The file format you want to shoot with—whether it's the ubiquitous JPEG or the increasingly popular raw format—can also influence the type of camera you buy. Let's take a look at the differences between these file formats.

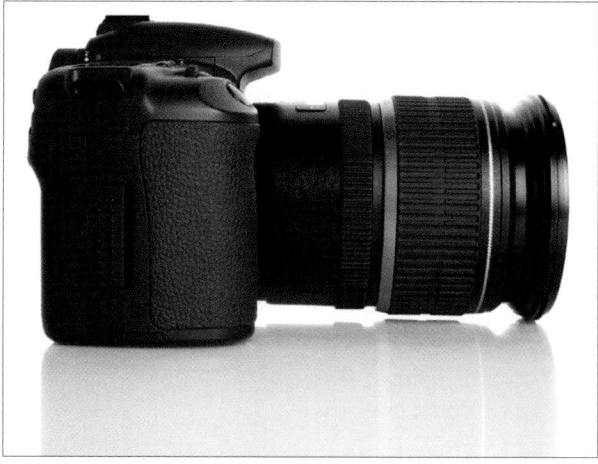

Figure 5.4 Side view of digital 35mm camera. © istockphoto.com/ jsemeniuk

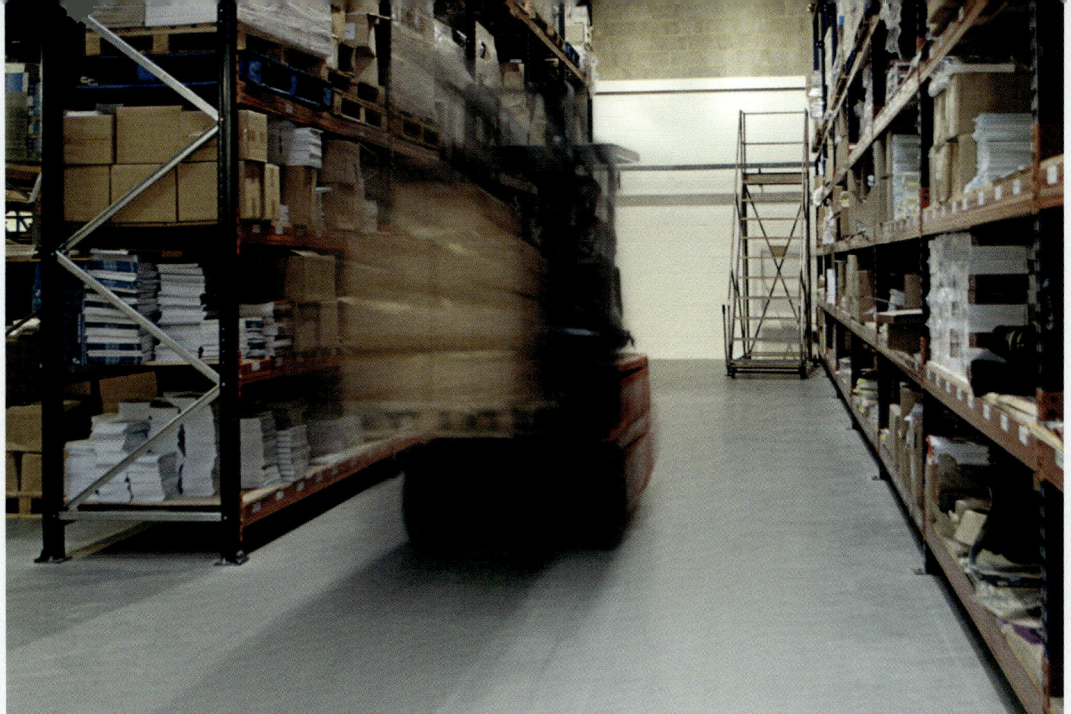

Figure 5.5 Busy Warehouse. Downloaded over 800 times.

Busy Warehouse

Creator	Carole Gomez (istockphoto.com/CaroleGomez)
Started	2005
Home	United Kingdom
Total portfolio	1,449 images
Total downloads	Over 22,000
About this photo	Carole says, "This image was taken on a Canon 30d. I shot this while doing a freelance project for a warehousing company. The company was happy to allow me to use some images from the day for stock in order to have a reduced project rate, and the employee shown was happy to sign a model release. I think the shot has been successful because there is just enough of the location to show that it is a warehouse, but little enough that it remains generic. The motion blur adds a sense of productivity and renders the product being moved more generic."
Carole's tip	"The best piece of advice I was given was to look at how images are being used in advertising. Understanding how imaging works within design is key to understanding how you can take a useful image for stock."

Raw vs. JPEG

JPEG is a very familiar file format. It is the file format of almost every photo on the Internet, as well as the file format that your phone's camera uses and likely the default file format on whatever other digital camera you own. If you've ever looked at a photo on a computer, the odds are that it was a JPEG.

Tip

It is tempting to buy the largest-capacity memory card so you can fit more images on a single card. Fitting all your photos on a single card sounds great until it fails and you lose everything. Consider buying smaller cards instead so that your risk of loss is reduced.

The reason for JPEG's popularity is that, by design, it does a great job of compressing image data to smaller file sizes with little or no visual difference from the original. A smaller file size is a great advantage for fitting more photos on a memory card or your computer's disk drive and for sending photos over the Internet.

The main downside of the JPEG format is that it uses *lossy* compression: It reduces file size by removing some of the original data from the image. The more compression you apply, the smaller the file size and, consequently, the more data that is lost from the original. Too much JPEG compression (**Figure 5.6**) will result in visible artifacts that look like jagged or blocky areas in your photo. It goes without saying that too much JPEG compression would result in a rejection at any stock site. Luckily, it is easy to avoid: Simply apply the least amount of JPEG compression possible when creating the file.

The other potential negative to shooting in JPEG mode is that it requires your camera to process the original capture data for output. To do this, the camera uses a combination of the settings you dialed in via the camera's menu options (such as color, white balance, sharpening, and contrast adjustments), and the programming instructions written into the camera's software. You'll often hear

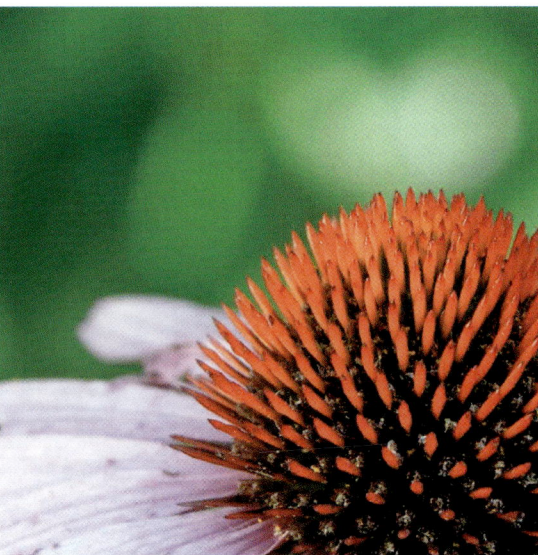

Figure 5.6 The telltale blocky-pixel look of too much JPEG compression. For a closer look, download from www.takingstockphoto.com/downloads.

this referred to as having the settings *baked in*. This means that by the time you first see that photo on your computer, it has lost some of the original capture data from both JPEG compression and whatever processing was done by the camera along the way.

This is not automatically a bad thing. It just means that you may have limited some of your post-processing options in the future since you can't unbake a cake. For example, if too much sharpening was applied by the camera, there is no way to undo that and start over from scratch. The damage is done.

Because of the smaller file sizes possible with JPEG, it makes a good output format for photos that will be distributed over the Internet (not to mention the fact that all the microstock sites require you to upload your photo submissions in JPEG format). But if you would like to have the opportunity to work with more of the original data captured by the camera when you sit down for editing, there is an alternative to consider: shooting in raw.

Keeping Your Options Open

Raw is not a specific file format, but rather a shooting mode that saves out the unprocessed image data from the sensor to your memory card. There are actually a great many raw file formats that are unique to different camera makes and models. Each camera manufacturer has its own proprietary raw format, with file extensions such as .cr2, .nef, .pef, and .raf, to name a few, and new formats appear with each new camera model. The primary benefit gained by shooting in raw mode is that you now have all the original data captured by your camera to work with and to process as you see fit. No data has been lost due to compression or by in-camera processing.

The flip side is that the file size of a raw photo is as much as four times or more larger than its JPEG equivalent. There are types of *lossless* compression formats for raw files, which will reduce the file size of a raw file, but these files will still be significantly larger than a JPEG. That means fewer photos per memory card as well as more disk space required for storage. In addition, since by design raw photo data is unprocessed, you will need to use some type of raw processing software before your photos are ready to be shared with the world.

Here's how I have approached this particular dilemma. When I first started shooting digital, JPEG was the only option my camera supported. As my skill improved and my interests in photography increased, I upgraded to a camera that produced a larger and better quality JPEG. When I reached the point of purchasing my first DSLR camera, which offered a raw format option, I stayed with JPEG because that was all I knew. It took me about a year to start testing the raw waters, and I did so by setting my camera to raw+JPEG mode, which meant the camera saved a raw file and a processed JPEG side by side. This seemed like the best of both worlds in terms of maximum flexibility, but of course it meant even more disk space was being used by twice as many photos. Eventually my confidence in my raw processing skills increased to the point that I abandoned shooting in JPEG (for stock purposes) completely and have never looked back.

I appreciate having as much data on hand as possible when processing my photos for output. As the software for processing raw data has improved, I have been able to go back and reprocess older raw photos with better results than were originally possible, something you cannot do with a JPEG photo. The price of hard drive storage has continued to decrease over time, so for me the trade-off in file size has been outweighed by the benefits of keeping an archive of raw image data. You'll need to make the best decision for your current needs. If you are not shooting in raw already, I strongly encourage you to at least try shooting raw+JPEG so that if/when the day comes that you are ready to give raw a try, you'll have an archive of raw files already on hand.

Key Camera Settings

If you're going to shoot JPEG, that means that your camera is the first computer that is going to process your photos. This in itself is not a bad thing, since the people who make those cameras are actually pretty smart folks. However, they

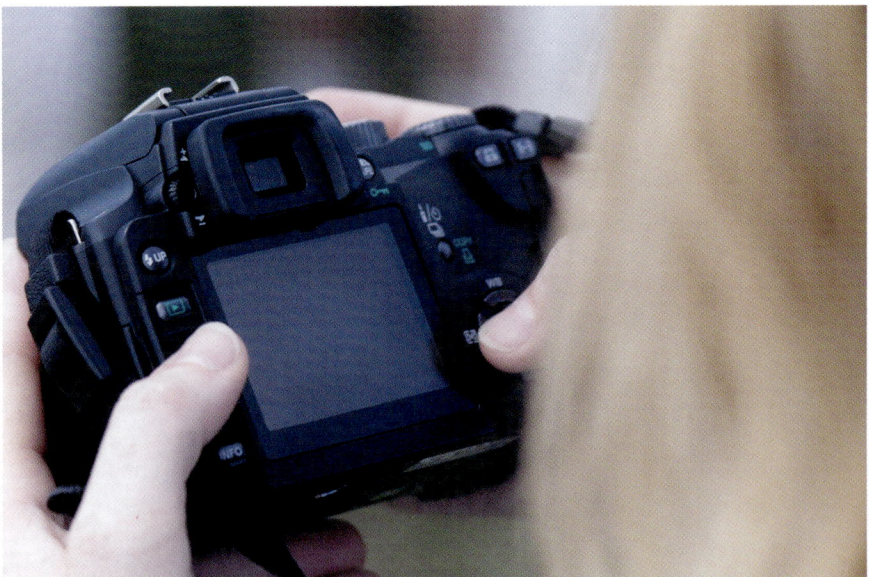

Figure 5.7 Choosing your camera settings.

are designing cameras to make pretty pictures, not necessarily pictures that will pass the standards for submission for stock. In this light, it is in your best interest to configure your camera to do the least amount of processing of your JPEGs as possible.

If you are shooting raw, you can skip this section because none of these settings will be baked into the raw photo's pixels. Your camera will save these settings as instructions in each raw photo's *metadata*, which is the non-image data section of a file format. If you are using the raw processing software provided by your camera's manufacturer, then it will read those instructions, and use them as a starting point for processing your raw files. However, you retain complete control for changing settings as you see fit since the data is unprocessed. If you use a third-party vendor's raw processing software (such as Adobe Camera Raw or Lightroom), then those applications will completely ignore in-camera processing settings, except for white balance, and have their own default settings to use as a starting point (more on this in Chapter 8).

Do Touch That Dial

Every camera's feature-set and menu offerings are going to be different, but there are several types of in-camera image processing that you should be aware of so you can make conscious decisions about what you want done to your photos. I'll assume you have already chosen to set the camera to the largest image size and least amount of JPEG compression (typically called "highest quality"), so here are the other settings to look for and configure:

> **Note**
>
> This may be one of those times to pull out the manual and decipher what all those symbols and labels mean.

- Sharpening: Turn this to the lowest setting the camera allows. Off is preferred. I'll discuss the role of sharpening in Chapter 8.
- Contrast: Set this to the lowest setting possible. You can always add more contrast later if desired.
- Noise reduction: Turn this off completely. This is one setting you want to apply just as little as is needed, and preferably after close inspection of the image on your computer.
- Color styles: This may be called saturation on some cameras. Use the setting that applies the least amount of color adjustment so that the colors in the photo most closely resemble the actual scene.
- Digital zoom: Turn off and never use. Digital zoom means your camera uses software in the camera to enlarge the center of the image captured to make the subject appear larger. This process is called *interpolation*, and most microstock sites will reject photos that have been interpolated to a larger size because the process can degrade the quality of the image detail.

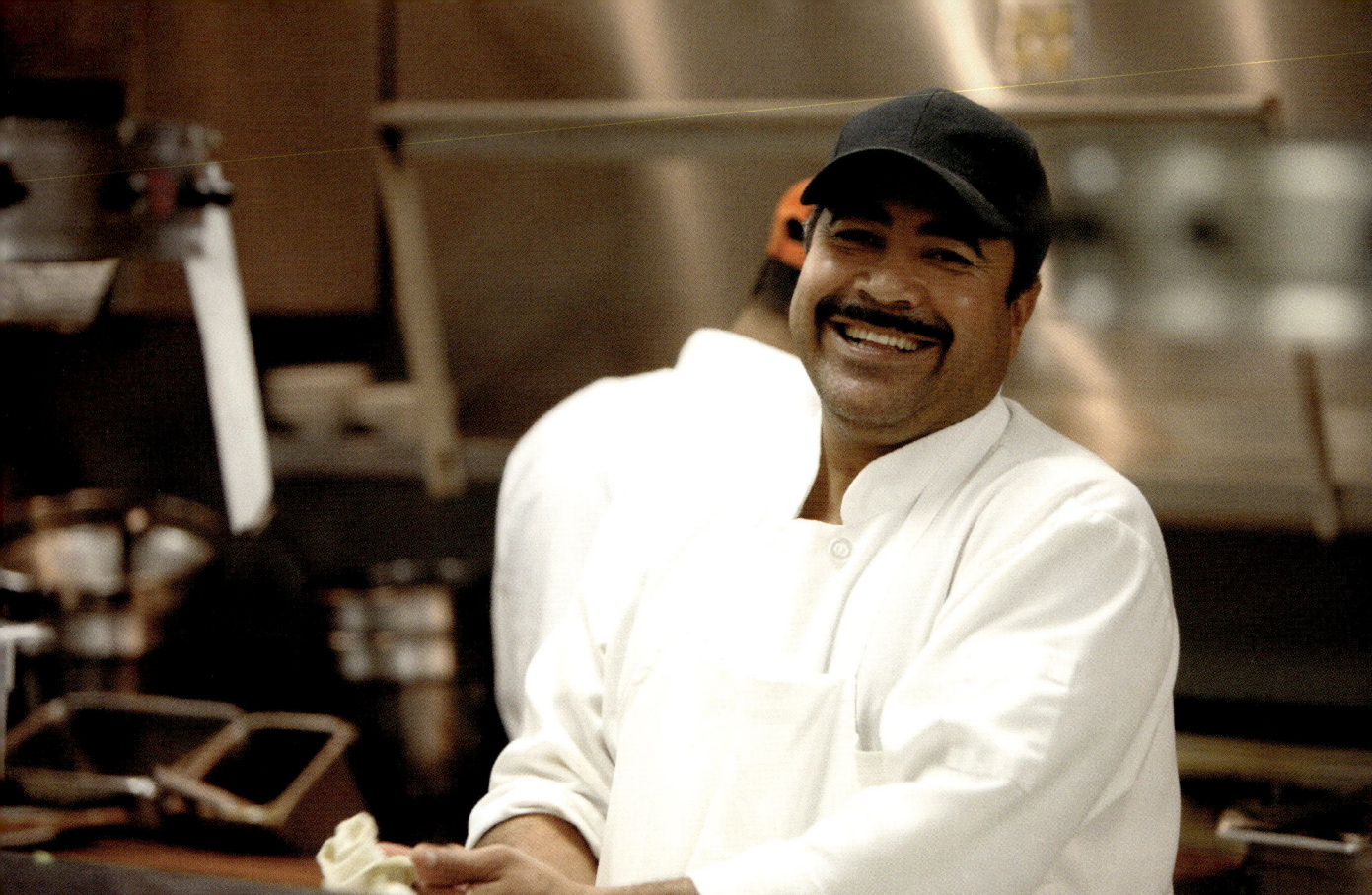

Figure 5.8 Chef. Downloaded over 1,300 times.

Chef

Creator	Stephen Walls (istockphoto.com/swalls)
Started	2004
Home	USA
Total portfolio	888
Total downloads	Over 25,000
About this photo	Stephen says, "I feel it's been so successful because of the natural look of the model. The smile is very nice, and he has a very friendly expression on his face. Another factor may be that it was shot in a real location and there must be a need for that look. It was shot with a Canon 5D using a Canon EF 70-200mm f/2.8 L IS USM lens."
Stephen's tip	"Follow your passion. Shoot what you like and learn as you go. You have many opportunities for growth and learning. Don't be afraid to ask questions."

My reasons for suggesting those settings are simply to provide you with the least processed version of your photo possible when shooting JPEG, so that you can have a more deliberate role in making those adjustments later in post-processing, and so that your camera won't make adjustments to your images that decrease their chances of getting approved. I do still think shooting in raw mode is preferred, but I realize you need to start where you are comfortable and get the best results possible.

Beyond the Camera

You can do a lot with just a good camera and lens. As you discover where the sweet spots are with any given camera/lens combination, you will probably find yourself wanting to acquire more equipment to expand your repertoire of subjects, technique, and style. I'm reluctant to encourage people who are new to shooting for stock to make large investments in new equipment, but I am not immune to the siren call of new gear, or the heady aroma of freshly unboxed electronics. So, if you have a couple hundred bucks just burning a hole in your pocket and you want to know one good investment to make, I suggest looking at some tools to help add or modify light.

I love sunlight for lots of reasons, and the fact that it is free doesn't hurt. However, depending on where you live in the world, the amount and quality of useful sunlight varies with the seasons as well as by the day. An off-camera flash or speedlight is an extremely versatile piece of equipment to add to your kit as soon as you can afford to do so. You can use it with available daylight to fill in shadow areas (called *fill light*), or you can use it in the absence of daylight to light a scene completely.

In **Figure 5.9** I used a single Nikon SB-800 speedlight to provide all the light in the shot. All I did was mount the speedlight on a spare tripod (though I could have held it in my hand, used a lighting stand, or put it on a table top) and direct the beam of light at the white paper behind the objects shown in the photo. In front of the objects and slightly to camera left, I placed a sheet of white foam core covered with aluminum foil, which reflected the light bouncing off the white paper back on to the subjects. Next to using daylight, this is a very simple yet useful way to start expanding your use of artificial light.

> **Tip**
>
> Head over to http://strobist.blogspot.com/ for an indispensible free resource for getting the most out of your off-camera flash.

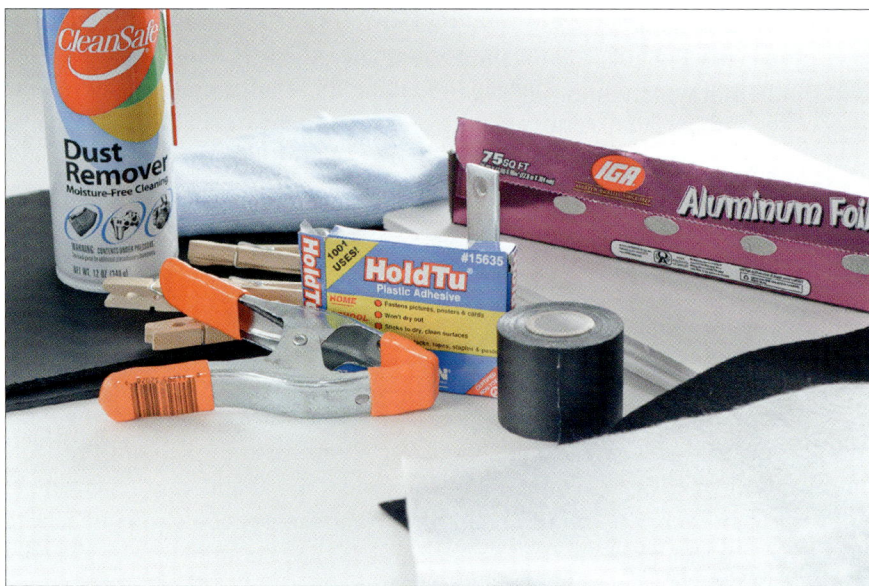

Figure 5.9 Inexpensive, yet essential, gear.

The objects in Figure 5.9 are some of the least expensive and most essential accessories I think you can add to your gear list. Here's what I included:

- White seamless paper: You can order this by the roll from any photography supply store.
- Gaffers tape: This cloth tape is easy to tear and has a strong bond, but can be removed easily without leaving a sticky residue behind. It's great for holding just about anything in place.
- Compressed air: A little blast of air is great for clearing dust off an object or insects off a flower. Removing distracting elements before you shoot is much easier than removing them in post-production.
- White and black foam core: Found at any craft supply store, foam core is light yet rigid, and can be used to either reflect (white) or block (black) light as needed.
- Aluminum foil: Highly reflective, easy to work with, and cheap.
- Clothespins and "A" clamps: You can never have too many hands for holding things right where you want them. Wooden clothespins are cheap and lightweight. When you need more holding power, pick up a few A Clamps (the orange-handled clamp in the photo) from your favorite photography supply store.

- HoldTu, Sticky Tack, or Blu-Tack: There are many different brand names for this reusable, putty-like adhesive. Handy for any time you need to temporarily hold something small in place.
- White and black felt squares: Pick a few of these up at the craft store for a few cents each. They make versatile light modifiers.

I directed the light coming from the speedlight in that scene by creating what is called a *snoot*, which is a sort of light-directing tunnel, out of a piece of black felt and a little gaffers tape. You can see what I mean in **Figure 5.10**, where I lit the scene using the same speedlight showing in the photo. The felt isn't lightproof, as you can see in that shot, but for this use that wasn't a problem.

Just like in the previous figure, I bounced the light off the paper in the back and then reflected it using foam core and aluminum foil back on to the subject (**Figure 5.11**). In case you are wondering how much difference that little piece of felt made, I took one more photo of the same scene in Figure 5.9, with the same exposure settings but without the snoot (**Figure 5.12**). As you can see, the light went everywhere and completely blew out the subject.

From this point forward you will continue to be faced with new decisions involving some sort of trade-off. I can't make those decisions for you, but I can encourage you to be thoughtful, to maximize the use from the equipment you already have, and to then discover all the little inexpensive ways you can expand your repertoire without mortgaging your future. Enjoy the process, focus on creating useful content, and know the next equipment upgrade can always wait until tomorrow. ■

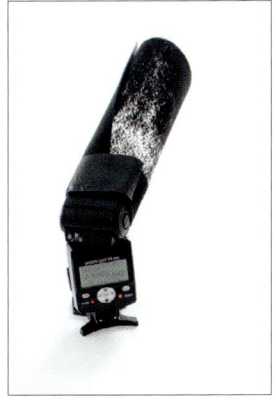

Figure 5.10 Light from a speedlight modified by felt and gaffers tape.

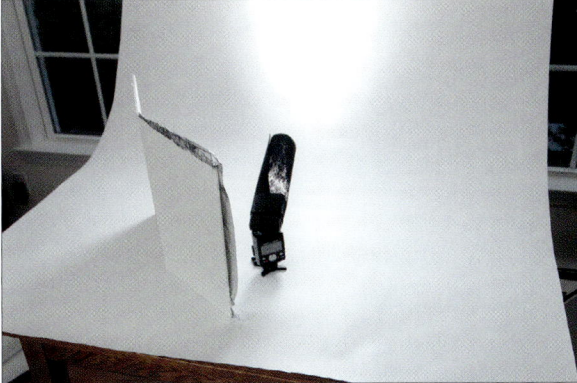

Figure 5.11 Lighting setup showing seamless white paper, single speedlight with felt square snoot, and white foam-core covered in aluminum foil reflector.

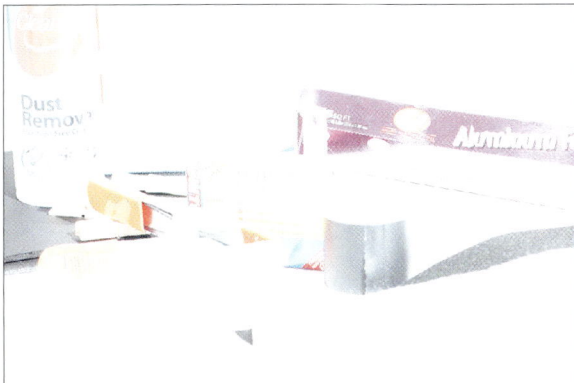

Figure 5.12 The difference a snoot makes. Same scene and camera settings as Figure 5.9, but without snoot on the speedlight.

6
Shooting Tips from the Pros

One of the aspects of photography that makes it so interesting and that keeps us engaged over a lifetime is that there is just so much to learn. Digital has made photography much more accessible due to the instantaneous feedback it provides, but digital has also brought additional layers of complexity as well as new tools to learn. I have to assume that you wouldn't be holding this book if you weren't already holding a camera, but that simple fact alone doesn't tell me much about what you already know about photography, or which photographic paths you want to follow. My primary focus in this book is to help you build a foundation for success in microstock, while helping you overcome many of the stumbling blocks encountered by all those who have gone before you. I simply cannot teach you everything you need to know about shooting every type of subject under every set of conditions.

However, there are shooting skills and knowledge—such as the importance of getting a proper exposure; how to use your camera's built-in computer to help analyze exposure; and knowing the important tasks required before, during, and after any type of photo shoot you encounter—that will continue to build that foundation. In addition, I want to expose you to some of the most successful microstock contributors I know. There are contributor profiles throughout every chapter of the book that provide excellent tips, but for this chapter I dug a little deeper with seven top contributors, whose combined lifetime download total is nearly 1.5 million, to get some of the shooting tips that have served them well along the way.

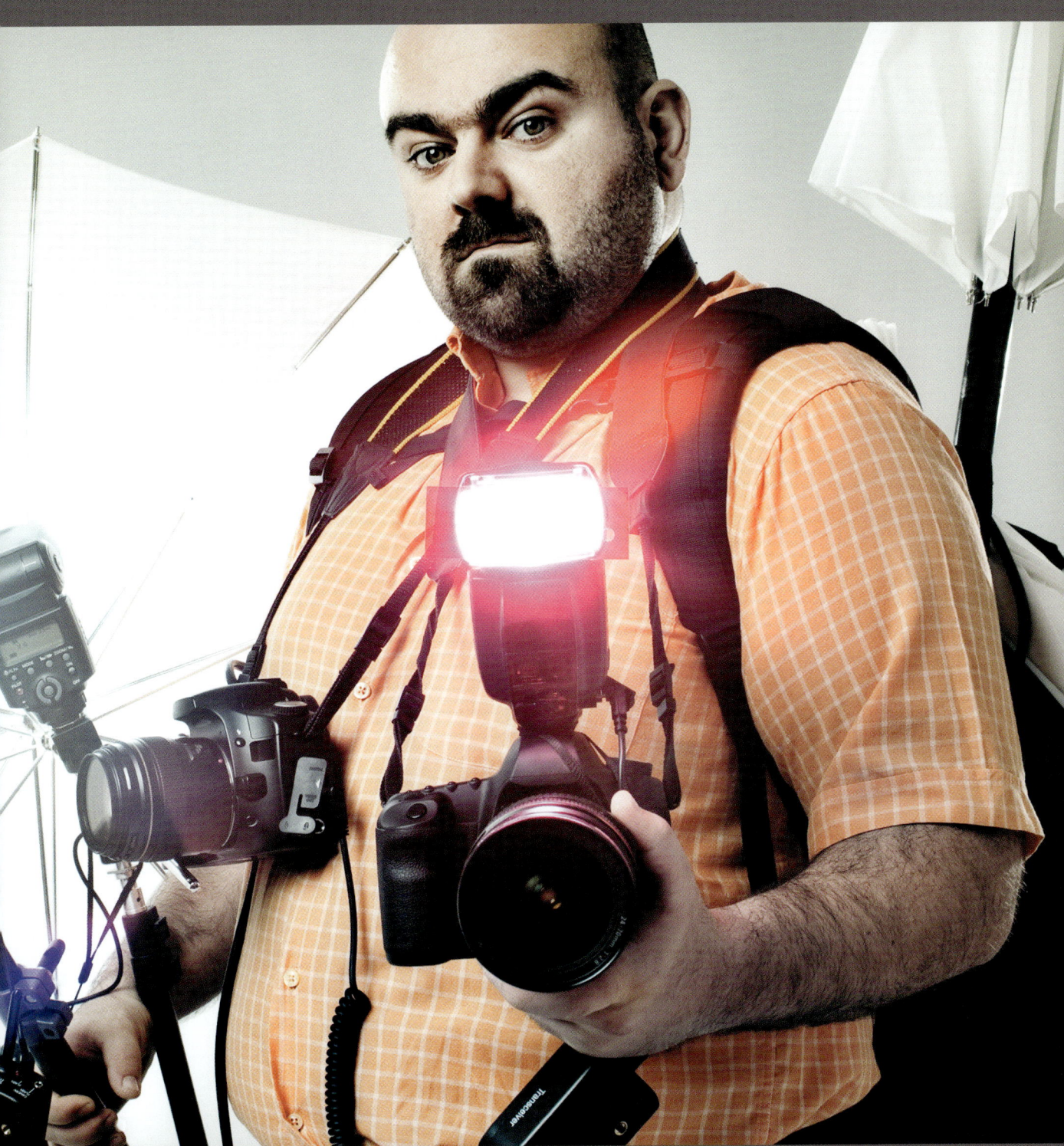
Figure 6.1 Photographer.
© Joan Vicent Cantó Roig

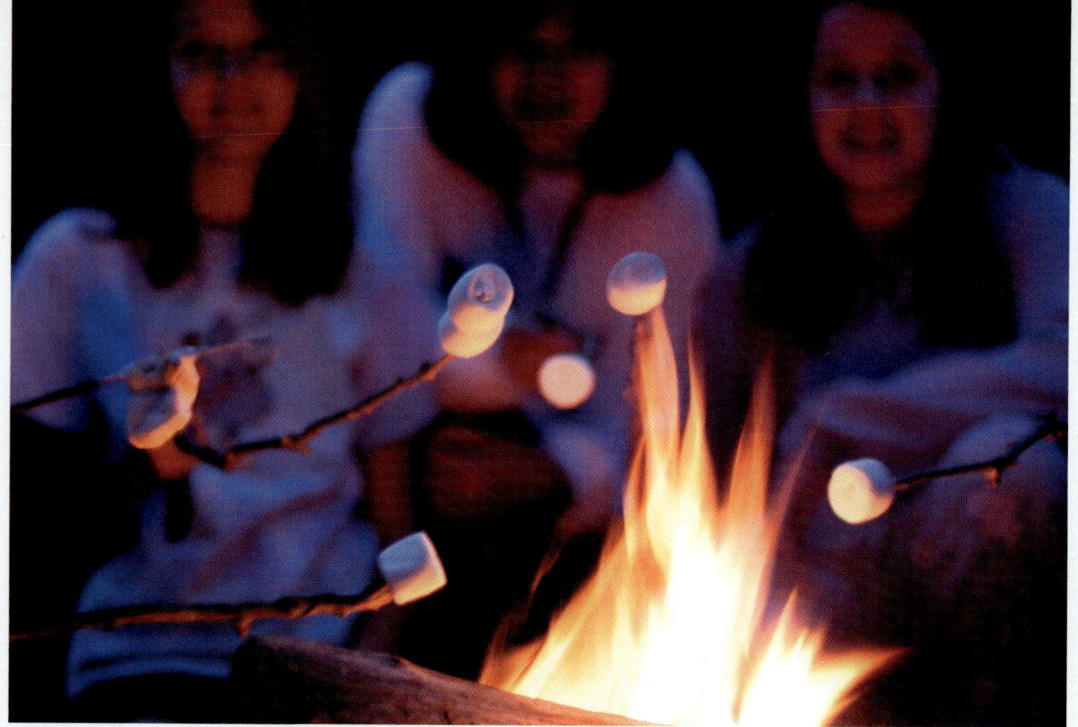

Figure 6.2 Marshmallow toasting. The image conveys a sense of fellowship of youth spirit in a positive way. It is taken from the visual perspective that makes the viewer feel like a part of the scene. There is a suggestion of people in the scene, but the girls' faces are blurred with a very shallow depth of field to suggest the background. The background is important but functions with the fire as an integrated composition.

Nancy Louie

Portfolio	istockphoto.com/nano
Started	2002
Total portfolio	959
Total downloads	Over 100,000

What is your background in photography?

I grew up with a darkroom in my basement and began developing my own film and prints when I was 10 years old. This was abandoned until I was a sophomore in art school when I took formal classes for a year and a half.

Go-to photo gear?

D700 and multiple speedlights.

Most essential gear beyond the camera?

A flash or two, with a method of diffusion.

What do you wish you knew when you started?

That Photoshop was used very differently by photographers than it is by designers. I also learned that the camera takes the image, but it's the photographer who makes it.

Favorite stock subject, and why?

People. It's always been people in all shapes and forms. I like relating to people and the interaction that yields results in depictions.

Snapshot of your workflow?

Shoot, offload to an external hard drive, and backup to DVDs or a second hard drive. Then I import into Lightroom with minimal keywording and perform minor tonal and white balance adjustments. If I see problematic interpretations in the RAW conversions in Lightroom, I will convert the images in Capture NX2 to note differences. All images are processed in Photoshop after initial RAW conversion. If logos need to be removed, it's done in Photoshop.

Tips for working with models?

After making suggestions to the model(s), listen to their input. I think you'd be surprised at what they come up with. It cements the importance of working with a model in a collaborative way if you can integrate. If they trust you, they will relax. Watch their movements carefully. They will often slip into a natural pose that's best for their depiction because they are relaxed. There's an art to what I call the "posed candid." If you connect to the model(s) that comes through in the results to the audience.

Strategies for coming up with concepts?

Immerse yourself in everyday living. I watch very little TV but always note commercials and look at my junk mail. I also keep a notebook. This is a great tool for setting goals, expanding ideas, and getting things on paper for those times when I'm unable to shoot. Ideas should not be tied to just the present.

Tips for shooting in urban environments?

I've found that the best time to shoot in a city is the very early morning on a Sunday. There is kinder light, and less traffic and people. Make sure you have enough light since tall buildings in a city often block light. If you are using artificial lighting, choose angles where it won't reflect in street-level windows.

Any last bit of wisdom to share?

Learn the technical side of your gear so you understand its limitations. You can't push something if you don't know where the boundaries fall. Rules are made to be broken, but you really need to know what they are before you can break them. You can't repeat success if you don't know what you did to obtain it.

The Importance of Good Exposure

Focus and exposure, if done poorly, are two factors that almost always guarantee rejection. Either a shot is in focus or it is not, and when it is not, the only recourse is to refocus and reshoot.

When it comes to exposure, it is not as clear-cut because of what is possible to adjust in post-production. While it is true that when shooting in RAW mode (and to a much lesser extent in JPEG mode) you have a bit of latitude to correct minor exposure problems (which we'll cover in Chapter 8), it is also true that the greater the corrections needed to fix exposure in post-production, the more likely you are to increase the visibility of noise or simply end up with a very overprocessed-looking photo. Remember, image inspectors are going to evaluate your photos at 100 percent (or 1:1 view), which is much less forgiving of technical flaws than you may be on your own screen.

Why give yourself less material to work with if you don't have to? Nailing a proper exposure is really all about capturing as much of the data as possible in a given scene. The light metering capabilities of digital cameras continue to improve, but it is still up to the human operator to evaluate the exposure of each capture.

Reading the Histogram

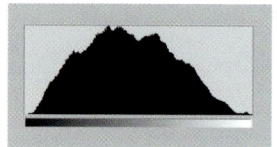

Figure 6.3 The histogram displays the pixels in your photo arranged from darkest on the left to brightest on the right.

> **Note**
>
> It is important to know that the in-camera histogram is based on the in-camera settings used to create a JPEG even if you are shooting in RAW mode.

Every digital camera is also a computer. One of the functions of your computer-camera is to arrange all the pixels in a given capture according to their brightness levels, from shadows (black) to highlights (white), and display them in a graph, called the histogram (**Figure 6.3**), that makes it easy to see at a glance on the camera's LCD screen where the majority of the brightness values happen to be, and where there aren't any at all. The distribution of these brightness values is called the tonal range. When used in conjunction with the actual captured photo, the histogram can help us evaluate if we exposed that scene in such a way as to have avoided losing any important data. Understanding the nature of the histogram now will also help when you see it later in your image editing software.

There is no single good histogram for all scenes, and the goal is not to get the best-looking histogram. The goal is always to maximize the capture of the important visual data in the scene. Let's look at some examples. Here are three photos, taken within a span of two minutes, along with the histogram for each. This is a scene where due to the partly cloudy sky and fast-moving clouds, the intensity of the light was changing quickly. The first photo (**Figure 6.4**) is overexposed and potentially has lost a lot, if not all, detail in the brightest highlights of the water. Notice how its histogram shows the highest number of brightness levels stacked up against the right edge, and almost no brightness levels on the left edge.

The Importance of Good Exposure 75

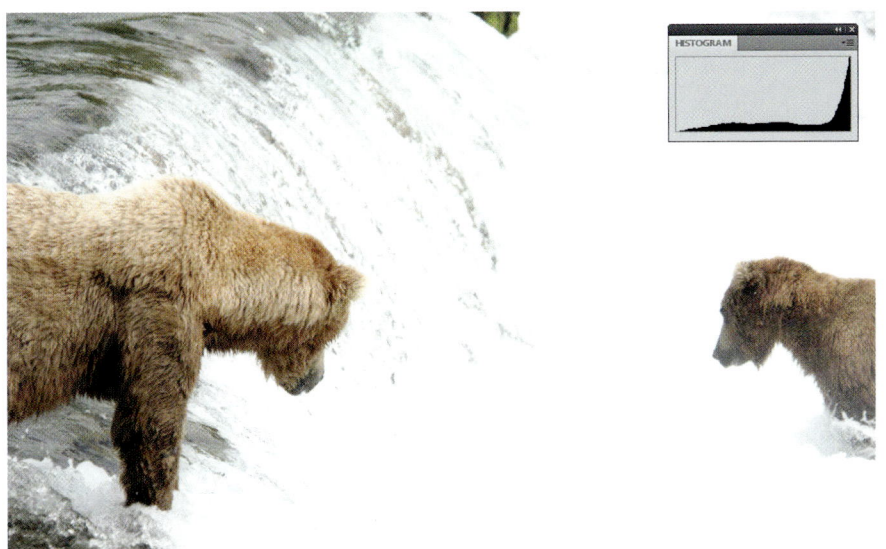

> **Note**
>
> You may need to consult the manual on this one if you don't know how to find the histogram on your camera.

Figure 6.4 This photo is overexposed and potentially losing highlight detail. The histogram is stacked up on the right edge.

In the second photo (**Figure 6.5**), I attempted to change my exposure settings to prevent overexposure, but went a little too far, and the result is slightly underexposed. Notice how the entire tonal range shifted to the left, pulling completely away from the right edge.

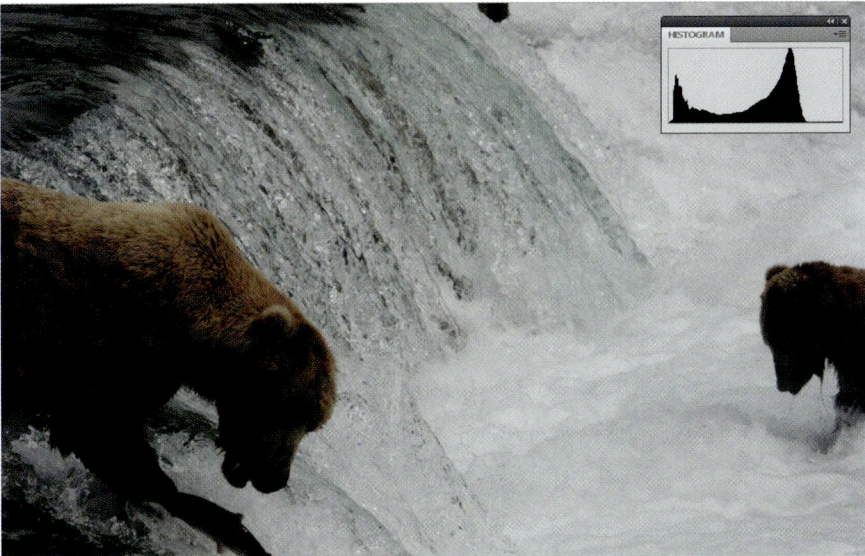

Figure 6.5 This photo is slightly underexposed. The highlight detail is captured, but recovering detail in the darker areas is likely to make existing noise more visible.

In the third photo (**Figure 6.6**), I readjusted my exposure settings. The light cooperated by not changing, and I was able to produce an exposure that was just right. By "just right" I mean the tonal range is distributed across the entire histogram, showing pixels in the shadows, midtones, and highlights, and while there are peaks in the highlight area of the graph, this is to be expected due to the amount of white water in the scene. I am fairly confident from looking at both the photo in Figure 6.6 and its histogram together that I can recover all important highlight data that may appear at first to be lost, while still retaining nice detail in the midtones and shadows, and overall good contrast.

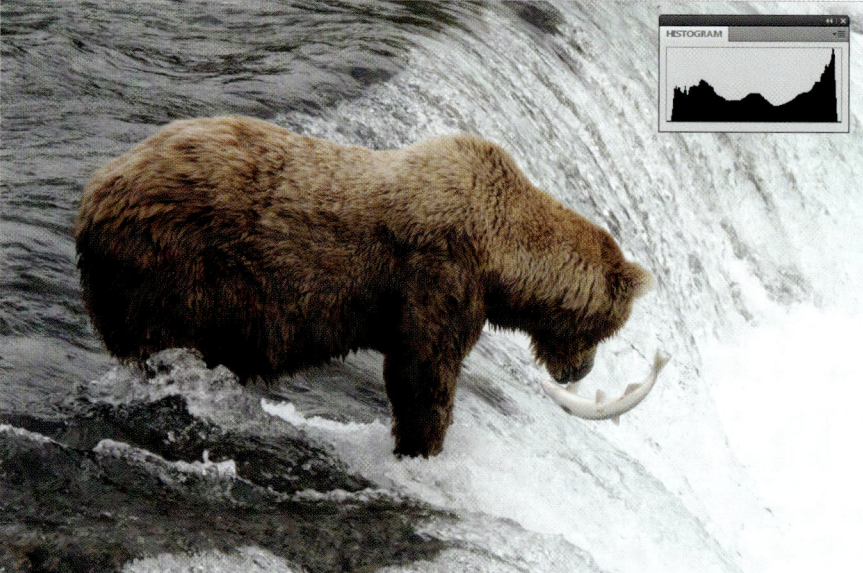

Figure 6.6 This photo is properly exposed for the scene. Highlight data is recoverable, and the wide distribution of tones across the histogram suggests adequate data at all brightness levels.

Some photos, because of the subject matter, will have a histogram that weighs heavily toward one end or the other of the tonal range without it being wrong. For example, the photo (**Figure 6.7**) of a single candle flame in an otherwise dark room has a histogram completely stacked up against the left edge (dark room), with just a tiny thin peak of a spike on the right (candle flame). That is the correct exposure for that scene. Similarly, you would expect that a photo of a small black ball on a pure white background would have most of its brightness levels stacked up on the right side (white background), with a small peak on the left (black ball). The detail in the photo is what matters most, and the histogram is just a tool to help you evaluate that when all you have is a small camera LCD screen, and the time to shoot is now.

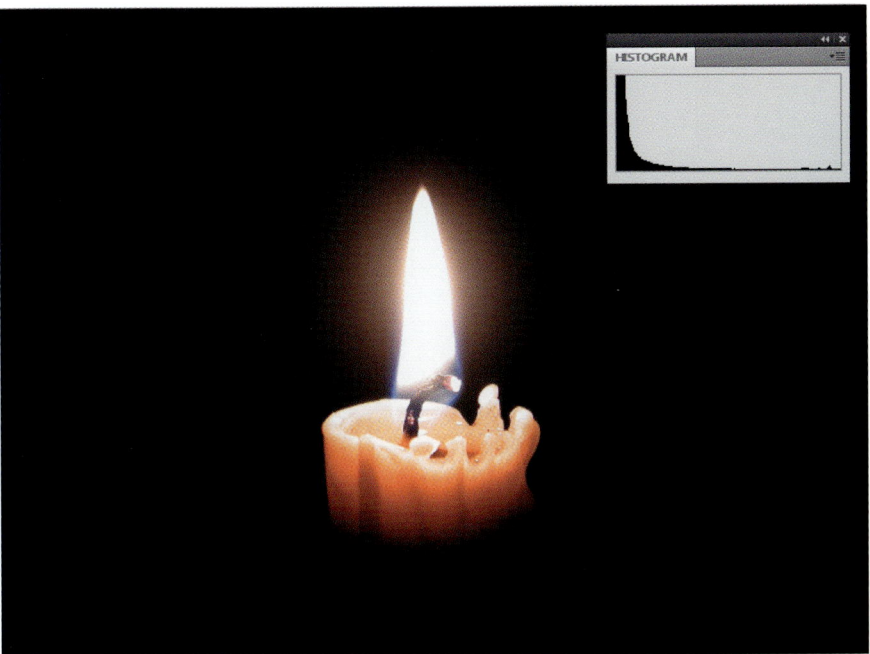

Figure 6.7 It is expected that a scene composed almost entirely of black regions would have a histogram stacked to the left.

Highlight Clipping Warning

In addition to the histogram, most digital cameras have a highlight clipping warning indication mode, commonly called the blinkies, because when it is turned on, any blown-out highlight area within the photo will blink on the LCD screen. I often find myself using this indicator first, and if there is no blinking and the photo otherwise looks well exposed, I'll just keep on shooting. At the first sign of blinking in an important highlight area, I'll switch to the histogram to try to evaluate if the overexposure is too great. For example, if you are shooting a scene that contains a highly reflective surface, like a chrome bumper, then you would expect to see some blown highlights in any reflections of the light source. However, if you are seeing that the white shirt of your subject is blinking then you need to evaluate the situation and change your exposure settings accordingly to preserve that important detail.

The key point to keep in mind when shooting is that if you nail focus and exposure, and can create a compelling and useful composition, then you've got a keeper on your hands, and that is what it is all about. It is always in your best interests to start with the best-quality capture possible, and not just hope you can fix it later in post-processing.

> **Note**
>
> As with histograms, you may need to consult the manual for your particular camera on highlight clipping warning as well.

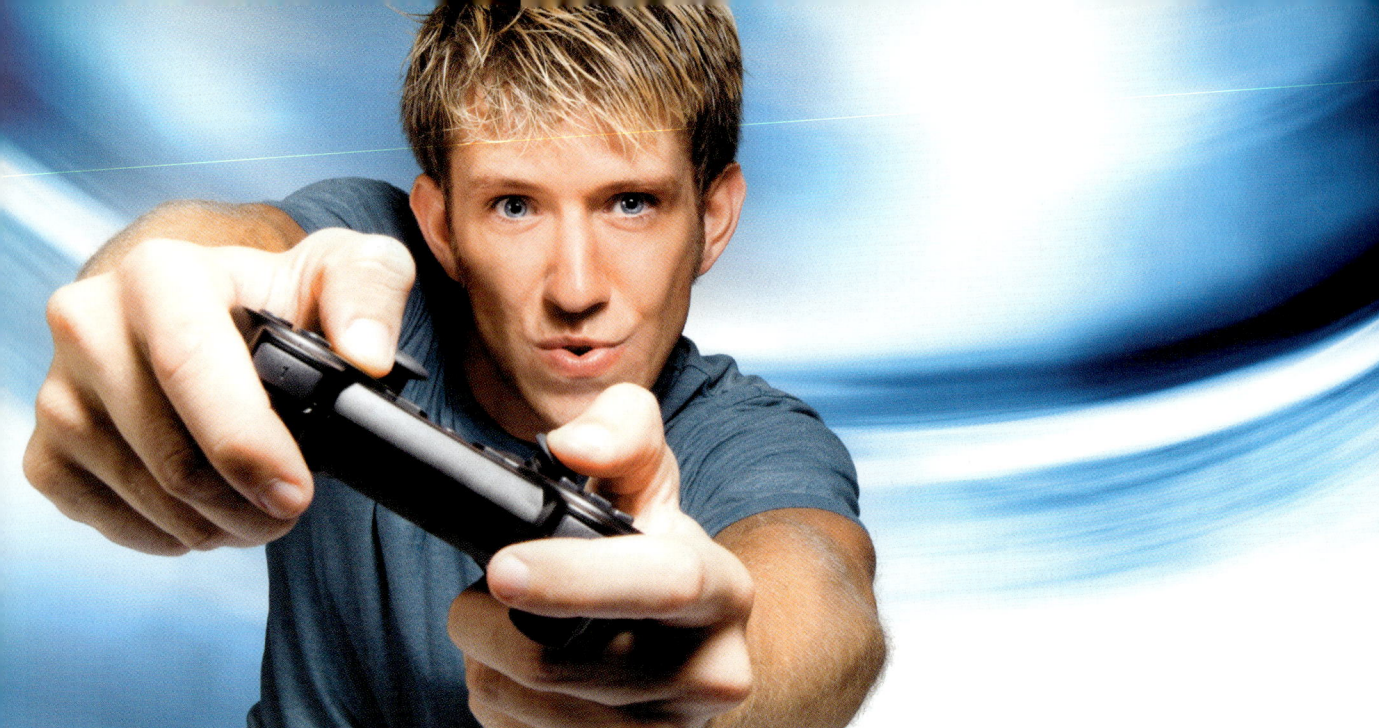

Figure 6.8 Game Playing. The colors complement each other while the background swirl draws your eye to the subject. It's simple and to the point but still shows energy and good framing, allowing your eye to flow through the whole photo.

Joshua Blake

Portfolio	istockphoto.com/joshblake
Started	2004
Total portfolio	1,682 images
Total downloads	Over 130,000

What is your background in photography?

I did take a home college course on photography while on tour in my performing group, but never really had hands-on training like I needed. It did teach me how to develop film and how the camera works, but that was also just as digital was becoming popular, and digital was definitely what I was more interested in. Most of what I've learned, I've got to credit to iStockphoto members and forums and, well, just by doing it.

Most essential gear beyond the camera?

I really love the studio lights. I work best with controlled lighting. I do enjoy working with reflectors and natural lighting outside as well, but I'm not as comfortable with them as I am in the studio.

Favorite stock subject, and why?

People playing characters! I love making "roles" for people and being crazy. People smiling are nice and OK, but if they are dramatic or theatrical in some way it is much more fun to work with and create. I love themed shots because it just makes things more fun to work with and shoot.

Advice for shooting self-portraits?

It depends on your camera and timer. My first camera had a flip screen and remote control where you could see the shot as you were in the shot so you could correct it, but if your camera does not have a way to do this, use something about the same height you are (hat rack, ladder, etc.) and place it about where you'll be standing. Focus on it and set the timer, quickly hop into the shot (moving the object out of the way), and hope for the best! It doesn't always work out, but eventually, you'll get it right.

White background tips?

It seems like it should be simple, but getting the lighting right is a challenge sometimes on white. Don't overexpose or go too bright with your lighting. I found you can always brighten up the exposure later in Photoshop or other editing software if you are unsure or just can't get it right, but when things are blown out from the start, it's really tough getting those details back in without reshooting.

How do you come up with concepts?

Look around you, listen to the gossip, find out what's hot in up-and-coming themes that people will be talking about and needing news about. When there's a story, they usually need images to support that story or theme. So find out what people need and then when you come up with an idea, try to think of a different and new way to look at that concept. That'll make you stand out from the rest because it will be different. It doesn't always have to be a new concept, though. You can do a very common concept all over again if you have a completely different way of looking at it.

Tips for working with models?

Don't be afraid to tell models what you are looking for from them. They want a good shot just as much as you do. Show them what you see on the digital display on your camera. Let them see what they look like so they know what needs to be changed.

Any last bit of wisdom to share?

Just keep it clean and simple. Let your image tell the story and don't confuse your audience. Let them see the point, easily.

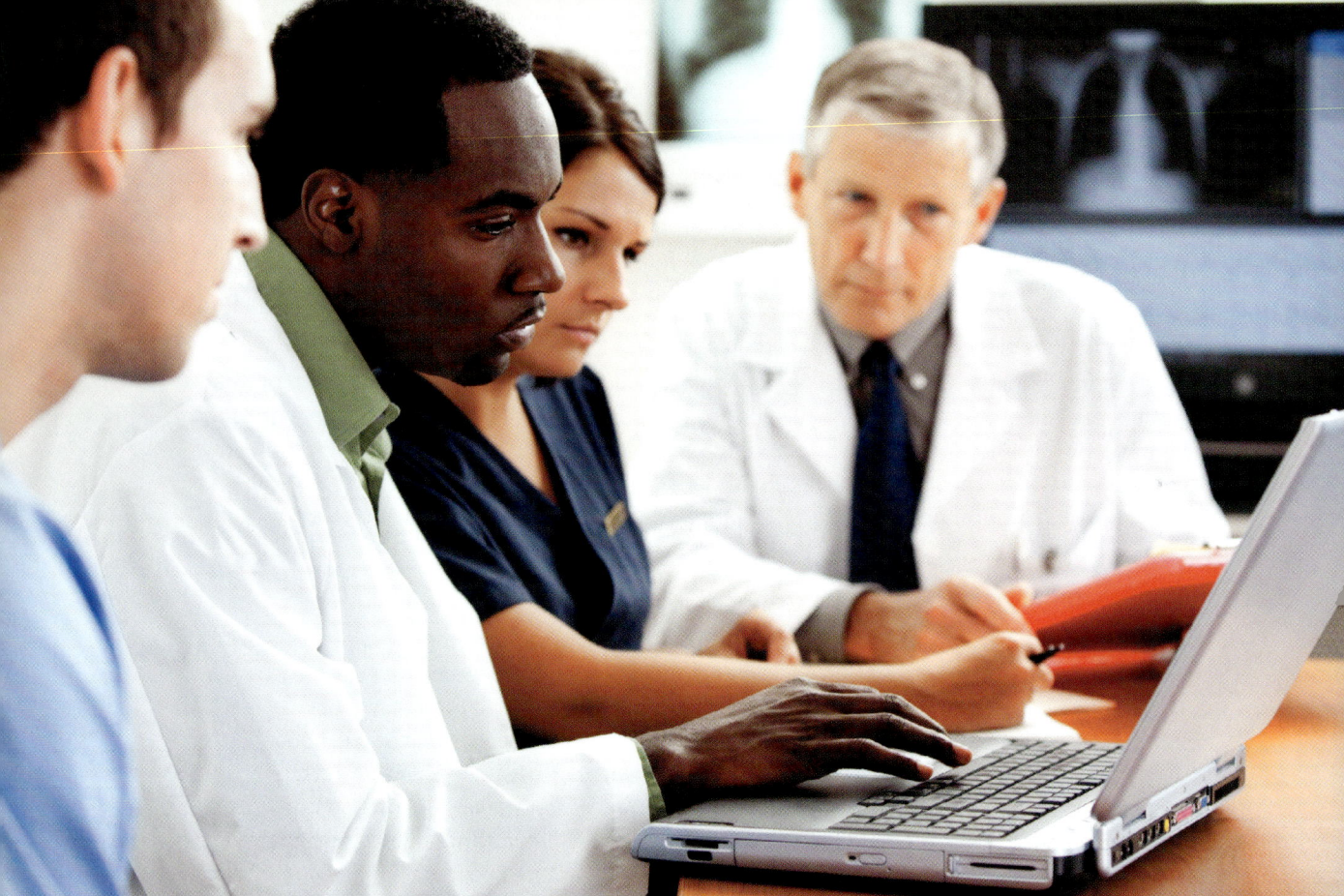

Figure 6.9 Doctors Checking Test Results. There's a variety of ethnicities and ages, but nothing that is inappropriate. There's real concern in the expressions. Also, the "investment" in reality works: the X-ray in the wall box, the image on the monitor—these things just don't magically appear on shoot day.

Sean Locke

Portfolio	istockphoto.com/sjlocke
Started	2004
Total portfolio	Over 8,600 images
Total downloads	Over 640,000

What is your background in photography?

My father used to travel internationally for his work and was always shooting slide film in countries like Pakistan, India, and China. Mostly he shot street images, just to document his travels, and we had a lot of slide shows at home. So, it was inevitable that eventually I'd get my own camera. I was in a pretty large high school that had a lot of elective classes, one of which was photography. We did get to develop the negatives and print black-and-white photos. Basic camera knowledge and terms like "dodge" and "burn" come from that class. Otherwise, my "training" is from reading the manuals, reading forums, experimenting, and a couple of books, like *Light: Science and Magic* by Fil Hunter, Steven Biver, and Paul Fuqua (Focal Press).

Go-to photo gear?

Canon 5dMk2, Canon 70-200 2.8 IS, 4 Alien Bees for in studio, or a 48" reflector outside.

Most essential gear beyond the camera?

Definitely Photoshop. There's always a logo popping up, or lint on a coat, or something. You can plan and plan, but things happen.

What do you wish you knew when you started?

You have to spend money to make money. I picked that up pretty quickly, though, when I got my first set of strobes very soon after I started to shoot with stock creation in mind.

Favorite stock subject, and why?

I really enjoy working with models. I like setting up for people shoots, directing the models, trying to get emotive responses to the setup, and then seeing them eventually used in an ad or article. The models seem to have a great time with it as well. It helps (I think) that I don't intentionally create themes that could lead to uncomfortable situations, either in subject matter, posing, or which models are working together.

Snapshot of your workflow?

I shoot in the studio or on location in RAW, then transfer images from cards to a portable hard drive as needed. I transfer all content from shoot to an external hard drive when I'm done. Finally, I work through folders, previewing in Adobe Camera Raw (setting white balance, etc.) and then do final processing on my best images in Photoshop.

Tips for working with models?

Set the scene with a good description of the "theme" and the situation they are in, so they understand how they are supposed to react. It also helps if the models know each other, either by being friends or having been shot together previously.

One important thing you do before shooting?

Make sure I have plenty of flash cards ready to hold the content. Even though I copy the images to a portable hard drive as I go, I don't want to overwrite anything until I confirm everything is there.

One important thing you do at the end of shooting day?

Turn off my Pocket Wizards (remote flash triggers) so I don't waste another set of AA batteries!

Top Tips for Your Next Photo Shoot

There's nothing wrong with a photo shoot that consists of simply grabbing your camera and walking out the door, but there are a number of ways to increase the chances of creating stock-worthy content, regardless of the subject matter. Put a little more thought and effort into each stage in the process, from preparing for the shoot, to the actual shooting day, and all the tasks needed at the end to wrap up successfully.

Get Ready

Over the years, I've noticed that one of the biggest factors that separates the pros from the rest is how much work the pros do before they even pick up the camera. Here are five tips to help you get to the top of your game:

1   Create a shoot list.

    This is all about pre-visualizing the themes, concepts, and ideas you want to communicate in your photos from a given shoot. Some people go so far as to create *storyboards*, which are a series of sketches that depict all the scenes they want to capture. I asked Josh Blake (profiled on page 78) about about his practice. "I usually draw a few hand sketches of what I'm looking for in the shoot. I also write down the main shots that I know I want to get for sure, otherwise I get so wrapped up in the shot, and getting the lighting right, and changing props/costumes/makeup, that I forget to get that one shot that I was really thinking would look cool if I tried," he says.

    Kelly Cline (profiled on page 90) adds, "It really helps to keep the shoot on track which maximizes the potential volume of output and usefulness of a particular item. This is especially true with food, since food has a tendency to have a very short life in front of the camera before it starts to droop, congeal, or wither. You really have to do everything you can to maximize your time."

2   Communicate with your models and team members well in advance.

    I know that for most of us, photography can be a one-person operation most of the time. As you grow and want to reach the next level, it's likely going to involve more people in the form of models, stylists (for food, people, animals, and even objects), and assistants. In those cases, be sure to send out multiple emails in advance of the shoot to provide information on the dates, times, locations, and requirements for a given shoot. Sean Locke (profiled on page 80), who works almost exclusively with models these days, says, "I make sure to send out several emails before the shoot, reminding them of the date/time, and what they are supposed to bring/wear. I also include the model release with the email, so they can get it signed ahead of time."

3. Scout the location.

   When you first have a concept or a theme in mind, it may require a specific location to make it work. Give yourself plenty of time to explore your surroundings and find that perfect spot, and get permission if needed. The location could be just the ingredient to add the level of authenticity to your shoot that puts it head and shoulders above the competition. Once you've got a location nailed down, be sure to pay it another visit a few days before the shoot to make sure nothing has changed that can affect your goals. Nancy Louie (profiled earlier in this chapter) had this excellent advice to offer: "Look immediately for problems. I note large mirrors or highly reflective areas or large objects that cannot be moved. Look for adequate space for the angles you want to shoot, and that there is room for the type of lighting you will use. I always try to scout at the time of day that I'd be shooting for both indoors and out. Always look for the electric outlet locations in the space."

4. Assemble the gear.

   In the 24 hours before the actual shoot, you want to use your shoot list to help gather all the gear you are going to need to get those shots, with that location in mind. This is the time to check that batteries are charged, memory cards are formatted, additional fresh batteries are on hand, and you have the specific camera body, tripod, stands, lenses, and lighting tools your shoot list requires. Do you have a backup camera body? Maybe not at the start of your career, but the next time you upgrade your camera, hold on to the old one as a backup. Make a checklist of all the gear you need, and check it twice. This list will serve as a reminder when you return, and check all the gear back in.

5. Reset the camera settings to a neutral state.

   I'm sure that like me, you are using your camera for all sorts of subjects and conditions. Hopefully, you are even experimenting and trying new things. Be sure to add in the pre-production step of loading your camera with a fresh battery and memory card, and firing a few test shots the night before. Check all your key camera settings, such as your ISO, white balance, metering mode, and image quality. Heaven forbid there is a technical problem with the gear, but better to know now than when you are on location.

Wrap it up with a good night's sleep so you are at your freshest mental state, which should help reduce simple mistakes and oversights on shooting day.

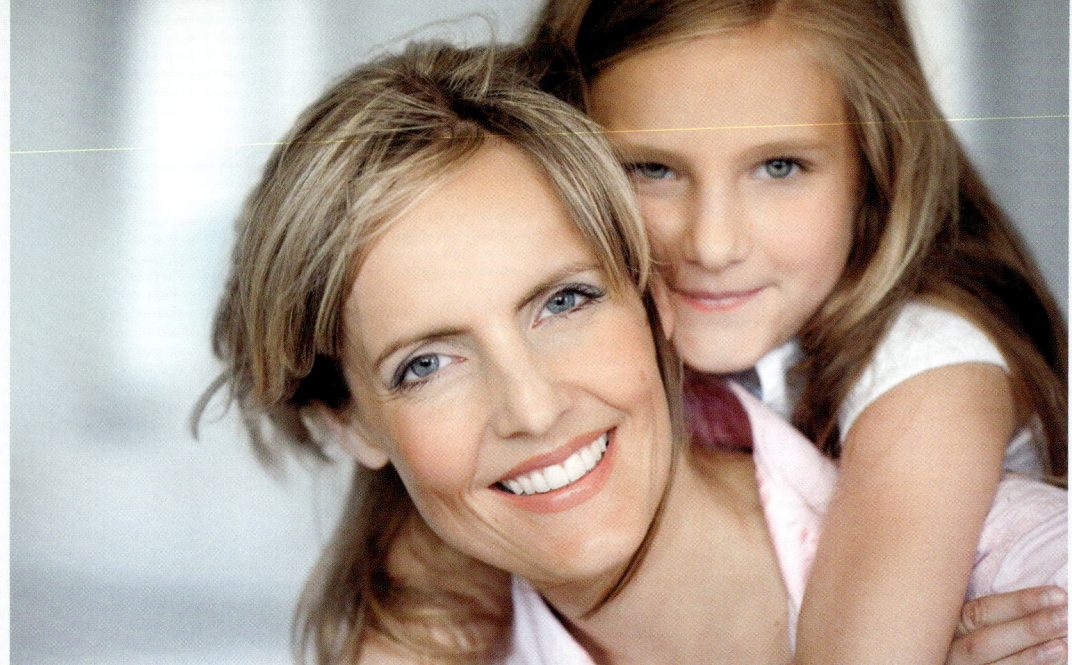

Figure 6.10 Mother and daughter. Happy family concepts are really popular; you can use this type of image for almost any market. I've seen this image on video software packaging and on an air conditioner ad. This was shot with daylight.

Katja Govorushchenko

Portfolio	istockphoto.com/iconogenic
Started	2005
Total portfolio	4,564
Total downloads	Over 220,000

What is your background in photography?

I'm not formally trained. My dad tried to get me closer to photography when I was very young. I liked it, but never thought to continue the development beyond travel snapshots. Eventually, I started to seriously play around with my husband's film SLR in 2004, and became dedicated to finishing and understanding everything in its manual. From there, I decided to make portraits of family members, and that's how all started.

What do you wish you knew when you started?

You know, you do photography because you already have something to tell, so basically, at any point that you start, you know enough. The rest is a matter of reading manuals and understanding commerce. I wish I knew more about importance of a good model and a good concept, instead of counting megapixels available on the market.

Favorite stock subject, and why?

Beauty visuals with women. I've always been fascinated with fashion and beautiful faces. I like dressing models up and indulging their vanity by making images absolutely perfect. I love working in *girly* teams. It is certainly more fun than shooting any other subject on your own.

How do you come up with concepts?

Shooting fashion has a lot to do with understanding women. Inspiration usually comes from my everyday activities as a woman. Even on the most dolled-up image, you still want to connect to women, so you've got to think—what are women busy with? What are their activities? Their hopes and their fears? As it turns out, makeup artists, hairstylists, or fashion stylists you work with already have a concept when they start working on a model. My task as the photographer is just to put their idea in the right light (literally).

Snapshot of your workflow?

I shoot on several flash cards. After a shoot, I copy everything to my hard drive, make selections, and throw away failed images. Processing always starts in a RAW editor, where I can fix overall lighting and colors. After that, I go to Photoshop and do a retouching on a working TIFF file, always in 16 bit. Then I save two versions of JPEG: large one for the stock website, and a small one for my personal site and to give to my models.

Tips for working with models?

Respect people you work with. All other things will grow naturally from it. A photographer should make his model a part of the process and inspire her. Make sure you communicate all terms to your models, related to licensing, model release, and copyright. When you work with people from non-professional environments, it is different in terms of communicating your ideas and especially in terms of making arrangements. Most disappointments I've heard from photographers come from mismatched expectations and careless deal making.

White background tips?

There are various types of white backgrounds available. The simplest is white wall. In my home, I use a 2.5-meter-wide paper roll, and sometimes I use a projection screen. Usually, you want your background completely white. Use a separate soft light source intended for background only. Usually, it's two sources, from left and right. It is up to you to allow fall-off onto your subject, but if you don't want it, make sure that the subject/model is far enough from the background and is not touched by that rear light.

Any last bit of wisdom to share?

Feel the freedom that stock photography gives you as an artist, as well as a commercial photographer. Don't feel intimidated by anything or anyone. Follow your own path and find a subject or a style you can't get out of your head: this will most probably become your signature and your success. Never stop learning and being critical.

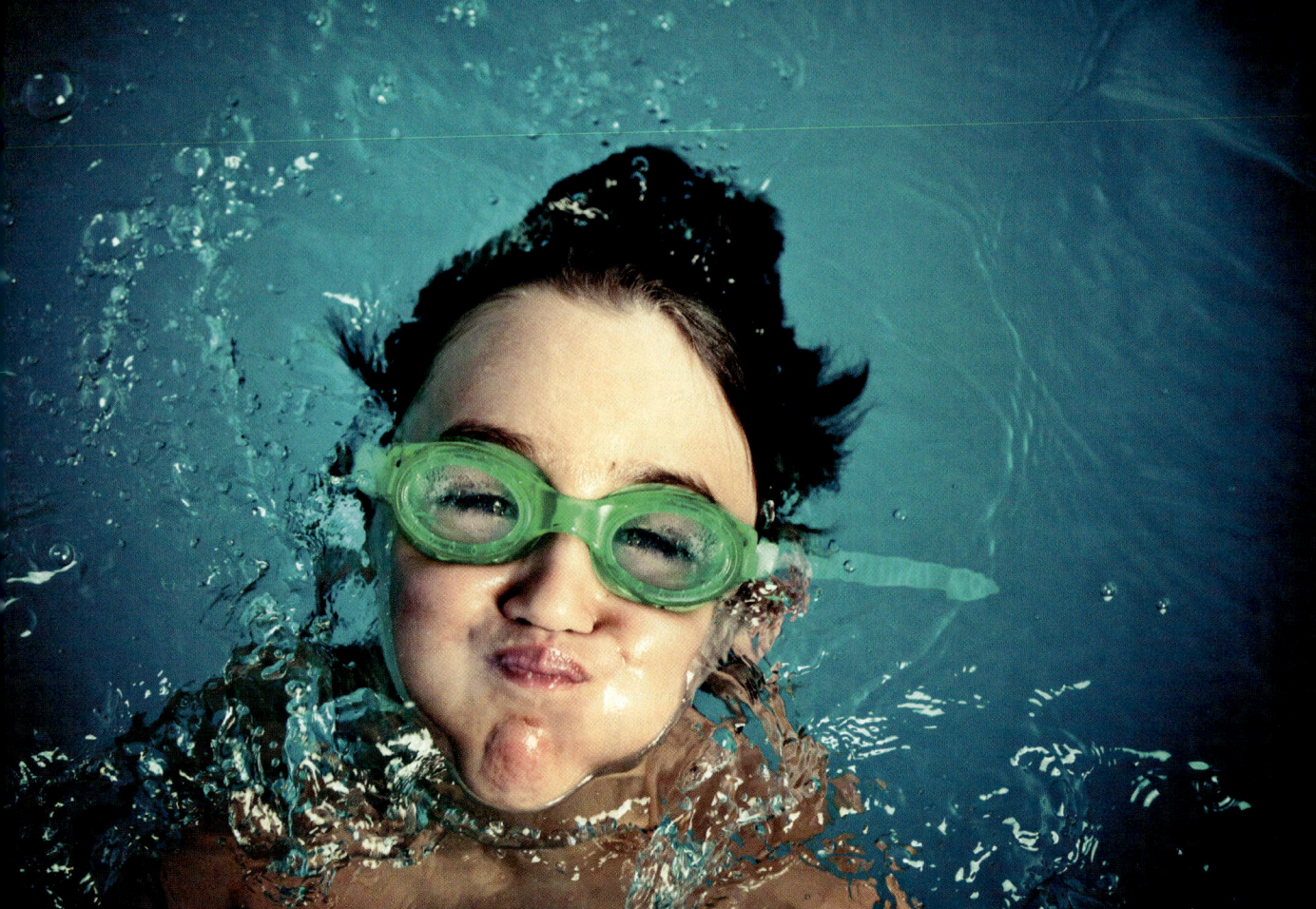

Figure 6.11 Kid Having a Good Time in the Pool. This was not planned. I was testing new remote flash triggers. This was the best shot of the day because I was pre-focusing. I tried to replicate the shot, but I never got the same happy expression. I guess luck is one of a photographer's best friends.

Roberto A. Sanchez

Portfolio	istockphoto.com/thepalmer
Started	2003
Total portfolio	6,640
Total downloads	Over 110,000

What is your background in photography?

I'm a graphic designer. I worked as an art director in Sweden, but I am now a creative director in Miami. I have no background in photography, except for the experience I've gathered working with photographers. I have been using Photoshop as my main retouching tool over the last 15 years in the business. All I have learned is self-taught.

Go-to photo gear?

Canon 5d Mk2 with Canon 24-70mm 2.8, 70-200mm f4, TS 90mm 2.8, and 135mm f2 lenses. Two Alien Bees strobes with beauty dishes, one Softlighter 60-inch umbrella, and the Apollo 28-inch soft-box.

Most essential gear beyond the camera?

Lightroom, Nik Color Efex, and Photoshop.

What do you wish you knew when you started?

Don't be afraid of working with models.

Favorite stock subject, and why?

People using weird props. The amazing possibilities that people give you—movement, feelings, expressions, poses—are endless.

Snapshot of your workflow?

I think of a concept or situation, then get props, model, and location. I shoot like a maniac—hundreds of photos—and then I bring them into Lightroom and do a lot of processing. Next is Photoshop for final retouching of each keeper image (most of the time using Nik Color Efex Pro), and after that, I upload to the site.

Tips for working with models?

I think it is good to be an easygoing person, show them respect, and act with confidence so they respect you. Most of the time I do work with my family and friends, which is easier for the level of comfort it gives you.

Any tips for a white background?

I love to shoot objects on white background. For a clear object, I like to surround it with black pieces of board (almost like a black box), and illuminate from behind with a bare-bulb flash, plus a frontal high soft light for fill. It produces very cool results.

How do you come up with concepts?

I think this comes from life experience. I'm very fortunate: I have been reading books since I was 5 years old. I'm an also a movie fanatic, and listen to music all the time. For me, it is about keeping your senses in action all of the time. Read facts, fiction, and novels, as they are your best friends.

Any last bit of stock photography wisdom to share?

Experiment with lights. Use continuous light, natural light, strobes, LED, and candles. Don't be afraid to crank up your ISO with modern cameras.

Day of the Shoot

Starting this day fresh, with all your prep work done, is going to help you get the most in terms of quality and quantity when it comes time to shoot. Here are five more tips to help you take it to the next level:

1 Double-check your gear before you walk out the door.

If you did your homework the night before, then this should be a quick confirmation that everything is as it should be. This is just too important to not take the extra five minutes to make sure you did in fact put the camera back in the bag after checking all the settings. Don't forget your shoot list either.

2 Prepare the scene.

You did the scouting, so you know right where to go. Whether it is just you and the great outdoors, or you've got a dozen models showing up in half an hour, take the time now to clear away distractions and set the stage. This is also a good time to be thinking about alternative options. Kelly Cline told me that she is always "making sure that I have a 'Plan B' in the event that an idea does not pan out or proves to be too difficult to execute." Things always go wrong on some level, but it is the pros who are prepared to roll with the punches and keep on shooting.

3 Change things up.

While your shoot list serves as an overall guide, take the time to mix up the angles you are shooting from, go high, go low, move way in, and move out. Shoot both horizontals and verticals. It is too easy, especially if you are using a tripod, to get locked into one way of shooting. Loosen that tripod up and shoot a vertical after each horizontal. You never know which angle may prove to be the most useful to your prospective customers. Once you've gotten everything on your list, and there is still time, circle back to any inspirations you had during the day and see what you come up with.

4 Do spot checks.

It is easy to get caught up in the shooting, and there's nothing wrong with that. Make yourself take time to spot-check the obvious things such as focus and exposure, but also on the less obvious such as the background. Is the background helping to communicate your intended message? Is it too busy, too bright, too dark? Are you noticing any problematic content that it would be easier to remove from the scene than to remove with software later? Did you brush all the lint off the model's clothing? Would a little burst of compressed air clear the bugs off that flower? Did you wipe down all the important objects with a lint-free cloth to remove the dust? Attention to detail is another factor that separates the pros from the pack.

5 Have fun!

> Pulling this off can be a lot of work, so be sure to build in breaks for yourself and your subjects. Having food and water on hand keeps everyone refreshed and in a good mood. If the situation allows, have some music playing in the background. Bring some crazy props that you may not even use, but could be just the thing to change an expression, or create a mood that is fun and lighthearted.

At the end of the day, if you've remained true to your vision, you'll not only have a lot of quality content to work with, but you'll feel satisfied by having had a great time making it happen.

After the Shoot

Whether you were shooting in your spare bedroom, an abandoned factory, the great outdoors, or a studio, there are a few things you want to make sure you always do to put a successful wrap on your shoot.

1 Clean up.

> Ugh. OK, easily the least sexy part of the entire process, but think of it more like helping you get set back up for the next shoot. You may have a location to put back together, so do it right so that you'll be allowed to come back in the future. You may have props to clean up and put away. Use the gear list you made the night before and check all your gear back in to be sure you didn't leave anything behind. Give your camera and lenses a wipe down on the outside, and learn how to clean your image sensor to keep it free of dust bunnies.

2 Back up your photos.

> Arguably this could come before doing any cleanup, but it really will depend on where you are when you were shooting, and what the subject matter happened to be. If you were shooting in your home or studio, then getting the backup started while you put things away works well. If you are on location and have a portable drive or laptop, then there is nothing wrong with multi-tasking by getting a backup going as you pack up the gear. Otherwise, this should be the first thing you do when you get home.

3 Don't forget the paperwork.

> Did I say clean up was the least sexy? This is a close contender. However, if you were working with models, be sure to collect all signed (and witnessed) releases before you let them leave the location (best to do on arrival, so no one gets away by mistake). Make a practice of taking a photo of the model holding the release. This helps you remember who is who, and serves as one more bit of proof that they did sign the release.

(continues on page 94)

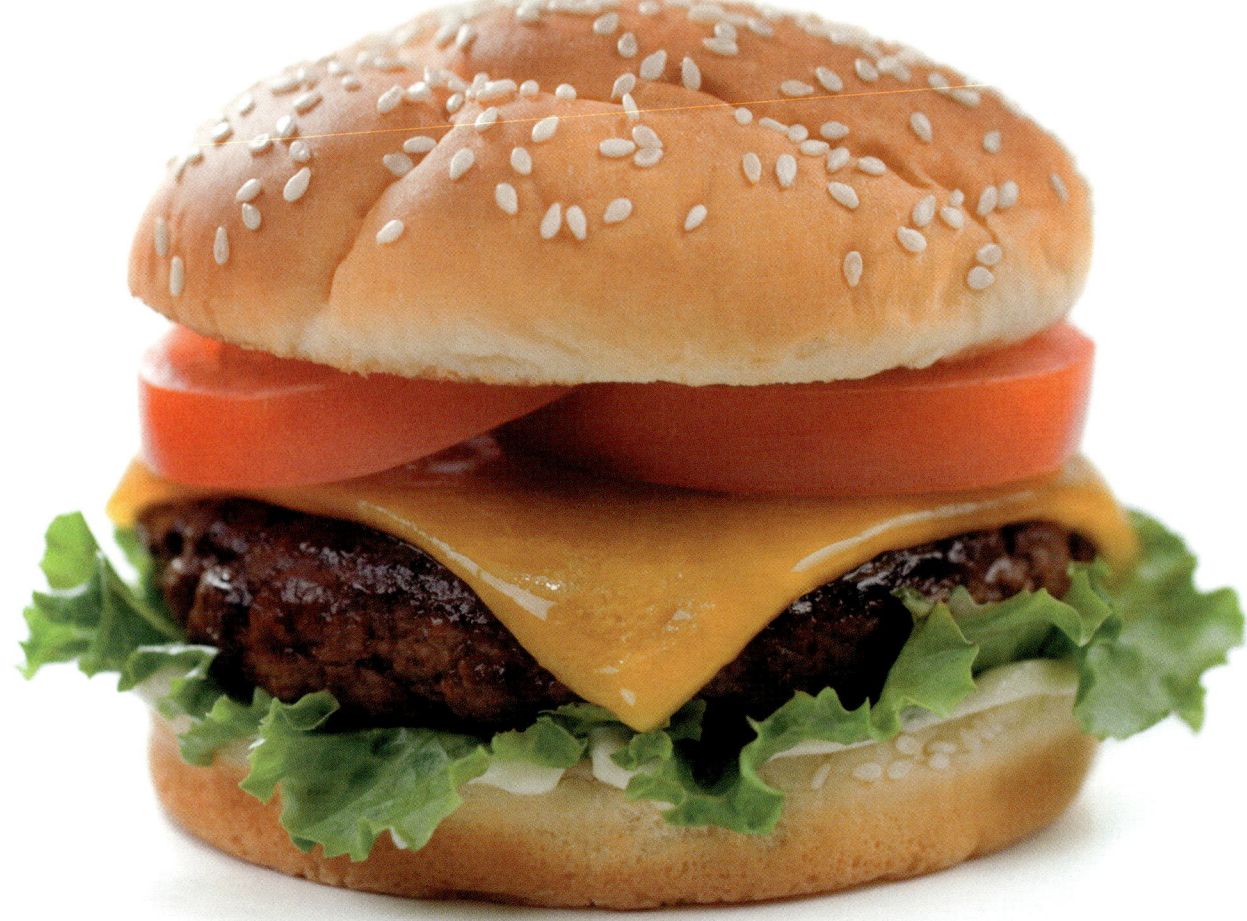

Figure 6.12 Cheeseburger. It's a simple cheeseburger, but it is iconic. It's not overly styled and it doesn't look fake. It's also isolated on white so the end-use possibilities are endless, since you can knock it out of the background and drop it into any design.

Kelly Cline

Portfolio	istockphoto.com/kcline
Started	2003
Total portfolio	2,035
Total downloads	160,000

What is your background in photography?

I've never had any formal training in photography. I tend to sort of go with the flow, and let the light speak to the camera, and let the camera speak to me. The first time I started taking photos was when I was very young, around 8 years old. My grandfather gave me an old Kodak Brownie. He was an avid nature photographer, so he would take us out on excursions strictly for the sake of shooting pictures. It was from him that I learned about apertures, shutter speeds, and film speed.

Go-to photo gear?

Bounces, bounces, bounces! Silver, gold, silver/gold, white—even paper towels and napkins can be used to bounce light. Also, I use a Canon 5D Mark II, with 85mm, 35mm, 50mm, 45mm TS-E lenses, and sometimes a Lensbaby when the moods strikes.

Most essential gear beyond the camera?

My tripod. While I don't use it exclusively, because there are some shots where hand-holding is just better or the only way to go, but I find it to be my most essential piece of equipment beyond the camera itself.

What do you wish you knew when you started?

Since I learned on the fly when it comes to stock, I don't feel like I really wished I knew more. About the only thing I wish I knew was that I would have enjoyed myself, and my career, this much so I could have started sooner.

Favorite stock subject, and why?

For me it is all about food. I'm a food geek, recipe developer, food writer and food stylist. It's a list of extracurriculars that goes very well with food photography. I love learning about food, ingredients, origins, and histories of food.

Snapshot of your workflow?

I start by creating concepts, sketching out the sets, constructing the sets, shopping for props and/or organizing props and color palettes. Then, I prefer shooting in small batches—sometimes tethered to my computer; otherwise I copy the cards to the computer and review the shots, so I can make adjustments where necessary to the set or lighting, and if necessary reshooting based on review. Once the shoot is done I import into Lightroom, perform basic RAW adjustments, and then transfer to Photoshop CS5 for further touching up. I enter metadata, and save a copy of the processed image as an uncompressed TIFF for archiving, then save a JPEG at highest quality.

Most important thing to keep in mind when shooting food?

It really is all about the lighting. Hard light can make the most beautiful dish look unappealing, especially anything with sheen. I prefer natural light.

What makes food different from other stock subjects?

For one, food is not an amateur model. Two, it doesn't talk back, and it goes right where I want it to go. It's not a diva, it won't get me in trouble if I need to touch it or adjust it. Food is base, and it speaks to the viewer. Everyone can relate and connect to food because we all need food to live. So I feel that food is approachable by those who view the photo, it makes you want it, touching upon that base primal need for nourishment, and it doesn't make you feel insecure about yourself.

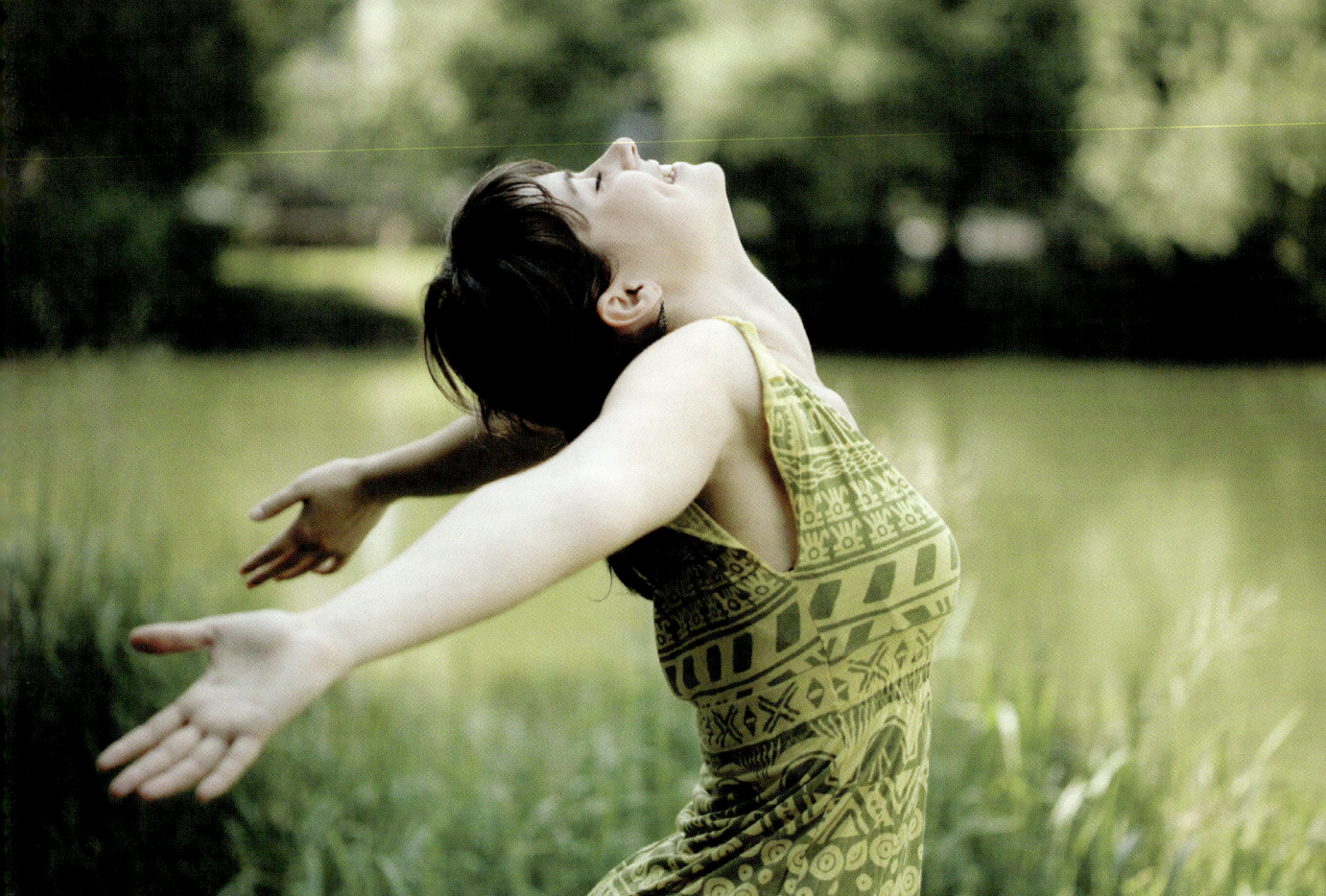

Figure 6.13 Enjoying the Sun. I just think that it's quite simple and symbolic at the same time. It is useful for a lot of concepts: green, fresh, and happy, which are three words that people want to think their lives are like.

Anna Bryukhanova

Portfolio	istockphot.com/anouchka
Started	2005
Total portfolio	5,758
Total downloads	Over 71,000

What is your background in photography?

I was learning journalism at Moscow State University and took some photography courses there. I wasn't interested in photography like I am now. It was just generic info about photojournalism and photography history—nothing that I could really use for stock photography. I got my first camera in 2003, and it was a surprise for myself, and everyone in my family, when I started making photos.

Go-to gear?

I'm shooting with a Canon 1Ds Mark III, and have lots of Canon lenses because I love them, and love to change them often. I would recommend any DSLR with one to two lenses for everyday use. If you shoot often, you will quickly understand exactly what piece of gear you're missing. It's a personal choice, depending on what you're shooting, the subject, location, and light.

What do you wish you knew when you started?

I wish I knew at the beginning how much satisfaction I would get from this activity. I think knowing that would have made me progress much quicker.

Favorite stock subject, and why?

People, and their lifestyle, and environment. That is what I like a lot, because it stops moments of life for eternity, and that is amazing, because nothing else can stop it like this.

Snapshot of your workflow?

I'm still trying to make my workflow more effective than it is right now. Like everybody, I make my choice after shooting, delete bad pictures, choose the best ones, convert them to 16-bit TIFF in a raw processor (Lightroom or Digital Photo Professional), put them in a special folder, then do processing in Photoshop, make the final JPEG, add keywords, and put them in another folder, ready for uploading.

Tips for working with models?

Be nice, be polite, and be relaxed, so the model sees you're in a good mood and can be relaxed, too. Humor is always very handy during shooting. Good background music is a must-have in studio. It can change the mood in a second. People will suddenly start dancing, and your shoot will be excellent with amazing results.

White background tips?

The best way to do a good shoot on white background is to make sure your lighting setup is correct. Typically, people shoot a subject on white using pretty simple setups, like two lights for background and two for model. This is a good basic setup, but you can always do more by adding a couple of lights for the model's hair and body lighting. Placing lights behind the model and directing it to model's shoulders and hair brings another dimension to your shoot on white.

Is there any last bit of stock photography wisdom you'd like to share?

The most important thing is to watch, to learn, to grow, to never stop shooting and uploading, and to love what you do. If you don't love it, just find something else to do. Earning money from this business does not come quickly. You have to love, and make an effort to love, what you are doing even more.

4 Review your photos.

After your photos are safely backed up, take a moment to enjoy all the work you did with a judgment-free review. You know you want to see them, so make this pass a focus on ensuring the backup is complete, the photos are corruption free, and you got all the shots on your list. Once you've confirmed all of this, it is safe to format those memory cards for the next shoot.

5 Unwind.

You just worked your butt off, and as much as you may have enjoyed it, do yourself a favor and decompress. Turn off the computer, stow the gear, and turn out the lights on your way out. I say this as someone who has burned the midnight oil one too many times. Eat a good meal, spend time with your loved ones, and do something that doesn't involve a glowing screen. You earned it.

Moving Forward

It has been my experience that the majority of microstock contributors are highly motivated self-directed learners. We learn from each other as well as from books, websites, and classes. This really is a lifelong process, and you will have many teachers along the way. There are two resources in particular that I have found so valuable that I made it a goal to find ways to get to work for both of them (and I did).

The first, and the one that I have gained the most from over the years, is the National Association of Photoshop Professionals. For an annual membership fee of $99 (at this writing), you gain access to a tremendous amount of training—covering photography, Photoshop, and Lightroom—both online and in print (Photoshop User Magazine); a very active member's online forum; and unlimited Photoshop, Lightroom, and photography gear Help Desk support. But what might be most valuable of all are the fantastic discounts on gear, training, and equipment from all the top vendors in the industry. You'll easily recoup your membership fee in no time at all. Head over to www.photoshopuser.com to learn more.

Many years ago, when I was first getting started in shooting for stock I picked up the book called *Understanding Exposure,* by Bryan Peterson (Amphoto Books), and the lights finally came on. I've recommended this book to everyone who has ever asked me what book they should get to help their photography. In 2009, I was researching online photography schools that could be a good fit for a Lightroom class I had in mind. When I discovered that Bryan Peterson founded his own school, called the Perfect Picture School of Photography (www.ppsop.com), I was immediately intrigued. What sold me on the school, though, was the fact that there is a lot of room for interaction between instructors and students, which is a real challenge in online training. PPSOP, as it is called, offers a wide variety of photography classes, ranging from 4- to 12-week sessions. If you are looking for an extremely accessible, yet structured, approach for expanding your photography skills, this is a good place to start. ■

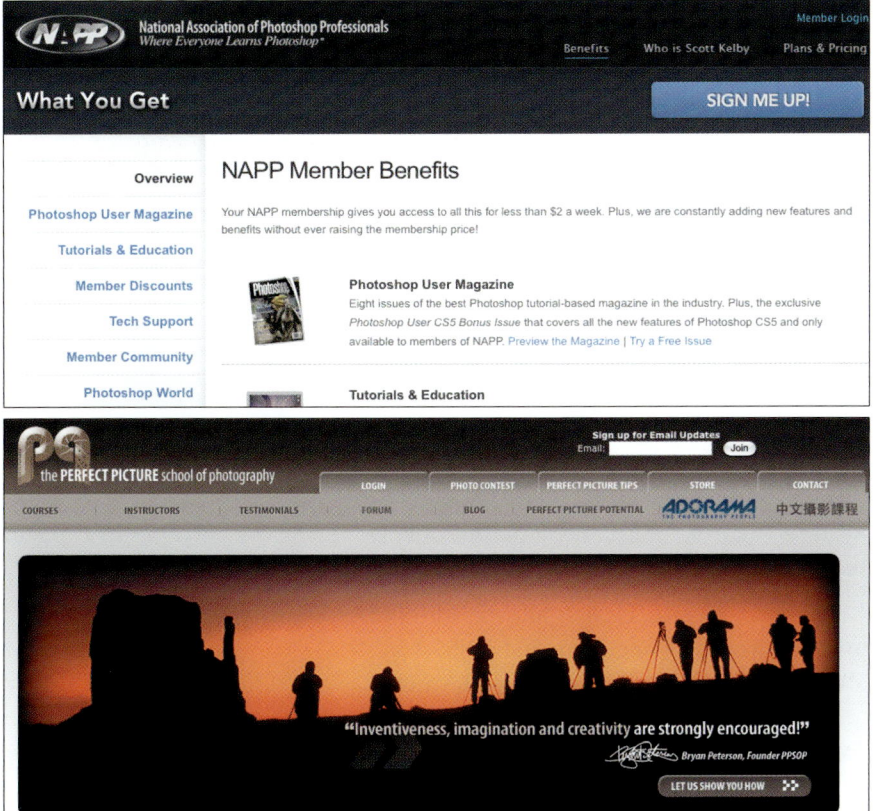

Figure 6.14 I write for Photoshop User Magazine and staff the Lightroom Help Desk for NAPP, and teach a Lightroom class at PPSOP.

7
Setting Up Your Digital Darkroom

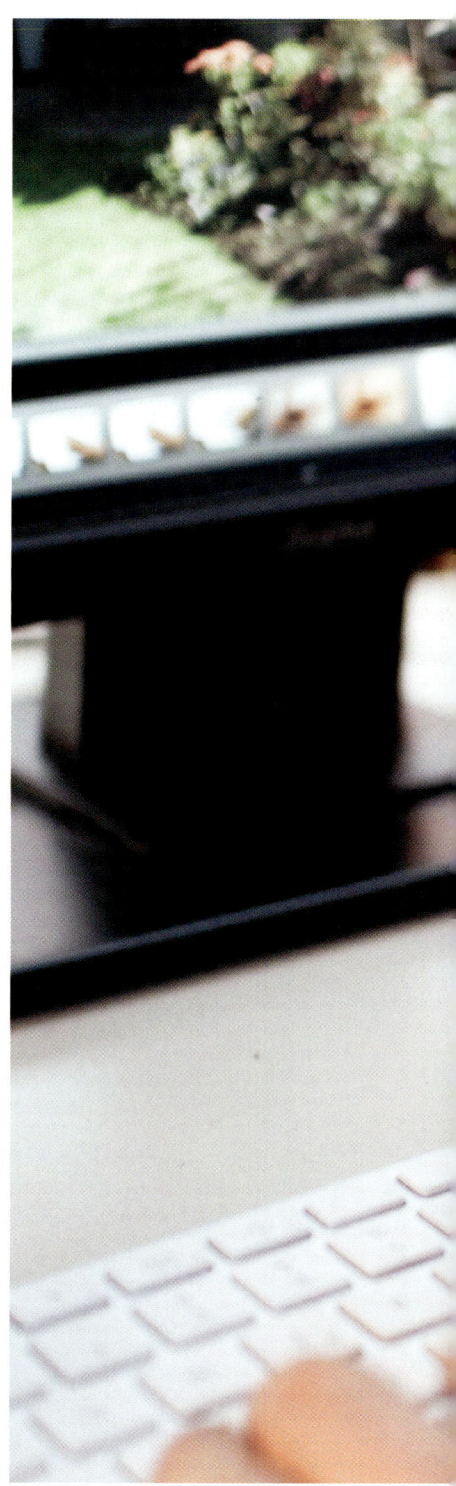

The digital darkroom is a place for both creativity and, equally important, data management. It is here that you will use all the tools at your disposal in an effort to create a final image on screen that matches the image in your mind's eye, all the while trying to preserve as much of the original data as possible (to minimize digital defects), and ultimately store duplicate versions in a safe backup location. Creating a system to view, store, organize, manage, retrieve, adjust, tweak, catalog, describe, and archive your photos is no small thing. This post-production part of your workflow requires its own set of equipment, and, of course, there is a range in complexity, quality, ease of use, portability, and cost to consider.

You will start with what you have, and as your budget allows, add and upgrade components over time to meet your growing needs and skills. Don't feel that you need to have it all out of the gate. Just like with your camera equipment in Chapter 5, first make the most of what you have and begin to identify places in your workflow where you want to improve the quality or efficiency of your process.

Hardware Choices

A computer and monitor are the bare essentials of your digital darkroom; if you don't have them, you'll need to go shopping before you can do much with your digital photos.

Desktop or laptop, Windows or Mac, are all equally irrelevant to the end user looking at your photos on a stock site. No one cares about what workstation was used to create the photos. The only person it matters to is you.

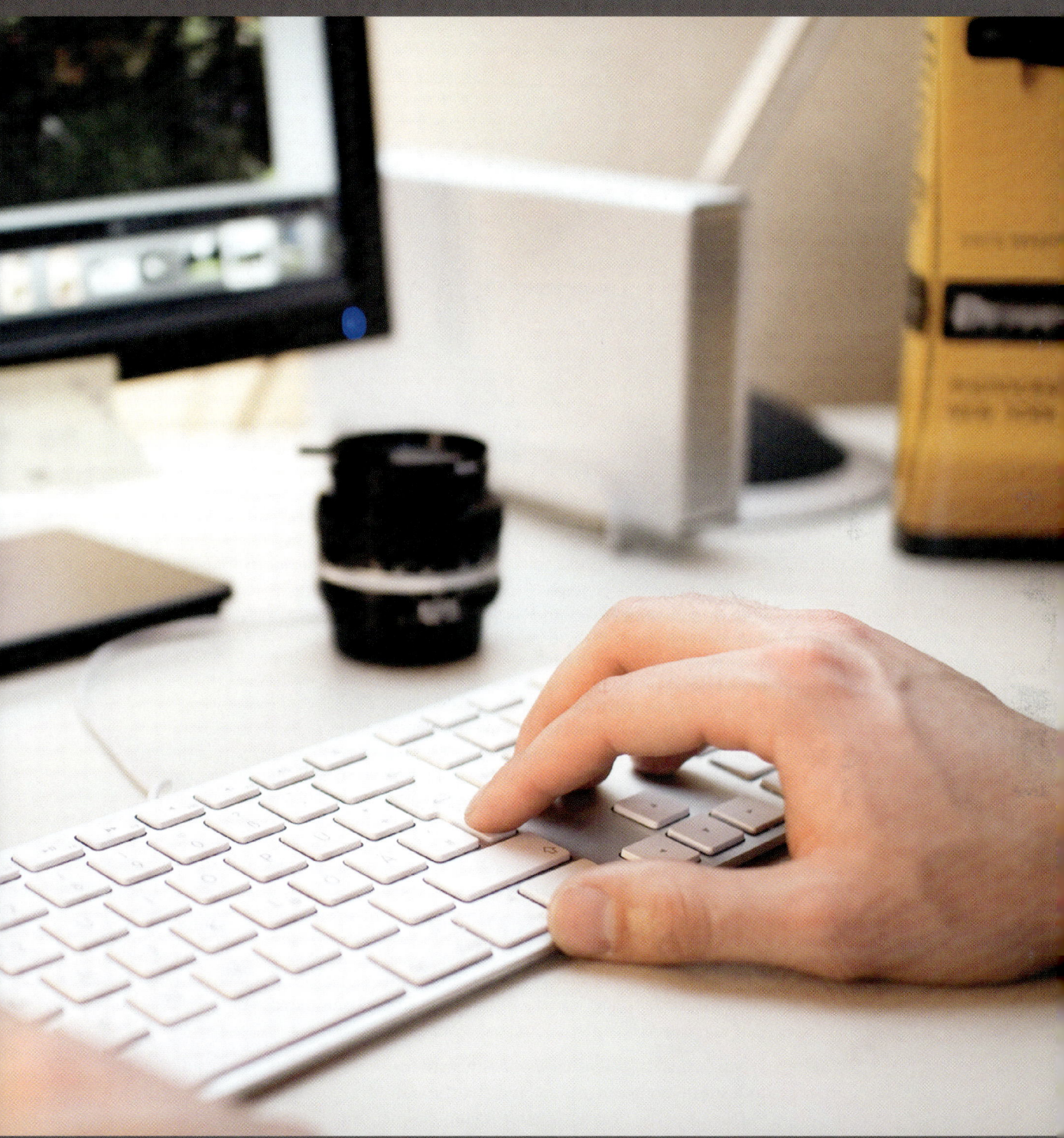

Figure 7.1 Photographer editing digital photos.
© Nicolas Loran (istockphoto.com/nicolas_)

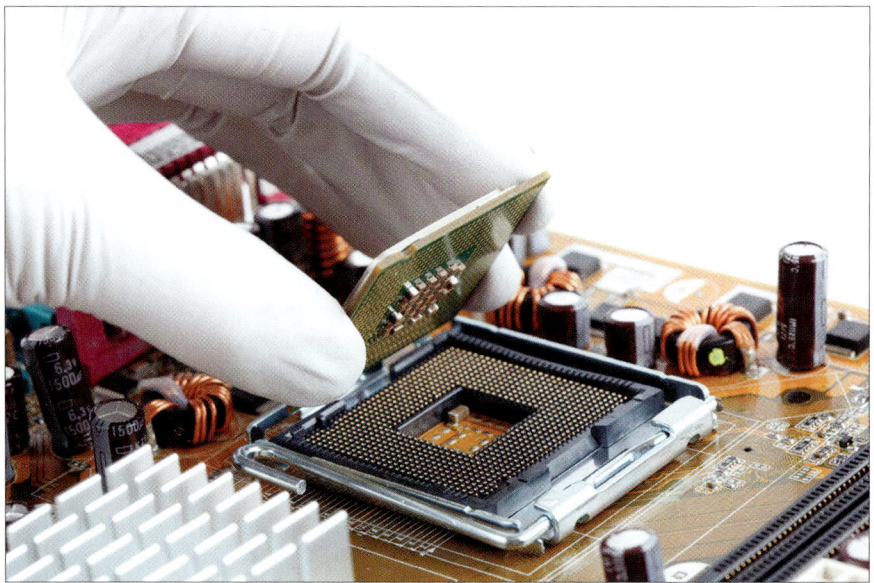

Figure 7.2 CPU Chip. © Khuong Hoang (istockphoto.com/fluxfoto)

These are your tools, and since you are going to be spending a lot of time with them, you need to choose the tools (within your budget) that you are most comfortable with on a daily basis.

Computer

I try to be as operating system–neutral (or platform-neutral) as possible. I use Windows and Mac computers. Over the years, and in different jobs, I have had both positive and negative experiences with both systems. I work on the Photoshop/Lightroom Help Desk for the National Association of Photoshop Professionals and help people with problems on both operating systems. There are pros and cons to each, but again, the operating system you choose will not make your photos look better.

When it comes to choosing between a desktop or laptop computer, the desktop will always win on performance at a given price point. More power under the hood translates into a much more efficient and pleasant editing experience. We are an impatient species. Having to wait while your system churns every time you make an adjustment starts to wear thin quickly.

When you shop for your next computer, it can help to start by considering the minimum requirements posted for the software you are planning to install. We'll talk software a little later in the chapter, but I don't think it will come as a surprise when I mention Photoshop as the industry standard in image editing. Photoshop CS5 was released in 2010 and lists the following minimum hardware requirements:

- (Windows) Intel® Pentium® 4 or AMD Athlon® 64 processor
- (Mac) Multicore Intel processor
- 1 GB of RAM
- 1024x768 display (1280x800 recommended) with qualified hardware-accelerated OpenGL graphics card, 16-bit color, and 256 MB of VRAM

Those are the minimums just to install the software. To actually enjoy using the software after installation, you want to exceed each of the minimums by a good margin. Whether you go Mac or Windows, having a multicore processor with at least 2 GB of RAM (preferably at least 4 GB) will make your experience so much more pleasant, efficient, and productive that it is worth the investment. If your computer is more than two years old (and it wasn't top of the line when you got it), then I think there is an upgrade in your near future.

In addition, you're going to need a lot of hard drive space to store all your photos. Trust me when I say that you will run out of space eventually, because you need internal drive space for the installation of all your applications along with ample free space for your operating system (and other applications) to use as *scratch disk* space, dedicated temporary storage used by some programs, for smooth operation. So, on top of all that you'll need to plan for additional storage for all your photos, video, and other data over time. External drives using high-speed (eSATA, FireWire, and USB 2.0) connections are great for extending your storage capacity without overfilling your primary internal drive.

Plan B (For Backup)

Although it is an additional expense, I can't stress strongly enough the need for a functioning data backup plan in place. Here are some key elements of a good backup system:

- Data is stored on at least two different storage devices.
- Backups run on an automated schedule so they are not dependent on you to remember.
- A copy of all data is stored in an offsite location.

You want your data stored on at least two different drives to protect against the eventual failure of your primary storage device. Every hard drive will die, and usually at the worst possible time. In addition to equipment failure, you need to be protected against theft and natural disaster. You can have a great local backup system in place, but (heaven forbid) if a meteorite turns your well backed-up office into a crater, it won't do you a bit of good. You need to keep a copy of your data at another location to truly be protected against the worst-case scenario.

A simple local backup can consist of your internal hard drive and a single external hard drive that you use to mirror (make an exact copy of) the data on your internal drive. Take it one more step and add a second external drive that you mirror to as well and keep that at an offsite location. There are a number of backup software packages to choose from, but check out ViceVersa Pro (www.tgrmn.com) for Windows, and ChronoSync (www.econtechnologies.com) for Mac as a starting point. The benefit of using dedicated programs like these is that you can schedule them to run automatically, and they are smart enough to mirror only the new or changed data, which is much more efficient than manually dragging and dropping files yourself.

Another hardware device worth checking out is a Drobo, www.drobo.com, which uses an array of hard disks in an easy-to-use package to back up your data and protect against equipment failure. In a nutshell, if any single hard drive in your Drobo fails, your data is still safely protected by the remaining disks. You just pop out the bad drive and insert a new one. I've been using one myself for over a year. I did have one drive fail (under warranty), and it really was a simple matter to replace the bad drive with no loss of data. The whole unit essentially acts like a single external hard drive despite consisting of multiple disks (although you can partition the device to act like multiple drives).

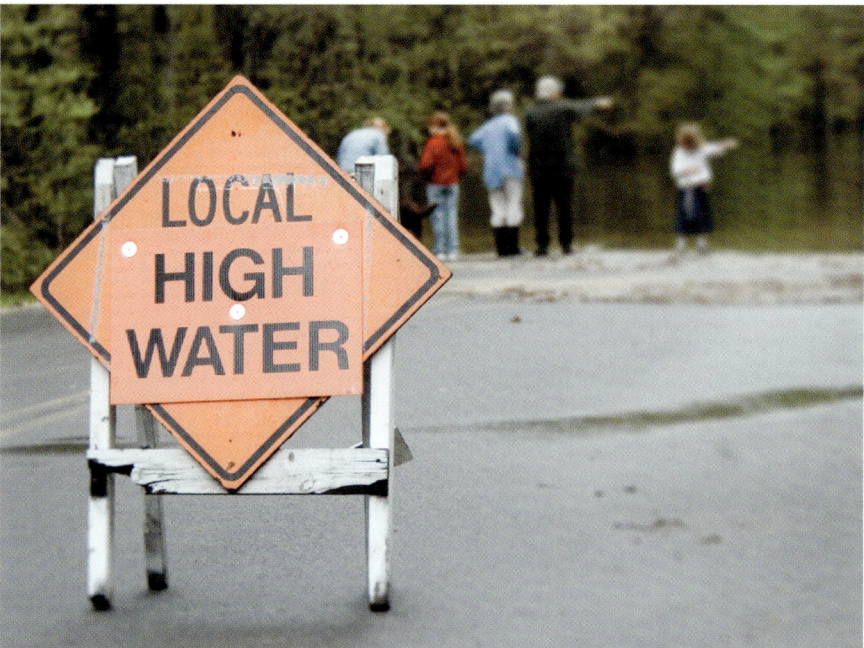

Figure 7.3 Disaster comes in many forms and it pays to be prepared. © Rob Sylvan

One last option to consider is online backup storage. The upside of online storage is that it is accessible from anywhere, happens automatically in the background, and ensures your data is safely stored in another geographical location from where you are. The downside is that it can take a really long time to get all your data uploaded depending on your Internet connection. I looked into a number of online solutions after a fire destroyed everything in my sister-in-law's apartment, including her computer, and settled on a service called Backblaze, (www.backblaze.com), because it offers a number of data retrieval options and will back up external hard drives (not all services will). It took over a month to upload about 700 gigabytes of data, but ever since, I've enjoyed the peace of mind of having my data far offsite.

Your Monitor

Of all your computer equipment, your monitor is going to provide the most help in improving your overall stock submission acceptance rate. Your monitor is both an output (it displays your photos) and input (you make editing decisions based on what you see) device in your editing workflow. If your monitor is not up to the task of correctly displaying your images, then you are working at a serious disadvantage. An all too common complaint from new contributors is that they just can't see the problems the inspectors are citing as rejection reasons. This is often the result of editing performed on a sub-standard monitor.

In some cases, it is the result of editing performed on a laptop. Most laptops (especially the cheaper ones) are designed for business tasks, such as spreadsheets, Word documents, and PowerPoint/Keynote presentations. The displays on these laptops are just not up to the task of helping you critically scrutinize your photos to the degree that stock sites require. If you are using a laptop because it is A) what you have, and B) otherwise meets all your needs, then I strongly encourage you to consider purchasing a better external monitor that you can run off your laptop for digital editing tasks. You'll get the added benefit of increasing your desktop space by using your laptop screen for less critical tasks while devoting full-screen real estate on your best monitor for image editing.

Likewise, if you are using a desktop computer package that was geared more toward the casual home or business user, then it is likely that the LCD monitor it came with just isn't going to do you any favors when it comes to editing your photos, and you are in the same boat as the laptop user above. Investing in a good monitor is similar to investing in better lenses for your camera. When it comes to your photography, the quality of the optics is too critical to skimp on. By the same token, there is little point in investing in a good monitor if you do not use it to its fullest.

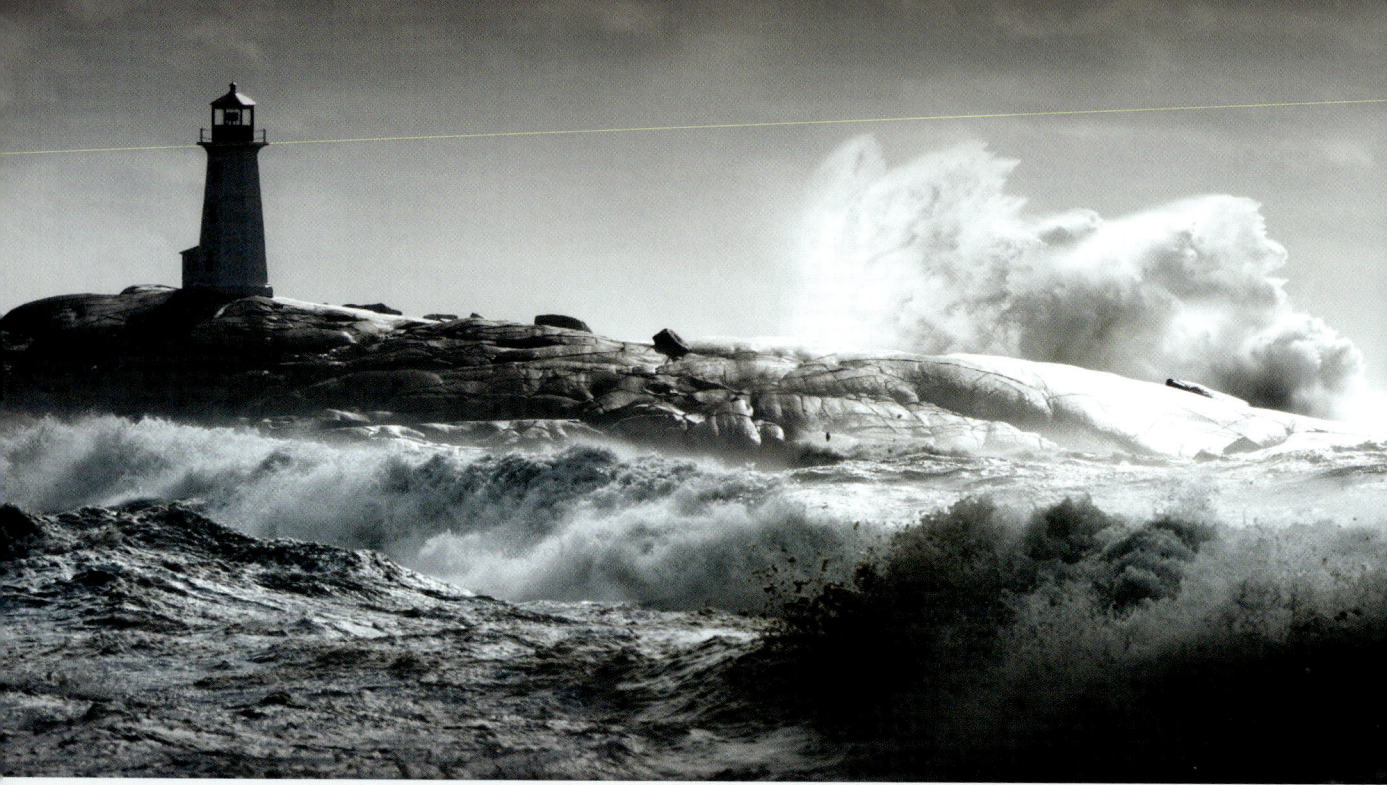

Figure 7.4 Ocean Fury. Downloaded over 1,500 times.

Ocean Fury

Creator	Shaun Lowe (istockphoto.com/shaunl)
Started	2004
Home	Canada
Total portfolio	2,573
Total downloads	Over 77,000
About this photo	Shaun says, "Shortly after Hurricane Noel passed by Nova Scotia I made my way to Peggy's Cove where I was thwarted by washed-out roads, high winds, and salt spray. Setting up on a few high rocks, a few friends and I waited for the moment we thought might happen. Small pockets opened in the cloud cover, providing intense sunlight set against the jet-black skies. It's the raw intensity of the shot that has made it one of my best sellers. It was captured with Nikon D70, Nikon 300mm F4 lens, and Manfrotto tripod."
Shaun's tip	"Find your own niche in the market and run with it. Learn every aspect of that niche, and immerse yourself (if you can) inside the culture of that niche to get a true feel for what the market is after."

Calibrating Your Monitor

Monitor calibration and profiling packages assist you in performing two important tasks: configuring your monitor to its optimal settings, and creating a custom monitor profile that accurately documents this optimal state. Every display installs a default monitor profile on your system and comes with a default configuration of settings. It has been my experience that, like most default settings, these are a good start, but possibly not the best configuration for editing your photos. The calibration process puts you in charge of determining the settings that are best for your system.

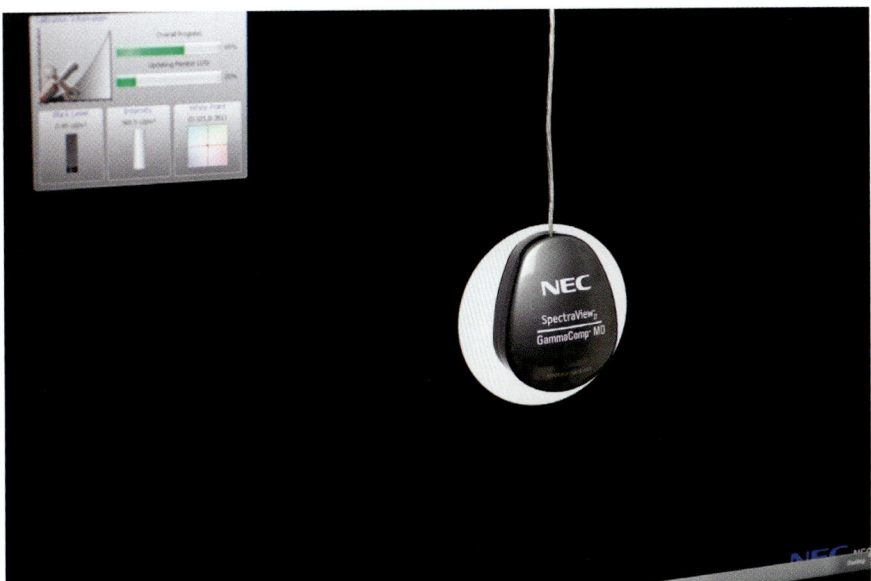

Figure 7.5 Calibration puck on an LCD monitor.

I know some of my peers have not always seen the point of using a calibration device and consequently don't use them now. From what I can see, it hasn't held them back, and I certainly respect their decisions. That said, I have been calibrating all of my displays (laptops, too) for years and in all cases I have preferred the calibrated result over the default. I also know that the people who are inspecting new microstock submissions are using calibrated displays. In addition, I have assisted people with display problems—such as thumbnails not displaying in Lightroom or display mismatches between Lightroom and Photoshop—that have been solved by properly calibrating and profiling their monitors.

The most painful part of the calibration process is the opening of your wallet to purchase the calibration package, as you can expect to spend upward of $150.

If you choose to go this route, and I encourage you to pursue it, don't buy the cheapest solution. I have had good experiences with both the i1 Display 2 from X-Rite (www.xrite.com), and the Spyder3Pro from Datacolor (www.datacolor.com). They are both designed for imaging professionals, have an intuitive interface, and most importantly, produce great results.

Technology in this area continues to improve. This is where you can really harness the power of the Internet to do some research before you buy. Ask in the contributor forums at the sites you are uploading to, check the reviews on Amazon, or talk to the folks in your local camera club/professional organizations. If you want to skip all that, then just pick up the industry standard i1 Display 2 and get on with calibrating.

Once you have a calibration package in hand, the process is as simple as following the series of onscreen prompts, and should take no longer than 5 to 10 minutes to complete. Recalibrate monthly to ensure everything is in top shape.

Software Choices

There is a wide range of image editing software. Balance your needs with your budget. There is no single right answer, and to be honest there are a lot of right answers based on the diversity of approaches I have seen other microstock contributors take over the years.

Ultimately, you will need software tools that allow you to access your photos in order to adjust exposure, tweak white balance, add contrast, change colors, remove distracting elements, crop, resize, reduce noise, increase sharpening, process raw photos (if you shoot raw), and correct lens distortions, to name some of the most common tasks. In addition you'll need to organize and manage your growing collection of photos, and edit metadata such as the keywords, titles, and descriptions required by stock sites.

> **Tip**
>
> Check Amazon.com for the best prices on software.

The best combination of software that I have found to fulfill all those tasks and more is Adobe's Lightroom and Photoshop. These are the industry standard image editing applications and have the price tag to prove it. Lightroom 3 costs around $300, while its much bigger brother Photoshop CS5 costs over twice as much. I honestly believe you won't find a more powerful image editing combination out there. That said, the price tag is steep, and I do have an alternative suggestion. Photoshop Elements 8 is a slightly watered-down (feature-wise) version of the full Photoshop, but at price of less than $100 (I purchased a copy for $50 after rebate) it can probably do everything you need, and it makes a great companion to Lightroom.

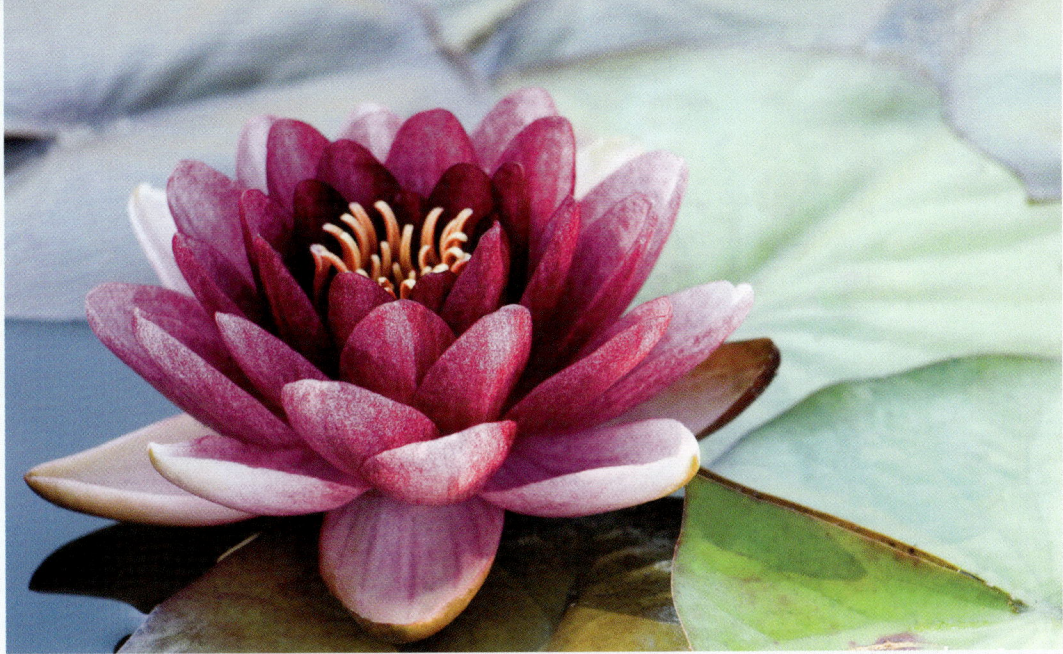

Figure 7.6 Hardy Waterlily 'Almost Black'. Downloaded over 375 times.

Hardy Waterlily

Creator	Zoran Ivanovic (istockphoto.com/zorani)
Started	2007
Home	Canada
Total portfolio	2,921 images
Total downloads	Over 10,000
About this photo	Zoran says, "For floral images, natural light qualities are the key for creating a great image. The colors have the right saturation, and the background doesn't overpower the image. Softer depth-of-field is usually required for this type of photo, while the main subject of the shot is kept in focus. The final shot had a number of bugs around the petals, but careful cleanup work in Photoshop allowed me to make this stock worthy. Captured with a Nikon D200, Nikkor 80-200mm f/2.8 lens, at ISO 100; exposure 1/6s at f/6.3."
Zoran's tip	"Creating images for stock is a business activity and requires all the steps needed to startup any type of business. It requires long hours, creativity, and lots of market research in regard to style, quality, and subjects that might be utilized for stock. Although having fun while doing the work is essential, doing the hard work (that is less fun) is crucial to receiving meaningful financial reward."

Why Lightroom and Photoshop (or Photoshop Elements)? Lightroom is a workflow tool designed to increase efficiency in processing your photos from start to finish. The program copies photos from your memory cards; provides organizational tools for managing your portfolio over time; can be used to add important titles, descriptions, and keywords that stock sites require; will handle 95 percent of the editing and adjustments you need to make; and save new copies for submissions to stock sites. There are some tasks that Lightroom is not designed to handle, such as combining multiple photos into a single final photo, removing distracting elements (like unwanted people or objects in the background), or making complex selections to apply adjustments to targeted areas. For the times when you need to get right down to the pixel level, you need a program like Photoshop or Photoshop Elements to get the job done. Lightroom is designed to work hand in hand with these editors, so it still fits in an efficient workflow when moving a photos between applications.

Is the only route to success through Lightroom and Photoshop? No, not at all. However, since they are so good at doing what needs to be done, offer versions for both operating systems, and are so widely used, they are the applications I will use to teach digital editing techniques in Chapters 8 and 9, as well as the file management and metadata editing skills in Chapter 11. Adobe.com does offer free 30-day trials for Lightroom, Photoshop, and Elements, so be sure to try before you buy.

Choosing a Color Space

> **Note**
>
> There is a whole lot more to understanding color spaces than I am able to address in this book, so if you are interested in diving deeper, I highly recommend *Real World Color Management* by Bruce Fraser, Chris Murphy, and Fred Bunting from Peachpit Press.

This is a subject that causes a bit of confusion, and for good reason, as it is not exactly intuitive and it involves numbers. Color space is important, though: As your photos move from your camera to your computer and then out into the world, it is very likely that their color space will change at least once, if not twice, which is neither good nor bad. But it is something you should be aware of and make conscious choices about each time it occurs. A basic understanding of what a color space is and how to use that knowledge to your advantage won't make you a better photographer, but can help you maintain the color appearance in your photos as they move through your workflow and out into the world.

Digital photos are captured in RGB, which uses the additive color model of combining a red channel, a green channel, and a blue channel to reproduce a range of possible colors. The outer limits of a specific range of possible colors, which is called its *gamut*, is defined by a specific color space within the RGB color model. There are three common color spaces you are likely to encounter when dealing with digital photos:

- sRGB (narrowest range of colors)
- Adobe RGB (slightly wider than sRGB, but much narrower than ProPhoto RGB)
- ProPhoto RGB (widest range of colors)

Each color space defines a specific range of colors, not number of colors (which is determined by the number of bits per channel covered later in this chapter), within the range of all the possible colors the human eye can see (and even beyond what we can see). There are no output devices, such as monitors and printers, that can reproduce every possible color that we can see in the real world. Our photos are only close approximations of the colors we actually see. So these various color spaces were created to help us translate the colors that exist in the real world to the colors that our cameras can capture to the colors that our monitors can display to the colors that our printers can print.

sRGB, Adobe RGB, and ProPhoto RGB are also called *working spaces*. Working space is the color space you do your image editing in. A device-specific color space defines a range of color that a specific device is able to reproduce.

For example, your monitor has a monitor profile that defines the range of colors it can reproduce. If you print with an inkjet printer, then you likely use a printer profile that defines the range of colors that your printer's inks in combination with a specific paper are able to reproduce. Beyond working spaces and device-specific spaces, there are mathematical color models that describe the full range human color perception called device-independent color spaces (such as CIELAB), which provide an absolute reference point for our computers to use when doing any conversion from one color space to another.

Color by Numbers

Computers only understand numbers. That means each individual color has to be defined by a number. For example, a single pixel of color could have a red value of 213, green value of 119, and blue value of 78. By themselves, those values are meaningless if not accompanied by a color profile that defines which color space to use to translate those numbers into the closest approximation of the actual color they are supposed to represent. Confused? Let's use a visual to help bring it home.

Figure 7.7 is a photo of typical New Hampshire autumn foliage on a sunny, blue-sky day. I opened that photo in Photoshop CS5 and placed three Color Samplers (one in the blue sky, one on a red leaf, and one on a yellow) that correspond to the #1, #2, and #3 shown on the Info panel. In the Info panel, we can see that sampler #1 shows R133, G141, and B203. Below the color samplers in the Info panel, you can see that the range of colors in this photo are defined by the ProPhoto RGB color space.

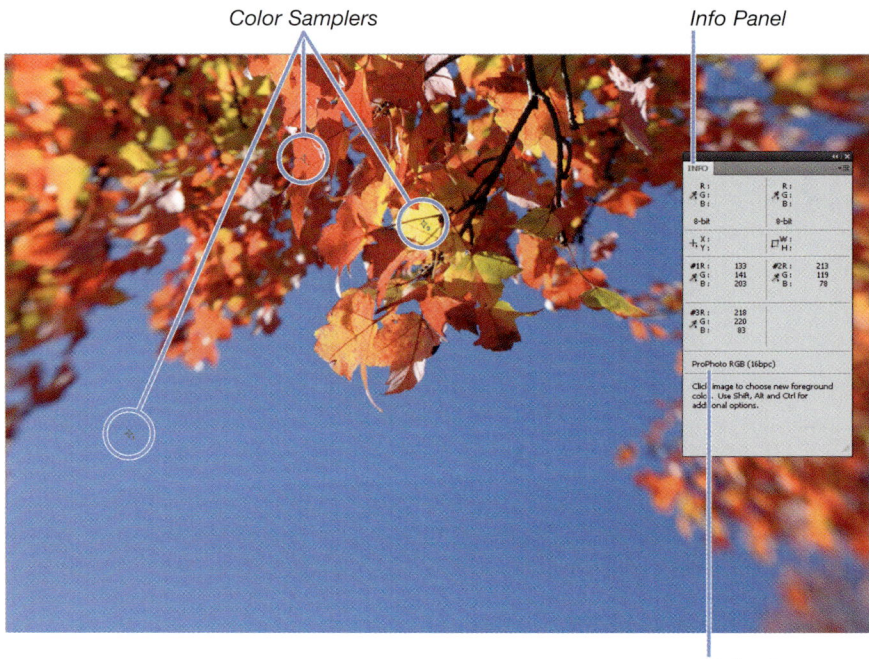

Figure 7.7 Photo in the ProPhoto RGB color space.

Now, let's see what happens if we tell Photoshop to keep those same RGB numbers, but use a different color space to determine which colors to display. You can do this easily in any version of Photoshop by using the Edit > Assign Profile menu. You can see the result in **Figure 7.8** where I assigned the sRGB profile to the same photo. Notice that the RGB numbers of all three samplers are exactly the same as Figure 7.7, but the colors displayed in the photo are very different (in a bad way). The two sets of numbers separated by the forward slash on the Info panel represent the before and after numbers, which in this case are exactly the same.

You might be scratching your head right now, so let me explain: The color profile and the RGB numbers are used together to properly display the colors in the photo. The same set of RGB numbers will produce different colors with different color profiles.

In addition to understanding the relationship between RGB values and color spaces, you need to wrap your brain around the concept of bit depth.

> **Note**
>
> You can download this photo and try it yourself by going to www.takingstockphotos.com/downloads.

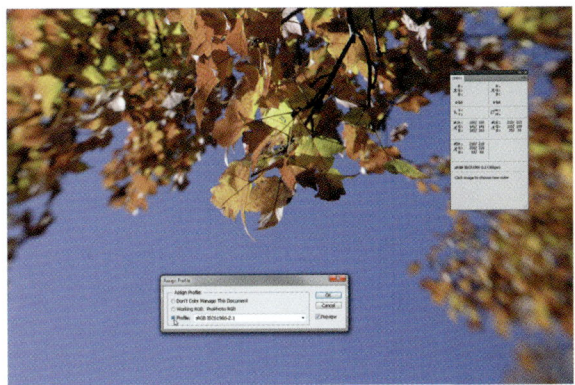
Figure 7.8 Assigning a different color space keeps the RGB numbers the same, but changes the color appearance.

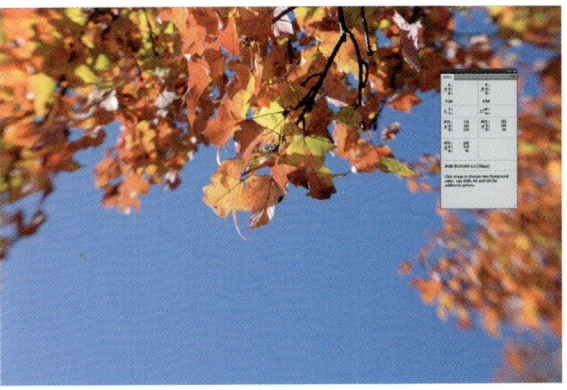
Figure 7.9 Converting between color spaces should result in similar color appearance.

Understanding Bit Depth

Color data in our photos is stored as a range of brightness levels, represented by grayscale tones, from black to white in incremental steps of gray, in each of the three RGB channels (**Figure 7.10**). Each brightness level in a given channel tells Photoshop how much of that color to include when combining the three channels to create the color image (recall R133, G141, and B203 from the color sample in Figure 7.7). The total number of grayscale tones that can be stored in a given RGB channel is what is known as its *bit depth*. The most common photo bit depth is 8 bits per channel, but we'll also encounter 16 bits per channel. Let's break it down.

Imagine a single pixel represented by a single bit (short for binary digit). That pixel can have only one of two possible values, either black or white. There's no room for shades of gray.

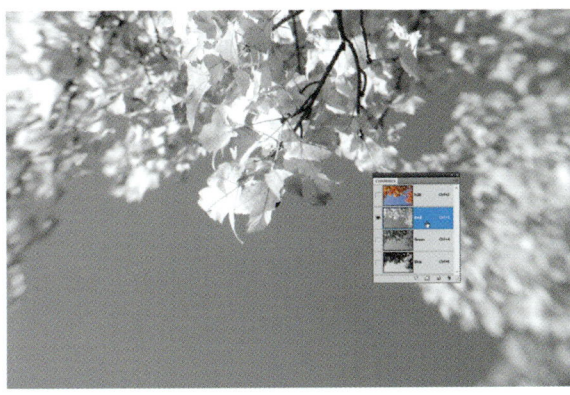
Figure 7.10 Photo from Figure 7.9, but just showing the Red channel. Brighter values correspond to higher amounts of red.

Now, imagine a single pixel represented by 8 bits. In the binary language of computers, that translates into 2x2x2x2x2x2x2x2, or 256 different values or shades of gray, ranging from 0 (black) to 255 (white).

A photo that is 8 bits per channel means that each red, green, and blue pixel is represented by 8 bits, or 256 possible values. The combination of all three channels means that 256x256x256, or 16,777,216, possible colors can be represented.

Computers store data as *bytes*; a byte is simply a grouping of 8 bits. Because of this, the next largest bit depth to consider is 16 bits per channel. This can be confusing because when shooting raw, our cameras can only capture 10, 12, or in some cases, 14 bits of data (depending on the camera model). However, since computers store data in bytes, raw photos are simply referred to as 16 bits per channel.

A photo that is 16 bits per channel means that each red, green, and blue pixel is represented by 16 bits or a theoretical (2x2x2x2x2x2x2x2x2x2x2x2x2x2x2x2) 65,536 possible values per channel. This is far more steps between black and white than the human eye can see, but all that data provides an excellent amount of head room for editing purposes, which is where the real benefit comes in. In other words, the more data that can be stored on an individual channel translates into having more data to work with as our photo travels through the editing pipeline.

Answering the Question

With that understanding, now you can determine the best color space and bit depth for your own workflow. The choice will be dependent on what file format you choose to shoot with on your camera.

If you shoot JPEG, then you will be working in 8 bits per channel because that is all JPEG can handle. In this scenario, configure your camera to save the JPEGs in Adobe RGB and set Adobe RGB as your working space in either Photoshop or Elements. If you use Lightroom to edit your JPEGs, then configure your external editor settings to also use 8 bits per channel Adobe RGB.

If you shoot raw, then it makes more sense to stay in a 16 bits per channel ProPhoto RGB space throughout your editing workflow because you retain as much of the originally captured data as possible during editing. Lightroom's working RGB space is a variation of ProPhoto RGB, so there is nothing to set there, but you'll want to configure your external editor settings to also be 16 bits per channel ProPhoto RGB, so that when you send copies to either Photoshop or Photoshop Elements, you still retain all that data until you decide you no longer need it.

An important 16 bit caveat: Not all filters and functions inside of Photoshop and Photoshop Elements will work with 16 bit files. That is not a problem, but it does mean you will first need to convert to a narrower color space, preferably Adobe RGB, and then convert to 8 bits per channel. Once you make the conversion, that data is lost from the file, but that's OK, because all of the major editing will have already been done. In the end, all files are going to wind up as 8 bit per channel JPEGs anyway, so it is inevitable. The benefits of 16 bits and ProPhoto RGB are in storing more data in your master files, and in having more data on hand for editing. You always want to move from the largest and widest space to the smallest and narrowest space. Think of it like a sculpture: you start with a large raw block of stone, and edit down to the smaller final creation.

Assignment

Here's a quick monitor test. Go to www.photofriday.com/calibrate.php and determine if you can see the full range of tones in the test image. If not, you may be missing out in seeing important detail in your highlights or shadows.

Evaluate your current hardware and software situation. Are you missing any components? Is there a possible upgrade in the near future? Figure out what component will give you the greatest boost in your workflow and start planning for it.

Download the sample photo shown in Figure 7.7 and go through the steps of assigning and converting color spaces to get a better feel for what is happening under the hood. www.takingstockphotos.com/downloads

Assess your current workflow and determine the points where you are currently changing color spaces and bit depth. Could you be making better use of a higher bit depth and wider color space earlier in your capture and editing stages? ■

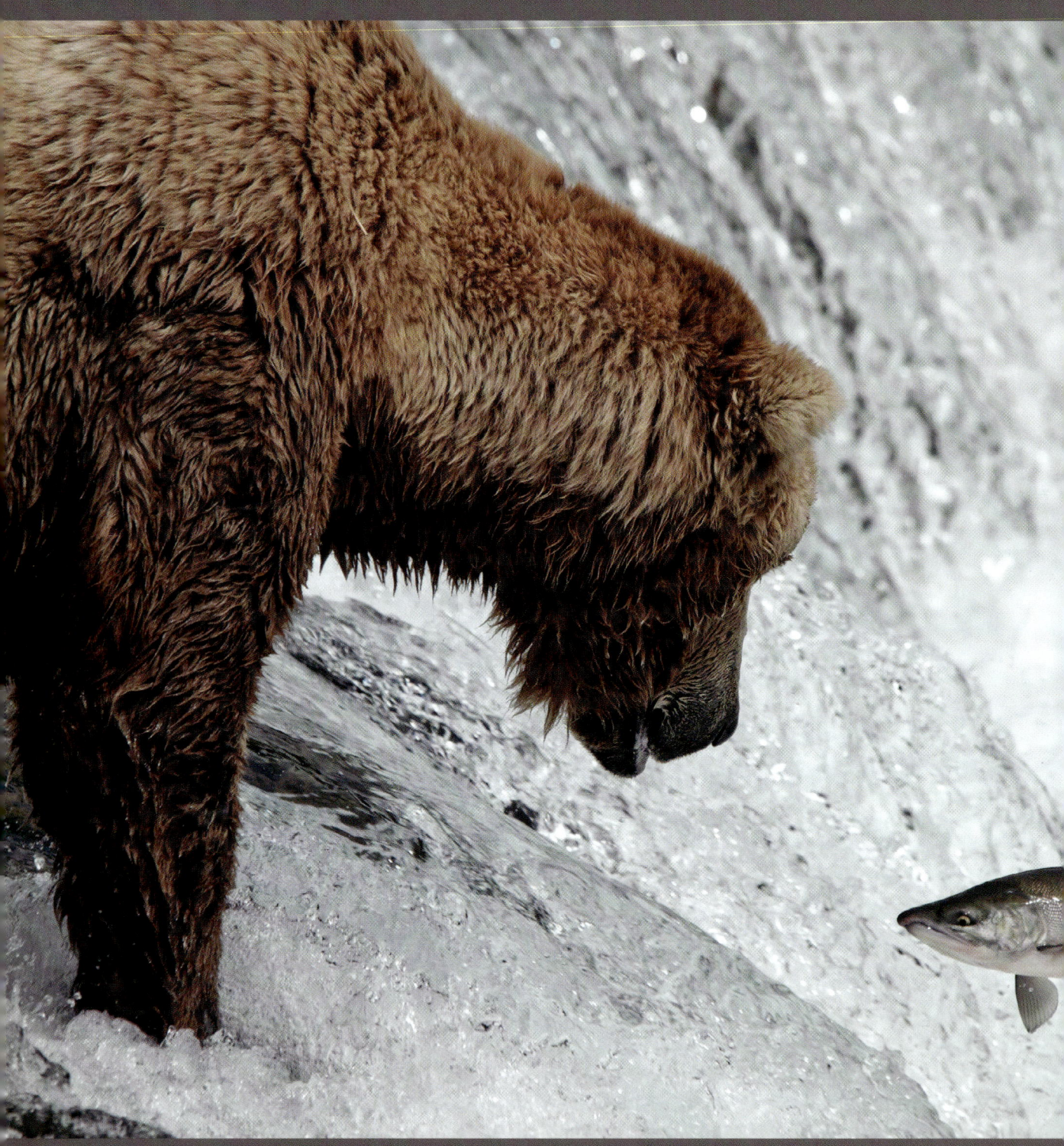

Figure 8.1 Brown Bear. Nikon D200 f/8.0 1/1000 sec ISO 320

8

Digital Editing Basics

The most important part of the stock photography workflow is what happens in your camera at the moment of capture. You need the best raw material to build the highest-quality images, and the work you did leading up to and including the moment of capture can be considered the acquisition of the building blocks of your image. Digital editing is the process of refining that raw material into the final image. In a raw workflow, there are a few basic adjustments—default rendering, white balance, exposure, contrast, noise reduction, and capture sharpening—you need to consider for all your photos as you process your shots. These are the same adjustments your camera makes if you were shooting in JPEG mode (based on your in-camera settings), but with a raw photo you are in the creative driver's seat. It is up to you to make the right decision each step of the way for the best output.

Back in Chapter 5, I discussed the pros and cons of shooting in raw mode versus JPEG mode, and I am working with the assumption that you have chosen to shoot in raw, or at least to step out of your JPEG comfort zone for now and give raw a try to see what is possible.

Focus on Quality

This is a critical point in your workflow. Just shooting in raw mode does not guarantee quality output. There are many opportunities in post-processing—exposure adjustments, noise reduction, color enhancements, sharpening, and so on—to self-inflict damage on an image. One of my main goals for writing this book is to help you reduce the number of rejections you might have gotten due to post-processing errors, such as:

- Failing to restore detail in vital highlight or shadow areas through poor exposure adjustments
- Not removing enough digital noise, those pesky unwanted discolored pixels that can appear in many digital photos
- Applying too much noise reduction, which has the effect of smudging and softening important edge detail
- Boosting saturation too high in an effort to enhance color, but resulting in overdone cartoonish results
- Over sharpening, which results in harsh and crispy edges on important details

The first step involves learning how to be your own worst critic before you start developing your photos. In Chapter 10 I'll give you lots of practice seeing your photos like an inspector, and then, in Chapter 11, provide a soup to nuts workflow for managing your photos and putting your inspector-vision to good use evaluating each shoot, but the key message I want to impart right now is this: don't waste time trying to save shots that are beyond saving. Invest your post-processing time and energy in only the keepers, and make notes about how to best reshoot the clunkers at a later date.

The reason for this is simple: The more adjustments you need to make to improve the original photo, the more likely you are to introduce new problems, waste time, and in the end, say something like, "I can't believe this was rejected after I spent hours working on it!" Every photo stands or falls on its own merits, and there are no points for effort.

In a perfect world, we start with the highest-quality capture possible, make as few adjustments as is necessary to smooth the rough edges, and then save out a final version that breezes through the inspection process. Since we are not in a perfect world, we need to come to grips with the less than perfect situations that arise, make the best decisions we can, and keep moving forward as efficiently as possible.

Work Smarter

As much as I enjoy the post-processing side of the equation, I think it is safe to say that we don't take photos just to spend time with them on our computers. While quality may be job one, job two has to be efficiency. Every photo cannot be treated as if it is your life's work. You do need time to go and create new photos.

The key to efficiency is to invest some time in learning how to master your tools, and then practice, practice, practice. Unfortunately, I can't teach the same processing steps in every possible application, but it is instructive to step through the actual processing I did on a not-so-perfect-world photo to show what is possible. If you don't use Lightroom 3, you will have to translate these basic steps into the application you have chosen to use. However, if you are using Photoshop CS5 with Camera Raw 6, then little translation is required since Lightroom 3's Develop module and Camera Raw 6 share the same tools, functions, and rendering engine. No matter what application you use, the basic types of post-processing adjustments that every raw photo requires are:

- Choosing a color rendering. Are you going for a neutral look? Something more vivid? Perhaps a black and white? The choice you make here will affect other settings down the road.
- Adjusting the white balance. This is a creative decision you need to make that affects the color casts in the photo.
- Adjusting exposure levels to improve the overall tonal range of the photo, while preserving important detail at the brightest and darkest ends, and accentuating contrast to make the image pop.
- Applying just enough capture sharpening to the important edge detail to overcome the inherent softness in raw captures.
- Evaluating and, if necessary, reducing unwanted noise without degrading detail.

To that end, I'll cover the basic raw processing steps you need to know in this chapter, and then follow up with tips for solving other digital problems in Chapter 9.

A Little About That Bear Photo

The bear and salmon photo at the beginning of this chapter (Figure 8.1) is one of my favorite photos I've ever taken. I had the opportunity to barter a day of Lightroom training in exchange for an all-expenses-paid photo-safari in Alaska. (It was an opportunity I can indirectly trace back to uploading my first awful sample photo to iStock back in 2002, but that is another story.) The reason I picked that photo was simply to show that a lot of what we shoot is under less than perfect conditions, and I don't want you to get the idea that perfection is the only thing that matters. Approximate perfection is a little more realistic.

The bear photo was taken with a Nikon D200, which is a good camera, not the best, but far from the worst, and I still shoot with it today. The location was Brooks Falls in Katmai National Park, Alaska, on a beautiful, partly cloudy day, which meant the light kept changing. Trying to expose properly for the bear, salmon, and the white water of the falls was a continuous challenge. I used a higher than normal ISO (320 in that shot) because I needed a fast shutter to freeze the motion of the jumping salmon, and with that fast of a shutter you can be less worried about noise.

The biggest problem to avoid, other than being out of focus, was completely blowing out the highlights, which according to the blinking highlight clipping warning on the camera's LCD screen at the time, it seemed to indicate that I had. It wasn't until much later, after downloading my memory cards, that I was able to evaluate if it was going to be a keeper or not. I suppose it is obvious I decided it was a keeper, but it came down to three essential factors:

- The composition was strong.
- The focus was on the right part of the scene.
- Exposure adjustments could be made to recover highlight data because I shot in raw mode.

In most cases, if you have those three things you probably have a keeper on your hands too. Let me show you the basic color rendering, white balance, and exposure adjustments I applied to that photo, then I'll switch to a different photo to look at noise and sharpening.

Setting Defaults and Creating Presets

In order to get the most out of a tool like Lightroom you need to learn how to use it as efficiently as possible so that you are not re-creating the wheel on every photo you process. Two of the most important things you can learn right off the bat are how to set custom default settings that are applied to your raw photos on import and how to create your own Develop presets, which are simply a way to preserve a configuration of settings for reuse.

By design, Lightroom applies default processing settings, such as white balance, brightness, contrast, sharpening, noise reduction, and so on, for each raw image file format it supports after the photo is imported into Lightroom. Even if an adjustment amount is zero, it is still a default setting. Every raw processor has to start somewhere, and since Lightroom can't read your in-camera processing settings, it has to have its own. However, these default settings are not carved in stone, and you can customize them to your own preferred starting point. One setting I suggest changing first is the default rendering based on your preferred camera profile.

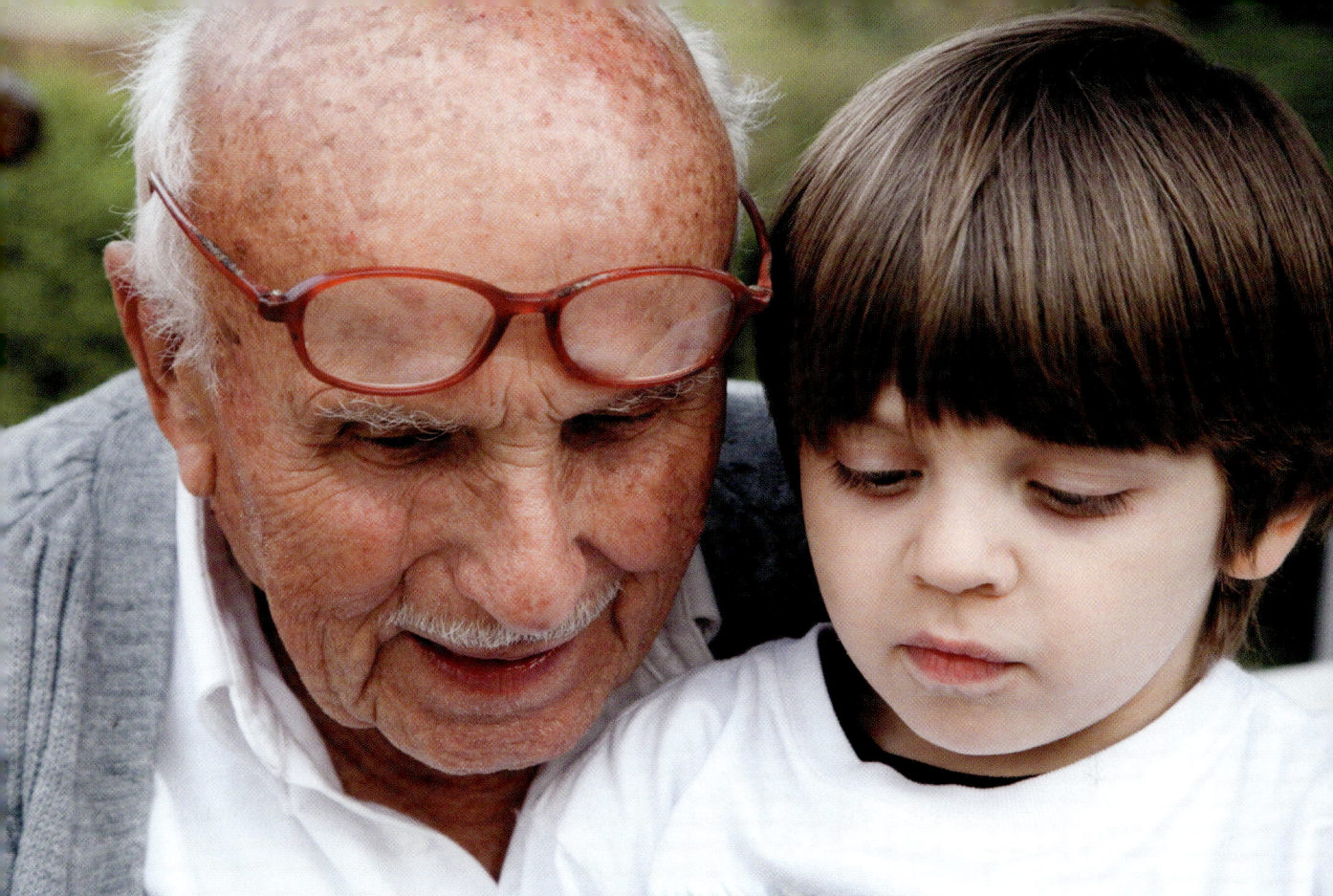

Figure 8.2 Two Generations. Downloaded over 800 times.

Two Generations

Creator	Slobo Mitic (istockphoto.com/slobo)
Home	USA
Total portfolio	Over 3,500
Total downloads	Over 57,000
Started	2005
About this photo	Slobo says, "The natural pose of models reflects a real-life situation that many people can identify with. It was taken with a Canon 5D with 24-105 F4L lens."
Slobo's tip	"Get a decent DSLR camera. Proficiency in post-processing is a must."

Choosing a Default Rendering

Most digital cameras have built-in options to apply various creative rendering styles to your photos at the time of capture, with names such as Portrait, Landscape, Standard, Vivid, and so on (though the exact names vary with each camera manufacturer). Each of these styles affects the color rendering—the essential look—of the captured image data. The style you choose is completely a matter of individual taste, but as I pointed out in Chapter 5, those styles aren't actually applied to the raw data. If you are using the software provided by your camera manufacturer, it can read the in-camera settings and apply the same rendering. But if you are using a third-party application, like Lightroom or Camera Raw, then you will have to manually choose the default rendering you prefer in that software.

Lightroom makes this possible through what it calls *camera profiles*, which are found in the Camera Calibration panel (**Figure 8.3**) under the Profile drop-down menu.

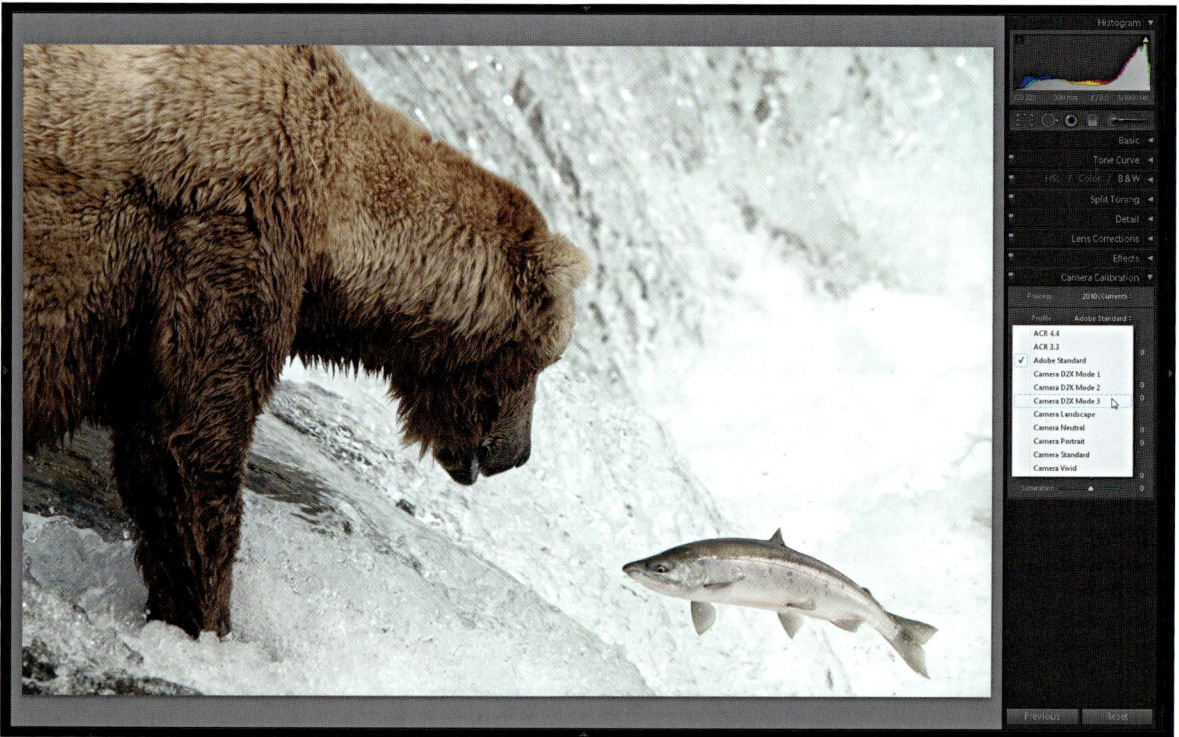

Figure 8.3 Choosing a profile from the Camera Calibration panel has a big impact on the overall color rendering of the raw photo. Compare against Figure 8.1.

Remember, a key benefit of shooting raw is that you can change this setting (and many others) non-destructively (meaning without harm to the original image data) at any point in your workflow. That said, you do need to start somewhere, so I suggest choosing the profile you want to be your default starting point. Here's how:

1. Select an unprocessed raw photo that is well exposed and contains a variety of colors to better help you evaluate the differences in each camera profile. Either a freshly imported photo or one you just haven't gotten around to working on yet is fine.

2. With that photo selected, press D to jump directly to the Develop module. The Camera Calibration panel is located at the bottom of the right side of the interface.

3. Experiment by expanding the Profile drop-down menu and selecting each available profile in turn to see how it affects the selected photo. As you try each profile, note how the colors change in the selected photo. Compare Figure 8.3, which uses the Adobe Standard profile, against Figure 8.1, which uses my preferred Camera D2X Mode 3 profile, to see the subtle difference it makes. Many people choose the profile that most closely matches the way the photo looks on the camera's LCD preview. If you configure your camera to shoot raw+JPEG, you can use the JPEG version as visual guide to help find the look you want.

4. Once you've decided on your preferred starting profile, hold the Alt key (Mac: Option) to change the Reset button (appearing directly below the Camera Calibration panel) to Set Default, and press that button. This will open the Set Default Develop Settings dialog box (**Figure 8.4**).

> **Note**
>
> Adobe has provided a limited set of camera style profiles for most of the current Canon and Nikon camera models. However, there is a means to create custom camera profiles for all camera models via the DNG Profile Editor. Go to http://labs.adobe.com/wiki/index.php/DNG_Profiles to download this free tool as well as find free tutorials.

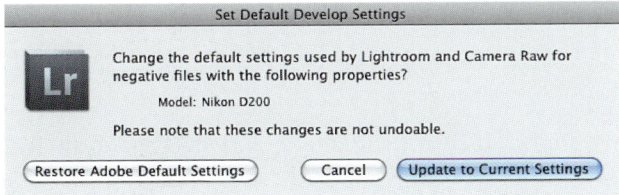

Figure 8.4 The Set Default Develop Settings dialog box.

5. Click the Update to Current Settings button to set the new default profile and close that dialog box.

From now on, all newly imported raw photos from that same camera model will have this profile applied by default. That's great, but (and this is a pretty big but) this process does not affect any previously imported raw files. So if you want to apply this same profile to existing photos, you will need to do that manually. The most efficient way to do that is to create a develop preset.

> **Tip**
>
> Although it says the changes are not undoable, it just means the Undo command won't undo the develop default settings. You can always repeat step 4 to either go back to the original Adobe default settings or apply a new custom setting.

> **Note**
>
> As you develop your photos further, you may find there are other settings you want to change to a different default value, and that is perfectly fine. Change only the settings you want to be used as the new default and repeat Step 4 to update to current settings.

Creating a Develop Preset

A preset is simply a way for you to save a collection of settings for reuse in a single click. These can range from simple things like camera profile changes to more complex multi-setting timesavers. Lightroom stores all of these in the Presets panel on the left side of the interface.

Now that you've set your default camera profile, let me show you how to save that as a new preset so you can apply it to any previously imported photos.

1 With this photo still selected, choose Develop > New Preset to launch the New Develop Preset dialog box (**Figure 8.5**). Name the preset the same as the camera profile to make it easy to remember.

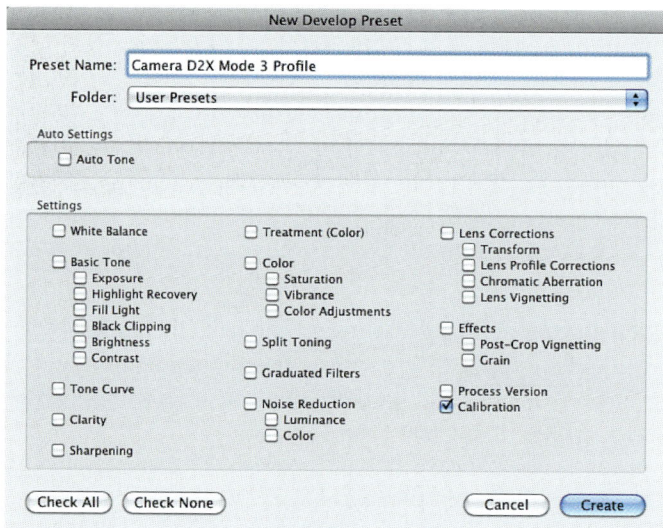

Figure 8.5 The New Develop Preset dialog box.

2 Click the Check None button to clear the dialog box, then check only the Calibration box. Click Create to save the preset.

3 Now you can press G to jump to Grid view, select all raw photos, and apply that preset via the Saved Preset menu in the Quick Develop panel (**Figure 8.6**).

This is just the tip of the preset iceberg of course, but it nicely illustrates the power of working with raw files. You are free to explore multiple creative paths in developing your photos without altering the original data in your photo, and you can continually take advantage of new rendering technology moving into the future. Keep the concepts of default settings and presets in mind as we continue to move through other essential adjustments.

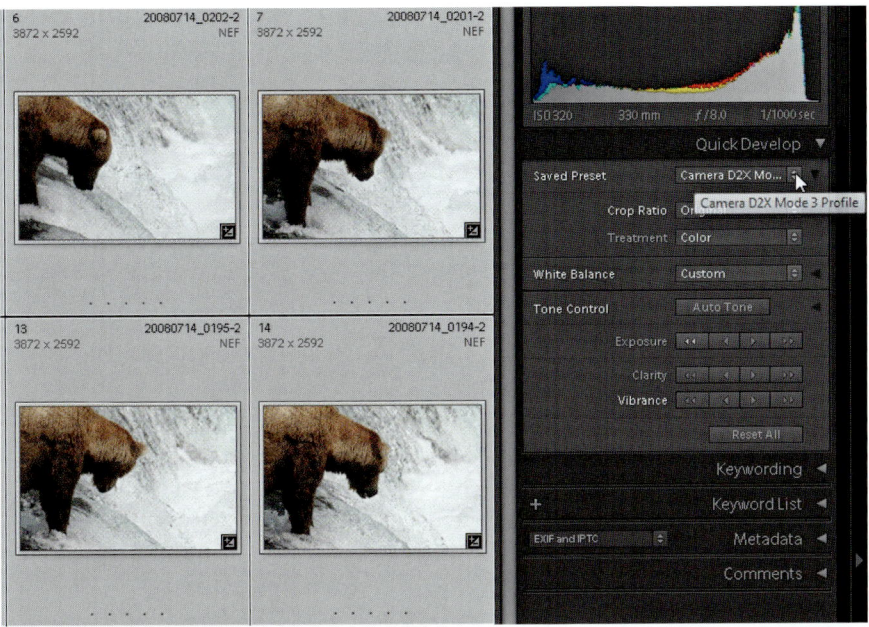

Figure 8.6 Applying a preset via the Quick Develop panel.

Adjusting White Balance

The white balance (WB) controls, both in your camera and in your software, are there to help you cope with color casts in your photos that result from light produced by different sources. Without getting bogged down in the technical stuff, you already know that things look slightly different under different light sources. Imagine the sickly green light of fluorescent light, the warm glow of a candle, or the harsh light of high noon. I'm sure you can see them in your mind's eye. Our brains do a great job of compensating for the different color casts produced by these light sources, but we still don't always see everything as perfectly neutral. We do see color casts depending on the light we are in, and those casts are intrinsically linked to how we feel about the scene we are viewing.

Imagine a romantic dinner for two. The incandescent wall lamps are turned down, and candle light flickers on the table. Now, imagine you close your eyes for a second and the restaurant has flicked on the overhead fluorescents because the staff wants to go home. Still romantic? No! If all light produced the same feeling, we'd all have switched over to fluorescents long ago. The quality and colors of light are very important variables for you, as a photographer, to use as effects.

This is not at all to say that removing or neutralizing color casts is wrong, because it isn't. It simply depends upon the photo, and it is your job to make the right call.

Using the Tools

Lightroom provides several tools for dealing with color casts. The tools can be used on JPEG or raw files, but you have more control with raw since the actual image data has not yet been rendered into pixels.

The first tool is actually your camera. The white balance setting you select on your camera will be interpreted by Lightroom, and this considered the As Shot setting you'll see by default. Depending on the photo, and your intentions, this may be a good enough starting point. If not, then you need to look at the Lightroom tools at your disposal, and there are three—White Balance Presets (WB), White Balance Selector tool (which looks like an eye dropper), and the Temp and Tint sliders—located in the top section of the Basic panel (**Figure 8.7**).

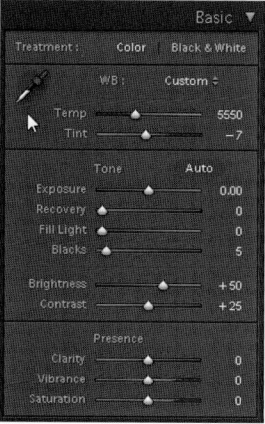

Figure 8.7 The White balance adjustment tools reside in the top section of the Basic panel.

> **Note**
>
> If you have a JPEG, TIF, or PSD file selected, you will only see As Shot, Auto, and Custom since the actual white balance setting was applied when that photo was originally rendered.

The WB Presets can be an easy starting point if the As Shot rendering is not working for you. Click the Presets drop-down menu (**Figure 8.8**) and select the preset that best fits the scene's lighting for that photo. Don't be afraid to try each in turn to see the differences. You might be surprised by which works best. While presets have recognizable names, some people are confused by Tungsten, which is simply the common light bulb (the filament inside the household light bulb is made of tungsten). The Auto setting is Lightroom's attempt to neutralize the image, while Custom appears the moment you start using the White Balance Selector Tool or the sliders.

Adjusting White Balance   **123**

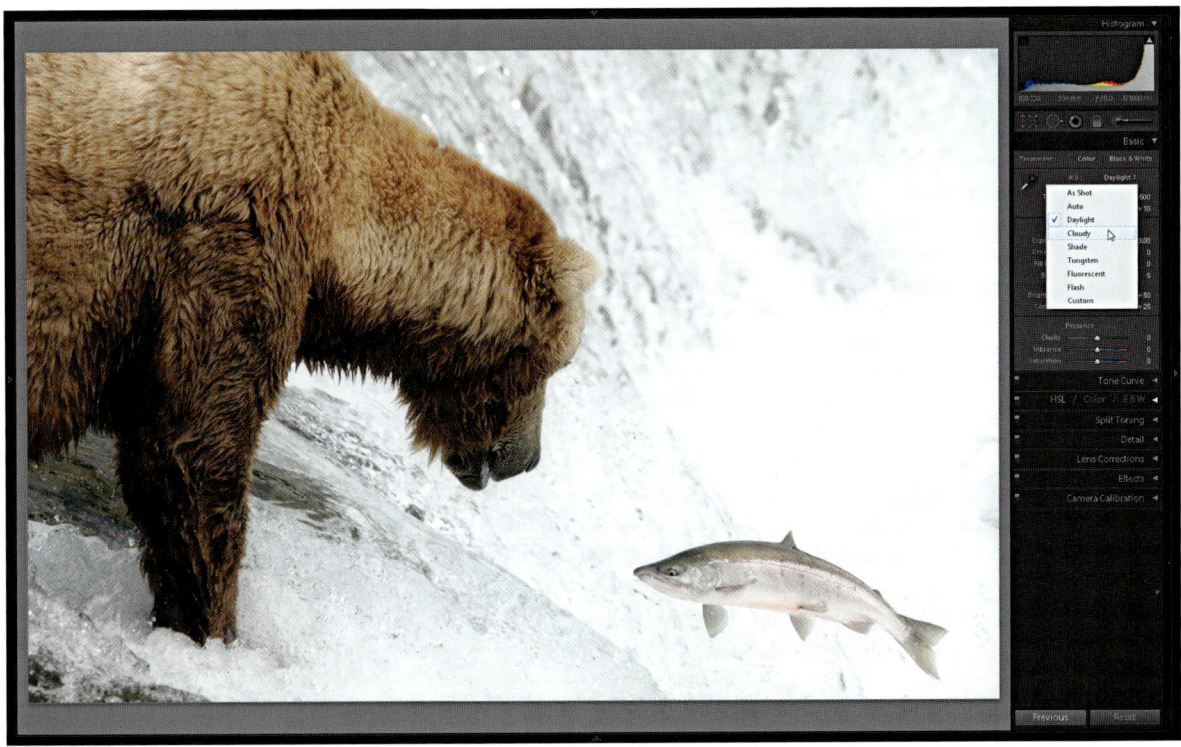

Figure 8.8 Compare the look of this Daylight preset setting against the look of the custom white balance I chose for Figure 8.10. It is subtle, but I preferred the custom.

My favorite custom approach is the White Balance Selector Tool because it is so easy to use. Here's how:

1 Press the W key or click the White Balance Selector tool in the Basic panel.

   When the tool is active, the cursor will change into an eye-dropper accompanied by a loupe that displays a zoomed view of the pixels directly under the White Balance Selector Tool (**Figure 8.9**). Under the pixel grid are the percentages of red, green, and blue contained in the center pixel. You want to *pick a target neutral*, which means click on a pixel that has R, G and B values that are pretty close together. I look for an area of pixels that should be a neutral light gray, such as the white water in that example.

2 Move the tool over the photo and choose a pixel that you want to neutralize. With a little looking, I found a nearly neutral point in my photo (Figure 8.9) and clicked on that spot, which caused Lightroom to adjust the R, G, and B values slightly to bring them even closer together, which adjusts the white balance for the entire photo. **Figure 8.10** shows a Before and After split view with the original As Shot white balance in the top half and the new custom white balance setting in the bottom.

Tip

Go to the View > Before and After menu to access all the Before and After view options.

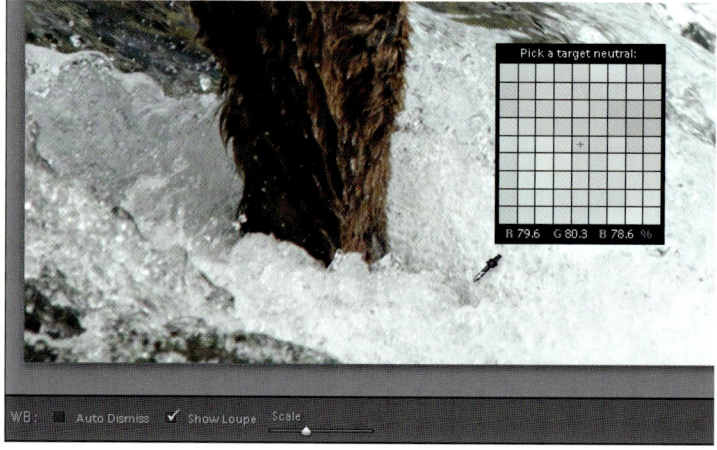

Figure 8.9 The White Balance Selector tool and accompanying loupe.

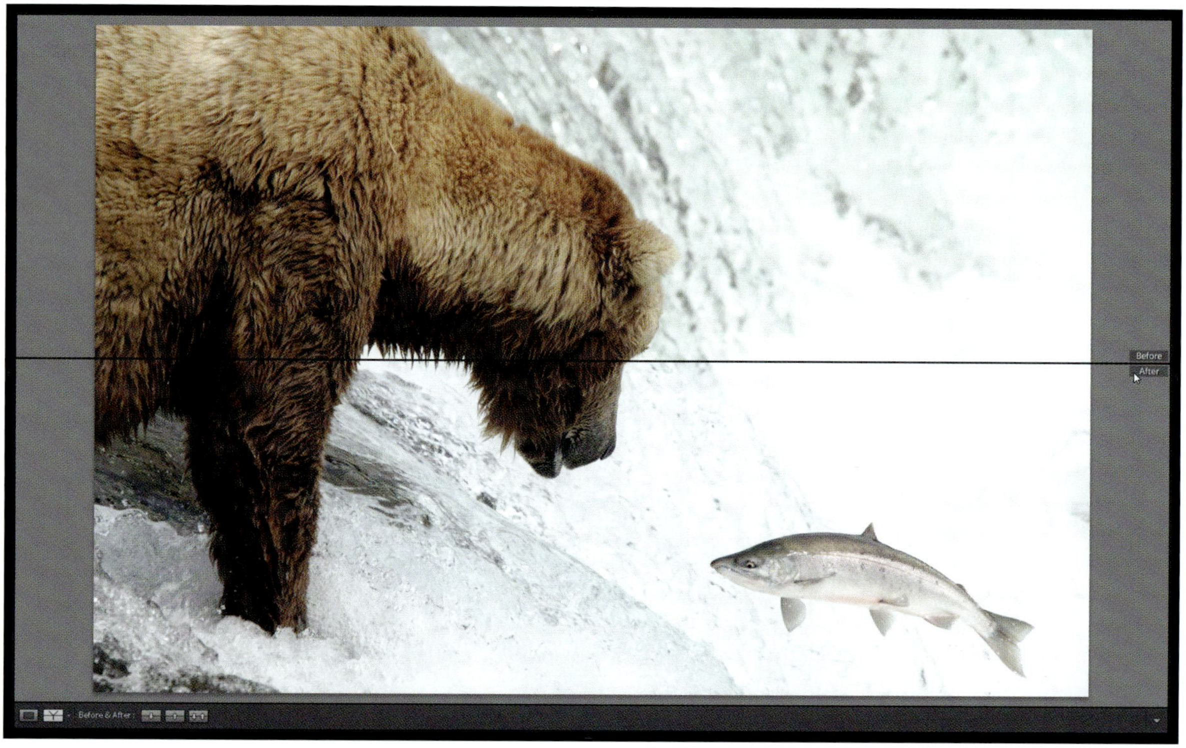

Figure 8.10 Compare the Before As Shot on top to the custom white balance on the bottom. White balance has a subjective element where there is room for more than one right answer.

Speeding Up the Process

Typically you'll have multiple photos in any given shoot that were all taken under the same lighting conditions. This is where Lightroom's Sync and Auto Sync functions come into play.

In Figure 8.10, I only had a single photo selected while I worked on adjusting the white balance, but I actually had a number of similar shots taken in that same light that could use that same exact white balance setting. When you've already applied a setting (or combination of settings) to one photo and you later decide you want to apply that same setting to more photos, you can use the Sync function:

1. With the adjusted photo still selected, select all other shots you want to adjust in the Filmstrip.
2. Click the Sync button to launch the Synchronize Settings dialog box (**Figure 8.11**).

> **Tip**
>
> You can hold the Ctrl (Mac: Command) key and individually select multiple files, or hold the Shift key and click the last file in a series to select them all.

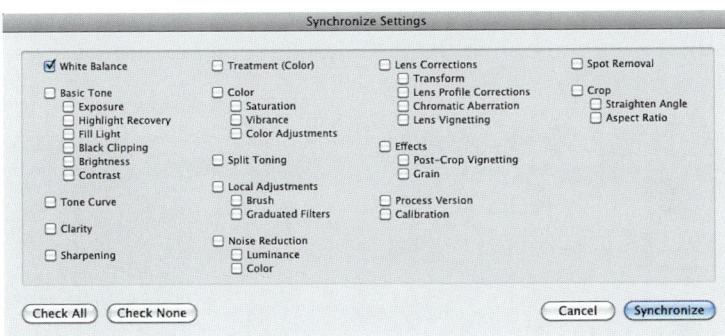

Figure 8.11 The Synchronize Settings dialog box.

3. Check the boxes next to all the settings you want to synchronize in all of the selected photos. In this case, we'd check White Balance. You are telling Lightroom to take the settings from the first selected photo and apply them to the rest of the selected photos.

The Sync button also has a hidden super power. Instead of working on one photo and then synchronizing those settings across multiple photos later, you can enable the hidden Auto Sync function and simply work on multiple photos at once.

Here's how: With multiple photos selected, hold down the Control (Mac: Command) button and watch the Sync button transform into Auto Sync. As you work on the active photo displayed in the work area, everything you do is equally applied to all selected photos automatically. This can be a huge time-saver when many photos require the same exact adjustments.

It is important to remember to disable Auto Sync—just click the button once more to revert back to Sync—so that you don't accidentally apply settings to other photos.

Making Exposure Adjustments

In Chapter 6, I discussed the importance of getting a good exposure when you are shooting in order to acquire as much data from the scene as possible without overexposing the capture to the point of data loss. If a photo is too overexposed, you won't be able to recover the important data in the blown-out areas, which will result in a rejection. If a photo is too underexposed and requires a drastic increase in Exposure, you run the risk of making visible all of the noise hidden in the darker areas of the photo, which will also result in a rejection. The goal of making exposure adjustments is simply to refine a good exposure as opposed to trying to salvage a poor one.

If you look at the histogram for this photo (**Figure 8.12**) you can see there is a lot of data stacked up on the right edge. If you press J to turn on the Shadow/Highlight clipping warning, you can see the areas of the photo that are currently clipped to pure white and contain no detail. However, because I shot in raw mode there is the opportunity to recover the lost detail in the highlights, as well as make adjustments to improve the total distribution of brightness levels throughout this photo to make it come alive.

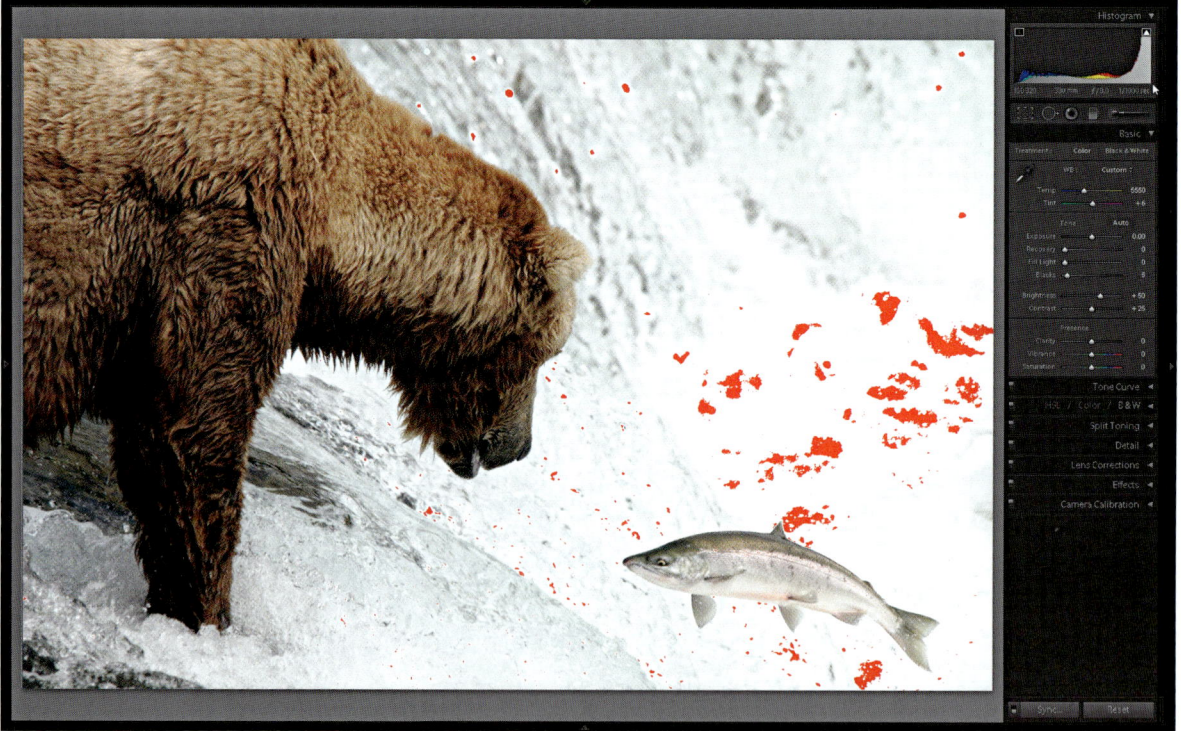

Figure 8.12 Photo displaying the red highlight clipping warning on the blown-out areas of the photo, and the histogram is all stacked up against the right edge.

Exploring the Exposure Adjustment Tools

Lightroom is designed to work from the top of the right-side panel group down as you make your adjustments. Starting in the Basic panel (refer back to Figure 8.7 for a better view), under the white balance controls, you'll see the Exposure, Recovery, Fill Light, and Blacks sliders, which have a direct link to the Histogram panel. In fact, if you move your cursor over any one of those sliders you will see the corresponding area light up on the histogram. Give it a try to see what I mean. The main goal of these four sliders is to work together to adjust the distribution of brightness values in your photo so that important highlight and shadow detail is preserved, without revealing underlying noise.

- Exposure, sometimes in conjunction with Recovery, sets the white point in your photo, which is the line between preserving detail in your highlights and pure white. Moving the Exposure slider to the left darkens the entire image, and moving it to the right brightens. On a properly exposed photo, you want the right edge of the histogram near to the right side without going past.

- Recovery's primary job is to recover lost highlight detail due to over exposure. Move it to the right to depress the highlights with minimal impact to the rest of the tonal range.

- Fill Light allows you to brighten up your shadows without much impact on the black or white points you set with the other sliders. It is great for adding a little brightness to subjects that were lit from behind. Move it to the right to brighten the shadow areas almost as if you added more light at the time of capture. Be careful, though; too big of an adjustment will bring out the noisier parts of the shadows.

- Blacks sets the black point in your photo, which is the line between having detail in the darkest shadows and pure black. If the left edge of the Histogram does not reach all the way to left side, try dragging the Blacks slider slightly to the right, which will increase the Blacks value and potentially add a bit more depth to an otherwise flat looking photo, which is a common cause for rejection.

The Brightness and Contrast sliders have a role here, too, and although they don't make areas of the histogram light up, they do affect the tonal distribution in your photo.

- The Brightness slider can be used to make global adjustments—shifting brighter (to the right) or darker (to the left)—to all the tones in your photo with minimal impact on the white or black point.

- When the Contrast slider is increased by moving the slider to the right, it shifts bright areas brighter and dark areas darker. When contrast is decreased by moving the slider to the left, it shifts bright tones darker and dark tones brighter.

Do take some time to make wild adjustments with each of these sliders to get a feel for how they work. Generally speaking, while keeping in mind that the preservation of detail is always your primary mission, for most photos, having a tonal range that results in an edge-to-edge histogram will suffer fewer rejections for exposure and lighting reasons. Please note, this type of result is not achieved through wild adjustments of any of those controls.

Practical Exposure Adjustments

> **Note**
>
> There are instances where blown-out highlights are acceptable, such as when the sun, or its reflection, or some other incredibly bright light source is included in the photos. These are called specular highlights and are acceptable in moderation.

With that in mind, refer to where we left off with my bear photo in (Figure 8.12). The biggest exposure problem is the blown-out highlights. I need detail in the waterfall to avoid rejection. Beyond that, there is actually a pretty good distribution of tones across the histogram. So, the first thing I need to do is see if I can salvage the detail in the highlights, and then fine-tune the overall tonal range. This is where the Recovery slider comes to the rescue. As you drag the Recovery slider to the right, Lightroom decreases the brightness in only the brightest end of the histogram and recovers any data that exists in the highlights. Not every photo will need the help of the Recovery slider, but it is a powerful tool.

I simply moved the Recovery slider to the right until the highlight clipping warning was gone, which brought back all the data in the highlights that first appeared to be lost.

In addition to the Recovery adjustment, I reduced the Brightness slider from +50 to +33, which reduced overall brightness and brought out more detail in the water (did I mention detail was important?). To compensate for the decrease in brightness of the bear, I bumped the Fill Light slider to +18. That was the full extent of the exposure adjustments for that photo. Refer to **Figure 8.13** for a before and after comparison.

Making Exposure Adjustments   **129**

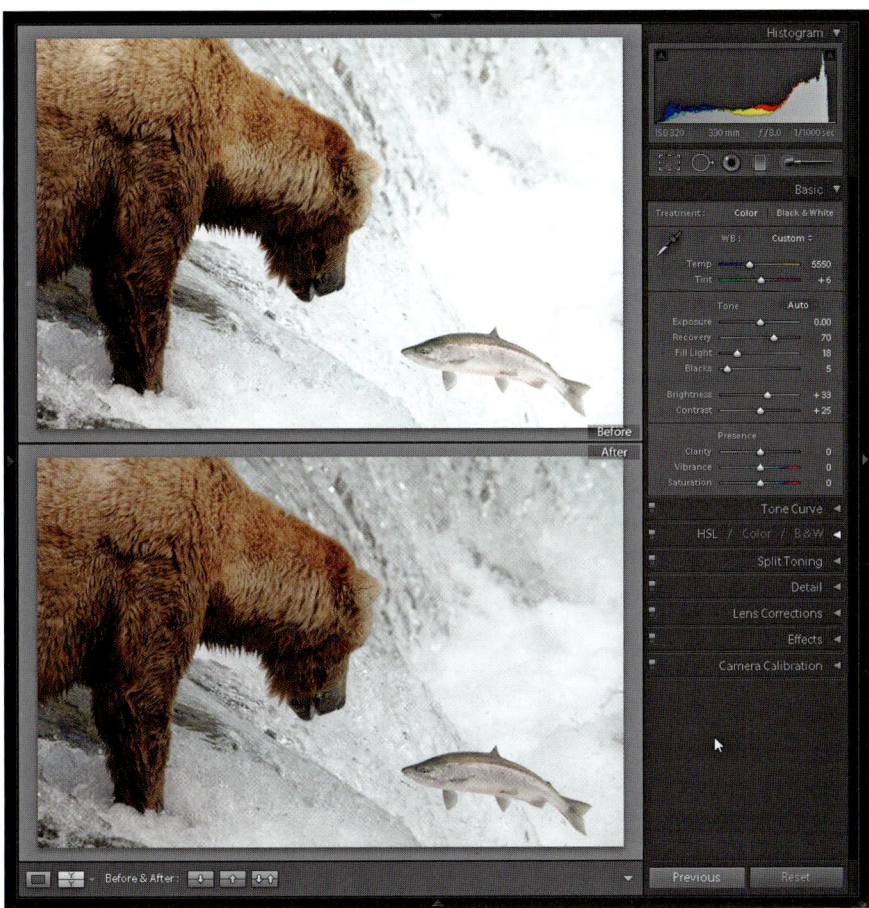

Figure 8.13 Before and after view showing recovered highlights and increased overall detail.

The Presence Controls

The last three sliders in the Basic panel (Figure 8.7) are Clarity, Vibrance, and Saturation. When used in moderation, the Clarity and Vibrance controls can really make certain photos pop.

- Clarity performs what is called a midtone contrast adjustment. Adobe originally wanted to name that slider Punch, because that is a good description of the effect it can have on your photo. There is a develop preset named General – Punch that sets Clarity to +50 and Vibrance to +25. It serves as a good starting point for many images.

- Vibrance is designed to have less of an impact on the most saturated colors in an image and instead focuses its attention on the less saturated colors. When used in moderation, it can really bring photos to life.
- Saturation affects all colors the same way, so when it is increased it runs the risk of over-saturating some colors to the point of losing detail. When decreased it can be used to remove all color from a photo.

For stock purposes, you want to use these controls with an extremely light touch if at all. In my brown bear photo, I did find that I could add a good amount of clarity, which added a lot more character to the raging water and also helped the subjects leap off the background. When making any adjustments, be sure to examine your photo carefully at 1:1 or 100% view to best evaluate the changes being made.

Sharpening for Stock

It is common to refer to a photo that is nicely in focus as a *sharp* photo. However, it is important to keep in mind that software sharpening cannot fix a photo that is not in focus, which is a common error made by new contributors. Software sharpening can only be used to improve the appearance of a photo that is already in focus.

Sharpening is really all about enhancing edges. When you take an in-focus photo and enhance edges of the image details, you can really bring that subject to life. Our eyes are drawn to detail. Software sharpening is a tool at your disposal to help lead the viewer's eye to the most important parts of the photo.

To oversimplify the process, sharpening works by increasing contrast along edges. The result of increasing contrast—pushing some pixels toward white on one side and some pixels toward black on the other side—along the edges creates what are called sharpening halos. The control of these halos is what the sharpening settings are all about.

The late Bruce Fraser advanced an approach to sharpening that separated out three distinct types—capture, creative, and output—that vary in technique and purpose. At this stage of developing a photo we are only concerned about the first type of sharpening, called capture sharpening, which is intended simply to compensate for the inherent softness in a raw photo. This is the type of sharpening that is performed using the sliders in the Sharpening section of the Detail panel (**Figure 8.14**):

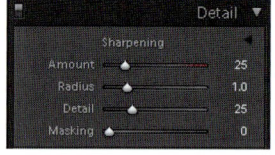

Figure 8.14 The Sharpening controls in the Detail panel.

- The Amount slider controls how much sharpening is applied to the photo.
- The Radius slider effectively controls the width of the sharpening halos. This is a key setting to get right and is based on the type of detail in the

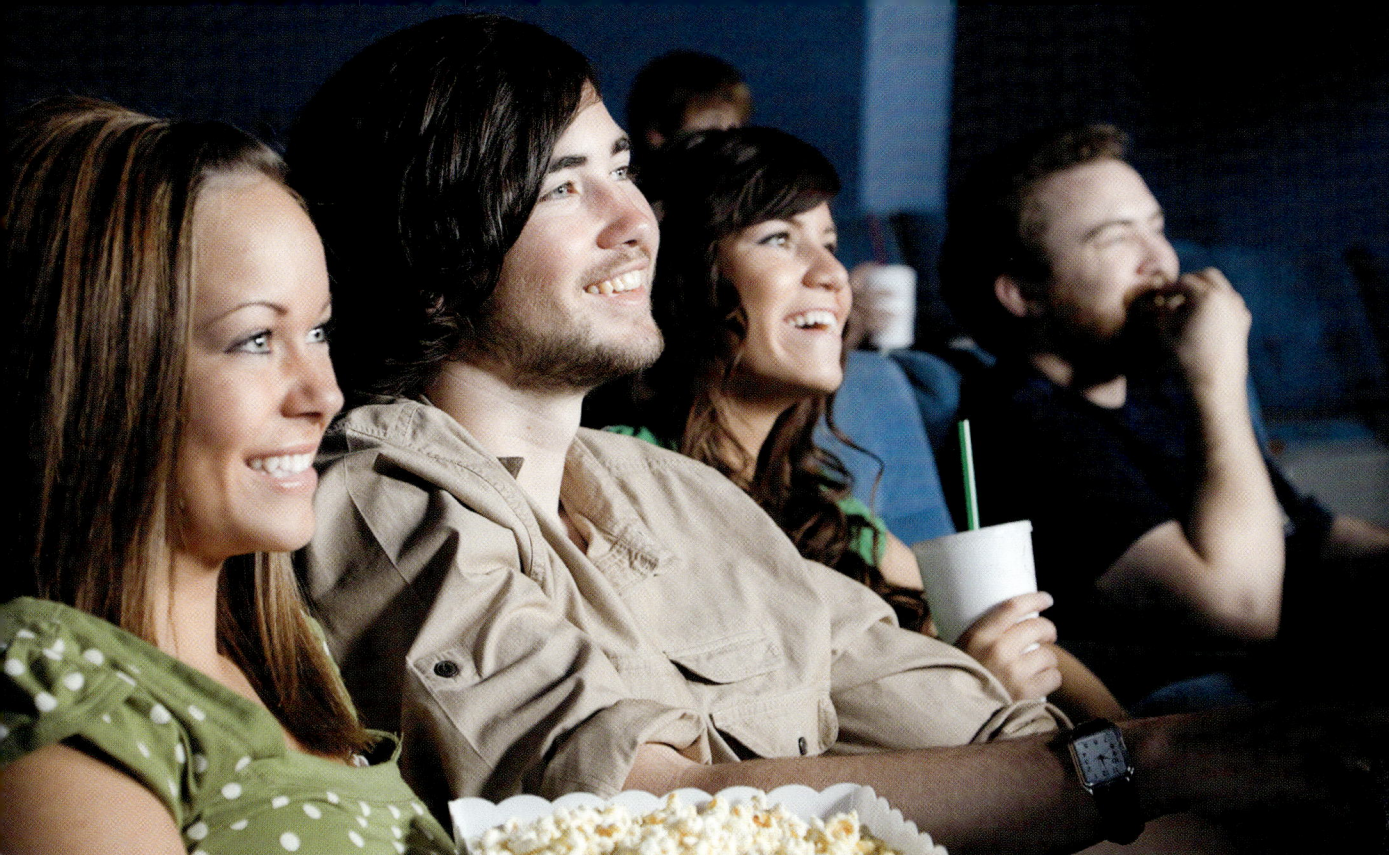

Figure 8.15 Young People in a Movie Theater. Downloaded over 1,100 times.

Young People in a Movie Theater

Creator	Rich Legg (istockphoto.com/leggnet)
Started	2005
Home	USA
Total portfolio	Over 6,000 images
Total downloads	Over 100,000
About this photo	Rich says, "Everyone likes going to a good movie and these people seem to be really enjoying the show. Additionally, I think the bright blue background, narrow depth of field, and use of props contribute to the success of this image. It was photographed with a Canon 5D using a Canon 24-105 f/4L lens. Lighting was provided by two 600ws monolights equipped with softboxes. The lights were placed at the front of the theater."
Rich's tip	"Don't try to shoot what you see others have had success with. Instead, find themes you love and shoot them."

> **Tip**
>
> There are two sharpening presets in the Presets panel—Narrow Edges (Scenic) for edgy texture, and Wide Edges (Faces) for wider smooth areas—designed to be good starting points for different types of photos.

photo. A photo with wide smooth areas and soft details like a face would typically do well with a Radius of 1.0 to 1.4. A photo with lots of small detail and edgy texture, like a tree and blades of grass, would typically do well with a Radius of 0.8 to 1.0.

- The Detail slider provides a means to suppress the visibility of the sharpening halos resulting from the Amount and Radius settings.

- The Masking slider controls what pixels in the image will be sharpened by masking out areas of the photo where you don't want any sharpening to be applied. This is an essential control for fine-tuning the amount of sharpening applied. This will become clearer in the coming example.

Making the Sharpening Adjustments

In the example photo (**Figure 8.16**), the subject, an Echinacea flower, is shown in sharp focus against a very out-of-focus background. This separation of detail makes it quite obvious what the photo is about, and it greatly simplifies the message. A hallmark of a good stock photo is that it communicates a clear message as simply as possible.

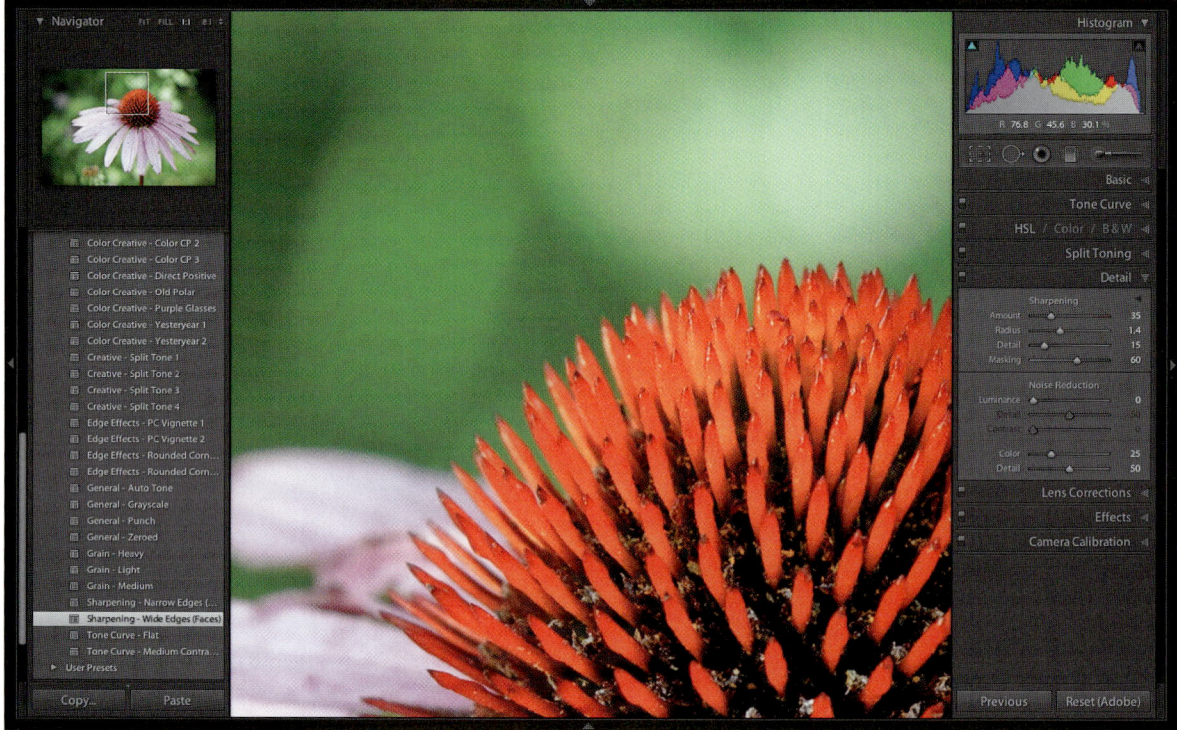

Figure 8.16 You always want to evaluate sharpening adjustments at 1:1 view.

The end result of a sharpening adjustment is more important than the order in which you move the sliders, and don't be afraid to come back and tweak some more after using the luminance noise reduction tools (covered in the next section on noise). That said, you need to start somewhere, so here are the steps I used to work on that Echinacea flower:

1. Click once on the photo to zoom in and then pan to an area of good detail. Zoom in to 1:1 view to best evaluate the adjustments you are making. It is a challenge to translate the important detail and texture from the image on my screen to the printed page you are viewing, so you can follow along after downloading this photo from www.takingstockphoto.com/downloads/.

2. In this example, I clicked on the Sharpening - Wide Edges (Faces) preset (in the Preset panel) since, like a face, this photo has lots of wide smooth areas. It will serve as a better starting point than the default settings.

3. Amount is subjective. Click on the Amount slider and drag first to the left, to decrease, and then slowly drag to the right while looking at the edges of the detail in your image. You can hold the Alt (Mac: Option) key to switch to a grayscale view to help evaluate detail without color distraction. Lightroom only applies sharpening to the luminance data, which is what you are seeing in that grayscale preview (**Figure 8.17**).

   Pan around the image as you make your adjustments to evaluate different areas. Don't be concerned if you see noise or other unwanted detail becoming more visible: This is normal, and we will address that later with the Masking control and really clean it up with the noise reduction controls in the next section. I chose an Amount setting of 45, because to my eye, it provided the best balance between increasing the visibility of important edge detail, without making it look too harsh or fake.

4. Now hold down the Alt (Mac: Option) key and click on the Radius slider to get a more accurate preview of what part of the image is affected by those settings. The Radius value contained in the Sharpening - Wide Edges (Faces) preset is a good starting point for this type of photo. If chosen correctly, you may not need to adjust this any further. For this image, I felt a setting of 1.2 worked best with the type of detail in this photo. Visually, the differences can be hard to see at first. Use the two presets mentioned in the tip to help get you in the right ballpark.

5. Adjust the Detail slider to suppress the visibility of the sharpening halos as needed. Again, hold the Alt (Mac: Option) key and click on the Detail slider to see a grayscale preview. I found a setting of 25 provided the best enhancement of the detail with room for further refinement from the Masking slider.

> **Tip**
>
> If you want to learn more than you thought possible about sharpening, check out *Real World Sharpening with Adobe Photoshop, Camera Raw, and Lightroom* (2nd Edition), by Bruce Fraser and Jeff Schewe. (Peachpit Press, 2009).

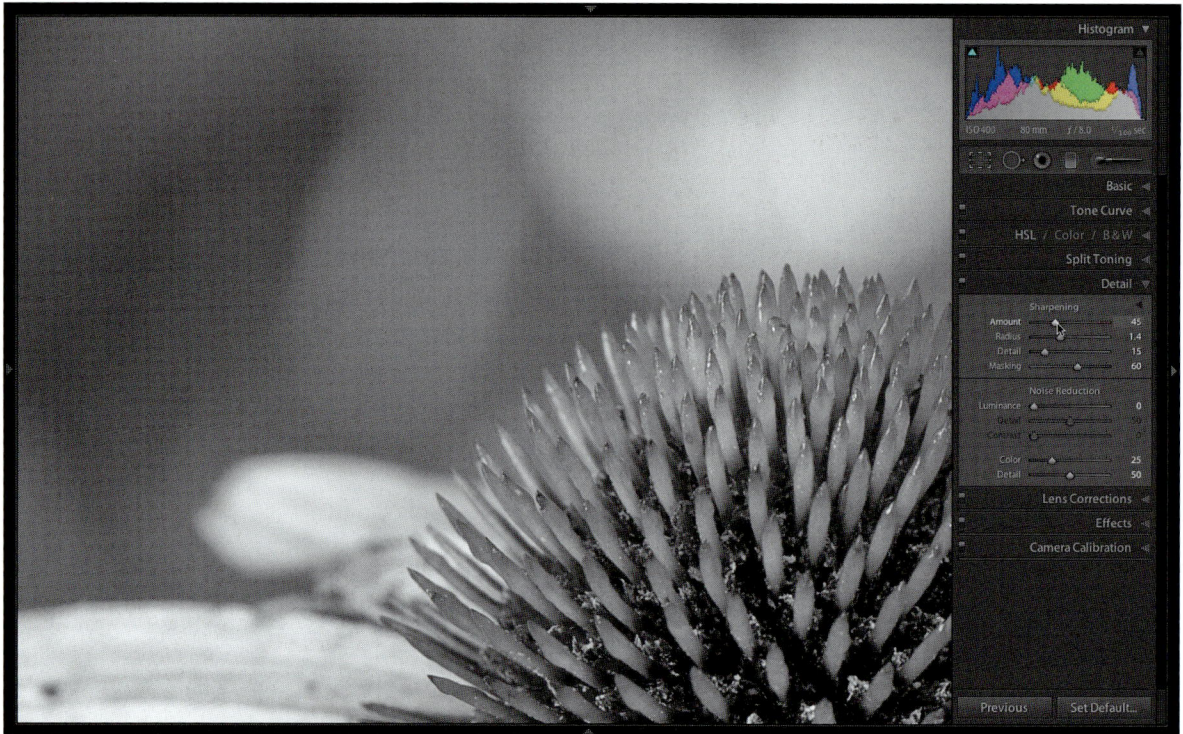

Figure 8.17 Sharpening applied to luminance data.

6. The Masking slider is how you can really focus your sharpening settings to just the edges that matter. Lightroom automatically detects the edges in the image and uses that information to create what is called a *mask*, which shields parts of the image from having any sharpening applied to it. When the Masking slider is set to 0 then no mask is present, and all areas of the image are sharpened equally. As the Masking slider is increased, more and more of the image is protected (masked) from having the sharpening applied.

This is a flower, with lots of soft wide areas of color. I don't want a crispy, edgy image. I want detail to be perceptible, but not overdone. It is always best to have less sharpening than more, so I often use a pretty high Masking setting. Hold the Alt (Mac: Option) key to get a glimpse of just the mask (**Figure 8.18**) as you move the Masking slider. The white areas of the mask are where the sharpening is being applied, and the black areas have none. I settled on leaving the Masking slider at 61, which protects the smoothest areas of the image, and focuses the combined sharpening settings just to the most important edges.

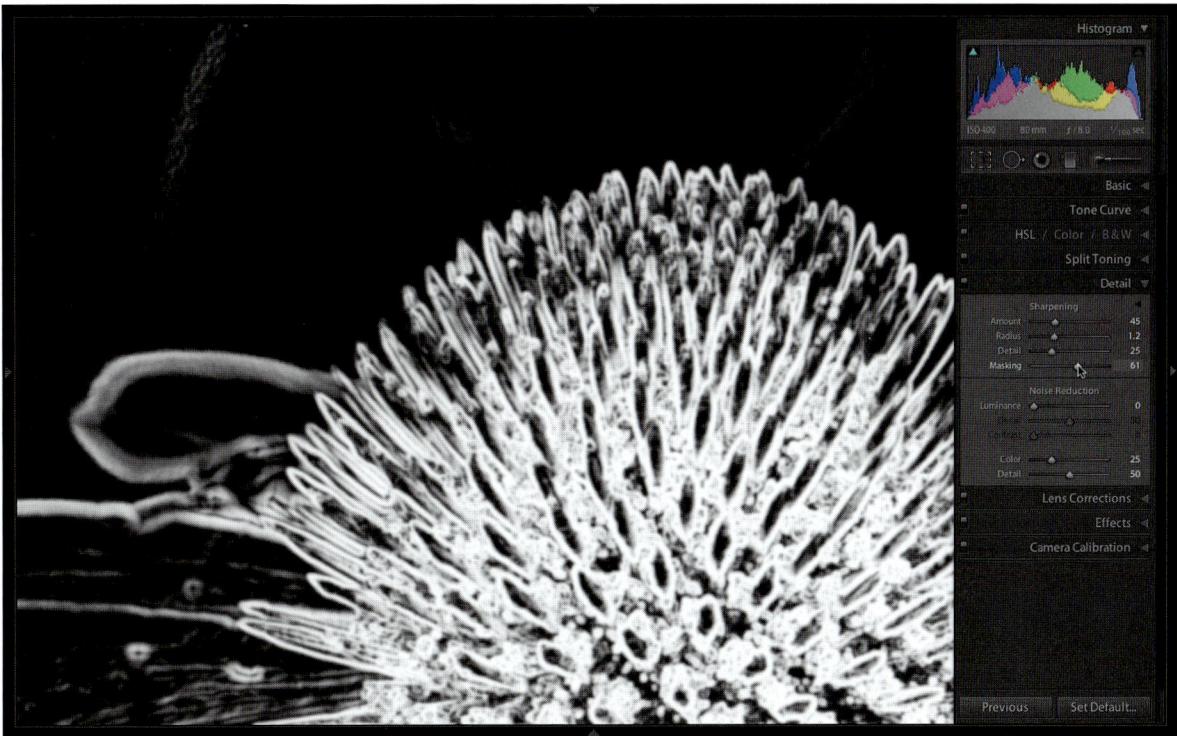

Figure 8.18 This shows the edge mask that determines where the sharpening is being applied.

Feel free to make exaggerated adjustments with each slider as you get a feel for how they work together. If your edges look too jagged or too pronounced, you may be heading into rejection territory for over-sharpening, so dial back the Amount slider and increase the Masking slider to be safe. You can reset all the sliders back to default settings by holding the Alt (Mac: Option) key and clicking Reset Sharpening.

Dealing with Noise

We've looked at the nature of noise as well as ways to reduce noise at the time of capture in Chapter 6, but there will still be images that require a little bit of noise reduction during post-processing. There are a host of software solutions for noise reduction, and if you've already got your favorite I won't try to change your mind. However, I will encourage you to test drive the improved noise reduction tools in Lightroom 3, which underwent a major overhaul in this release.

The goal of noise reduction software solutions is to minimize the appearance of digital noise without sacrificing critical image detail. You need to know that stock photos are just as often rejected for the overuse of noise reduction software (**Figure 8.19**) as they are for just having too much noise. Your job is to use just enough (and possibly a little less) noise reduction to minimize the appearance of noise in the worst areas, while maintaining sharp details. Too much noise reduction turns pixels into mushy blobs of color that are no more pleasing to the eye than the original noise.

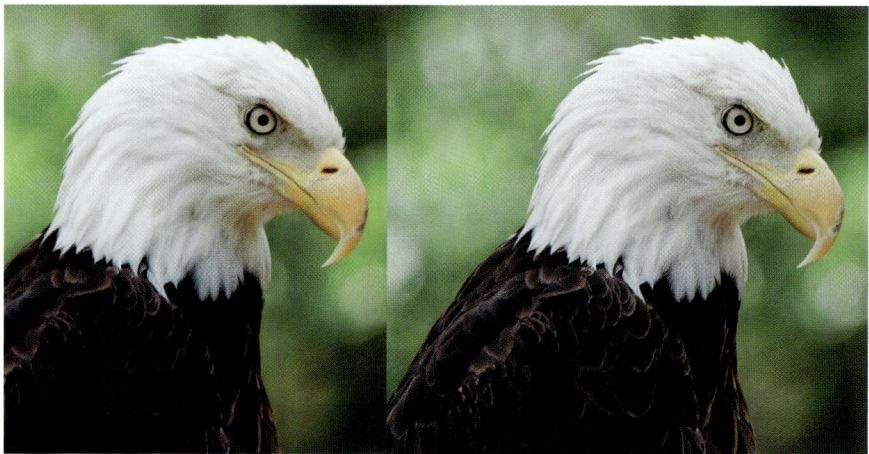

Figure 8.19 Left side photo shows how too much noise reduction has smoothed out important detail. Right side contains critical detail in eyes and feathers. Download and view at 1:1 for best comparison. www.takingstockphoto.com/downloads/

Remember, too, any acceptance or rejection is the result of a cumulative number of factors, so a photo with a strong composition and useful concept can get away with having a little more noise than a photo with less going for it. In other words, don't waste time reducing noise on a photo that might be rejected for some other reason.

There are two types of noise— Luminance noise (**Figure 8.20**), which has more of a characteristic of film grain, and color noise (**Figure 8.21**), which presents as random pixels of color almost like Christmas tree lights—and correspondingly two sets of controls for dealing with each type (**Figure 8.22**). I over-emphasized the noise in Figure 8.20 and Figure 8.21 to help it show better in the book, but noise is best evaluated digitally at 1:1 view, so download the examples to get a closer look.

Dealing with Noise **137**

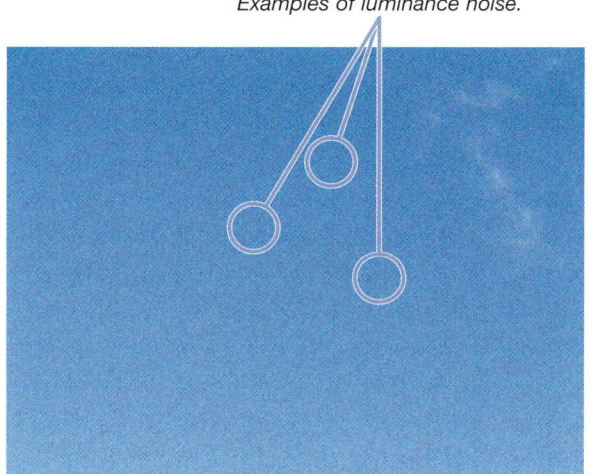

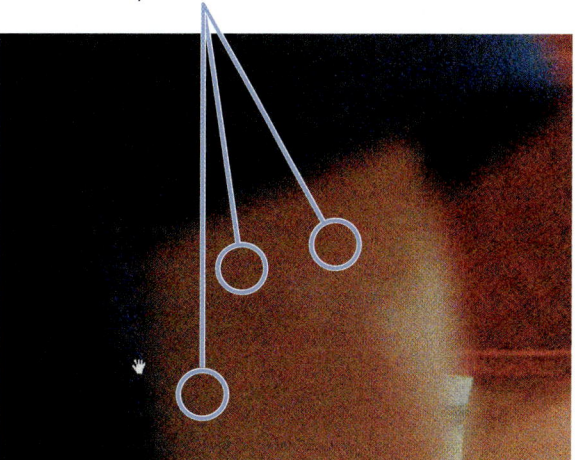

Figure 8.20 Luminance noise has a grainy appearance. it's a common problem in blue skies for some cameras.

Figure 8.21 Color noise has a random, color-speckled appearance. it's often caused by high ISO settings and long exposure times.

Luminance noise reduction is set to zero by default, as it is less often a problem than color noise. Color noise reduction is set to 25 by default, which is intended to be a good compromise between color noise reduction and detail preservation.

Making the Adjustments

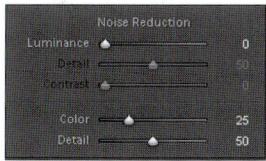

Figure 8.22 Lightroom's noise reduction sliders in the Detail panel.

The Echinacea flower photo we've been working on was shot at ISO 400 on purpose so we'd have more noise to reduce. To really see what is happening here you need to download the photo from www.takingstockphoto.com/downloads/. To help illustrate the effects of the adjustments, start by turning the Color slider to zero. While not the noisiest image I've ever seen, if you zoom to 400% and look in the darker regions, you will see both the rainbow-speckled sign of color noise and the grainy appearance of luminance noise quite easily. Let's walk through the steps to reduce that noise as best we can while still preserving important detail.

1. As with sharpening, you want to zoom to 1:1 view to see the effects of the settings you apply.
2. Pan to an area of the image that shows both noise and important detail.

3. Start with the Luminance slider and slowly drag until the grainy areas start to smooth out. As you see the grainy areas smooth out, drag the Luminance slider back to the left to bring back a little grain. A general rule of thumb: apply less than you think and make your primary focus the preservation of detail. A setting of 25 is probably the highest you will want to use to avoid rejection. I chose a setting of 16, which appeared to reduce the noise enough and preserved more detail.

4. Leave the Detail and Contrast sliders in their respective default settings. These have little effect on low noise images such as this, and high ISO images are unlikely to be good candidates for microstock outputs.

5. (Optional) You may want to re-tweak your sharpening settings after reducing the luminance noise.

6. Click on the Color slider and slowly drag until the color noise is removed. Similar to the Luminance slider, the default setting of 25 is likely the highest you want to use for the sake of detail preservation. I felt a setting of 16 here too was sufficient for reducing the noise enough and saving the detail in the flower. Leave the Detail slider at the default.

The goal should always be to remove enough of the noise to prevent it from being a visual distraction while maintaining crispness in the important detail areas to enable it to pass inspection at 100% or 1:1 view.

> **Tip**
>
> You can visit my Lightroom-centric blog at www.lightroomers.com, which is chock-full of free tutorials and tips intended to help you master a Lightroom workflow.

Assignment

If you're not shooting in raw mode already, this is a great opportunity to start.

1. A free 30-day free trial of Lightroom 3 is available from Adobe. I highly recommend you download a copy and give it a test drive to see what is possible.

    adobe.com/products/photoshoplightroom/

2. Set your camera to shoot both raw and JPEG (or just raw if you prefer). Choose a shooting assignment from Chapter 3 and create some photos. Import those photos into Lightroom and do the following:

    A. Configure your custom default settings.

    B. Create a preset with those same settings and apply the preset to other photos from that shoot.

    C. Choose your top 3 to 5 keeper photos from that shoot and apply white balance, exposure, sharpening, and if needed, noise reduction adjustments.

3   Head over to www.takingstockphoto.com/downloads/ and download the sample photos for this chapter. All your image evaluations need to be done on screen, so the more practice you have the better! ■

9
Avoiding Rejection

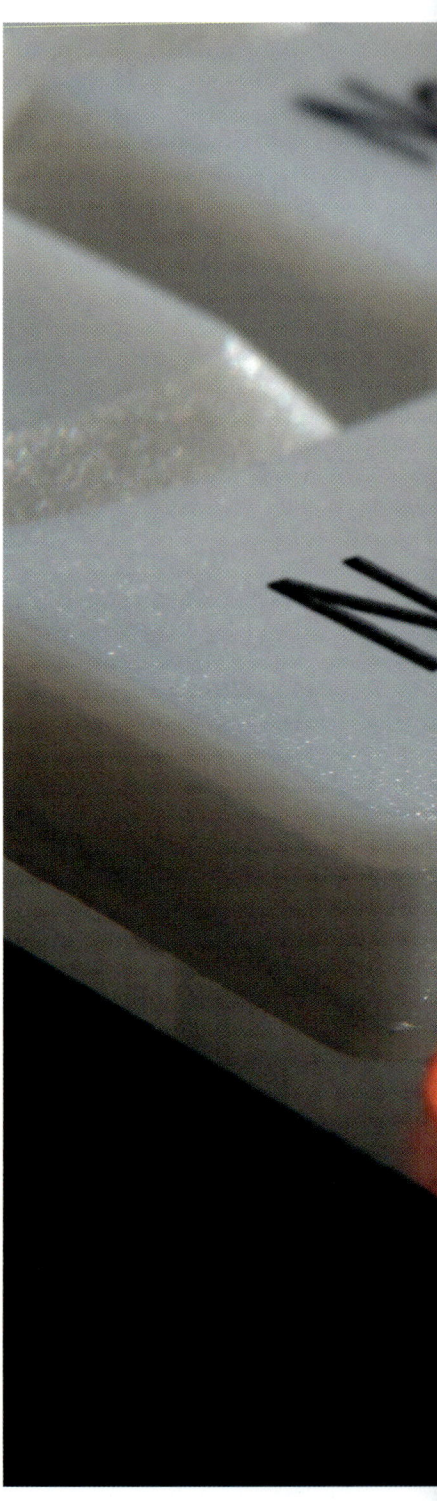

Anyone submitting work to a stock site has felt the sting of rejection. No one likes it. It can be both a source of frustration and a learning opportunity, so don't let it get you down. I wrote this chapter to help you learn how to avoid it (or at least reduce its frequency) in the first place. Up until this point in the workflow, we have focused on setting up to create the best capture in camera, then to do the least harm to get the best results doing your basic raw processing. In this chapter, I want to focus on specific tips to deal with real-world situations that simply require digital intervention, follow up with some advice about not going too far in your editing efforts, and leave you with a couple of low-key enhancement techniques.

I know I've said this in multiple places throughout the book, but only because it bears repeating. A photo's usefulness as stock, quality of lighting, and strength of composition can trump minor technical flaws. Too often rejection notices are doled out to people who invested too much time in trying to repair minor technical flaws in an otherwise bad original. Be tough when selecting your keepers, so that the time you invest fixing problems is time well spent.

Digital House Cleaning

Neatness counts. There are all manner of nuisance problems—dust, hair, sensor spots, *hot pixels* (pixel points of brightness that appear on some sensors), and noise—that can detract from an otherwise good capture. Then there are legally problematic content—logos, copyrighted works, and people without release forms—that simply need to be removed before submission

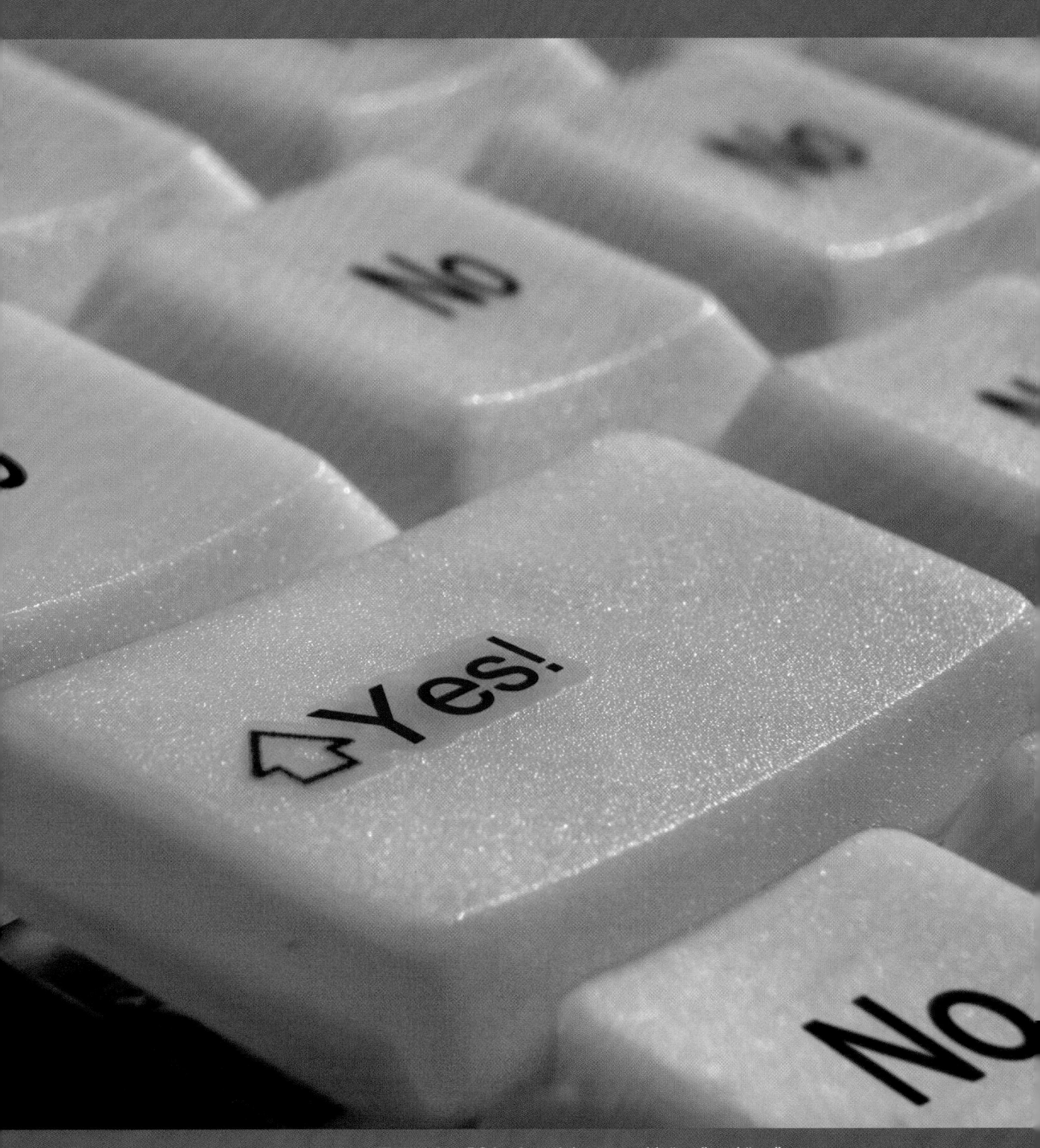

Figure 9.1 PC keyboard: buttons with "yes" and "no."
© Alexander Novikov (istockphoto.com/AlexanderNovikov)

to avoid rejection. It's best to keep such content out prior to capture, but that is not always practical or possible. In those cases, you need to decide if it is worth your investment of time to do a software fix.

The tools I turn to for solving these problems are Lightroom 3 and Photoshop CS5. However, problems can be solved with other software choices as well. For someone just starting out, Lightroom 3 and Photoshop Elements 8 make a very powerful combination for about half the price (or less) of the full Photoshop CS5. In fact, I feel so strongly about it that I'll use either Lightroom 3 or Elements 8 for solving all the problems presented in this chapter. Can you use any recent version of Lightroom, Photoshop, or Photoshop Elements? Yes. Can you other image editors? Sure. Use what you have and what you are comfortable with, but know there will be differences in tools and approaches from what I demonstrate here.

The Dreaded Purple Fringe

> **Note**
>
> You can download the photo in Figure 9.2 and follow along by going to www.takingstockphoto.com/downloads/.

Chromatic aberration is a common problem and almost always an instant rejection. That fringe jumps out like Vegas neon to inspectors, so learn to look for the telltale saturated purplish, bluish, or reddish fringe along the edges of high contrast in your photos when performing your initial inspection at 1:1 view. Can you see the bluish edge along the green leaves as well as the branches in **Figure 9.2**? The problem occurs when the lens fails to focus all the wavelengths of light onto the same focal plane, or if it magnifies certain wavelengths differently from the others. It is more common in cheaper lenses due to quality of glass, or when using a wide aperture with a high-contrast background. Lightroom 3 has tools to help reduce the visibility of chromatic aberration in the Lens Correction panel (**Figure 9.3**). This panel is new to Lightroom 3 (and Camera Raw 6.1) and provides a set of tools for dealing with geometric distortion, lens vignette, and chromatic aberration. One approach, using the Profile tab, is to create (or use an existing) lens correction profile for your specific camera and lens combination. I don't have a profile for the lens I used to capture the photo in Figure 9.2, but check out the Note in the margin to learn more about creating your own profiles. The other approach uses the options in the Manual side of the panel.

Digital House Cleaning 143

Examples of purple fringe.

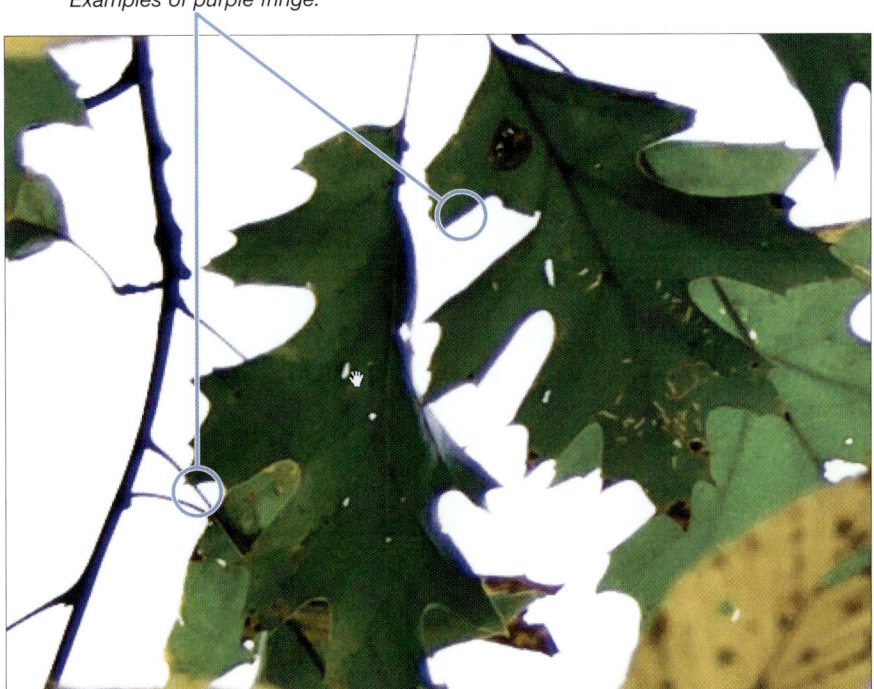

Figure 9.2 Notice the bright color fringe along leaf edges and branches as seen at 3:1 view.

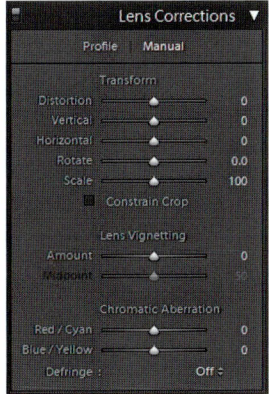

Figure 9.3 The Manual tab inside the Lens Corrections panel.

> **Note**
>
> Head over to http://labs.adobe.com/technologies/lensprofile_creator/ to download, and learn about, the free Adobe Lens Profile Creator.

The quality of the results from these controls will vary with the severity of the fringe in question. This is a visual process, and I find zooming in to 3:1 helps you to see the effects of the sliders while you are working. But keep in mind you only need it to look good for the stock site's image inspectors at 1:1 view. Your job is to tweak the Red/Cyan and Blue/Yellow sliders as needed to reduce the visibility of the fringe as much as you can. Hold the Alt (Mac: Option) key while dragging the Chromatic Aberration sliders to see a preview of just the colors affected by that slider, which really helps you to see what you are doing. Setting the Defringe drop-down menu to All Edges can sometimes offer further subtle improvement. Don't worry about getting it perfect here (unless you can with some images); just minimize its visibility as much as possible (**Figure 9.4**), and don't make it worse. Here's where having an external image editor like Elements is needed to finish the job.

> **Note**
>
> Before you send a copy with your Lightroom adjustments to any external editor, you want to make sure all your basic adjustments (such as white balance, exposure, capture sharpening, and noise reduction) are done so that they too are applied to the new copy.

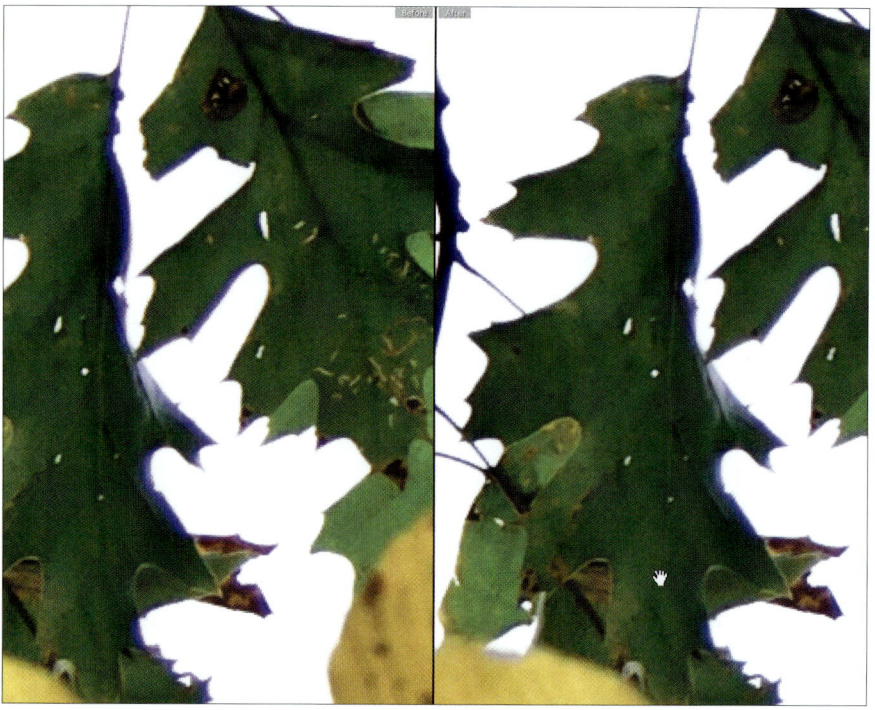

Figure 9.4 This split Before and After view (View > Before/After) shows the unadjusted image on the left and the corrected version on the right. It's improved, but not as good as we need to prevent rejection.

There are a number of ways to correct for chromatic aberration in Elements, but here is one of my favorites that is both effective and simple:

1. In Lightroom, press Ctrl–E (Mac: Command–E) to send a copy with Lightroom adjustments to your primary external editor.

   If you are working with Elements I suggest configuring Lightroom to send copies in 8-bit Adobe RGB, but if you are using the full version of Photoshop I suggest 16-bit ProPhoto RGB. The difference is that Photoshop Elements is very limited in its ability to edit 16-bit images.

2. Once the copy opens in Elements, select the background layer in the Layers panel and press Ctrl–J (Mac: Command–J) to duplicate that layer.

3. Select the top layer and choose Filter > Blur > Gaussian Blur. When the Gaussian blur dialog box opens, set the Radius to 15 pixels and click OK.

4. Back in the Layers panel, with the top layer selected, change the layer mode from Normal to Color.

Double-click the Magnifying Glass icon in the Toolbar to zoom to 100 percent. All signs of the fringing should be gone. However, the colors overall probably look a little duller. Let's fix that with a trick for using layer masks in Elements:

1. Select the bottom layer and click the Create new adjustment layer icon at the bottom of the Layers panel (half-moon icon) and choose Brightness/Contrast. This will place the adjustment layer between the duplicated layers.

    Elements supports layer masks, which help us combine multiple layers together, but doesn't provide a simple way to add a layer mask as in the full version of Photoshop. We're only going to use the Brightness/Contrast adjustment layer to take advantage of the built-in layer mask so that we can combine the original color of the bottom layer with the fringe corrections in the top layer.

2. Select the top (blurred) layer and choose Layer > Create Clipping Mask, which means that everything in that top layer has to pass through the layer beneath it to become visible, and visibility is now controlled by the layer mask on the Brightness/Contrast adjustment layer.

3. Click on the white layer mask itself to make it active (**Figure 9.5**), and choose Edit > Fill Layer. When the Fill Layer dialog box appears, set Use to Background color (which should be black by default when the layer mask is active) and click OK.

    The white area on a layer mask reveals the contents of that layer (or clipping group in this case), while the black area hides the layer. We hid the entire corrected layer, so that we can now bring in only the corrected edges while preserving all the good color in the original.

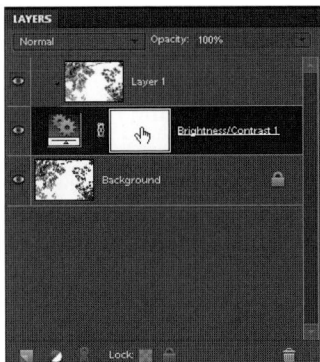

Figure 9.5 Layers panel showing the clipping group formed by the top two layers with the layer mask active.

4. With the layer mask still active, select the Brush tool from the Toolbar (press B), and using a soft-edged brush set to white, paint over any areas of remaining purple fringe to reveal the corrected version of the layer.

Even in an image with a lot of edges like **Figure 9.6**, it won't take more than a few minutes to quickly remove any remaining fringe. Download the example photo and give it a try.

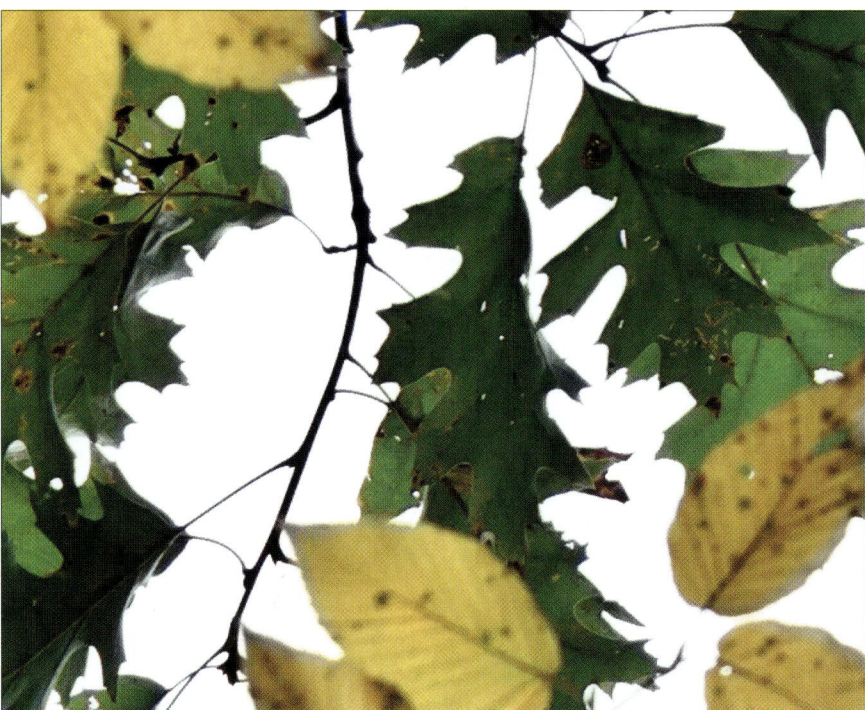

Figure 9.6 Final version with all fringe removed.

Cropping for Composition

Getting the composition right in camera is always preferred, but there are times when it is not possible or it just doesn't happen. In those cases, cropping software comes to the rescue. I prefer to do my cropping in Lightroom because it is non-destructive to the original (meaning I can always go back and readjust or remove my crop). Cropping is sometimes one of the first things I do before any of my other processing steps. The reason? There is no reason to adjust exposure levels on an element in a photo that is going to be cropped from the final version. If there is a distracting element near the edge of the frame that you know is ruining the shot, just get rid of it right away.

> **Note**
>
> Lightroom's histogram updates after you apply a crop. So it can make a lot of sense to crop first and make exposure adjustments later.

Digital House Cleaning   **147**

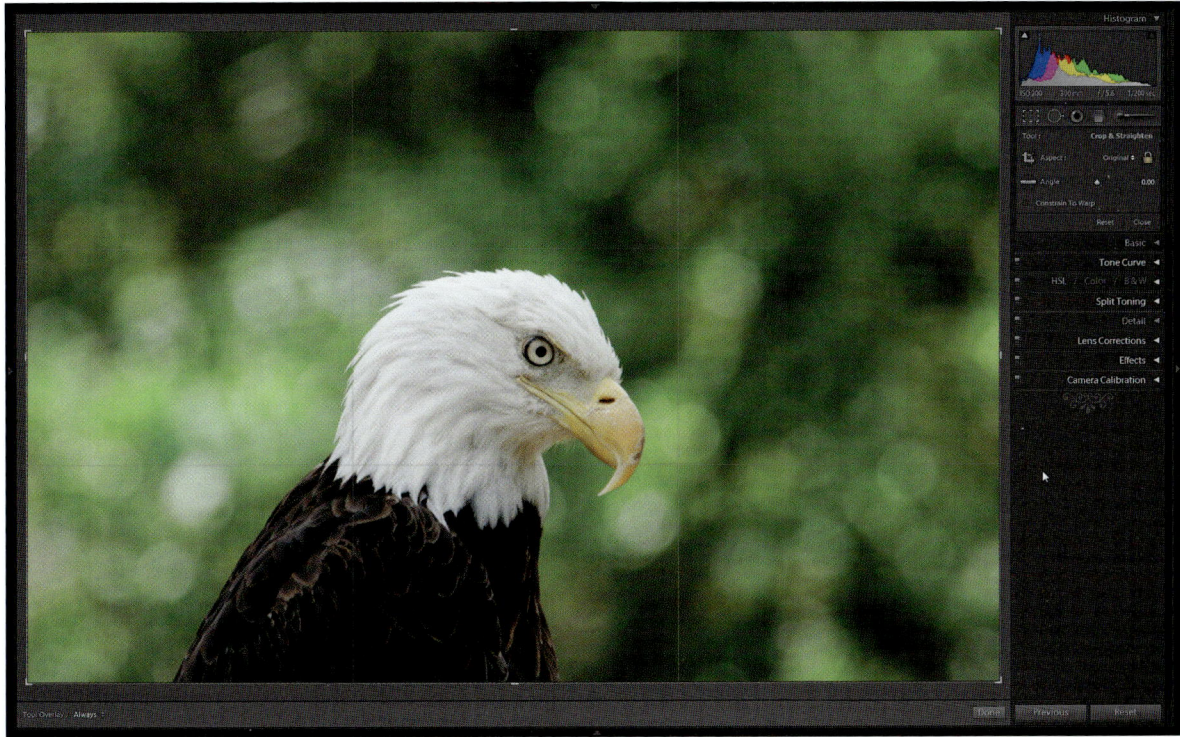

Figure 9.7 Weak composition caused by subject centered in frame.

That being said, in Chapter 3 I discussed the importance of leaving space in your photos as a selling point for designers who might want to put copy there, and that still holds true. The uncropped photo in **Figure 9.7** has a very loose composition, but it is possible to improve the composition by cropping away excess pixels and still leave breathing room copy space.

To crop in Lightroom:

1 Select the photo and press R to jump to the Crop tool.

   This will bring you to the Develop module (if you are not there already); expand the Crop panel on the right, and place your photo inside the crop rectangle. By default, Lightroom displays an overlay that neatly divides your photo into thirds. Based on the rule of thirds, this overlay can be very useful in finding the strongest composition. Generally speaking, a focal point in your photo that aligns with the intersection of two gridlines results in a stronger composition. There are six different overlays to choose from, and you can cycle through each one by pressing the O key (or choose Tools > Crop Guide Overlay).

> **Note**
>
> You can download the photo in Figure 9.8 and follow the exercise below by going to www.takingstockphoto.com/downloads/.

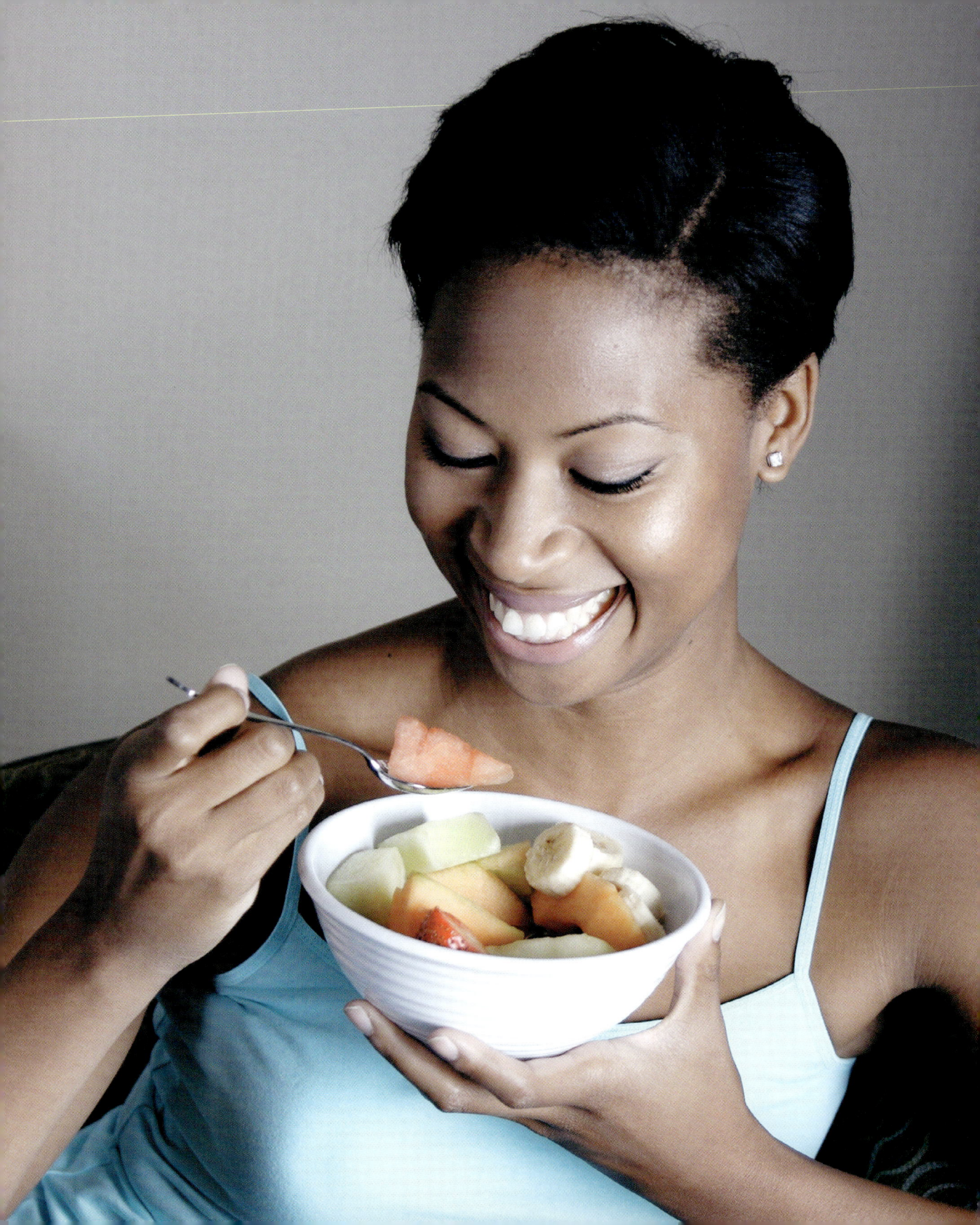

Healthy Eating

Creator	Li Kim Goh (istockphoto.com/gollykim)
Started	2005
Home	USA
Total portfolio	1,203
Total downloads	Over 38,000
About this photo	Kim says, "I was just starting photography at the time, so I was using a Canon XTi with a 50mm 1.8 lens and a reflector. I think it is the natural lighting and the healthy lifestyle subject matter that makes this image successful. The young and beautiful African American model is a plus."
Kim's tip	"Don't go crazy buying an expensive camera and lens right away. A camera doesn't take good pictures, people do, and you can still get really nice pictures with an inexpensive camera, just like me."

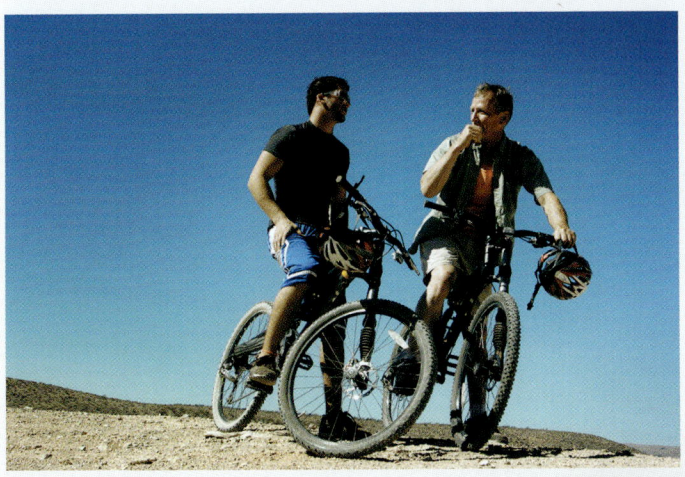

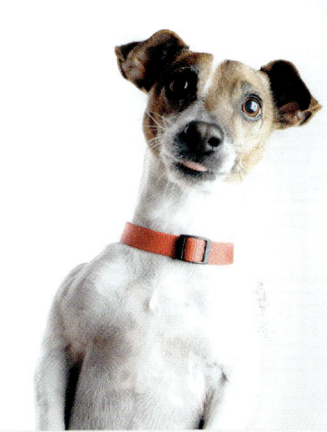

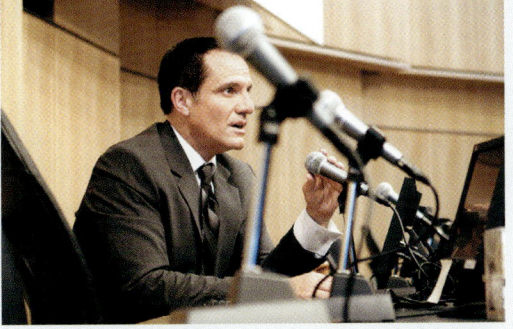

Figure 9.8 Healthy Eating. Downloaded over 600 times.

Figure 9.9 Father and Son.

Figure 9.10 Ding Dong.

Figure 9.11 Councilman.

> **Tip**
>
> Press the L key to switch to Lights Dim mode, which dims everything outside the crop rectangle. Press L again to go to Lights Out and leave only the area inside the crop rectangle visible. Press L once more to turn on the lights.

2. Choose a desired aspect ratio from the Crop Tool panel.

   The aspect ratio of an image is just a way to describe the relationship between the longest edge and the shortest edge. For example, a square image has a 1:1 aspect ratio because both sides are the same length. As one side increases more than the other, the shape becomes a rectangle. The aspect ratio for most photos produced by a digital camera is 1.5:1, or more commonly referred to as 3:2.

3. Resize the crop rectangle by clicking and dragging any corner or side. Keep the lock icon closed to maintain the aspect ratio as you resize the crop.

4. Position the photo by clicking and dragging the photo into place behind the crop rectangle, which remains fixed in the center of the screen (**Figure 9.12**).

5. Press H to hide the overlay and evaluate the composition, and press H again to bring it back. Once you've decided on a final composition, press R to exit the Crop tool.

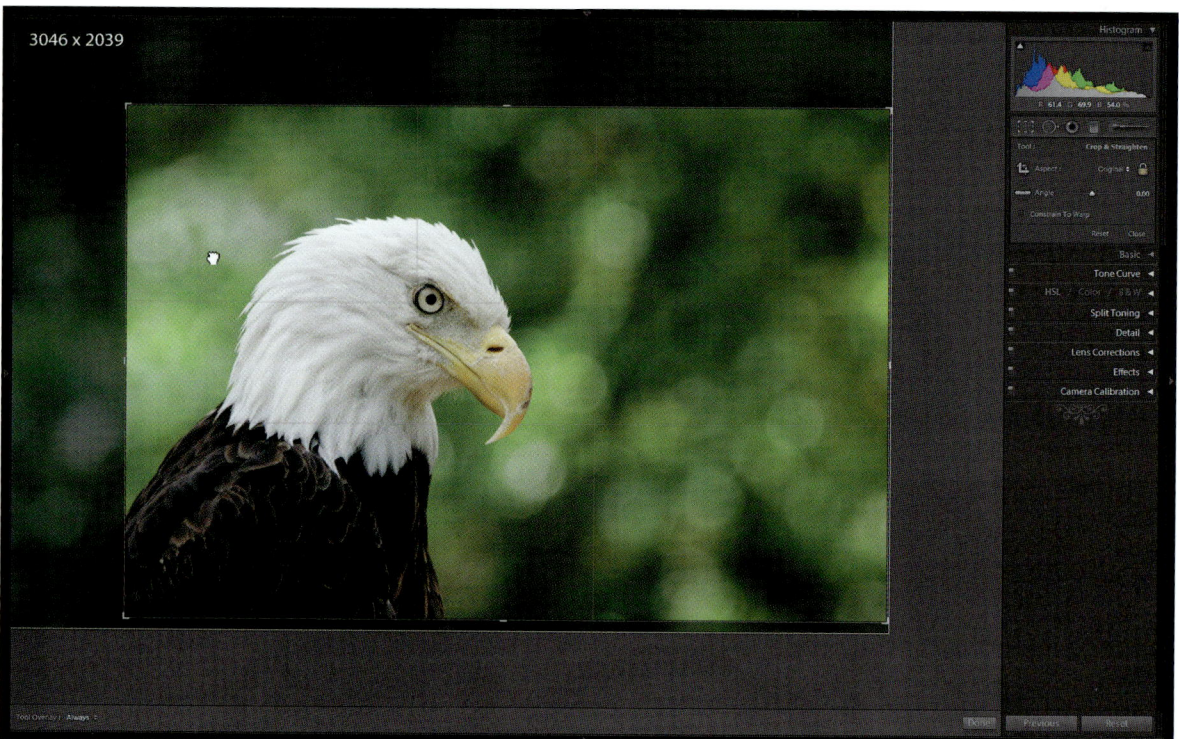

Figure 9.12 A much stronger composition results after cropping.

You might be concerned about the final size of your photo, which is understandable. If you crop off too much, you may have a great composition but a tiny photo. In my experience, a good composition trumps size, but even I have my limits. I try to keep all my final sizes above 6 megapixels, which is more than enough for a wide range of uses. The vast majority of images downloaded from microstock sites are destined for an online project, so while larger file sizes tend to bring in more money per download (because the costs of licenses tend to be based on pixel dimensions), better-looking files tend to bring in more downloads. This is a subjective call, and you are in the driver's seat.

One last point to consider: It is not unusual to have a designer pop into the iStockphoto forum and complain that photographers are cropping their photos too tightly. Designers often want more flexibility in choosing how, if at all, a photo gets cropped based on the needs of their project. While I completely understand their desire to have that flexibility, it is unfortunately not in your best interests to upload a photo that is too loosely composed. For one, it runs a greater risk of being rejected (rejection can depend on other factors, which we'll cover in the next chapter, but a weak composition is not going to help put you into accepted territory). The second reason is that potential customers are making their first decision to choose an image based on a rather small thumbnail. A small subject in a weak composition is just not going to make as many people click.

Ultimately, it is your photo and your decision, but it is my experience that a strong composition is not only going to help you get past the inspectors, but bring in more downloads. That said, you need to keep usefulness as stock in mind as you are cropping. Envision your photo in a project all the way through your workflow.

> **Tip**
>
> Press I to show the Info Overlay. Choose View > View Options and configure it to show Cropped Dimensions. This way, you'll see a live update of the final cropped pixel dimensions in the upper-left corner of the image (visible in Figure 9.12).

Removing Distracting Elements

Lightroom's Spot Removal tool is good for just that: removing spots. The first part of your processing should include examining the photo at 100% or 1:1 view. If you discover a sensor spot, hot pixel, or some similarly unwanted blemish, press the Q key to jump to the Spot Removal tool (**Figure 9.13**). Here's how it works.

1. Adjust the Size slider until the Spot Removal circle is larger than the spot you want to remove.
2. Set the edit mode to Heal for best results.
3. Click on the spot and drag the circle to an area of the photo that contains similar pixels without any spots.

    Lightroom will use the pixels at the chosen destination to heal the area within the circle you clicked on.

> **Note**
>
> You can download the photo in Figure 9.12 and follow along by going to www.takingstockphoto.com/downloads/.

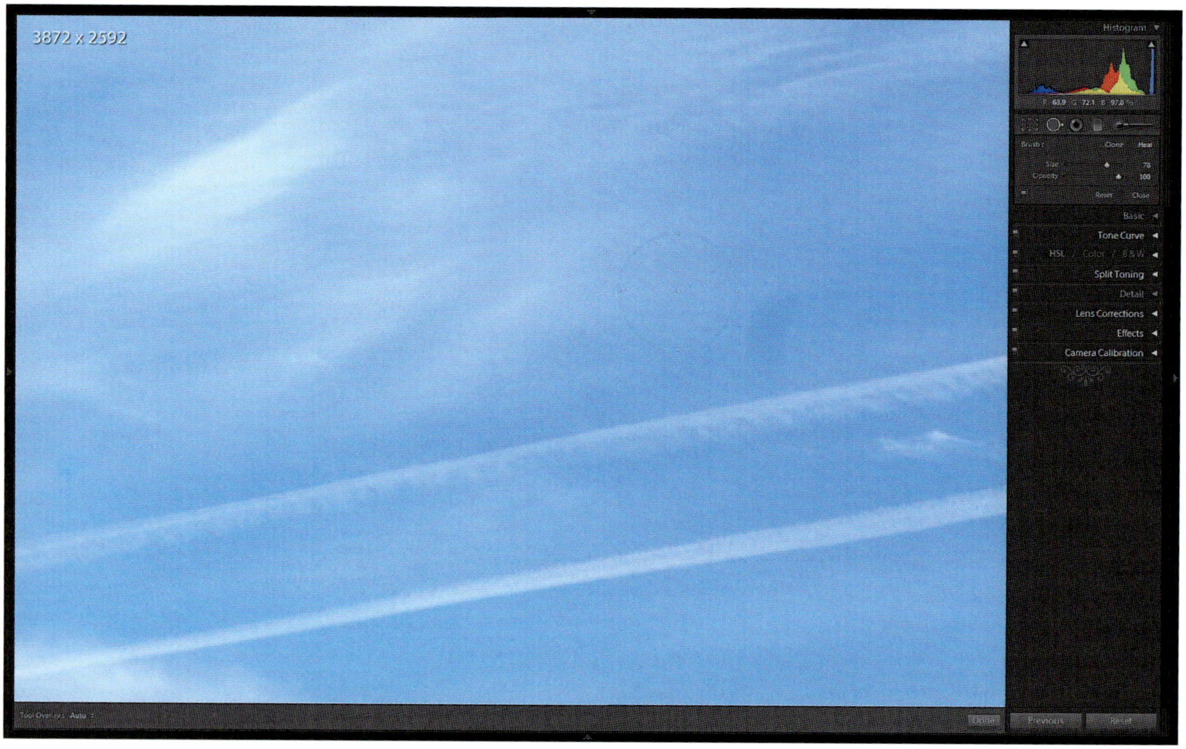

Figure 9.13 Sensor spots, caused by dust on the sensor, show easily in blue skies and smaller apertures.

> **Tip**
>
> Here's a great way to examine a photo. Zoom to 1:1 view and press the Home key, and Lightroom will jump to the top-left corner. Press the Page Down key to step through viewing the entire photo until you reach the bottom-right corner. You won't miss a spot.

4. Resize and reposition the Spot Removal tool circle after clicking on the spot as needed for best results (**Figure 9.14**). Press H to show/hide the circles to evaluate the job.
5. (Optional) Adjust the opacity slider as needed to reveal original pixels for more realistic blending.
6. Press Q to exit the tool.

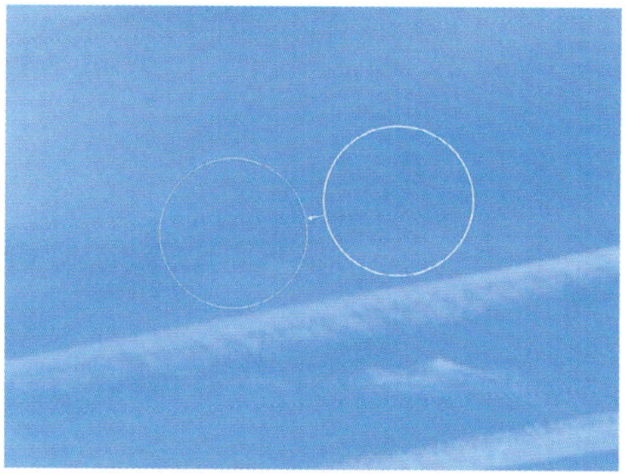

Figure 9.14 Sensor spot removed.

Digital House Cleaning **153**

If you need to remove anything more complicated than a spot, it is time to head over to Elements to take advantage of the advanced cloning and healing tools, as well as the ability to work with selections and layers. You only want to make this move after your basic processing adjustments are complete because at this point Lightroom is going to create a new copy that includes all your Lightroom adjustments, and it will open this new copy in Photoshop.

> **Note**
>
> You can download the photo in Figure 9.14 and follow along by going to www.takingstockphoto.com/downloads/.

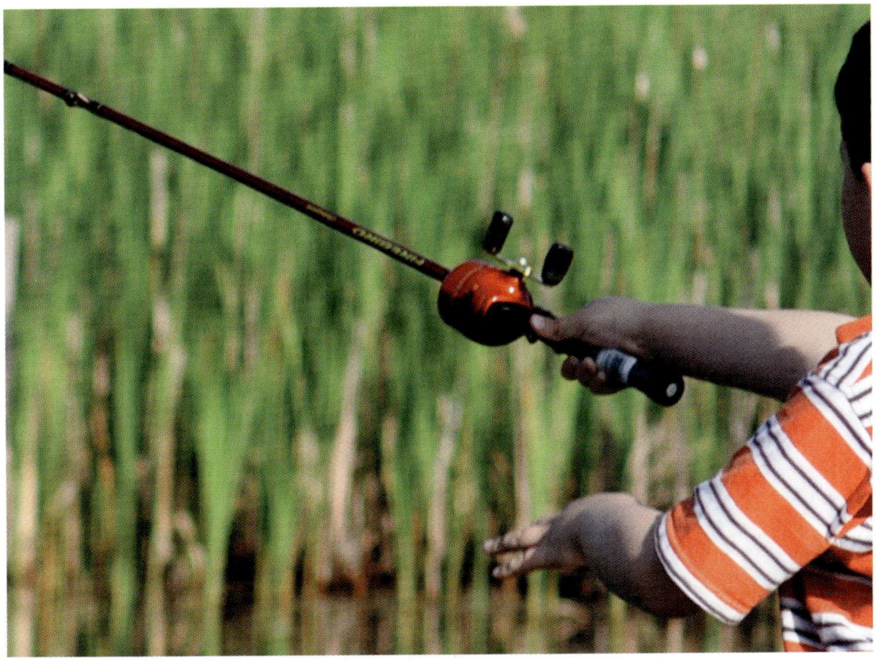

Figure 9.15 The logo on the fishing rod would be cause for rejection. Remove it.

Figure 9.15 is a photo of my son fishing displayed at 100% view in Elements. There is a barely legible logo at the base of the fishing rod that would trigger an automatic rejection. Stock is all about generic scenes with generic equipment. If you're ever unsure about whether to remove some similarly questionable content, just remember this simple phrase, "When in doubt, clone it out," and wonder no more. The basic process is the same for any element you want to remove from a photo:

> **Tip**
>
> Set the zoom level greater than 100% when working in a small area to see what you are doing more easily.

1 Click the Create new layer icon at the bottom of the Layers panel (looks like a page curl) to add an empty layer above the background layer.

2 Select the Clone Stamp Tool from the Toolbar.

3 Check Sample All Layers in the Options Bar so that the Clone Stamp will take pixels from the bottom layer while you work on the empty layer.

Performing our cloning work on the empty layer leaves the original bottom layer untouched, which provides the means to fix any mistakes you make while working by simply erasing the mistake on the top later. Having the cloned pixels on their own layer also provides more flexibility in blending the new cloned area with the original image through layer masks and layer opacity adjustments.

4   Use the Left Bracket key to reduce the brush size or the Right Bracket key to increase the brush size as needed to match the size of the area you want to cover.

5   Hold the Alt key (Mac: Option) and click on the area you want to use to sample pixels to apply to the area you want to remove. In this case, I clicked an area of the rod that was a solid color just above the logo.

The Clone Stamp tool works by allowing you to take pixels from the sampled area and then paint with them, so you want to choose a sample that closely matches the area you want to correct.

6   With the empty layer active, begin painting over the logo (or whatever it is you are trying to remove).

The goal is to make the scene look as if that element never existed. Don't just make a logo illegible or a person unrecognizable. Take your time and make the item completely disappear (**Figure 9.16**).

> **Tip**
>
> For this sort of detailed painting with pixels, I find having a pen tablet makes the job much easier. Lightroom, Photoshop, and Photoshop Elements all work really well with a pen-input tablet. Go to www.wacom.com to learn more about these devices.

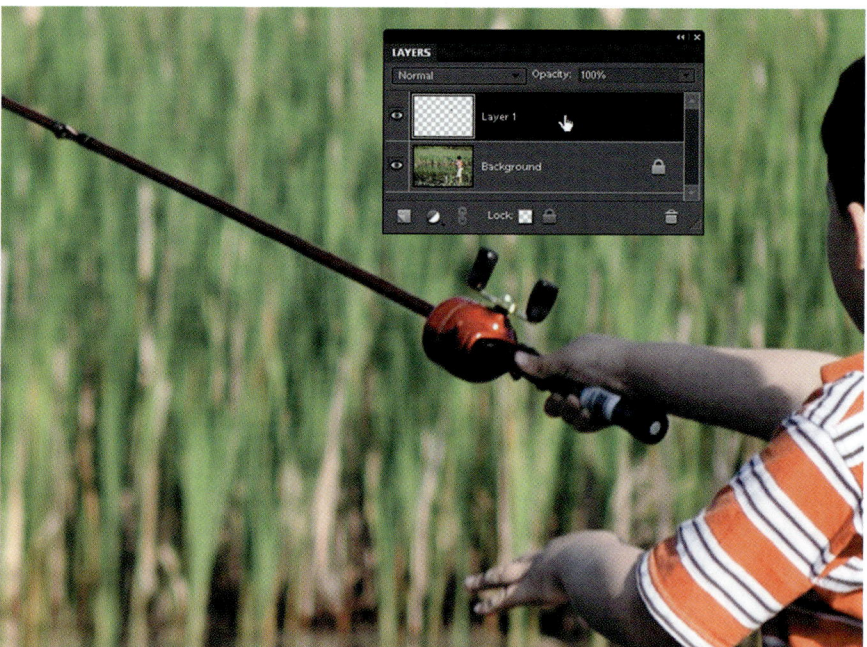

Figure 9.16 What logo? Careful application of the Clone Stamp has removed all trace of the logo's existence.

Downsizing to Fix Minor Problems

One of the most frustrating causes for rejection people struggle with has to do with digital *artifacts*. Artifacts is a rather vague and loosely applied way to say that a photo's pixels did not look quite right. The problems are most commonly caused by:

- Too much noise reduction, resulting in mushy detail that is then over-sharpened in an attempt to compensate for the mushiness.
- Luminance noise that was not reduced effectively.

The best ways to avoid artifacts are to shoot with enough light that you can get a good exposure at a lower ISO, and to use a faster shutter speed, which should reduce the noise problem at the root. In addition, apply as little noise reduction as possible, and preferably only to the most affected areas of the photo. Finally, apply capture sharpening in conjunction with your noise reduction, paying specific attention to the Masking slider so that you are only sharpening important edge detail and not unwanted artifacts.

As a coup de grâce, if you have a large enough photo to begin with (such as any photo over 8 megapixels), try resizing the photo smaller as a final step. The process of making the photo smaller, called *downsizing*, averages surrounding pixels together to reduce the total number of pixels in the photo. The end result is that it will appear sharper and lessen the appearance of artifacts. How much smaller should you go? That will depend on how large your photo is to start, how much help it really needs from this process, and what is the smallest size you want the photo to be for licensing. As a rule of thumb, I try to never resize my photos smaller than 6 megapixels. Obviously, the less you reduce the better, but don't be afraid to reduce the original by 500 to 1000 pixels as it may be just the thing to get your photo accepted.

> **Note**
>
> Generally speaking for most microstock sites, you don't ever want to make your photos larger than their original dimensions, called upsizing. This will cause an automatic rejection at iStockphoto. Upsizing results in new pixels being created from neighboring pixels, which can degrade detail.

While you can downsize on export from Lightroom by checking the Resize to Fit box on the Export dialog box and entering the desired size, I prefer to use Elements so that I can immediately see the result and either undo or downsize further. Here's how:

1. With the photo open at 100% view in Elements, choose Image > Resize > Image Size. This will open the Image Size dialog box.
2. Check the Resample Image box (**Figure 9.17**). Leave the other boxes checked.
3. Choose a resampling algorithm. I prefer to use Bicubic Sharper, which does add a little sharpening to the mix. If the result looks too crunchy, undo and try Bicubic instead.

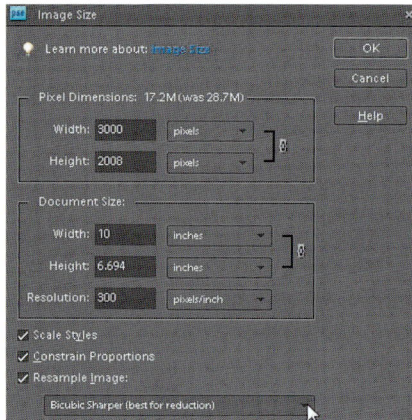

Figure 9.17 Image Size dialog box.

4 The amount will vary for the reasons I stated earlier, but a good start is to reduce the pixel dimensions by 500 pixels and see how it looks.

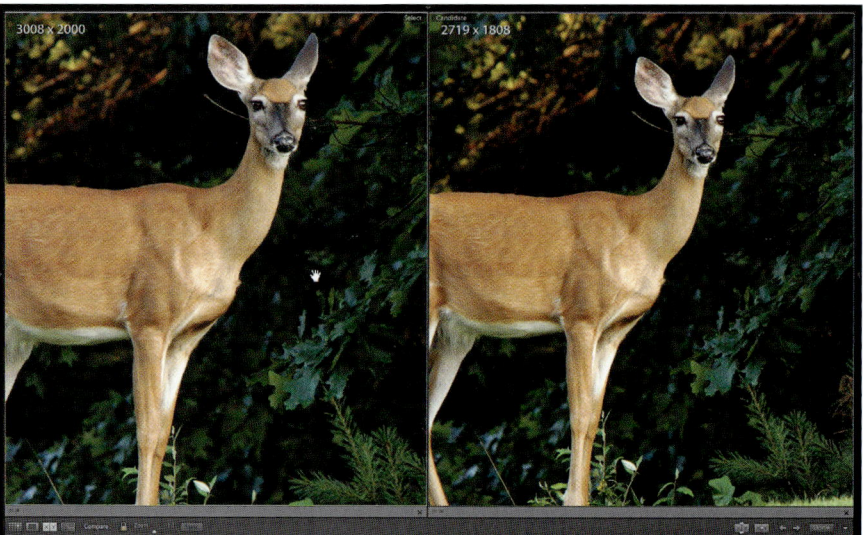

Figure 9.18 Before and after downsizing.

The photo (**Figure 9.18**) was originally taken with my Nikon D70 in 2006. I increased the ISO to 640 so that I could increase the shutter speed enough to hopefully reduce the chances of introducing motion blur caused by camera shake, since I was hand-holding my 80-400mm lens. The deer was kind enough to pause on the hill long enough for me to capture a few frames. Even after noise reduction I didn't like the look of the pixels in the background behind the deer. A slight downsizing did the trick.

This photo also serves as a good example for why you should start shooting in raw now. In 2006, I processed the original raw file as best I could with Lightroom 1, and then applied a lens blur to the background in Photoshop to further reduce the noise (because Lightroom's noise reduction wasn't as good as it is now), before finally downsizing to help it pass inspection. **Figure 9.19** shows the originally approved 2006 version on the left with the recently re-processed with Lightroom 3 and Photoshop Elements 8 version on the right. If I had shot in JPEG mode back in 2006, I never would have been able to reprocess that shot so well and make such an incredible improvement. I still chose to break my rule of thumb and resized it below 6 megapixels to ensure it passed inspection (and it did), but for a 640 ISO shot I'm very pleased.

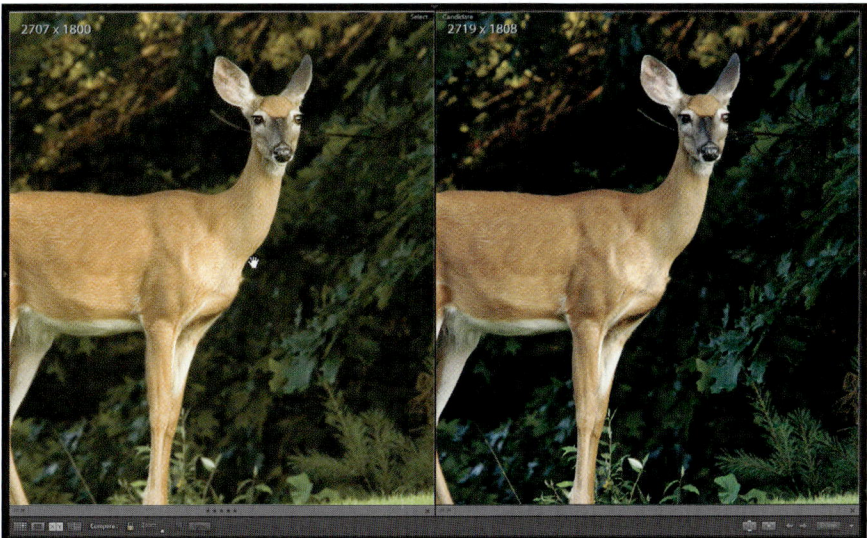

Figure 9.19 The difference improved software can make.

Avoid Overprocessing

Conventional wisdom in the world of microstock says to submit photos in as close to their unaltered state as possible to avoid rejections for *overfiltering*, which essentially means you went a little too far in your attempt to enhance the look of the photo. Generally speaking, stock is intended to be someone else's raw material, so theoretically, the more *enhancements* you apply to a photo, the greater the potential to make it less useful to future customers because they can't undo your enhancement.

Let's take an extreme example, like performing a simple conversion to grayscale. By taking all the color out of the photo, you have effectively made that photo useless to every customer who wants a color photo. At the same time, you are only appealing to a much smaller potential audience who does want a grayscale image, but who could easily convert the photo to grayscale on their own. I can already hear you say, "But I intended it to be that way!" OK, that's legit. The thing is, when submitting for stock, you are not submitting work to be hung in an art gallery. In this scenario, your work is being reviewed by people tasked with approving potentially useful raw stock content. So, there is nothing wrong with your intentions; it's just that your intentions may not fit well with this outlet.

Now, I am not saying you can never take creative license with your stock submissions. There are many examples of extremely successful stock content that have been heavily touched by the hand of Photoshop. I'm just trying to give you the heads-up that not only does it take a little time to master the technical aspects of certain Photoshop techniques, but just as importantly, it takes time to master knowing when to use which technique on which photo. I will take the liberty of quoting fellow iStockphoto contributor stacey_newman, who came to the following conclusion after getting a series of what she called "experimental motion blurs" accepted. She wrote, "Proof, I guess, that if something is done well, processing is acceptable."

I know it seems blindingly obvious, but it is tricky to pin down the exact meaning of *done well* across all the various image reviewers across all the various stock sites. The further you venture beyond the basic raw processing steps outlined in Chapter 8, and the digital housekeeping techniques in the preceding sections, the further you head into subjective territory, which can lead to inconsistent approvals and rejections, and a lot of frustration.

Here are some techniques practically guaranteed to trigger nearly universal rejections for overprocessing:

- Just about any straight application of any filter in Photoshop's Filter menu, except for intentional tweaks with Lens Correction, Blur, Noise, and Sharpen. I'm sure there are various techniques that utilize one of the other filters as a secret ingredient that produces stellar results, but as a general rule of thumb, avoid Photoshop filter fantasies.
- A simple conversion to grayscale and then bringing back color in one element of the photo.
- Adding borders, signatures, or watermarks of any kind. Save those for Flickr.
- Sloppy removal or replacement of some element in the photo (such as trying to make a logo appear illegible instead of removing it as if it was never there).

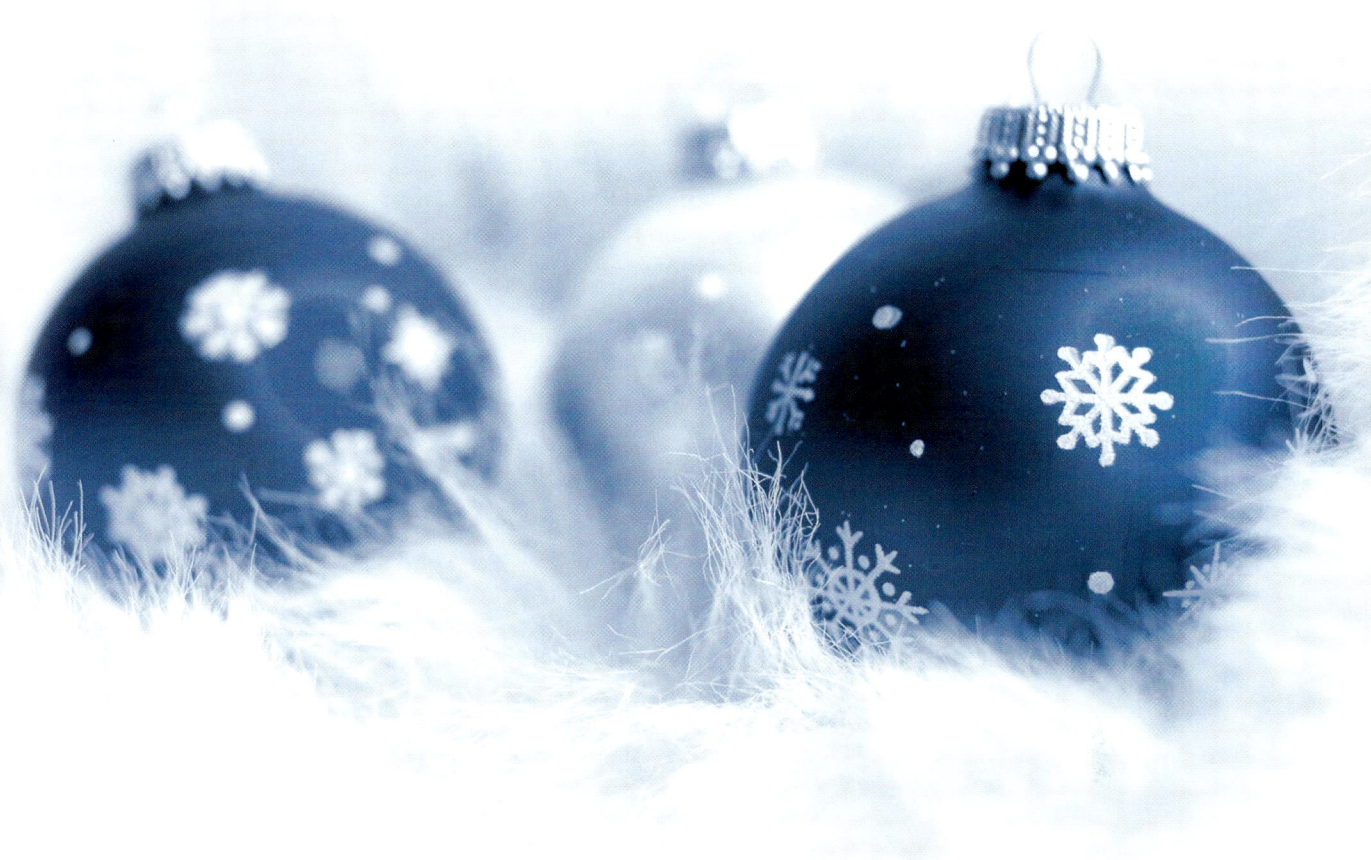

Figure 9.20 Wintery Decorations. Downloaded over 5,700 times.

Wintery Decorations

Creator	Shawn Gearhart (istockphoto.com/ideabug)
Started	2005
Home	USA
Total portfolio	1,758
Total downloads	Over 40,000
About this photo	Shawn says, "I believe this image has been successful because of its softness and simplicity, and also because the monochromatic blue tones give it a cool, wintery feel for the Christmas season. Captured with a Nikon D70, Nikkor 28mm f/2.8 Lens, AlienBees B800, and 60-inch Photek Umbrella."
Shawn's tip	"Try to compose photos with the designer in mind. Rather than centering the object/person in the frame, move them to the left or right. This gives room for designers to add text over the image without covering the main subject."

So, with that said, you may be wondering, "What can we do?" The list of possible acceptable enhancements is longer than I could possibly cover here, but I do want to share two techniques that can be used in a lot of situations, and as always, with a very light touch. Back in Chapter 1, I said I would share the processing steps I used with my Christmas tree photo (refer back to Figures 1.4 and 1.5 to see the before and after versions) to help make it pop. Beyond the basic processing steps covered in Chapter 8, the next few sections will walk you through the two simple enhancements you can try on your own photos.

The technique of darkening the edges of a photo to focus attention on the center, referred to as a *vignette*, has been around for many years, but still proves to be quite popular due to its simple effectiveness and ability to work well with a wide range of subject matter. There are many ways to add a vignette, but since we have been primarily using Lightroom 3 and Photoshop Elements 8, I want to show you one method in Lightroom 3 (which also works in Camera Raw 6) and follow up with another version in Photoshop Elements 8 (which works just as well in the full version of Photoshop).

Adding a Vignette

Note

This technique can be applied to both raw and non-raw files.

All of the controls we need are found at the top of the Effects panel (**Figure 9.21**) in Lightroom's Develop module. The name, Post-Crop Vignetting, is intended to differentiate it from the Vignetting slider in the Lens Corrections panel, and simply means that Post-Crop works with photos that have been cropped in Lightroom as well as those that have not been cropped at all. Post-Crop Vignette is completely intended for stylistic effect. Here are the available controls:

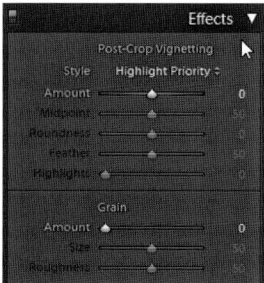

Figure 9.21 The controls in the top of the Effects panel are devoted to applying vignette effects.

- The Style drop-down menu offers three choices that affect how the vignette effect interacts with the image. The Highlight Priority option puts the focus on preserving and recovering highlights, but at the potential cost of color shifts, while the Color Priority option attempts to avoid color shifts, but cannot protect or recover the highlights. Paint Overlay just adds in either black or white pixels to the existing pixels in the image. Try each option and go with the one that suits the photo and your vision.

- Amount controls how much of the vignette effect you want to apply, and if it is dark or bright. A negative value creates a dark vignette, while a positive value creates a bright vignette. Dark vignettes are the most common choice.

- Midpoint determines how far into the center the vignette can extend. A low value extends the vignette further toward the center, while a high value keeps the effect just on the edges.

- Roundness affects the shape of the inner part of the vignette. A low value moves toward rectangular, while a high value moves toward circular.

- Feather adjusts the softness of the transition of the vignette from the edge to the center. Lower values trend toward harder transitions, while high values increase the softness of the transition.

- Highlights only comes into play with the Highlight Priority or Color Priority styles enabled, and allows you to basically brighten any highlights affected by the vignette to somewhat counter the effect in a more natural way. It is a subtle control that won't be needed on most photos.

My goal for applying a darkening vignette to my Christmas tree photo was an attempt to help make that tree look like it was the one warm light in a dark cold place. I just wanted to darken the outer edges a little bit in preparation for the reverse vignette I'll cover next.

In this case, I set Style to Color Priority since I am more concerned about preventing color shifts, set the Amount to -10 until I could just start to see the effect, nudged Midpoint up to 78 to push the darkening away from the center, decreased Roundness to -66 to further push the darkening effect toward the edges, and left Feather and Highlights at their respective default settings. Keep in mind that it is perfectly normal to go back and forth between sliders and re-tweak after each adjustment. These controls all work together, so sometimes you need to over-adjust to see the effect and then dial it back down to Earth.

At this point, I am ready to add the final touch in Photoshop Elements to really make that tree pop. If Photoshop Elements (or the full version of Photoshop) is your primary external editor for Lightroom, you can press Ctrl-E (Mac: Command-E) to send a copy with Lightroom adjustments right over. We'll pick up in Photoshop Elements in the next section.

> **Tip**
>
> Hold the Alt (Mac: Option) key to change the Post-Crop Vignetting label into a Reset button to zero out all the sliders in a single click. Double-click a slider to reset it to its default.

Creating a Reverse Vignette

In the previous technique, we darkened the edges to make the center area appear brighter. In this reverse vignette technique, we're going to do the opposite and brighten the center slightly while keeping the edges mostly unchanged. We'll need to call upon the layer mask trick I showed you previously in the purple fringing section to make this work. Here are the steps:

1. Duplicate the Background layer by pressing Ctrl-J (Mac: Command-J).

2. Select the Background layer to make it active, then click the half-moon-looking Adjustment Layer icon at the bottom of the Layers panel and select Brightness/Contrast. This is that layer mask trick we used before (if you are using the full version of Photoshop you can just apply a regular layer mask).

3. Select the top duplicate layer to make it active, then choose Layer > Create Clipping Mask. This just forces the top photo layer to pass through the layer mask on the adjustment layer (full Photoshop users don't need this step).

4. With the top photo layer still selected, click the layer blending mode drop-down menu at the top of the Layers panel and choose Screen. Your background photo should immediately become much brighter.

5. Reduce the Opacity of the top photo layer to around 20%. This is subjective and will vary with each photo. In general, we don't want to over do it, so err on the side of lower opacity.

6. Click on the layer mask to make it active.

7. Select the Brush tool, and configure a large soft-edged brush set to paint with black. We want a large soft-edged brush to make the transitions between the brighter center and darker edges as smooth as possible.

8. Here's the fun part: With the layer mask active, we're going to paint back the edges of the original photo on the Background layer. By using a brush and a layer mask, we have much more flexibility to adjust the effect of the vignette than is afforded by the Lightroom Effects panel. This is especially true when, like my photo, the subject is off center.

Tip

Reduce the Opacity value of the brush in the Options bar to better blend the transitions between dark and light.

This is intended to be a subtle effect. I am not trying to put a lighthouse on my front lawn. I just wanted to give that tree a little bit of a boost. Compare **Figure 9.22**, which just has the original Lightroom vignette, to **Figure 9.23**, which is the final result after both techniques. As I said, there are a lot of ways to achieve a similar end, but I hope you can see the world of possibilities that exist using these techniques in concert and independently of each other. Always ask yourself this important question before applying any enhancement technique: "Does this effect/trick/tip help enhance the core message this photo is intended to communicate?" If you can't honestly answer "yes," then you might be heading into the Photoshop fantasy zone, which is a really fun place to visit, but you don't want to bring your stock there.

Assignment

Head over to www.takingstockphoto.com/downloads/ and download the practice files for the purple fringing, cropping, spot removal, and logo removal techniques and practice each exercise.

Choose a few of your own photos to try the vignette techniques in various degrees and ask yourself if it helps or hinders the communication of that photo's message. Remember, rejection can result from sloppy editing, too, so practice, practice, practice.

Grab a free 30-day trial version of Lightroom 3 and Photoshop Elements 8 (www.adobe.com) if you don't have them already. ■

Avoid Overprocessing **163**

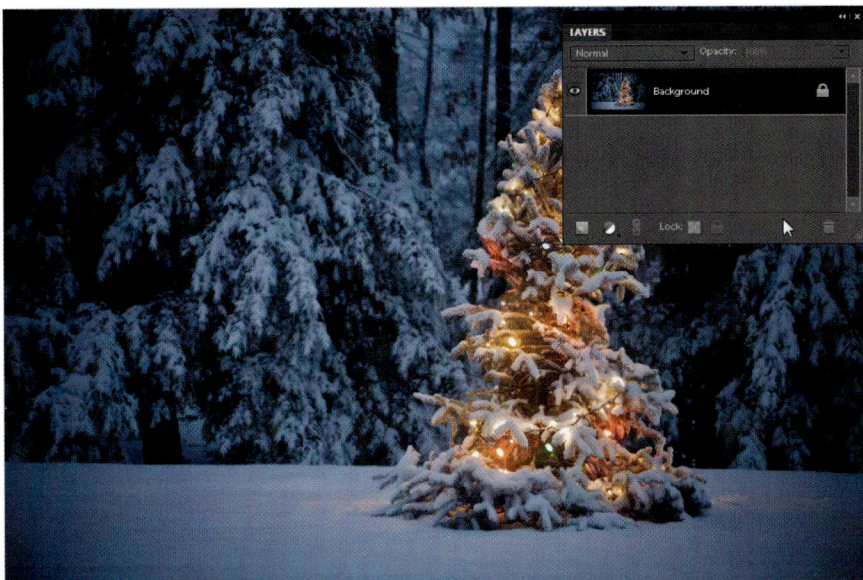

Figure 9.22 The results of the Lightroom Post-Crop Vignette.

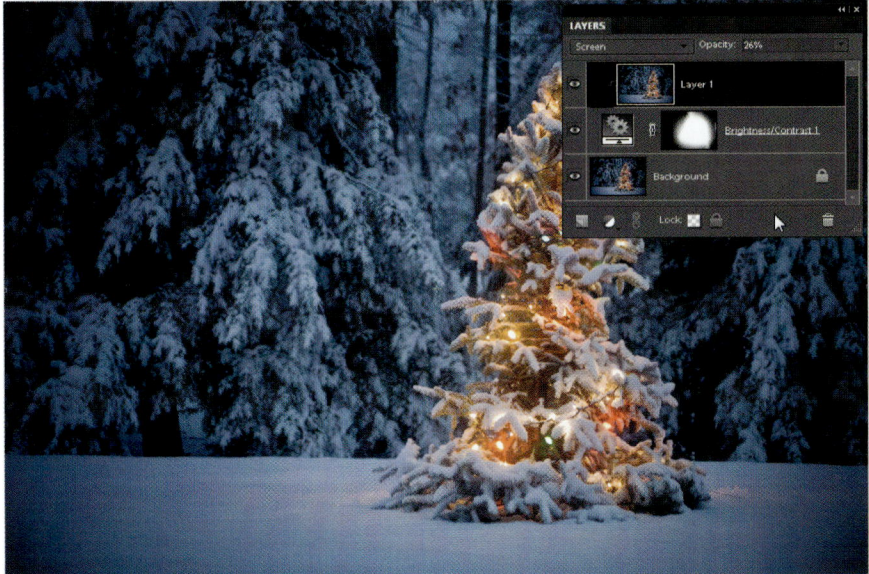

Figure 9.23 The final result combining both types of vignette. The Layers panel shows the arrangement of the three layers used.

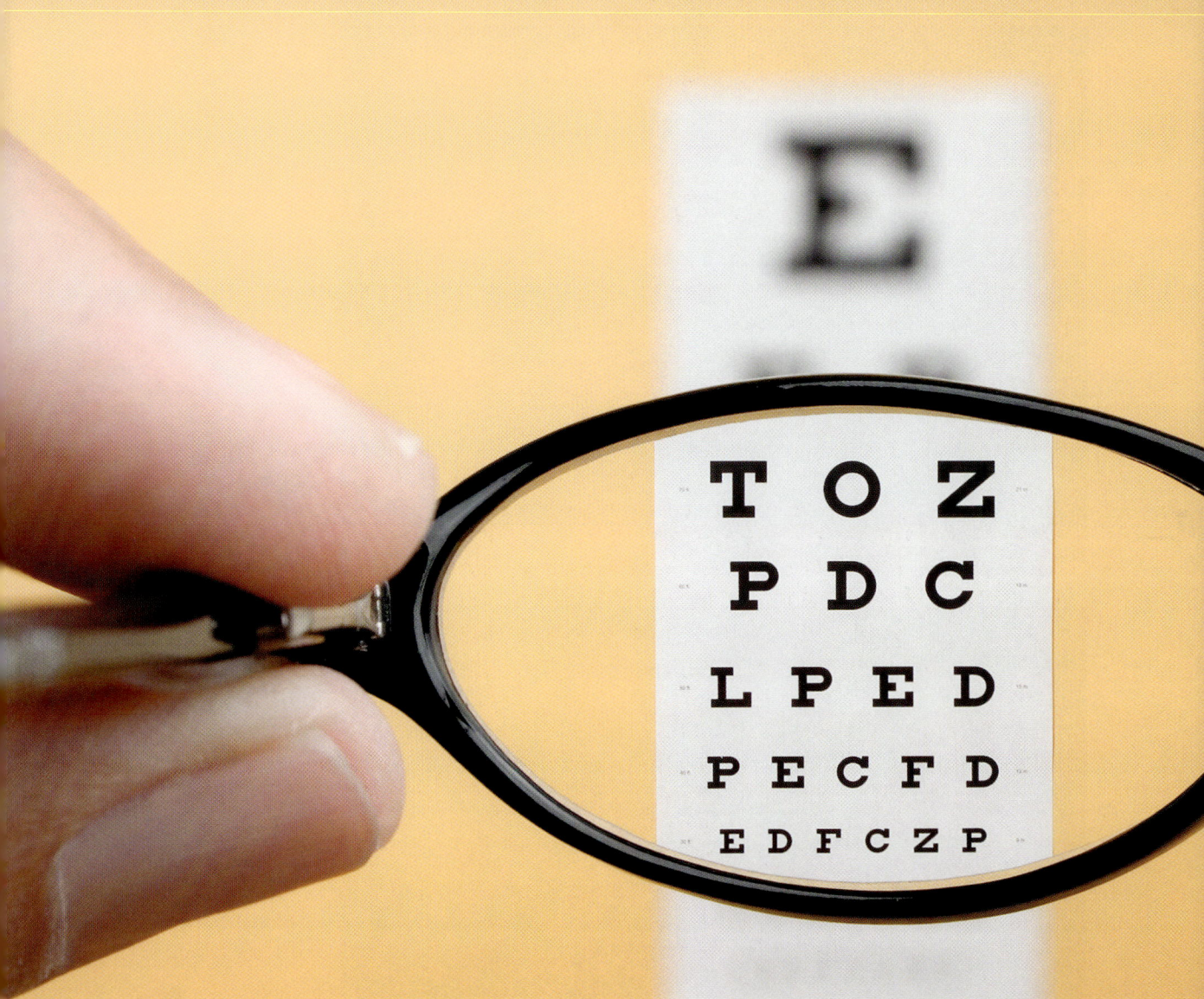

Figure 10.1 Eyeglasses.
© Gene Chutka (istockphoto.com/gchutka)

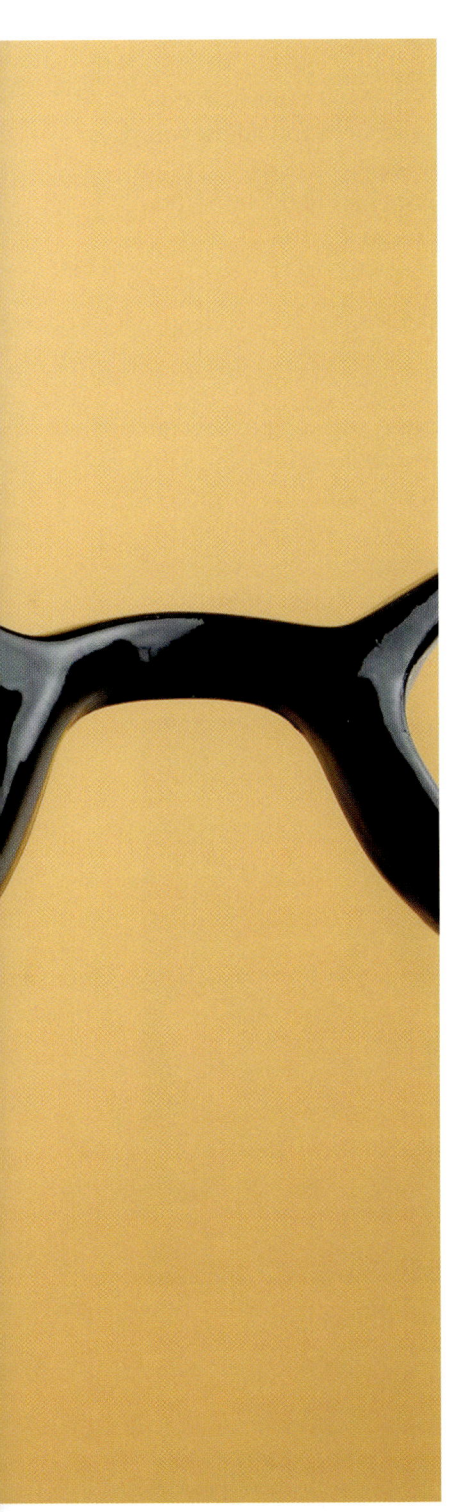

10
Seeing Like an Inspector

The most significant obstacle to overcome when you produce photos for stock is how you judge your own finished work. It is perfectly natural to have emotional attachments to your photos due to the combination of the experiences that occur in their creation. Everything from the pre-production visions in your mind's-eye, to what happened when the photos were captured, to everything you put into them during post-production can affect your perception of the final output.

Unfortunately, these attachments cloud our objectivity and cause us to overlook flaws and problems that are more easily spotted by a neutral observer. This puts us at a serious disadvantage, because the person who will review our stock submissions has no emotional attachments to our photos, which are just the next collection of pixels to appear on his screen. We need to learn how to become a little more detached so that we can start to see our photos through a more objective set of eyes.

It is also very common for new contributors to have little experience in critically viewing other people's photos. Sure, we all love to look at pretty pictures, but how often have you really scrutinized someone else's photos at 100 percent to evaluate focus, noise, and sharpness, in the context of its quality of composition, lighting and subject matter, all the while keeping vigilant for legally problematic issues? This is what the photo inspectors do every day, multiplied by hundreds of photos. The long-term benefit of an inspector's photo-immersive experience is a calibration of what to expect when they are viewing different photos. If you only ever critically examine your own photos, it puts you at an additional disadvantage, because you lack a sense of where your work fits into the larger context of work produced by your peers.

These problems are surmountable, though, with skills that will come with experience and practice. Being aware that the issues exist can help you adjust your expectations when getting started, and propel you to take the necessary steps to expand your vision. You are the first and most important part of the inspection process, so let's talk about how to get yourself up to speed.

Being Your Worst Critic

This isn't about self-loathing. This is about being as objective as you possibly can when viewing your photos at different points in your workflow. The goal is the management of your expectations, the preservation of your time, the creation of a clear path for growth, and increasing the acceptance rate of your submissions. All of this adds up to a much more profitable, productive, and satisfying experience over time. There are several points in your workflow that you will need to examine your work and make decisions about where to focus your energies or cut your losses. Inspection is a continual process.

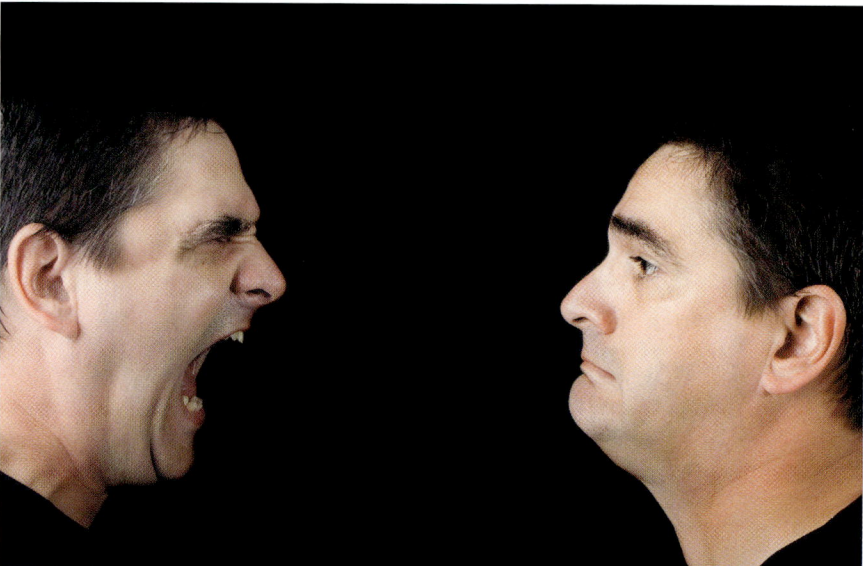

Figure 10.2 Mad at Me. © Randolph Pamphrey (istockphoto.com/imbarney22)

Capture Time

I admit to sometimes being a first-class *chimper* when out shooting. Not heard of chimping? You know the move. You've just fired the shutter and without hesitation you rotate the camera to see the preview appear on the back of the camera's LCD as the photo is saved to your memory card (**Figure 10.3**). It is fun to see what you have just captured, and enjoying yourself is a significant reason to be out shooting in the first place. That said, there is a time and place for everything, and you certainly wouldn't want to miss a shot because you were too busy staring at the back of the camera. Of course, there is useful information to be gained via that LCD preview, so check focus occasionally, make sure you are exposing properly (see Chapter 6), use the tools at your disposal to take corrective action, and take pleasure in what you have captured. I encourage you to save the serious review session for when the shooting is over, and you can put those photos up on the computer's screen. Light can be fleeting, so capture it while you can.

As you are shooting (and chimping), keep the following questions in mind:

- Are you working inside the sweetspot of your equipment?
- Is the subject so unique/compelling it is worth moving outside the sweetspot?
- Are you meeting your original goals for why you went out shooting that day?

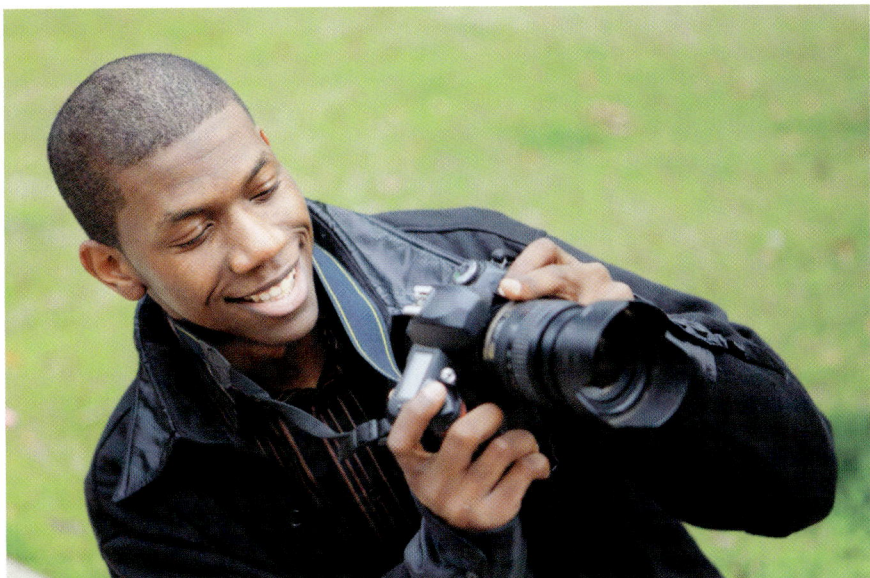

Figure 10.3 Great Shot. © Nathan Jones (istockphoto.com/bjones27)

First Review

So now the shooting is done, and you are dying to dive in and see what you've got. Not to be a killjoy, but I do want to point out that you are probably not in your most objective mental state at this point, so you may want to refrain from making any final decisions on this first pass. Your hopes may be so high that you are overly critical of your work. One of the simplest ways to add a lot more objectivity to your process is to increase the amount of time between when you create the captures and when you sit down to separate the wheat from the chaff. Make your immediate first pass and satisfy your curiosity. You may even be able to take some corrective action and reshoot if time allows, but then give yourself 24 hours to transition out of the moment before you bring out the axe. You'll be surprised at how much more effective you'll be with just that bit of distance.

> **Tip**
>
> Be sure to create backup copies as soon as possible after shooting so you are not relying on a single memory card to safeguard your work.

Post-production

You've invested all that time in the shoot, you've been thorough in making your selects for processing, and now you're darn well going to get some photos ready for uploading. Try just focusing on the very best two or three, process them well, and prepare them for uploading. Let the rest sit on the bench until you've gotten some feedback on your star players. Investing your energy on a few sure winners, running them up the flag pole, and then waiting to see who salutes can be incredibly valuable in helping you decide if it is worth your time to go back and process the next group of selects from that shoot.

Objectivity Practice

Working with your own photos will only get you so far. To gain proficiency in being objective, you need to get access to as many photos created by other people as you can, then sit down and view them as if you were in charge of accepting or rejecting them for your own stock site. You'll already be far more objective since you have no emotional connection, but the main goal here is the calibration of your eyeballs to the gamut of what is possible, and to gain a better sense of where your own work fits on the spectrum. That may seem like a tall order, but there are a number of resources for (legally) getting access to other people's work.

First, make a habit of regularly downloading the free photos that various stock sites offer as customer incentives. These are typically found on the site's home page, but you should also sign up for any customer-focused newsletters that are offered, as links to free photos can be included in these as well. Aside from being free practice material for you, these photos have already passed their initial round of inspection, and very likely a second round of inspection.

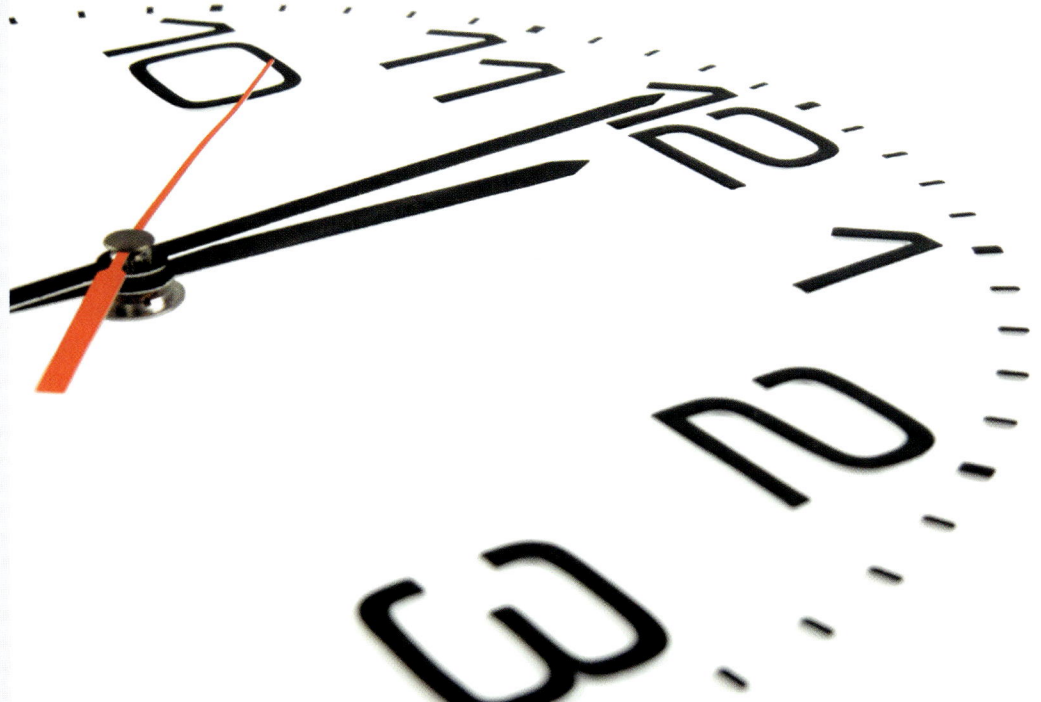

Figure 10.4 One Minute to Midnight. Downloaded over 1,200 times.

One Minute to Midnight

Creator	Susan Trigg (istockphoto.com/trigga)
Started	2005
Home	Australia
Total portfolio	1,689
Total downloads	Over 54,000
About this photo	Susan says, "It has strong visual impact and can be used for a variety of concepts, such as New Year's Eve, climate change, urgency, and opening hours. Captured with D70s, 50 mm micro, and studio strobe."
Susan's tip	"It's important to review images at 100 percent for quality issues, and also review them at thumbnail size in terms of composition, impact, and lighting. Buyers first see images on the site in this tiny size, so images need to entice them to take a closer look. Once the buyer decides to download your image, make sure the full size image lives up to the promise so they want to buy from you again. Repeat business is as important in the microstock industry as in any other."

> **Note**
>
> When you are evaluating accepted photos at various sites, it is helpful to look for the upload date. The more recent the better. Standards do evolve over time, and evaluating photos approved several years ago are a poor gauge for current standards.

This won't give you a lot of material to work with in the beginning, so also consider investing a small amount of your earnings in purchasing some credits at a site of your choosing. Then do a series of targeted searches on subjects you are interested in shooting. Evaluate the thumbnails. Which catch your eye? Why? If the site offers a zoom function, take the time to zoom in to 100 percent and evaluate. Pick one of the best shots and use your credits to download the largest size. There's no harm in checking out the competition to see how you measure up. You want to get a feel for what is acceptable quality.

In addition, get involved in the contributor community at each site. There are so many people who are walking the same path and will share what they've learned along the way. At iStockphoto, there is a dedicated Critique Request forum where people can post their rejected images and get free feedback from their peers (inspectors chime in, too). It is a huge opportunity not only for feedback, but also for any contributor who wants to gain experience calibrating his or her eyeballs to see like inspectors do because you can download the full-sized versions of the rejected files and look at them up close and personal. This is probably one of the best learning tools in existence. Download the photos, take part in the discussions, listen to the feedback, offer your own, and watch your learning take off.

As you begin to make connections with other contributors, I encourage you to reach out to some of them and even consider creating your own critique group. I know a number of contributors who have formed these groups over the years and have benefited from the experience. You end up with a whole team of people with whom you can share, evaluate, cheer on, and talk shop.

Developing an Inspection Workflow

It's time for a little role-playing. Put yourself in the shoes of an image inspector. You're getting ready to sit down and examine several hundred photos. What do you need to get the job done? There isn't any magic here. You need a large, good-quality, and calibrated monitor for viewing each photo at its best, and a color-managed, image-viewing application (such as Photoshop or Photoshop Elements) that will respect the embedded color profile of each photo and allow you to easily zoom to 100 percent to inspect the photo at full size. That's it. The rest is up to your eyes and brain to methodically check each photo for any problems that could result in a rejection. You need to remain as objective as possible. Each photo stands or falls on its own merits, and there are no points given out for effort.

You might think of the act of inspection as something that only happens at the end of the workflow, but as I've tried to continually stress, when you are in the inspection seat of your own process, it should be happening all the time. It is in your best interest to spot and take corrective action as early in your process as possible. That said, one of the most important times to inspect is the last step, before you submit your work to the various stock sites, so that you can potentially spot any problems you overlooked before they are out of your hands.

I'll talk about how to organize your photos in the next chapter, but one simple tip is to create a single upload folder, into which you will save a final copy of every photo you plan to upload. I can't tell you how often I see people with uploader's remorse, trying to cancel an upload after the fact because they realized they either uploaded the wrong photo, the wrong version of the photo, or a last-second-look revealed a problem they missed. There is no reason to waste your time this way. By placing a copy of all final versions in a single folder, inspecting that folder one last time, and then only uploading photos pulled from that folder, you can eliminate these all too common rookie mistakes.

Creating an Upload Pre-flight Checklist

Put on a cup of tea or coffee (save the hard stuff for later), pull up your comfy-yet-ergonomically-designed office chair, fire up your file browser and image viewer, and let's get down to work. None of the criteria we're using should be new to you at this point, but that doesn't mean you won't find a problem that has escaped your notice up until now, which is exactly why we are here.

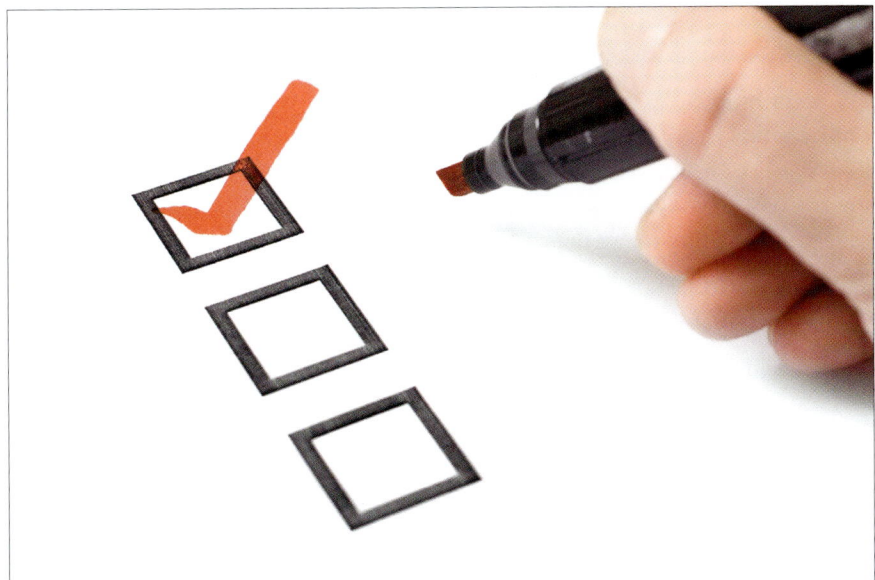

Figure 10.5 Red Positive Tick. © Robert Hadfield (istockphoto.com/NuStock)

The first thing an inspector is going to see is a thumbnail of some size. The thumbnail provides the first impression of the subject and overall composition, and it is exactly what customers are going to see when they view search results on a stock site. Remember, the thumbnail is what sells your photo to the customer. Generally speaking, each stock site displays a small thumbnail of about 100 pixels on the longest edge in the search results, as well as a larger thumbnail, anywhere between 300 to 500 pixels on the longest edge depending on the site. So choose a similar size for first viewing your own photos. Ask yourself the following:

- Can I tell what the subject is from the thumbnail?
- Does the thumbnail have enough visual impact to make a customer want to click in for a closer look?

Inspectors aren't going to reject your photo based on the thumbnail, but honestly, it can set a tone, and as the saying goes, you only get one chance to make a good first impression. If you answered a solid "no" to either of those questions, it's not a deal-breaker. Just note it and move forward. Not every photo is going to have a strong thumbnail, and that's OK, if the photo is otherwise useful and technically sound.

Open the first photo into your image viewer, and make it as large as you can and still see the entire photo edge to edge. Ask yourself the following:

- Does it appear properly exposed?
- Does the lighting work?
- Does the composition support the subject and does it make it more useful?

The more times you can say "yes" here, the better. When you view the entire photo at this larger size, you can get a good sense of what the subject matter is, how it works in that composition, and the overall impact of the image. Every photo doesn't have to knock your socks off, but if you are seeing problems at this stage, it isn't going to get better once you zoom in and examine at full size.

OK, zoom in to 100 percent view, start at one of the corners, and work your way across every inch of that photo. Ask yourself the following as you progress:

- Is the subject in focus where it needs to be?
- Is there adequate detail in the shadows and the highlights?
- Have I reduced the luminance and color noise to an acceptable level without sacrificing important detail?
- Have I removed any sensor spots, hot pixels, or other distracting flaws?

- Have I reduced all chromatic aberration along the high-contrast edges?
- Did I remove all logos or other trademarked content?
- Do I have model releases for all the people I am using as compositional elements in this photo?

If you answer "yes" to all of those questions, that's great: Those photos are ready to upload. If you answered "no" to any of those questions, or you weren't sure, then I suggest removing those shots from the upload folder. You need to decide it if it is within your abilities, and worth your time, to make the necessary adjustments to those photos to change the answer to "yes." If you do go back to the drawing board with some, then you should repeat the inspection process by saving a final copy back to the upload folder, and going through the above checklist again.

Dealing with Rejection

It is inevitable. Even after all the work you have done prior to submission, you're still going to encounter rejected submissions from time to time. There are no automated or mechanical aspects to the inspection process at any site. At the other end of your stock submission is another human being who has been trained to evaluate each image according to that site's standards for acceptance. It is never personal. Honestly, it is far easier for them to accept a submission than it is to reject, so if you did get a rejection, there was some reason, some issue, that triggered that person to take that action.

I can tell you from my own inspection experiences that I absolutely loved seeing good work come through the queue and accepting it into the collection, because it is faster and more satisfying. Rejecting new submissions is a pain. Unless a photo is horribly flawed (which is rare), it takes longer to evaluate a so-so photo, and then you've got to provide a rejection reason before moving on to the next photo. There is no joy in rejection.

We've all had work rejected, and there's no shame in it. What you are hopefully coming to understand is that the line between acceptance and rejection is not thin and black, but rather wide and gray. That means there's a level of subjectivity that is inherent in any human process. Don't waste energy hoping for more consistency in the process because that is outside of your control. Learn to roll with the feedback, improve your game, cut your losses, and check your ego.

> **Tip**
>
> You're going to need some place on the Web to upload your photos in order to share them with your peers. If you don't have a website, some of the more popular (free) options are www.vox.com and www.dropbox.com.

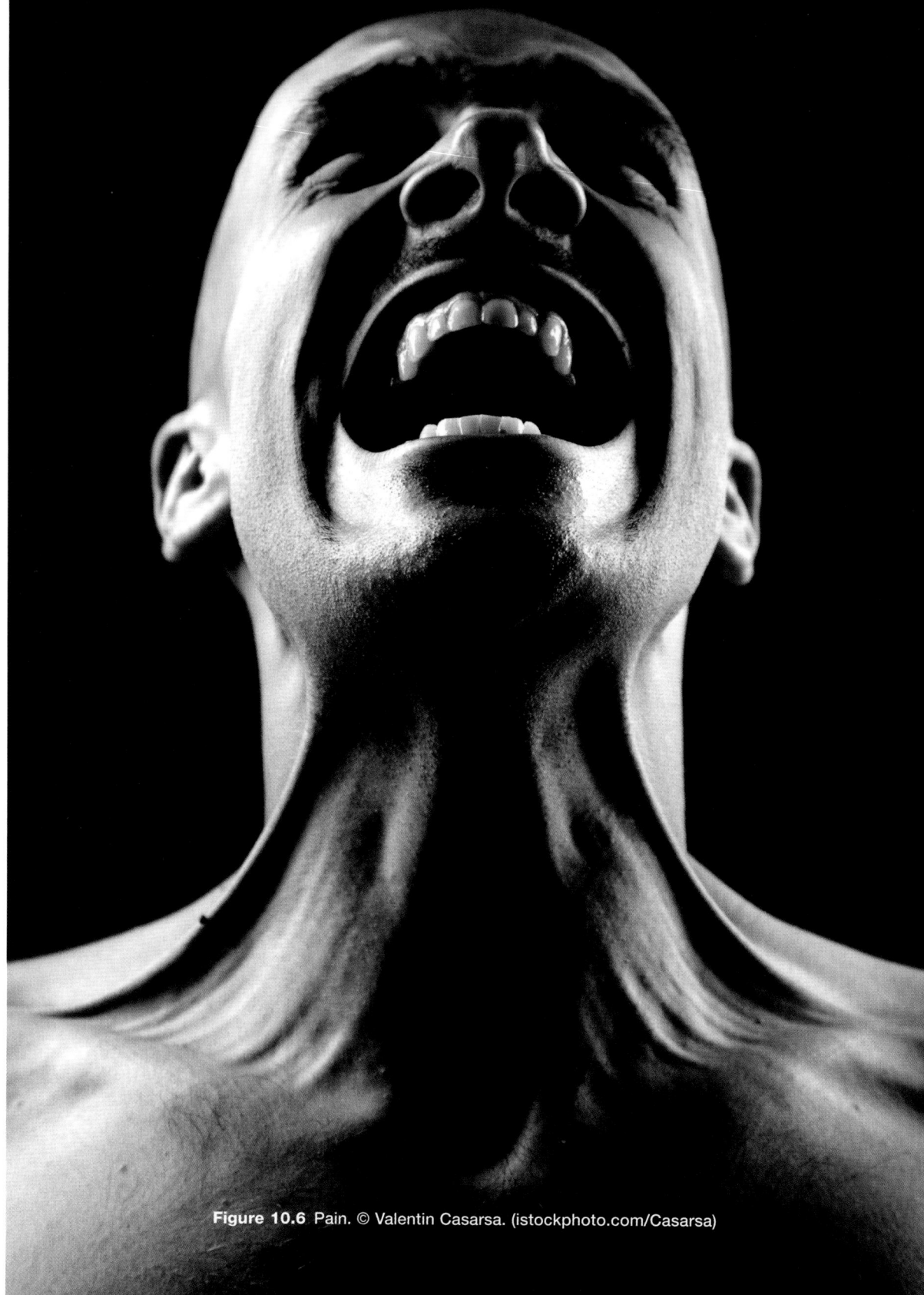

Figure 10.6 Pain. © Valentin Casarsa. (istockphoto.com/Casarsa)

Should the day come when a rejection email lands in your inbox, the first thing to do is figure out what triggered the rejection. Sometimes we miss the small problems that are an easy fix, such as a missed logo that didn't get cloned out. If that is the case, then it is worth your time to make the fix and resubmit. If you're not sure what the problem really is, and you believe that the concept, composition, and lighting is otherwise solid, then it is worth your time to seek some outside help from your fellow contributors via a critique forum. Let some fresh (and neutral) eyes take a close look at your work, and be open to the feedback. Once you have a handle on the problem, it is up to you to decide to either salvage the reject or reshoot with an eye toward improvement. Although it may seem like more work, I'm a bigger fan of a reshoot than a salvage job whenever reshooting is possible because it is a new opportunity to take all the feedback and create an all-around better shot.

Yes, there will be photos that for any combination of reasons are just not possible to reshoot. When faced with such a situation, invoke the 24-hour rule: Close the email and step outside. Put a little distance between the feeling of rejection and your decision about how to proceed. Postpone all decisions until tomorrow, and be amazed by the amount of clarity a day can bring.

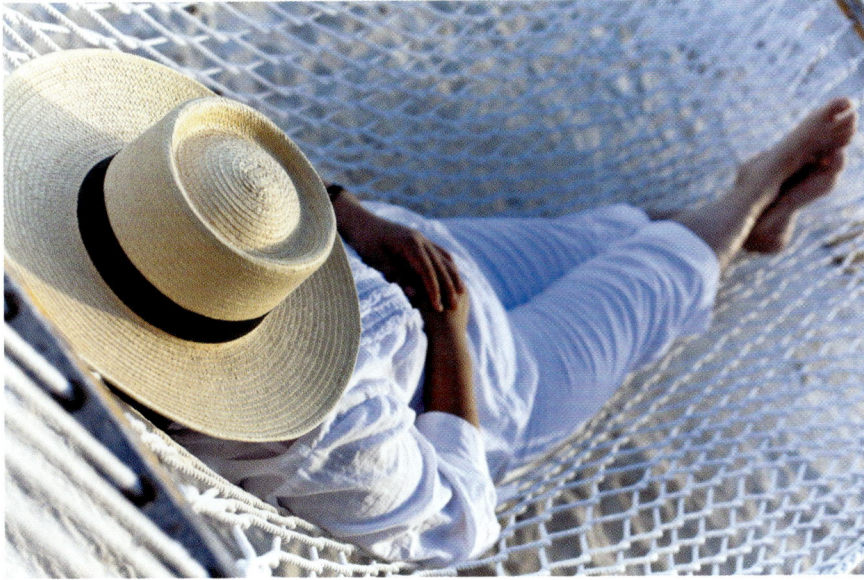

Figure 10.7 Relax. © Jill Chen

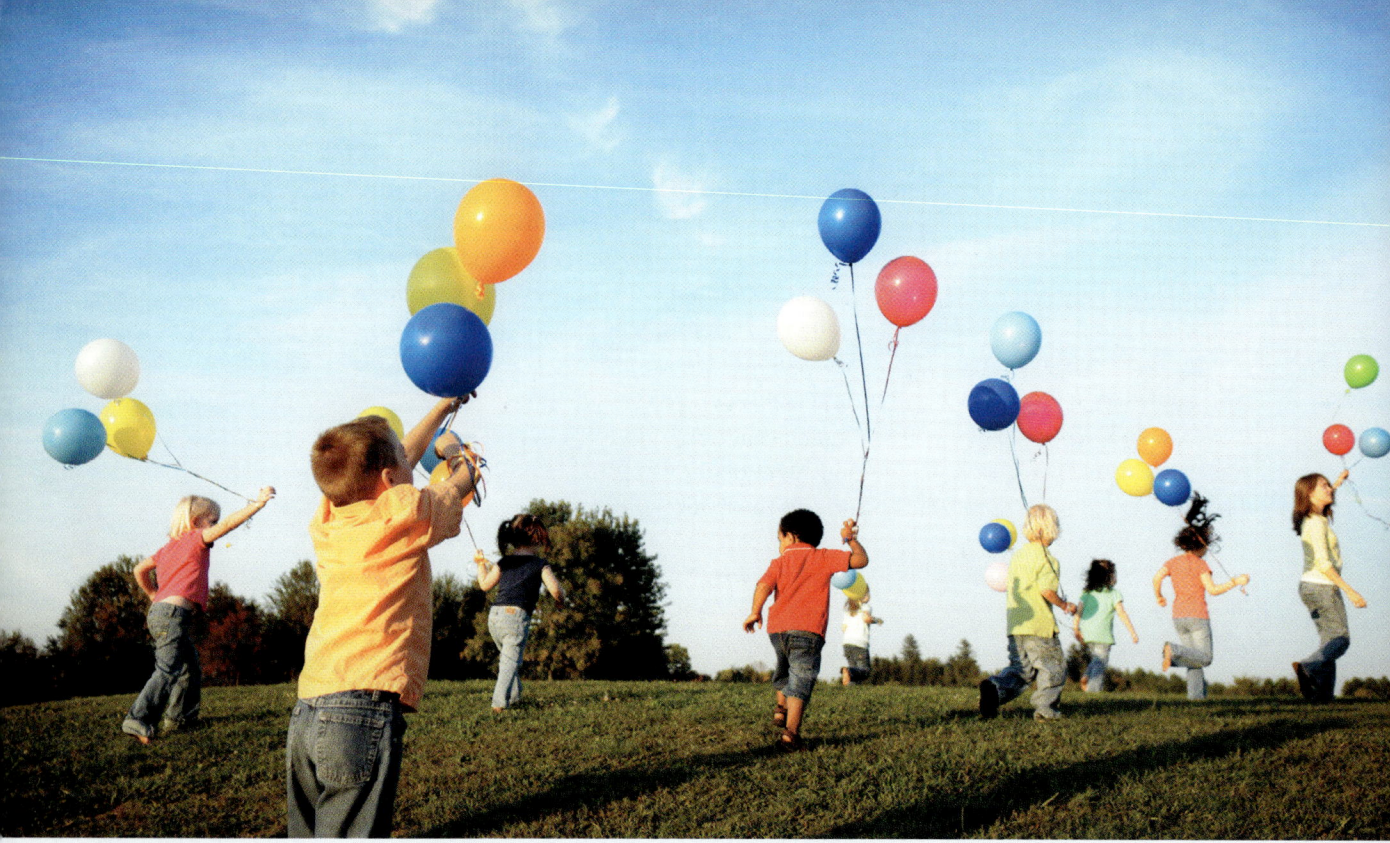

Figure 10.8 Group of Kids Running with Balloons. Downloaded over 1,300 times.

Group of Kids Running with Balloons

Creator	Rosemarie Gearhart (istockphoto.com/ArtisticCaptures)
Started	2006
Home	USA
Total portfolio	2,339
Total downloads	Over 69,000
About this photo	Rosemarie says, "This image has sold well because of the bright, vivid colors and because of the freedom and carefree nature of childhood that it portrays. It was captured with a Nikon D300 and Nikkor 17-55mm f/2.8G lens."
Rosemarie's tip	"When working with groups of children for stock photography, it is much easier if the children already know each other. Utilizing a club, church group, siblings, or cousins will make your job a lot easier. Have a lot of things planned for them. Keep the action constant but focused on what you want to accomplish. Never force a child to participate. Know that things won't go as planned and be prepared to go with the flow."

Assignment

To help you on your way to earning your inspector badge, I have put together a collection of full-sized JPEGs for you to review. You can download them in a Zip file from www.takingstockphoto.com/downloads. These are all my own photos that I rejected, and I have included a text file that explains why I rejected each one. These are very typical of the types of photos I have seen submitted over the years, and I encourage you to put each photo through your inspection process (with the checklists provided in this chapter) to see what reasons you choose before referring to the text file I included. The goal is to help calibrate your eyes to what will get your work rejected so that you can set your own bar higher. I want you to be able to recognize these problems early in your workflow, so that you can take corrective action, and invest your energy on your best work.

Repeat the same process with all of the approved photos you've downloaded from the various stock sites, whether they are the free samples or the ones you've paid for, and work on calibrating your eyes to what acceptable quality looks like, and aim higher still. ■

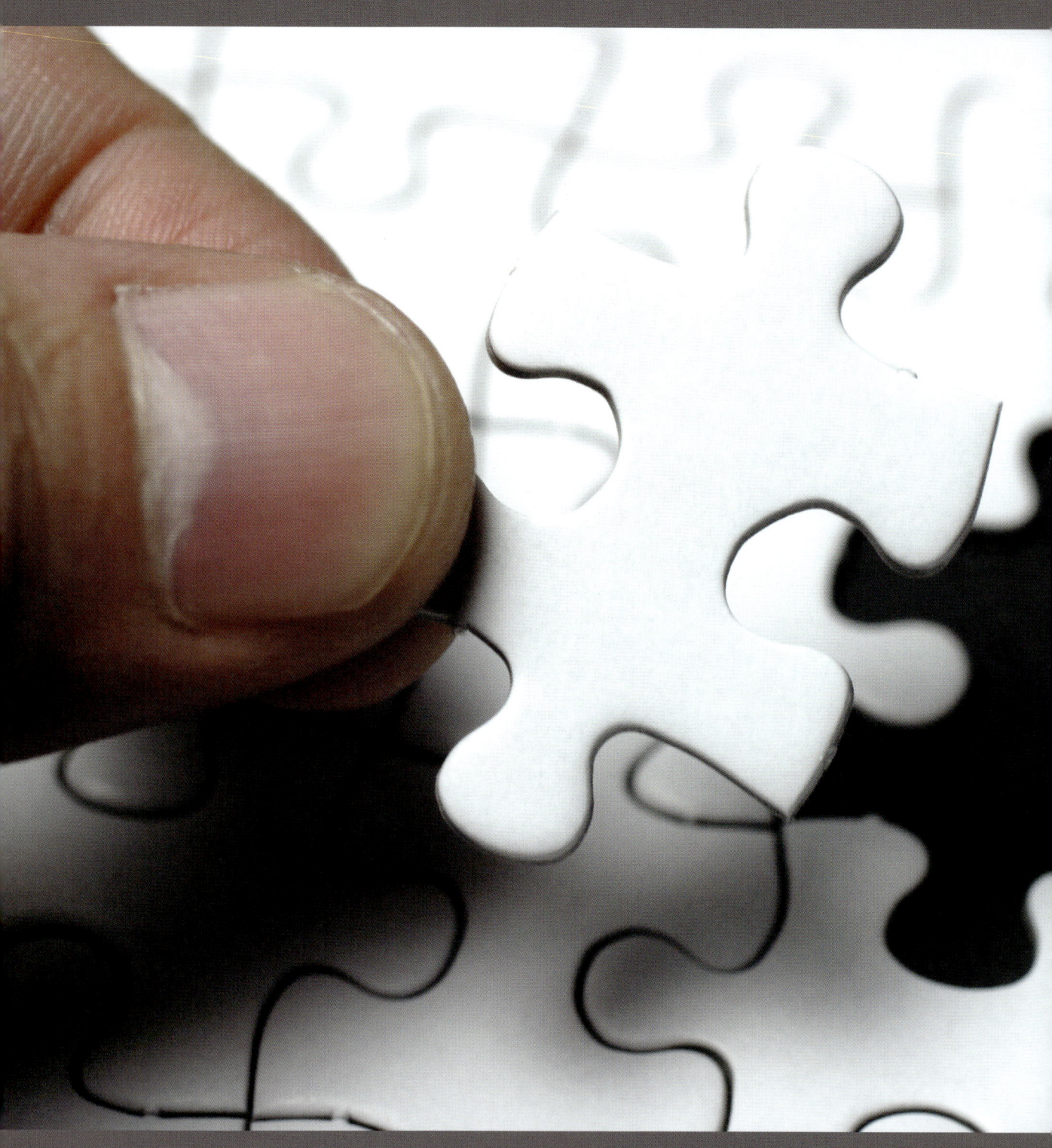
Figure 11.1 Finishing Touch.
© istockphoto.com/blackred

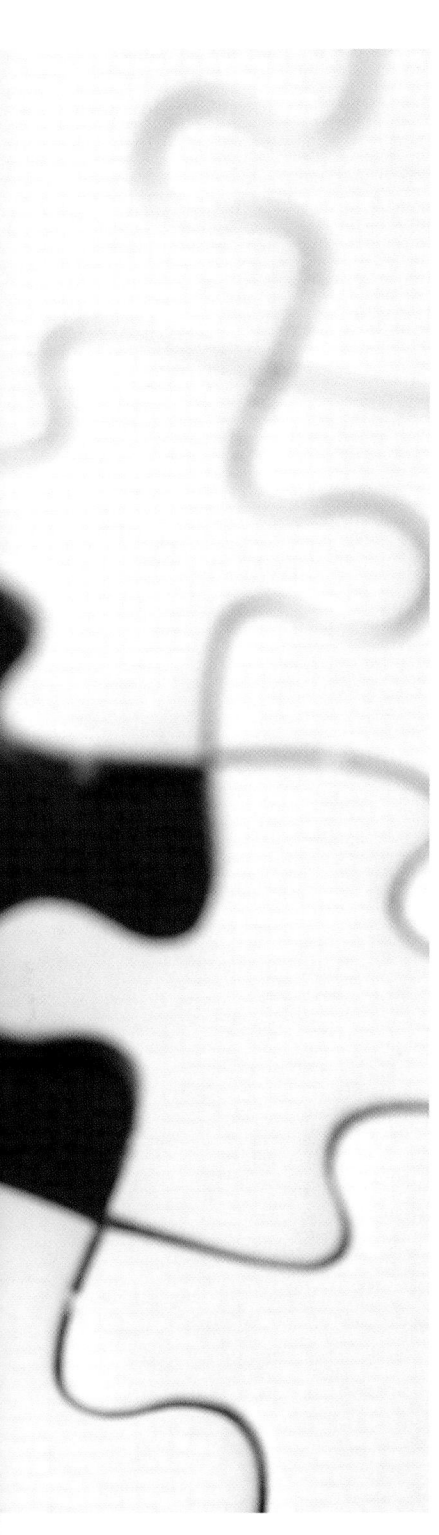

11
Putting It All Together

We've covered the sexy stuff—taking, creating, and processing your photos—and now it is time to dig into the more mundane, but still vitally important, tasks—such as file management and metadata insertion—required for preparing your stock submissions. Just as with processing our photos, software tools are required to get these jobs done. And this is one more reason why I have been working with Lightroom for the last three-plus years. I have found greater efficiency from having a single application that can take me from start to finish, aside from the occasional side trip to Photoshop (or Elements), and perform all the tasks required to submit my work as stock, as well as any other photographic projects I pursue.

If you're not using Lightroom 3, and that is perfectly fine, then you'll still learn about tasks you need to complete, but you'll need to apply that information in the application(s) you are choosing to use. The software is not really the key; it is doing all the steps—such as backing up memory cards, applying copyright metadata, organizing your files, choosing your picks, and applying titles, captions, and keywords—in the most orderly and efficient manner as possible so that you don't miss anything and don't get bogged down in the details. There are many roads to the finish line, and if you have certain systems that already work for you but are different from mine, then keep on keeping on.

I use the word workflow a lot, but what I mean is that over time we develop systems for completing common tasks that are required for getting in-camera work ready for the world. Each of these tasks contains steps of their own, but when strung together, the steps form a continually tested and well-worn path that helps us become more efficient and produce better work. Feedback, in the form of frustration, success, loss, and enjoyment, helps us to refine our processes and tweak our steps. A workflow is not something carved in stone, but rather a living, breathing set of actions that grows and changes as we grow and change as photographers. I am not doing all the same things today the same way I did 10 years ago, and I am quite certain I won't be doing all the same things the same way 10 years from now. What I humbly want to offer you is a view of the cumulative knowledge I have gained, in the hope that you will find key elements that you can take away and use to construct your own system.

First Things First

It is in your best interests to treat the contents of your memory cards like gold. You may not know the true value of what you have on that card for days or months or even years later, so make the first action of your after-capture workflow the duplication of the contents of your memory card onto at least two other storage mediums, before you format that memory card and put it back into service.

This is one of the most fragile points in the workflow, because unless you are shooting with a camera that has dual memory cards, or are shooting tethered, with photos being saved to the card and computer simultaneously, then your precious photos only exist on a single, tiny, highly portable, easily lost memory card. If you are shooting in the studio, at home, or otherwise near your computer, the logical choice would be to copy your memory card on to one of your drives as soon as you are able. Having your photos on one memory card and one hard drive sure beats just a memory card, but chances are you are going to want to format that memory card pretty soon (so you can add more photos to it), but then you are down to just having your photos on one hard drive, which is not ideal. Let's look at two other options.

Backups on the Go

Note

Don't format your memory card until after your photos have been safely copied to your primary storage so that you always have two copies at all times.

One way to address the issue is with a portable photo storage/viewer device. I picked up an Epson photo viewer (there are other brands that perform the same function) a couple of years ago, and it has gained a permanent home in my kit. These devices are essentially battery-powered external hard drives with built-in card readers that allow you to simply pop in a memory card while out shooting, and back it up on the spot, which gives you two copies on two storage devices. This can provide an incredible amount of peace of mind until you are able to copy another set of those photos to your primary storage device, and include them in your next full system backup.

Some of these devices also include an LCD screen for previewing your photos (which is fun on the ride home), as well as output ports for transferring data to your primary system. They can be pricey (several hundred dollars or more), so shop around.

Software Solutions

Another method to achieve early redundancy in your workflow is to use software that can copy your photos from your memory card to two different drives at the same time. This way, you create a duplicate set of originals right out of the gate, to provide a safeguard until your full system backup runs. This might sound confusing at first, but if you think about it, few people are likely to run a full system backup more than once a day (most people are lucky to back up their data once a week), so the potential exists for your photos to be left out of your backup system anywhere from hours to days. Lightroom has a memory card backup function built into the import process, which I'll cover later in this chapter within the context of the entire Lightroom import process, but there are other applications that have memory card backup functionality, too, such as ImageIngester (www.imageingester.com) or Photo Mechanic (www.camerabits.com), which are both excellent programs in their own right, and they offer a host of other features for managing your photos. The point is, just using your operating system's file browser to copy the photos off the memory card is slower, doesn't offer as many features, and leaves you without a backup. So check out each application (there are likely to be others) and focus on the core task: backing up your photos as soon as possible.

> **Note**
>
> It is best to format your memory card in the camera, so that the card is set up the way the camera requires, after verifying the photos have been safely duplicated and are corruption-free, as opposed to using software to delete or format the cards.

Why not use this early duplicate set as your regular backup system? I prefer a backup system that is a complete mirror of my primary storage, so that should the primary fail, it is a simple matter to seamlessly replace the lost data with the backup. The import backup that I describe here is a one-time backup of the memory cards. As soon as I start working with my photos and deleting the real duds, creating new versions, and possibly renaming existing files, my primary storage is no longer in sync with this import backup copy. So I treat the import backup as only a temporary backup to allow me to safely send my memory cards back into duty, and once my full system backup is up to date, these temporary backups are discarded.

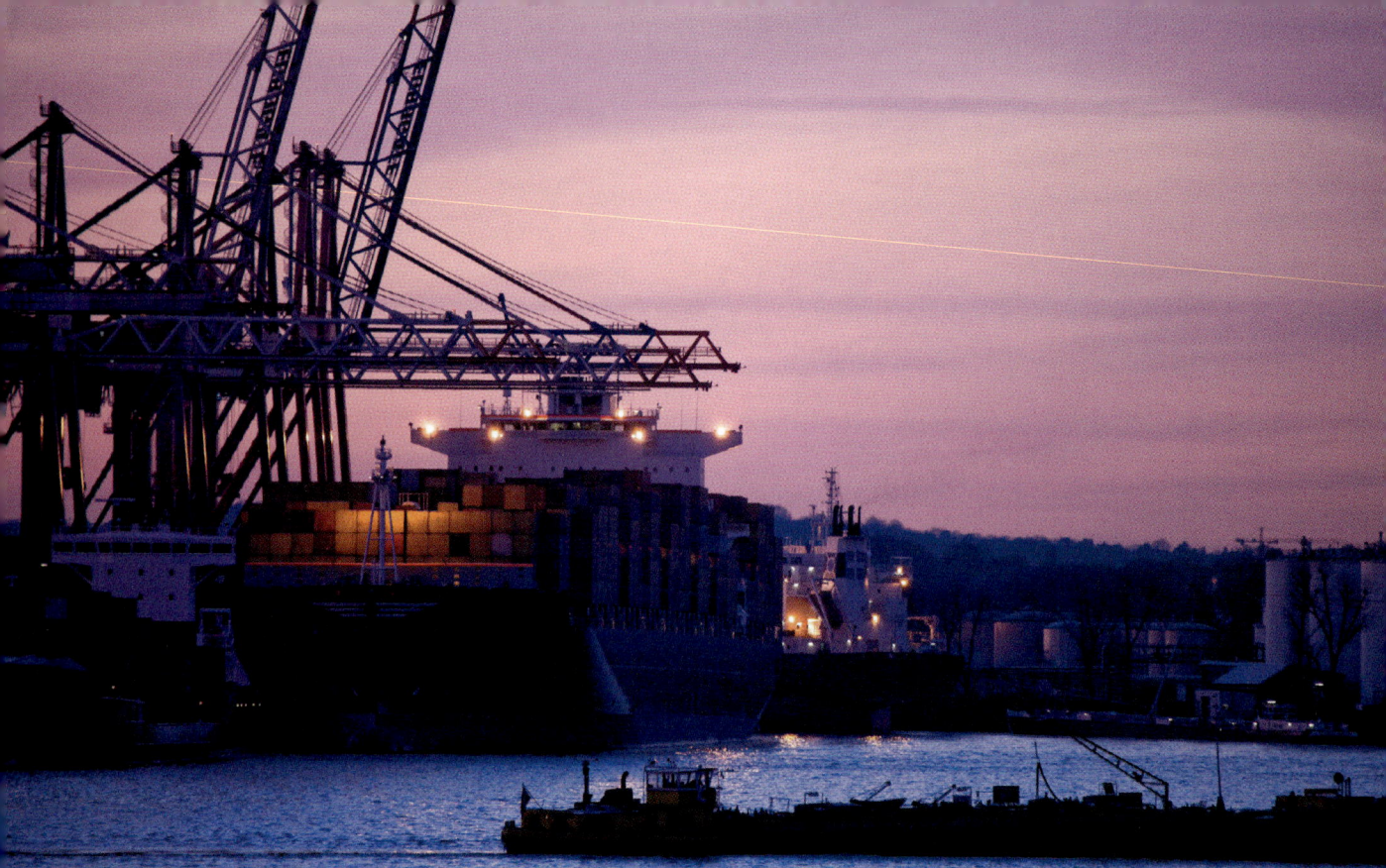

Figure 11.2 Container Terminal, Harbor. Downloaded over 200 times.

Container Terminal, Harbor

Creator	Arne Thaysen (istockphoto.com/goldhafen)
Started	2005
Home	Germany
Total portfolio	1,259
Total downloads	Over 36,000
About this photo	Arne says, "The color concept/scheme of this photo is key to its success. The high contrast and saturation create a vibrant look, which is emphasized in the mix of cool daylight and warm artificial light. The colors match well and create a serene and moody atmosphere. Captured with a Canon EOS-1Ds Mark II and 100-400mm lens."
Arne's tip	"Patience and anticipation make a great photo. Take your time, wait for and anticipate the perfect moment. Use a tripod, create a sophisticated composition, and wait for the right light and action to happen."

Importing into Lightroom

I've been working with photographers (at all levels) with Lightroom since it came out, and while people are usually impressed with its image-processing ability, they are commonly confused by the role of the catalog, as well as the whole import concept. So, before we dive into the how-to, let's take a peek under the hood.

Lightroom is a photo editor built upon a database. Inside this database, commonly referred to as the *catalog*, is all the data about your photos. This includes all the EXIF metadata created by the camera at the time the photo is taken (things like shutter speed, f-stop, and ISO) as well as all the data you add in Lightroom (such as keywords, titles, captions, ratings, and so on) and all the adjustments you make in the Develop module.

The import process is simply the doorway to the catalog. During the import process, Lightroom creates a new database entry for every photo and fills that entry with all the information contained in each photo's own metadata as well as each photo's file name and its location on disk. That is the sole purpose of importing. However, there are a few other tasks that can be accomplished via the Import dialog that save you time and effort, such as:

- Copying photos from a memory card to a destination of your choosing
- Copying photos from a memory card to a secondary destination for backup
- Converting copies of the photos to DNG (Digital Negative) format, and saving them to a destination of your choosing
- Renaming the copies
- Applying common metadata you want embedded in all of your photos
- Applying specific develop adjustments through saved presets

While most new imports into Lightroom will come from memory cards, it is also just as easy to import photos that are already on your hard drive, in which case Lightroom simply notes their current location and imports all existing metadata into the catalog. At no time are your photos actually *inside* of Lightroom. Lightroom does create previews, which are essentially JPEG copies, of all your photos and stores the previews in a special cache alongside the catalog file. Your actual photos will always be on your hard drive at the location of your choosing. With that in mind, let's move on to how the import process works.

Note

Remember, when you open Lightroom, you are really opening a catalog file, and then accessing and changing the data contained within that catalog. You can't open Lightroom without also opening a catalog.

Note

DNG is Adobe's Digital Negative format, which is essentially an openly documented file format for storing raw photo data. You can learn more about DNG by going to www.adobe.com/products/dng/.

Import Interface Orientation

It feels a little odd to call something that takes over your entire screen a dialog box, but while the Lightroom Import dialog box might be overwhelming at first, it is logical in its design. Let's step through it in a logical fashion.

On the left side, you will choose the source location of the photos to be imported. This can be a memory card, optical drive, or hard drive. The selected source in **Figure 11.3** is a memory card.

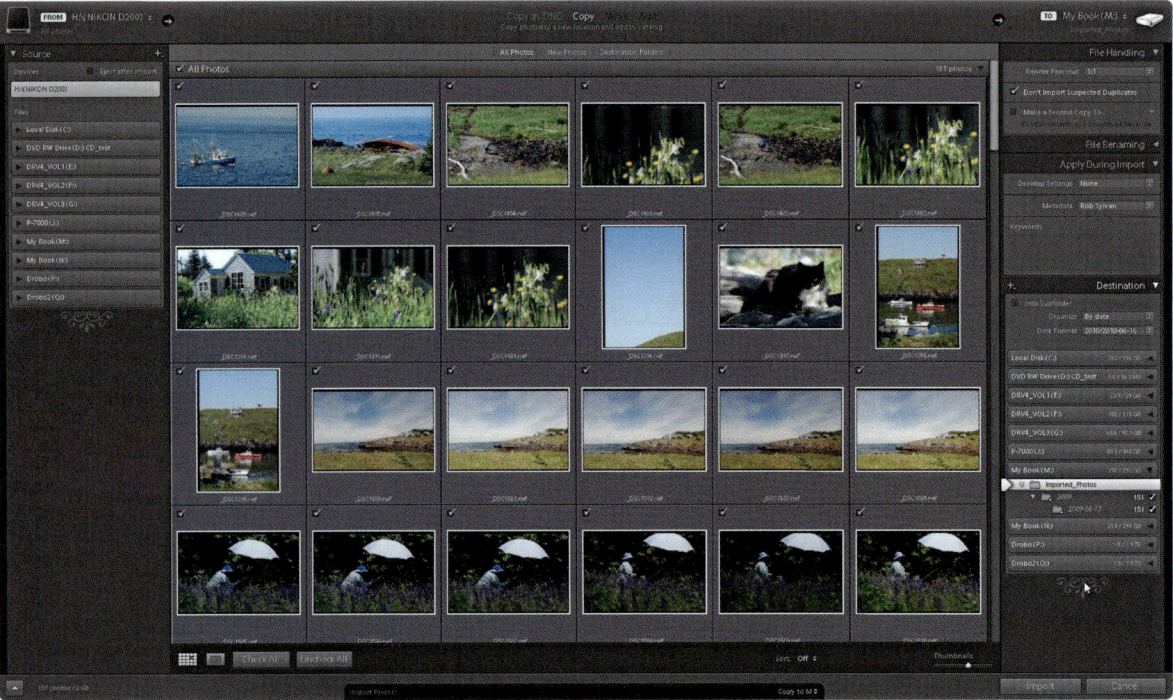

Figure 11.3 The Import dialog box.

The center of the screen is dominated by the thumbnails of the selected source location. Directly above the thumbnails are the options that control if you also want to copy these photos to a new destination, or simply add the photos to the catalog without changing where the source photos are located (use this for photos already on your drive). I recommend against ever using the Move option because Copy is safer, since it does not delete the originals as part of the process. I prefer to copy, verify that the copy was successful, and then manually delete instead of move. The Move option will be unavailable when a memory card is the source for this reason. The checkmarks on the thumbnails indicate which photos will be imported.

The right side of the dialog box is dedicated to configuring what you want to happen at the destination. It is here that you can choose to designate a secondary location for backup copies, change the file names of the new copies, batch-apply metadata and develop settings, and, of course, choose where on your drive you want the primary source copies to be located.

Once you become familiar with the way this dialog box works, you can click the arrow in the lower-left corner and switch to the compact view, which shrinks the dialog box down to focus on the bare essentials. Click the same arrow a second time to revert back.

A Typical Import

The most common import scenario we face is bringing photos from a memory card to their new permanent home on your disk drive of choice. Let's walk through the steps.

1 With Lightroom open, choose File > Import Photos, or click the Import button in the Library module, to launch the Import dialog box.

2 Select the source location that contains the photos you want to import (**Figure 11.4**). In this case, I chose the memory card in my card reader, but you have access to all the other drives and connected devices on your system.

3 Configure the type of operation you want to take place (**Figure 11.5**).

   Choosing Copy is the most common option, but if you want to also convert to DNG at this time you can choose Copy as DNG instead. See my previous note to learn more about the benefits of DNG. If you want to import existing photos on disk, choose Add.

Figure 11.5 Choosing the type of operation.

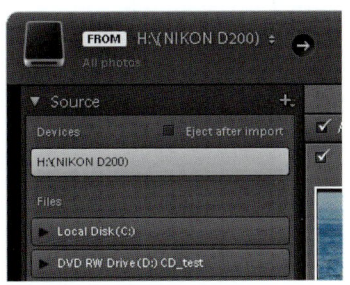

Figure 11.4 Selecting the source.

4 Deselect any photos you do not wish to import by unchecking the box on each thumbnail.

This is helpful for any obvious inside-the-lens-cap shots or other misfires, but I don't advise spending too much time weeding the garden at this stage. There will be time for that later. That said, you can double-click any thumbnail to zoom in for a closer look, and double-click again to return to the thumbnails.

5 Configure the File Handling panel (**Figure 11.6**).

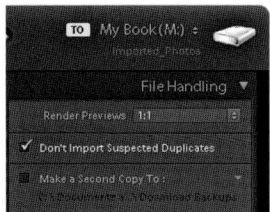

Figure 11.6 The File Handling panel.

The Render Previews drop-down menu allows you to schedule Lightroom to completely render all previews of your imported photos immediately after the import process is complete. Lightroom will render previews as needed automatically, but it can help speed your after-import workflow to have all the 1:1 (full size) previews already rendered. So in a stock workflow, I suggest setting this to 1:1.

When checked, Don't Import Suspected Duplicates means Lightroom will prevent any duplicates (same file name, capture date, and file size) from being added to the catalog. This is worth keeping checked at all times.

If you have not already backed up your memory card to another drive prior to import, then all you need to do is check the Make a Second Copy to box and choose a folder on a different drive than the one chosen in the Destination panel. I didn't check that box because my card is already backed up on my portable drive, but I want to point out this second copy option exists if a portable drive doesn't suit your needs. Both options achieve the same duplication end result.

6 (Optional) Choose a file name template.

When using a copy operation, you have the choice of renaming your photos as part of the process by checking the Rename Files box in the File Renaming panel, which provides access to a number of preset naming templates and an editor with which to customize your own. Leave the box unchecked to retain the camera-generated file names. You can always use Lightroom to rename photos later if desired.

7 Apply develop settings and copyright metadata (**Figure 11.7**).

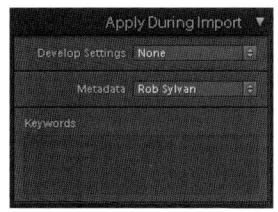

Figure 11.7 The Apply During Import panel.

Because I customize my default settings for raw photos (as described in Chapter 8), I tend not to apply Develop Settings via presets during import, but the option exists.

However, I do highly recommend applying a basic metadata preset that contains your copyright and contact information to every import. I'll show you how to create a custom template in the next section, so that all you need to do is select the template from the Metadata drop-down menu and the information will be applied to each imported photo.

There is a Keywords field in this panel, but I advise that you to leave it empty and do all your keywording later in the process. Anything entered into this field will be applied to every photo you are importing.

8 Choose the destination drive and folder (**Figure 11.8**).

This is the actual location on the drive to which you want Lightroom to save the copies of your photos. The Destination panel displays all available drives, and even shows how much free space is left on each drive. Select the drive you want, and drill down to the folder that contains your photos.

At the top of the panel, you can check the Into Subfolder box and create a new folder on the chosen drive if needed. The Organize drop-down menu provides the option to let Lightroom automatically create new subfolders based on the capture date of each photo by using the By date option, or you can choose Into one folder, and Lightroom will save all copies into the designated folder.

I prefer a date-based structure because it is simple, automated, and scalable. I use collections, metadata, and keywords to find photos later, so I don't rely on descriptively named folders for organization. There is no wrong answer, and I know many smart folks who prefer descriptive names. Trust your gut.

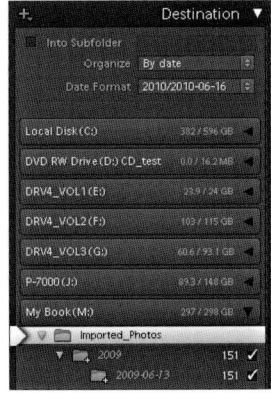

Figure 11.8 The Destination panel.

That may seem like a lot to configure, but one of the great things about the Import dialog box is that all the settings (except for the Keywords field) are *sticky*, meaning the next time you see the Import dialog box, it will display all your previous settings. Over time, you'll simply need to give the screen a once-over to confirm settings, and click the Import button at the bottom before heading off to refill your coffee cup.

> **Tip**
>
> At the bottom of the dialog box under the thumbnails is the Import Preset drop-down menu, which allows you to save various configurations of settings for reuse and easy access.

Creating a Metadata Preset

Previously, in the steps for configuring the Import dialog, I mentioned the importance of embedding basic copyright and contact information into the metadata of each of your photos. This is a free and easy way to help keep your name associated with your photos. Embedded metadata can easily be stripped out of a photo by anyone with the intention of doing so, but don't do the work for them! While inspecting photos, I have occasionally discovered people attempting to pass off the work of others. I can tell because the actual copyright holder had the foresight to embed his or her name and contact information in the photo's metadata. It really is worth doing and a snap to set up. Here's how:

1 Go to Metadata > Edit Metadata Presets to launch the Edit Metadata Presets dialog box (**Figure 11.9** on the next page). You can also access this from the Import dialog box by clicking the Metadata drop-down menu and choosing Edit Presets.

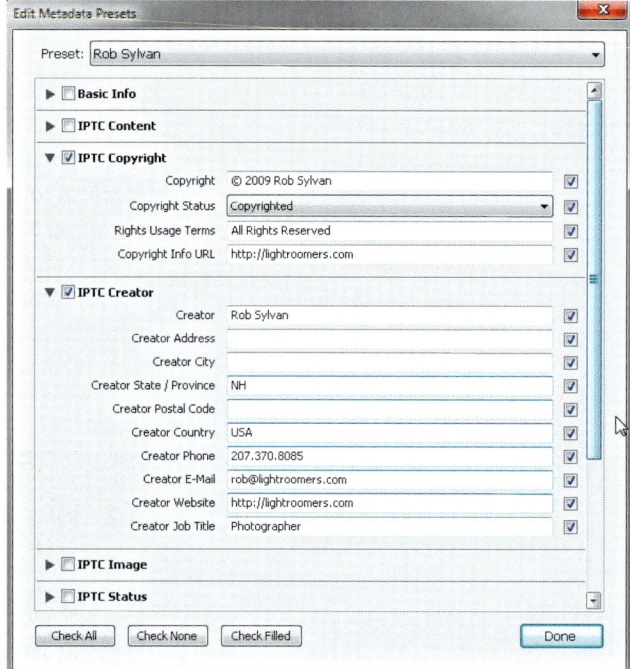

Figure 11.9 The Edit Metadata Presets dialog box.

2   Complete all of the fields in the IPTC Copyright section. You can create a © symbol on Windows by holding the Alt key and pressing 0169 on the numeric keypad, or on the Mac by pressing Option–G.

3   Enter your name in the Creator field of the IPTC Creator section, and then complete as much of the contact information fields as you want. At a minimum, enter an email address so that it would be possible for someone to make contact.

4   Complete any other fields you want to apply to every photo you import. You may not enter any more, but scroll through the dialog box and get acquainted with what is included. You can create multiple metadata presets and in time, you might create ones that are specific to certain locations, models, or jobs.

5   Click the Preset drop-down menu and choose Save Current Settings as New Preset. This will open the New Preset dialog box, where you enter a name and click Create.

6   Click Done to exit the dialog box.

Once the import process is complete you will have copies of all your photos saved to your chosen destination, an additional set backed up to a second drive, your metadata preset applied to all photos, and your Lightroom previews in the process of being rendered. Now the real work begins.

Wheat from the Chaff: Reviewing

OK, now that you are seeing all your imported photos inside of Lightroom's Library module, it is time to roll up your sleeves, and take a closer look at your new photos. When you are looking at rows of thumbnails in the Library module, that is called Grid view (**Figure 11.10**). This is a very helpful way to look at your photos, so helpful, in fact, that you can press the G key no matter where you are in Lightroom, and you will immediately jump to Grid view. A close companion of Grid view is Loupe view, which is how you can look at a single photo in more detail. You can jump to Loupe view from anywhere in Lightroom by pressing the E key. You will spend a lot of time jumping back and forth between those views, so make a practice of using those shortcuts for greater efficiency.

> **Tip**
>
> You can increase the size of Grid view thumbnails with the + key, or reduce the size with the - key.

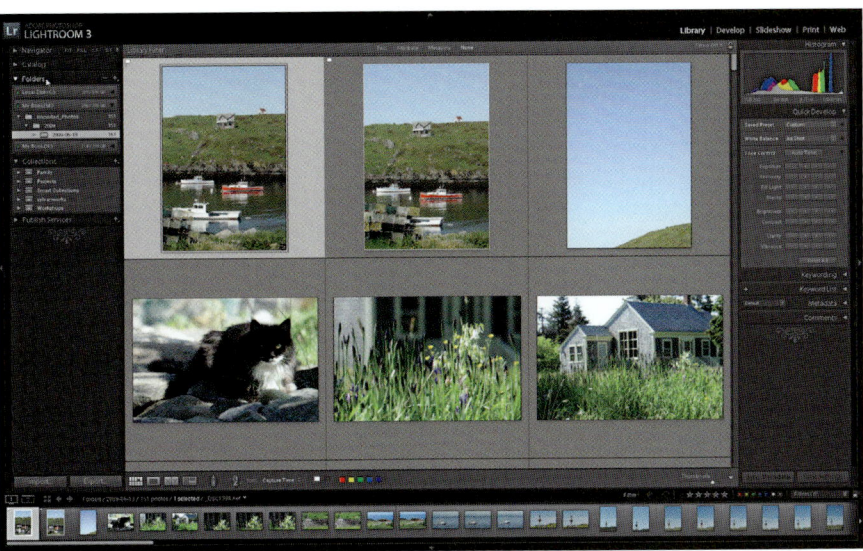

Figure 11.10 Recently imported photos shown in Grid view.

I also want to point out two panels—Folders and Collections—on the left side of the Library module (**Figure 11.11**), which are used for organizing your photos. The Folders panel is where all your imported folders will appear and where you can always go to access the photos that reside in a given folder. The Collections panel is where you'll find all of your collections. This is a sort of virtual folder that only exists inside the catalog. The key concept to keep in mind is that your photos will always reside in a single *folder*, but they can be added to any number of *collections* as you wish, to fit your organizational needs. We'll look at some ways to use collections a little later on in this chapter.

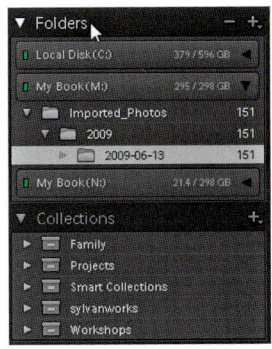

Figure 11.11 The Folders and Collections panels.

Be prepared to do the reviewing process of your photos in several passes. In fact, the first time you see your photos, just run right through them. I know you're dying to see them up close and personal, so just go to it and enjoy reliving the moments from when you were shooting. This is supposed to be the fun part, after all. Wait until you are ready for the second pass to make any decisions.

Decision Time

After you've made your first giddy pass (and possibly even had a good night's sleep), you should be ready to put on your inspector goggles (see Chapter 10) and get down to the ruthless decision making needed to determine which photos make the cut and are worthy of your time to develop further. The seemingly small decision you make now to *not* process a borderline reject photo can translate into saving you hours of developing time, days of waiting to find out it was rejected, and buckets of angst over having wasted all that time in the first place. Do yourself a favor and set the bar high. It may feel painful in the short term, but you'll thank me for it later.

Lightroom has a brilliant method for making this inspection task as efficient as possible with a few keyboard shortcuts and a simple labeling tool called Flags (**Figure 11.12**). There are three states of "flag-ness":

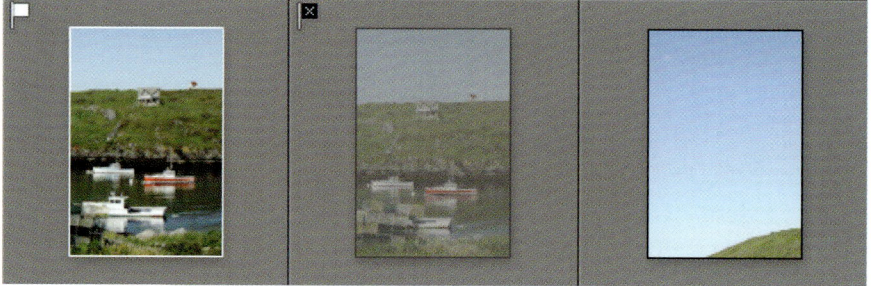

Figure 11.12 From left to right, Flagged, Rejected, and Unflagged.

> **Note**
>
> Applying a reject flag does not actually delete the photo. Think of flags as a simple notation device for your own use. You can change any flag state at any time.

- Flagged: Commonly called the *Pick* flag, it is used to identify your keepers or picks. It is represented by a white flag, and its keyboard shortcut is P.
- Rejected: This is used to identify the photos you want to remove/ignore/delete. It is represented by a black flag with an X in the middle. Its keyboard shortcut is X.
- Unflagged: Not flagged or rejected are represented by no flag. This keyboard shortcut is U.

With those three keyboard shortcuts in mind, let me introduce you to a menu option that will increase your reviewing speed. Go to the Photo menu and select

Auto Advance. Now, as soon as you apply any flag state to a photo, Lightroom will automatically advance focus to the next photo in line. Armed with that information, let's walk through the steps to efficiently evaluate and select your keepers:

1. Expand the Folders panel, and select the folder containing the photos you want to review.
2. With the first thumbnail in the grid selected, press E to jump to Loupe view.
3. Evaluate the Fit Screen zoom level.

   The default view in Loupe view is Fit Screen (where you can see the entire photo at once). At this zoom level, you can evaluate the composition and look for any other obvious problems such as under- or overexposure. If a slight crop can't improve the composition, or the exposure problems are beyond repair, then press X to flag as rejected and automatically move to the next photo. Otherwise, move to the next step.
4. Press Z to zoom in to 1:1 view.

   Pressing Z will toggle you between Fit Screen and 1:1 zoom levels.
5. Press the Home key (on your keyboard) to jump to the top-left corner of the photo.

   You need to evaluate every inch of your photo at 1:1 because that is what the inspectors will do. The Home key will always take you to the top-left corner and allow you to methodically scroll through the entire photo without missing a spot.
6. After inspecting that section of the photo, press the Page Down key to advance to the next section of the photo. Continue pressing the Page Down key, after evaluating each section, until you reach the lower-right corner.

   At 1:1 view, you can effectively evaluate focus (which is critical), take note of fixable problems (like sensor spots, purple fringing, and minor noise), and ultimately decide if this is a photo you want to spend time processing in Develop. If it is out of focus, then press X and auto advance to the next photo. If all the detail is missing from important highlights or shadow areas without hope of recovery, then press X and move on. If composition is good, exposure is good, and focus is sharp, then press P (to Pat yourself on the back), and move on to the next.

You want this procedure to be quick and smooth. Don't hem and haw over every photo. If you get to a photo that you find is too hard to decide between X and P, then don't sweat it; just press U to automatically advance without applying a flag, and you can revisit (and most likely reject) it later. With a little practice, you can quickly P, X, and U your way through hundreds of photos in no time at all.

> **Tip**
>
> You can hide all side and top panels quickly to maximize screen real estate for evaluating your photos by pressing Shift+Tab. Press T to hide the Toolbar under the photos. Use the same shortcuts to bring them back.

Collecting the Keepers

Now you have a folder full of flagged photos. We really just want to focus on the picks, but you might be wondering what to do with the rejects. There is no wrong answer here, but I prefer to delete my rejects. If I really felt they were beyond saving, then I don't need to waste disk space on them. If you are not ready to delete, just let them be, and we'll work around them. If you are ready to say good-bye, select Photo > Delete Rejected Photos, and have Lightroom gather up all the rejected photos in that folder and prompt you with the option to Delete from Disk (gone forever), Remove (just removes them from Lightroom's catalog), or Cancel.

Here's how you can leverage the database side of Lightroom to use the flagging work you just did to show you just your picks, while leaving the rejects and unflagged photos behind. I'd like to introduce you to smart collections. A smart collection is a way to automatically group photos together based on specific criteria that you decide. For example, let's go through the steps to create a simple smart collection that uses the folder name and flag status to group all of our picks together.

1   Choose Library > New Collection Set.

   A collection set is a way to group and organize collections within the Collections panel. This menu command will open the Create Collection Set dialog box. Enter a name for the shoot you are working on. I named mine Monhegan Island, which is where I was shooting on this particular day. Click Create to add the collection set to the Collections panel.

2   Right-click the collection set you just created and choose Create Smart Collection.

   This will open the Create Smart Collection dialog box (**Figure 11.13**).

3   Enter a descriptive name for the smart collection.

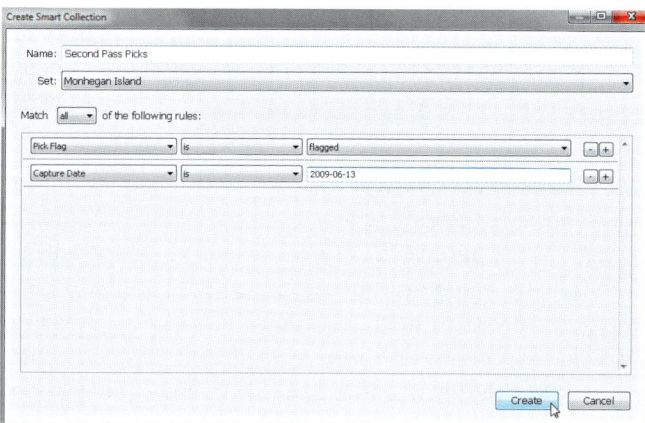

Figure 11.13
Create Smart Collection dialog box.

4   Click the drop-down menu for the first rule shown and select Pick Flag, and set it to *is flagged*.

5   Click the plus sign at the end of the first rule to add an additional rule.

6   Click the drop-down menu for the second rule and select Folder, set it to *contains*, and enter the name of folder.

   I chose Folder as my criteria, but when you click the rule drop-down menu, you will see a wide range of criteria from which to pick. If you had photos that ranged over several days of shooting, then try Capture Date set to a date range instead. This is a very powerful way to leverage the database. Experiment with rule combinations to tailor the smart collections to your way of working.

7   Click Save to add the smart collection to the collection set.

Lightroom will then automatically gather up all photos that meet those criteria and assemble them in that smart collection. You now have all your picks neatly grouped and organized, and you no longer have to look at your Unflagged and Rejected photos that are excluded from this smart collection. You can remove photos from this smart collection by changing the flag state to Unflagged or Rejected (if you find you were too generous in your earlier appraisal). Likewise, you can go back to the original folder and Flag any other photos you decide you want to include. Moving forward, we'll just be working with our picks, to add titles, descriptions, and keywords to our masters before taking them into Develop to make them look their best.

The Wonderful World of Metadata

The quality of your photos may get you in the door of each stock site, but there are three types of metadata you need to add to your photos—titles, descriptions, and keywords—in order for image consumers to find your photos among the great sea of existing stock content. Each stock site uses this data in slightly different ways, but this metadata is the key to making your photos more findable by both the internal search mechanism each site has, as well as external search engines (such as Google).

Lightroom has a suite of tools in the Library module to help you add this information efficiently. When the final versions of your photos are exported out of Lightroom, all of the titles, descriptions, and keywords you've added will be written to each photo, which in turn is read by each stock site's ingestion process, and then used on each website to help people find the photos. It is also important to mention that each site has standards for proper metadata entry, and a poor job of keywording (typically due to adding irrelevant keywords) can result in rejected submissions.

Search Engine Optimization

The majority of stock sites rely solely on keywords for their internal search mechanisms (Dreamstime is a notable exception for including title, description, and keywords), but all sites show some combination of title and description on each photo's display page as part of their search engine optimization (SEO) efforts. A large percentage of any website's traffic arrives via search engine results, and stock sites try to optimize the code on their Web pages to gain greater visibility in the search results.

Here's an example: Open your Web browser and go to images.google.com, which is Google's image search portal. Enter "geese migration" (without the quotes) and check the first page of results. At the time of this writing, one of my geese migration photos from Chapter 3 (**Figure 11.14**) was the first result. There are many factors that affect search placement, and getting to be the first result is not realistic for all photos, and not really the goal. This is simply to illustrate that you have a role in the process, so make the most of it.

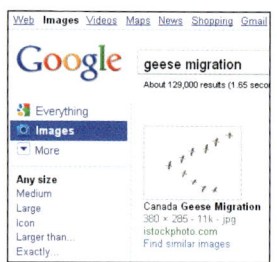

Figure 11.14 Google images search result for geese migration.

Clicking on that thumbnail takes you right to the file detail page for that photo on iStockphoto (**Figure 11.15**). That is exactly the kind of traffic the site likes to have. When you look at the actual page on iStockphoto, you will see that the title I entered, "Canada Geese Migration" is used as the page's Title tag (which is the HTML code that displays a page's title in your browser's Title bar). The page title is a very important factor in SEO terms.

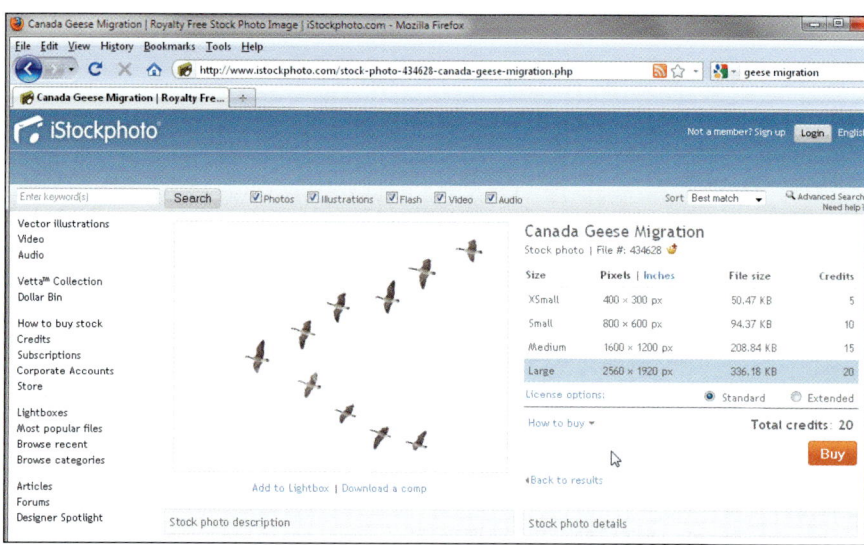

Figure 11.15 File detail page on iStockphoto showing how the title and description are used.

Another important factor is the file name of the page and of the image itself, and that title information was used in both locations making the link to that page www.istockphoto.com/stock-photo-434628-canada-geese-migration.php. The supporting textual information on that page is another factor, and that is where the photo's description, and to some extent its keywords, can also play a part. Shutterstock actually uses the photo's description for the file detail page's Title tag and file name in the same way.

To this end, you want to keep your titles short, relevant, and to the point. Here are some tips for good titles:

- Resist the temptation to get cute or clever.
- Use the most important words at the beginning.
- Focus on the key message that photo communicates.

The description area is where you can expand on the message in the title and even provide additional important detail, such as geographic location or some other relevant information a customer might find helpful in deciding if that photo is right for a certain project. When entering geographical information, keep in mind that you are dealing with a global audience, and country names are important to include. I live in New Hampshire, and half the towns in my neck of the woods are named identically to towns over in England. If I take a photo in Manchester, it is important for me to be complete and provide "Manchester, New Hampshire, USA" to help avoid embarrassing mixups for potential customers. Let's walk through the actual process of entering titles and descriptions with our smart collection of picks.

Adding Titles and Descriptions

The Metadata panel (**Figure 11.16**), located on the right side of the Library module, provides a number of different ways to view the metadata associated with the selected photo. Click the drop-down menu in the Metadata panel header to explore each of the view presets and see what fields they contain. There's a lot of data in there, but for our purposes, we only need access to two fields for adding a title and a description to each photo we plan to submit for stock: Title and Caption.

Here's how to make short work of all the titles and captions for your collection of photos:

1. Select the first photo in the collection.
2. Click into the Title field and enter your title.
3. Press the Tab key to jump down to the Caption field and enter the description.

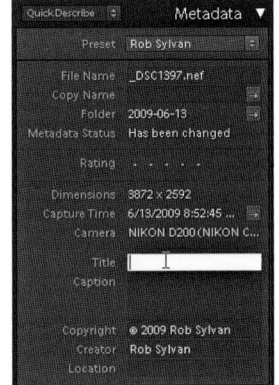

Figure 11.16 The Metadata panel set to Quick Describe view.

> **Tip**
>
> Lightroom doesn't provide support for customizing metadata views, but there is a plug-in that does. Check out the Metadata-Viewer Preset Builder: www.regex.info/blog/lightroom-goodies/metadata-presets.

4   Hold the Ctrl key (Mac: Command) and press the right-arrow key to move to the next photo in the collection with the Caption field still the active field.

The Ctrl (Mac: Command) arrow key trick works with both right and left arrows (in case you need to step back to an earlier photo) and regardless of what field you are editing. This allows you to keep your hands on the keyboard as you move through your photos without ever leaving the active metadata field.

5   After entering the caption for that photo, press Shift+Tab to jump up to the Title field and enter the title. When an editable field is active, pressing Tab jumps to the next editable field, and Shift+Tab jumps back to the previous field. However, keep in mind that if no text field is active, pressing Tab will show/hide both side panels.

6   Continue the process of entering the data in all those fields for the remaining photos in the collection.

With titles and captions completed, you will be primed for entering keywords. If you prefer to enter keywords first, that's fine. Do what works best for your workflow, but I find the process of entering titles and captions makes keywording much more fluid because your mind is already full of descriptive words about those photos, and you can refer to the entered titles and descriptions as reminders.

Keywording 101

The primary function of keywording, whether you add the keywords in Lightroom or any other program, is to describe your photos using the most relevant words possible to facilitate finding those photos later just by calling on a specific keyword. That's really all there is to it. I have seen a lot of people agonize over keywording as if they were tasked with curing cancer. The cause for their angst is the fear that somehow they just might miss the one critical keyword that every customer uses to find that particular photo, but somehow it escapes their notice. Relax. Focus. It isn't that complicated. Here's what you need to worry about:

- Don't be wrong. Seems obvious, but if you are not sure of the exact name of something you need to do your research, don't guess.

- Don't stretch. Stretching involves adding keywords for items that are technically included in the photo but are not important or relevant to the message of the photo.

- Be careful using conceptual keywords. Just because you once found the view from the top of a mountain to be inspiring, it doesn't mean that every photo of a mountain top deserves the keyword *inspiration*.

I asked Jordan Lane, the manager of Search Data at iStockphoto, what he knew about customer search behavior, and what tips he could pass along to contributors wanting to keyword effectively. According to Jordan, "Searchers, generally speaking, search broadly. It's not as important as you think to add excruciating amounts of keyword detail about your image, especially if you find keywording unpleasant or dull; the ones that pop in your mind right away will be the ones that sell your image."

You see, the most important competitive edge you can have in your keywords is to be relevant. Relevancy is highly rewarded because relevant search results make customers happy. Happy customers spend money. Happy, spending customers makes stock sites happy. Happy stock sites work to find ways to make relevant images appear higher in search results. This is a very positive feedback loop, and your goal should be focused on getting your photos into the loop. Relevant keywords are the most obvious keywords.

Jordan had more advice: "Niche images, particularly scientific images, definitely benefit from more detail, as searchers familiar with a given subject will search on more arcane terms related to their field of choice. That said, make sure things are accurate when dealing with niche subject matter, it's better to be too broad than to be detailed and wrong. A real lab tech is going to know that the man with the test tubes full of green food coloring and dry ice isn't actually mapping the human genome. If keywording is a process that takes you 30 minutes per image to even come up with a basic set, it's probably more trouble than it's worth to come up with extras for very general images. If you can blaze through a file and effectively keyword it in a few minutes, it might be worth the extra time to capture the little things."

Let's look at an example to bring this home. My Christmas Tree photo (**Figure 11.17**) has managed to be found over 5,600 times in the last three years. I applied 20 keywords to that photo, and for the purpose of this book I asked iStock to tell me the order of most relevant to the least ones based on customer behavior. This is how it looks from most to least: Christmas, Christmas tree, Snow, Winter, Tree, Christmas Decoration, Lighting Equipment, Holiday, Christmas Lights, Outdoors, Photography, Decoration, Evergreen Tree, Morning, Color Image, Nobody, Cold, Multi Colored, Copy Space.

From what they told me, the top ten keywords did the lion's share of the work in bringing in those 5,600 downloads. Is it really surprising to think that the majority of traffic came to this photo via the keyword *Christmas*? Of course not. Should I have not bothered including the last 10 keywords? No, those are still helpful, but keywords like Photography, Nobody, Color Image, and Copy Space are really there to help the *power searchers*, the people who like to drill deep down in the results using multiple keywords. For example, someone looking for a photo of a Christmas tree without any people in the scene could use the combination of Christmas tree AND Nobody, with the expectation that the search results would not include any photos of people. It's always good to help the power users!

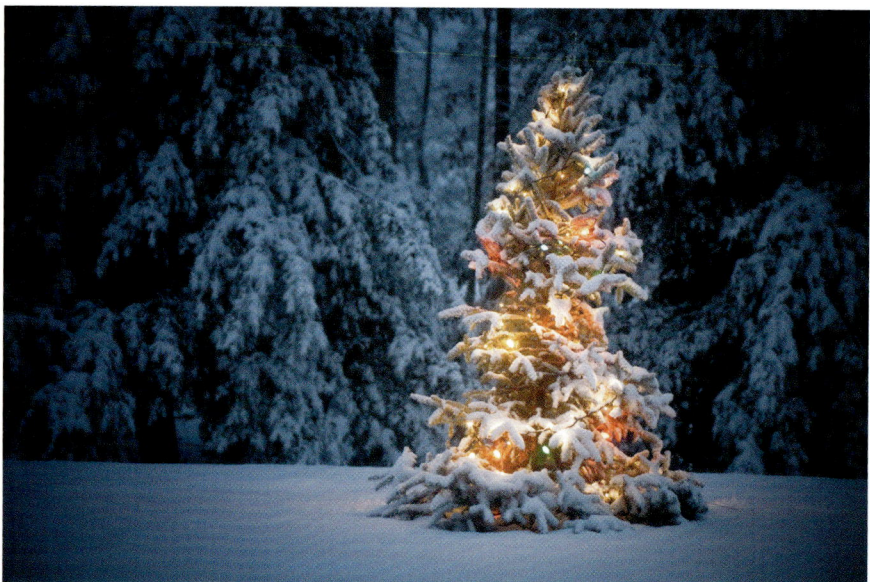

Figure 11.17 Christmas Tree.

How about if I added the keyword *Santa*? No, the photo is about Christmas, but there is no jolly old elf in that photo; that would be wrong. What about *Snowflake*? There is snow on the ground, but it isn't snowing and there are no visible flakes; that would be stretching. What about the concept of *Goodwill*? Christmas as a holiday is evocative of many things to many people, but this particular photo does not at all communicate goodwill. For every keyword you consider adding, you need to ask yourself a few questions, such as:

- Would a customer performing a search with just that single word expect to find my photo in the results?

- Does my photo communicate that keyword in a significant way?

If the answer to either question is no, then that is not the right keyword for your photo. If you can honestly answer yes, then you are on the path to keywording righteousness. If you are thinking *maybe*, then that means *no*. Sorry. Refer back to Chapter 3, and try to see your photos through the eyes of a designer. Think about how you envisioned your photos being used when you created them. Think about the types of searches a given designer might use to find your photo. Keywording with the needs of the customer in mind is one of the surest ways to avoid rejections due to poor keywords, commonly referred to as *keyword spam*. With that in mind, and your titles and descriptions freshly embedded in the Metadata panel, let's get down to the task at hand.

Creating a Keyword List

One of the hardest aspects to keywording is creating a logical keyword structure, or hierarchy, to keep your keywords organized and to make the process of applying them to your photos more consistent and efficient. You can build you own, and keep adding to it over time. If you want to explore a time-saving shortcut to getting your hands on a pre-built keyword list with over 11,000 terms, you can invest $69.99 in David Riecks' *Controlled Vocabulary Catalog*, which comes in the form of a text file you can import into Lightroom. This is a big expense for someone just getting started, so file the ideas away for now if you found yourself instinctively clutching your wallet (or your heart). For me, I just figured how many hours it would take me to complete such a thorough list and decided my time was dearer than the cash. There's a host of free resources and tutorials on how to approach and complete your keywording tasks on David's site, worth a visit for everyone: at www.controlledvocabulary.com

A controlled vocabulary is simply a way to structure a set of terms in a consistent and logical manner. In some cases, a controlled vocabulary can also include synonyms, plural and singular forms of a word, and even other languages. iStockphoto's entire search system has a massive controlled vocabulary under its hood that allows a customer to search a single term, like say *orange*, and then be asked to clarify if they are looking for *orange* the fruit or *orange* the color (or both). More importantly, it allows for the translation of the word *orange* across 10 different languages. Not every site uses a controlled vocabulary, so make sure you spend time getting familiar with the nuances of each site's keywording standards.

Lightroom's Keyword List panel (**Figure 11.18**) allows you to import a custom keyword text list (as mentioned previously), or create your own from scratch. Trust me when I tell you that it will make your life much easier to have a keyword list, even a very basic one, started before you actually begin applying keywords to photos. For example, I have a number of shots of my dog in my portfolio, but I also have a number of other pets in my home, so I created a simple keyword structure that reflects my pet reality, which is shown in Figure 11.18. Here's how to start creating your own:

1   Click the + icon in the Keyword List panel header, which will open the Create Keyword Tag dialog box (**Figure 11.19**).

2   Enter the name of your keyword tag. In my case, I started with *animals*.

> **Tip**
>
> You can build a keyword list in any plain text editor, which some people prefer over creating it in Lightroom. Lightroom-news.com has an excellent cheat sheet to get you started: http://bit.ly/keywordList.

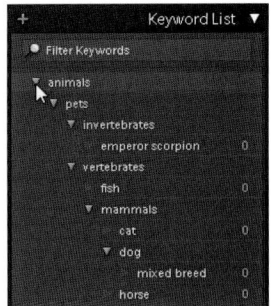

Figure 11.18 Keyword List panel showing a simple animal keyword structure.

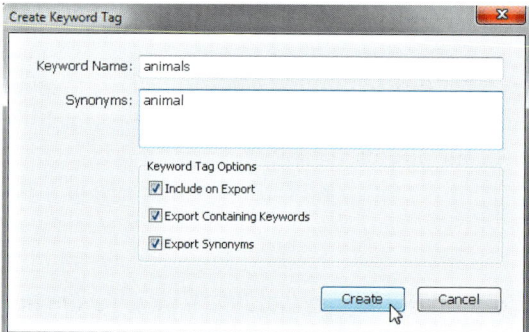

Figure 11.19 Create Keyword Tag dialog box.

3 Enter any important synonyms in the Synonyms field.

   This is where you might enter plural or singular versions of the word, synonyms, or even relevant key phrases. In my case, I only added the singular form of the word, *animal*.

4 Check the Include on Export box.

   You can leave this box unchecked when you want to add a word to your keyword structure that is meaningful to your system, but that you don't want to apply to exported photos. For example, if I added my dog's name as a keyword, I would not include it on export as it has no relevancy on a stock site.

5 Check Export Containing Keywords if desired.

   This tells Lightroom to include any keywords above this word in the hierarchy, if applicable.

6 Check Export Synonyms to add all your synonyms to the exported copy of your photo.

7 Click Create to add that tag to the Keyword List panel.

From there it is a matter of repeating that process for each keyword you want to add. Here are a few more things you need to know about creating a keyword list:

- Right-click a keyword to explore the pop-up contextual menu and find the commands for renaming, editing, and deleting existing tags, as well creating new tags.

- You can drag and drop one keyword into another to create a parent-child relationship.

- The Filter Keywords field at the top of the panel allows you to enter tags and reduce the visible keyword list to just tags that contain that word (makes handling large keyword list much simpler).

To give you a head start, and to let you take a closer look at the keywords in Figure 11.18, you can go to www.takingstockphoto.com/downloads/ and download a

> **Tip**
>
> Brainstorming relevant words for a given subject or photo can be hard. There are two free tools, created by other micro-stock contributors, that will help grease the gears: the PicNiche Toolbar (www.picniche.com) and the Keyword Wizard (www.deepmeta.com/Tools/Wizard/).

text file containing those tags and bring them right into your catalog. Save the animals.txt file to your desktop, then go to Metadata > Import Keywords, select the animals.txt file, and click Open. Be sure to check out the tips and resources I've included in this section. Once you have the beginnings of a keyword list, let's start applying those words to your photos.

Applying Keywords

There are a number of ways to apply keywords to photos in Lightroom. I'm not going to show you every possible way, but I will show you what I think is the most efficient, and dare I say almost fun (OK, that's a good example of stretching). We're going to use our keyword list, the Filter Keywords field (if you have a long list), and what Lightroom calls the Painter Tool (**Figure 11.20**), which lives in the Grid view Toolbar. The Painter Tool looks like a spray paint can, and functions in a similar fashion. The *paint* in this case will be a keyword or string of several keywords. Once the Painter Tool is loaded, you just click and drag it over all the relevant photos showing in Grid view. Here are the basic steps:

Figure 11.20
The Painter Tool.

1 Press Ctrl+Alt+K (Mac: Command-Option-K), or click the Painter Tool icon in the Toolbar, to enable the Painter Tool.

2 Click the Paint drop-down menu in the Toolbar and choose Keywords.

The Painter Tool can be used to paint on a range of other information.

3 Press Shift-Alt-Ctrl-K (Mac: Shift-Option-Command-K), or go to Metadata > Set Keyword Shortcut, to open the Set Keyword Shortcut dialog box (**Figure 11.21**).

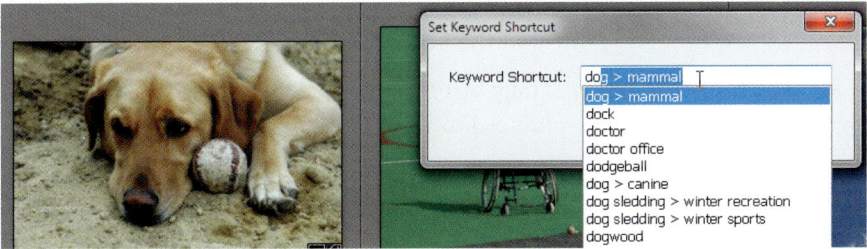

Figure 11.21 Keyword Shortcut dialog box displaying possible tags from my keyword list.

This is the quickest way to *load* the Painter Tool. You'll also see why I encouraged you to create your keyword list first, because as soon as you start typing a keyword into the Keyword Shortcut field, that database action kicks into gear, and Lightroom displays a list of all possible matches from your existing keyword list. You can press Enter to select the highlighted keyword, use the mouse to click on a tag showing in the list, or keep typing to enter the full word.

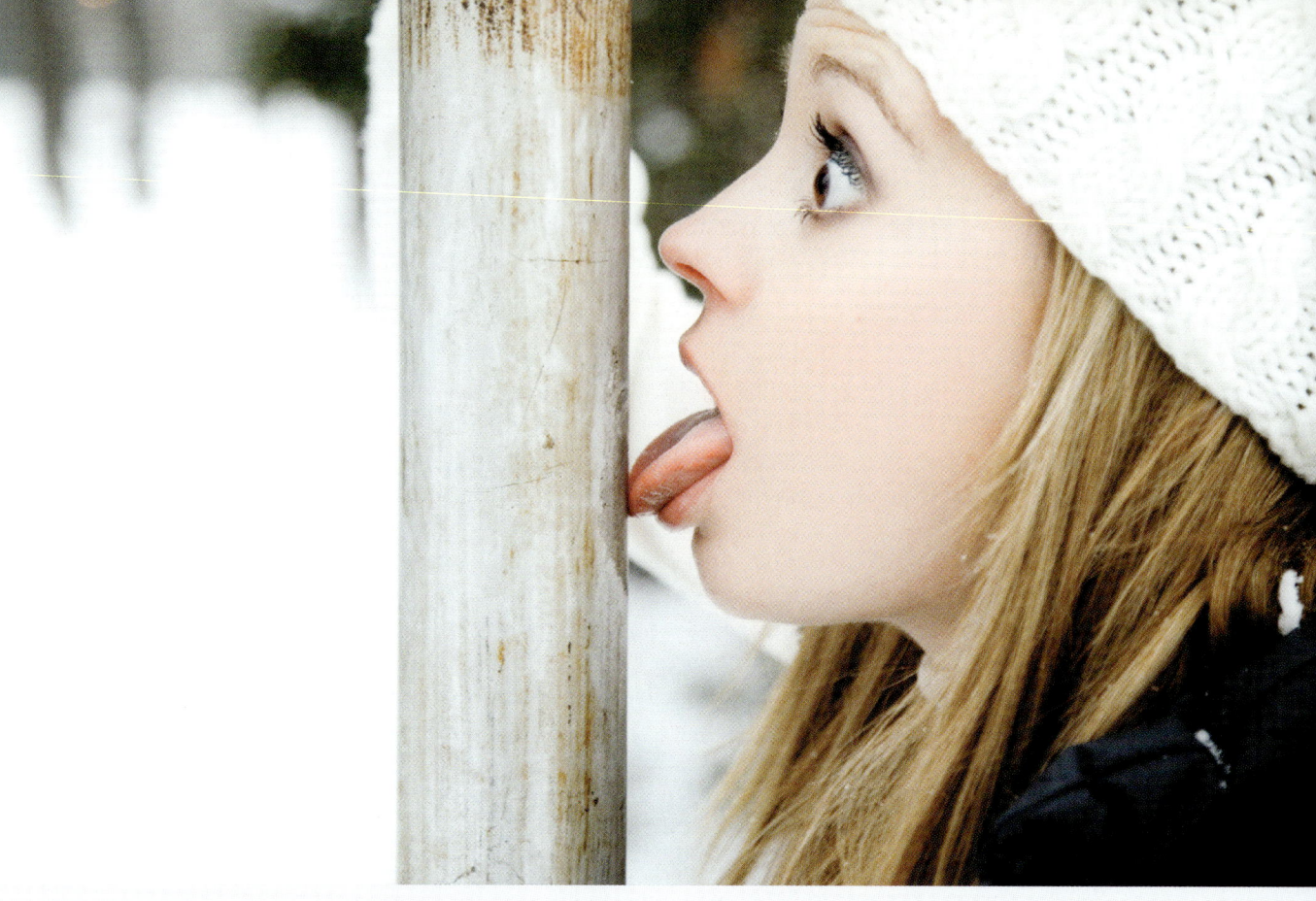

Figure 11.22 Sticky Situation. Downloaded over 800 times.

Sticky Situation

Creator	Joey Boylan (istockphoto.com/kangah)
Started	2004
Home	Canada
Total portfolio	3,966
Total downloads	Over 62,000
About this photo	Joey says, "This photo was successful because it is a situation we all can relate to, and it can be used in a variety of ways. It is a humorous photo, which can be applied to a variety of situations, plus it has copy space for graphics and text. It was captured with a Canon 1Ds MarkII."
Joey's tip	"It takes a lot of hard work, but don't give up. If you receive a rejection for a file, take it as constructive criticism and learn from it, and you will see yourself improve."

4 (Optional) If you want to apply additional keywords at the same time, then type a comma after the first word, and start typing the next keyword. Repeat as needed to load all the relevant keywords you want to apply.

5 Click and drag the Painter Tool over all relevant thumbnails (**Figure 11.23**).

Lightroom will display a "keywords assigned" message as they are applied. If you should over-spray onto the wrong photo, just hold the Alt (Mac: Option) key and single-click that photo to remove the misapplied keywords.

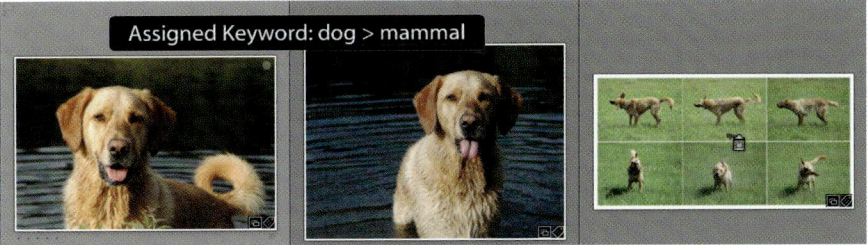

Figure 11.23 The Painter Tool applying keywords to three photos at once.

6 After applying those keywords to all relevant photos, call up the Keyword Shortcut dialog box to clear it out and load it with a new set of keywords.

I find that using the Painter Tool in conjunction with my keyword list is fast and efficient for large batches of photos. If the Painter Tool isn't working as well for you, keep in mind that you can always drag and drop photos onto keywords in your list, or drag and drop keywords onto your photos. There's always more than one way to get the job done.

What matters most, is that by the end of this process, you will have copied all your photos to your primary storage, backed them up, applied your copyright and contact information, identified all your keepers, and added an SEO-minded set of title, description, and keywords to all your picks. From here, you'll move on to making them look their best (see Chapters 8 and 9), before exporting final copies (see Chapter 12) that have all the work you've just done baked into the JPEG files you upload. ■

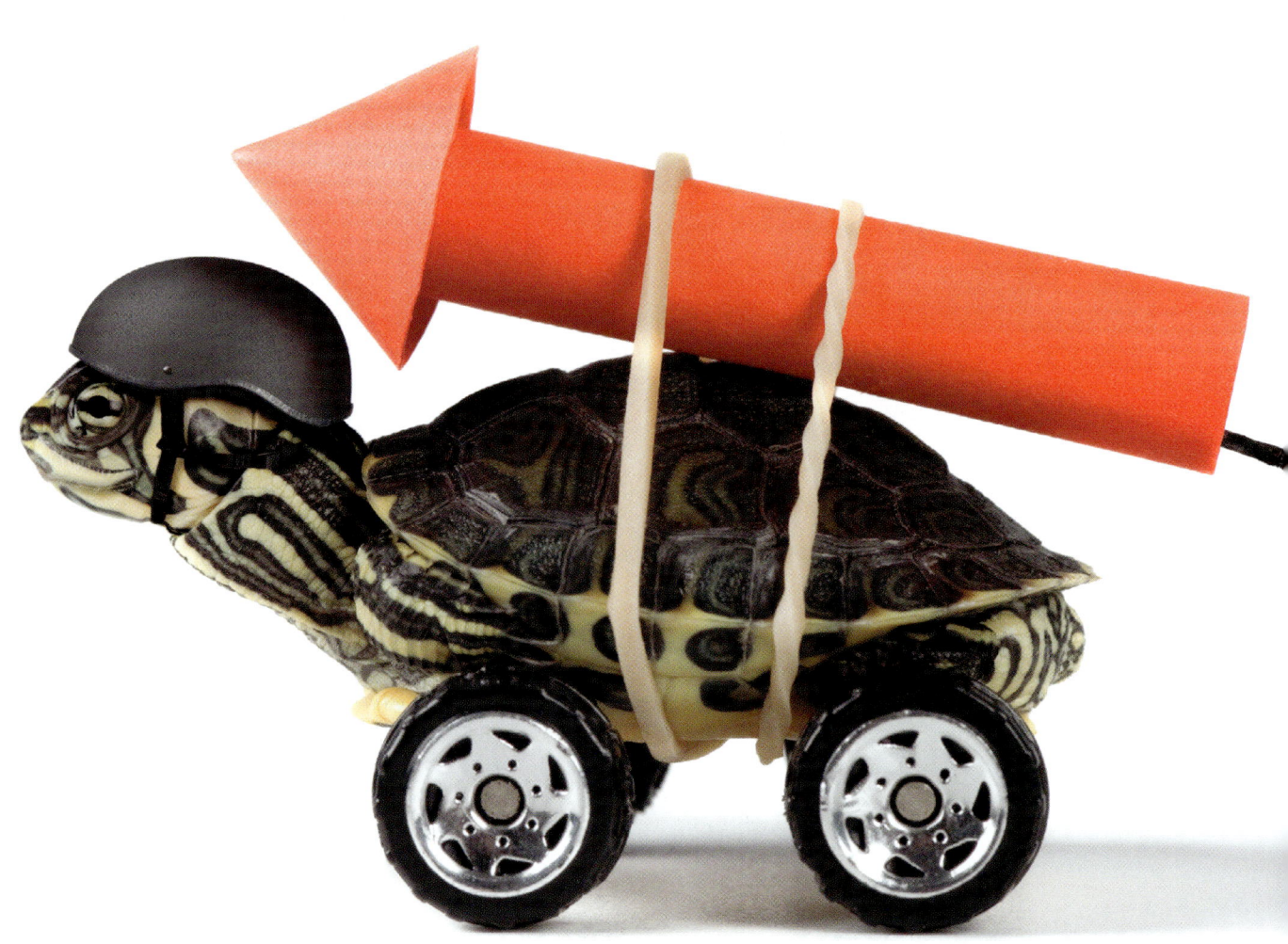

Figure 12.1 Stunt.
© istockphoto.com/craftvision

12
Moving Out into the World

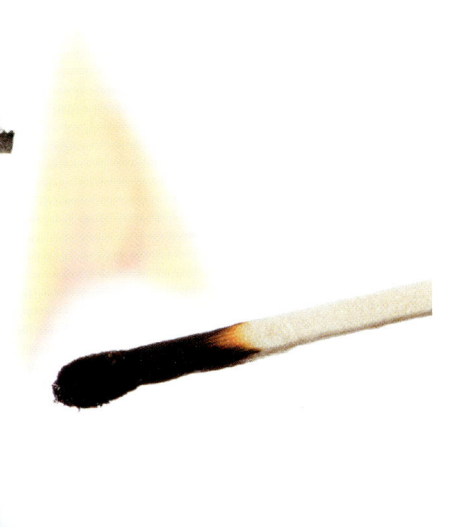

Consider this graduation day. Congratulations! Before you take everything you've learned up to this point and head out into the world, I want to arm you with some tips on how to prepare your final copies for submission, how to ace any entry exams you may face when setting up your contributor accounts, where to find additional online resources to help you succeed, and close out with a few parting words. Let's get to it.

Save Your Final Versions

I've shown you how to get your photos into Lightroom and how to use Lightroom to process them to look their best. So I wanted to close out the book with how to save the best quality copies. One of the most important things to keep in mind when working with Lightroom is that it never applies any changes to your originals; instead, it will only apply the adjustments you make to copies that are saved during some type of output. "Output," in Lightroom terms, can mean printing, creating a slideshow, creating a Web gallery, or exporting copies. For the purpose of preparing an output for stock, there are two methods of exporting copies that you can use; one is called Export and the other is Publish Services.

Lightroom Export

Prior to Lightroom 3, the Lightroom Export process was the only way to create copies of your photos with your Lightroom adjustments, based on your chosen output settings. The basic workflow is simple: you select the photos you want to export in Grid view and choose File > Export (or click the Export button), then configure the specific file settings—such as file type, file size, color space, and destination folder—in the Export dialog box (**Figure 12.2**) according to the needs of your output. When the export process is complete, you have a folder of photos that match your specifications.

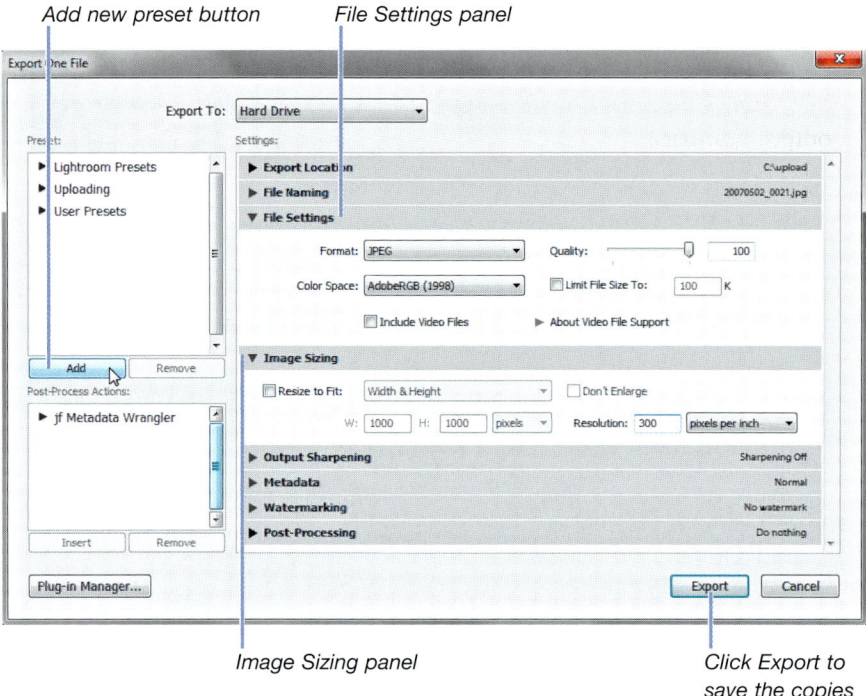

Figure 12.2 Lightroom Export dialog box.

When exporting your photos for submission to microstock, there are a few settings you need to get right:

- In the File Settings panel, choose JPEG as the format, set the Quality slider to 100, and choose AdobeRGB as the color space. Honestly, choosing sRGB as the color space is not a wrong answer, but Adobe RGB is the most often recommended choice between the two.

- In the Image Sizing panel, uncheck Resize to Fit so that Lightroom does not change the pixel dimensions of your exported copies, and set the value in the Resolution field to 300 pixels per inch. The pixels per inch setting simply writes that value into the photo's metadata, and it is solely for the benefit of customers who expect that number to be there because they were taught 300 pixels per inch equals high quality.

- In the Output Sharpening panel, uncheck the Sharpen For box so that no additional sharpening is applied to your copies. This setting is used for applying output sharpening to photos heading to an online printing service, or for photos that will only ever be displayed on screen. Since we don't know the final output destination of our stock photos, it is best to do no further sharpening.

- In the Metadata panel, leave both boxes unchecked. If you check Minimize Embedded Metadata, your keywords, title, and description will be stripped out. There's no reason to write keywords as Lightroom Hierarchy for this output destination.

It is entirely up to you where you save your photos on your drive prior to uploading and what you name them. When the dialog box is configured to your liking, and you've double-checked all the settings, do yourself a favor and click the Add button in the Preset section and save all your settings as an export preset that will recall these settings with a single click when preparing future stock submissions.

There is nothing wrong with continuing to use the Export dialog box with Lightroom 3 for saving out your final copies, but the new (with Lightroom 3) Publish Services panel in the Library module offers an interesting option to consider.

Lightroom Publish Services

You can think of Publish Services (**Figure 12.3**) as a sort of managed export. Just as with a typical export, you can save copies of photos to local folders on your drive. However, the difference between a Lightroom export and the Publish Services panel is that the latter creates a connection between the originals in your catalog and the published copies (at the location of your choosing) that you can manage from within Lightroom over time. In other words, you can assemble a special Lightroom collection of your top stock picks and publish (just like export) them to a folder on your hard drive, and then if you need to make changes to any of those published copies, such as if you get a rejection, you can make the correction in Lightroom and easily republish the improved version to resubmit.

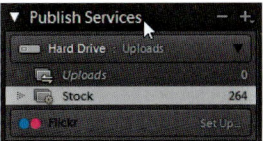

Figure 12.3 The Publish Services panel in Lightroom's Library module.

I really like the idea of having Lightroom manage my master originals inside the catalog, and at the same time, have a permanent home on my hard drive for the actual final copies I submitted for stock. Furthermore, I feel it is vitally important to give those final copies one last quick (but thorough) inspection before uploading them, and I mean specifically the copies saved out by Lightroom in this instance. You always want to visually inspect the actual photos you are uploading because those are the copies that the inspectors will be checking. You can catch any output configuration errors you may have made (like accidentally resizing too small, or even worse, resizing larger), or any technical problems you missed earlier in the process.

Note

Publish Services also has the potential to directly publish photos to some photo-sharing sites, like Flickr, but as of this writing, I do not know of any such options to publish directly to a stock site.

> **Tip**
>
> To learn more about the other Publish Service possibilities, such as Flickr, Smugmug, Facebook, and so on, head over to www.*publish.lightroomers.com*.

Let's go through the process of setting up a Publish Service that saves copies to a folder of your choosing on your hard drive to help clarify how this works. When you first expand the Publish Services panel (Figure 12.3), you will see two publish connections: Hard Drive and Flickr. The Hard Drive type of connection is designed for publishing copies to a local or shared drive, which is the one we want to set up:

1. Click Set Up on the Hard Drive connection in the Publish Services panel to launch the Publishing Manager dialog box (**Figure 12.4**), which should remind you of the normal Export dialog box (Figure 12.2).

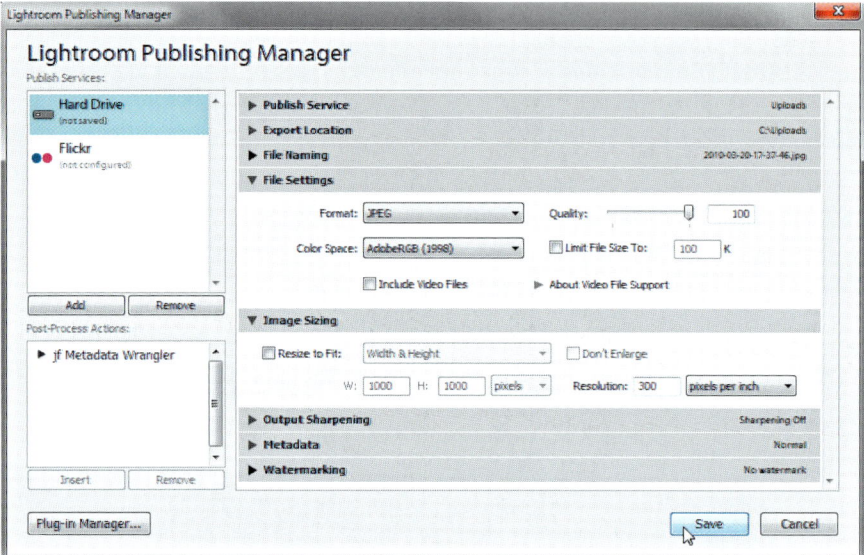

Figure 12.4 The Publishing Manager dialog box.

2. Enter a short, yet descriptive name for this connection in the Publish Service panel, which will be displayed later in the Publish panel. I named mine Uploads.

3. Choose the Export Location, which is where on your drive you want Lightroom to publish these copies. This is an important one to get right the first time because it can't be changed without deleting the entire connection and starting over. I created a folder on my drive called Uploads and used that.

4. Configure the remaining panels the same exact way as I describe for the Export dialog box in the preceding section. You will find all the same panels, named the same way, performing the same functions as the Export dialog box.

5. Click the Save button to save your settings and exit the Publishing Manager.

Now you could stop there and simply drag and drop your top picks to that new Uploads connection to create a batch for publishing, but I want to give you one more tip that utilizes the power of smart collections (see Chapter 11) to automatically collect all your final stock picks for you.

1. Right-click on the connection you just created and choose Create Published Smart Folder from the contextual menu.

   This will launch the Create Published Smart Folder dialog box, which is 100 percent identical in looks and functionality to the Create Smart Collection dialog box in Chapter 11 (Figure 11.13).

2. Customize the rules you want to use to automatically assemble your final versions into this Smart Folder.

   I took the easy way out and simply added the keyword <<STOCK>> to all my final masters. The only rule I use for my Smart Folder is to find all photos in my catalog with that keyword. This is a simple way to add photos for output as well as quickly find them all through a keyword search inside of Lightroom. There's no wrong answer here, and you might have different criteria, so experiment with what works for you.

3. Click Save to create the Smart Folder, and it will immediately pull all your photos together.

Think of that connection as a bit of a cross between a Lightroom smart collection and a real folder on your drive. You see the master copies in Lightroom, but once published, new copies will exist in the designated folder on your drive. Next comes the actual "publish" part of the process:

1. Click on the Smart Folder you created in the Publish Services panel to see the photos displayed under New Photos to Publish (**Figure 12.5**).

2. Click the Publish button (below the panel). As the copies are published to the designated folder, you will see them move under the Published Photos heading (Figure 12.5).

3. When the publishing is complete, right-click on the connection and choose Show in Explorer (Mac: Show in Finder) to open the folder and see the new copies.

Now you have a folder full of copies ready to upload to whichever stock sites you choose. Lightroom will track your masters, and any time you make the slightest change, from adding new keywords to making an exposure adjustment, Lightroom will put those changed folders in a Modified Photos to Re-Publish queue inside that connection (Figure 12.5). Clicking Publish will update the copies in the folder on your drive accordingly.

The same goes for any rejects that are beyond saving (hey, it happens). If you decide (or it gets decided for you) that one of your picks just doesn't make the cut, then all you need to do is change the aspect of that photo that caused it to be included in the smart folder to begin with. In my case, I just remove the

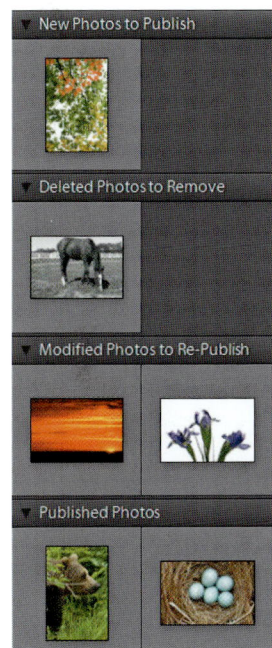

Figure 12.5 Lightroom manages your photos in various queues depending on what needs to happen with them next.

<<STOCK>> keyword from that photo, and Lightroom moves it to the Deleted Photos to Remove queue (Figure 12.5). The next time I click the Publish button, that original photo will be removed from the Smart Folder and the copy will be removed from the folder on disk (the actual master copy is not deleted or harmed in any way).

The Publish Service output option certainly requires more initial setup than a typical export, but once it is created, you've got a live mechanism for continuous output and management of your stock submissions. I've just showed you the basics. You can create multiple connections and use a wide range of criteria to meet your needs as time goes on.

Now that you know how to get your copies ready for submission, I want to give you a few final tips for getting the most out of the experience as you venture out into the world of microstock.

Establish a Name for Yourself

One of the very first things you'll do when you create an account at any stock site is to choose a username (sometimes called a member name or nickname). A lot of people don't give this much thought when they are first starting out and can sometimes choose a name they may later regret because it doesn't sound professional, is hard to spell, or just easy to forget. Perhaps their nickname from their college days came to mind, or they just use their XBox gamertag for everything. There's nothing wrong with choosing a creative or clever name, or even something odd like "suckaheadjivemamacow" (true story) if that is what you really want to do. But you may not want to go through your microstock life being known as "crawlinghomedrunk" (true story). I've seen many people build their careers from their start in microstock, so ask yourself:

- Do you have a blog or website that might suggest a good name?
- Do you have an existing business that you want to tie into?
- Do you want to carry the same name across all sites?
- Do you want to carry the same name across other social media outlets like Twitter or Flickr?

I'm not trying to make this more complicated than it needs to be, or even suggest that the first name you pick is carved in stone, as most sites should allow for you to change your username (though I can't claim for certain that all will). I just want to suggest that you give it some thought now, because down the road you may find it harder to switch—and you lose any name recognition you may have built with customers—or you may find that all the really good names, like "shooterguy," are already taken. Just keep in mind that this will be the name that people will come to know you by, and that many people may never even know your real name.

Going through the Application Process

While creating accounts at each site is free and relatively painless, some will require you to read through their contributor manual, submit sample photos, and possibly even take a short quiz before they let you begin uploading your work. Of the five sites I suggested checking out in Chapter 2, only Shutterstock and iStockphoto require submitting samples before getting approved. These are also the two most profitable sites for most people, so it is worth your time to get the green light as soon as possible.

My hope is that all the material in this book will get you through the door easily, but here are a few important tips to keep in mind:

- Submit your best work. This is your chance to show what you are capable of, so don't mess around with snapshots on your hard drive from your last vacation. Go out and create some stock with intention.

- Keep it simple. Don't go gear crazy. Think simple compositions that communicate a simple message.

- Keep it clean. Watch out for the easy technical problems that inspectors hone in on like bloodhounds.

- Choose a diverse range of subject matter. Ten variations of an apple on a white background will get you sent to the back of the line. Play to your strengths and interests, but show some variety.

If you encounter a quiz in the application process, you should be well prepared, so don't sweat it. These are pretty much open book quizzes anyway, since there is no time limit and you are on the Internet. Their purpose is really just to make sure you've read that site's contributor guidelines. Usually, the safest, most cautious answer is the correct one (especially in regard to model releases, property releases, and respecting copyrights of other artists). In addition, since becoming a contributor brings the potential to start generating income, some sites also require that you submit a scanned (or photographed) copy of your driver's license or equivalent photo identification. This is just to verify you are who you say you are, you are of legal age (18), and your address matches the address in your account.

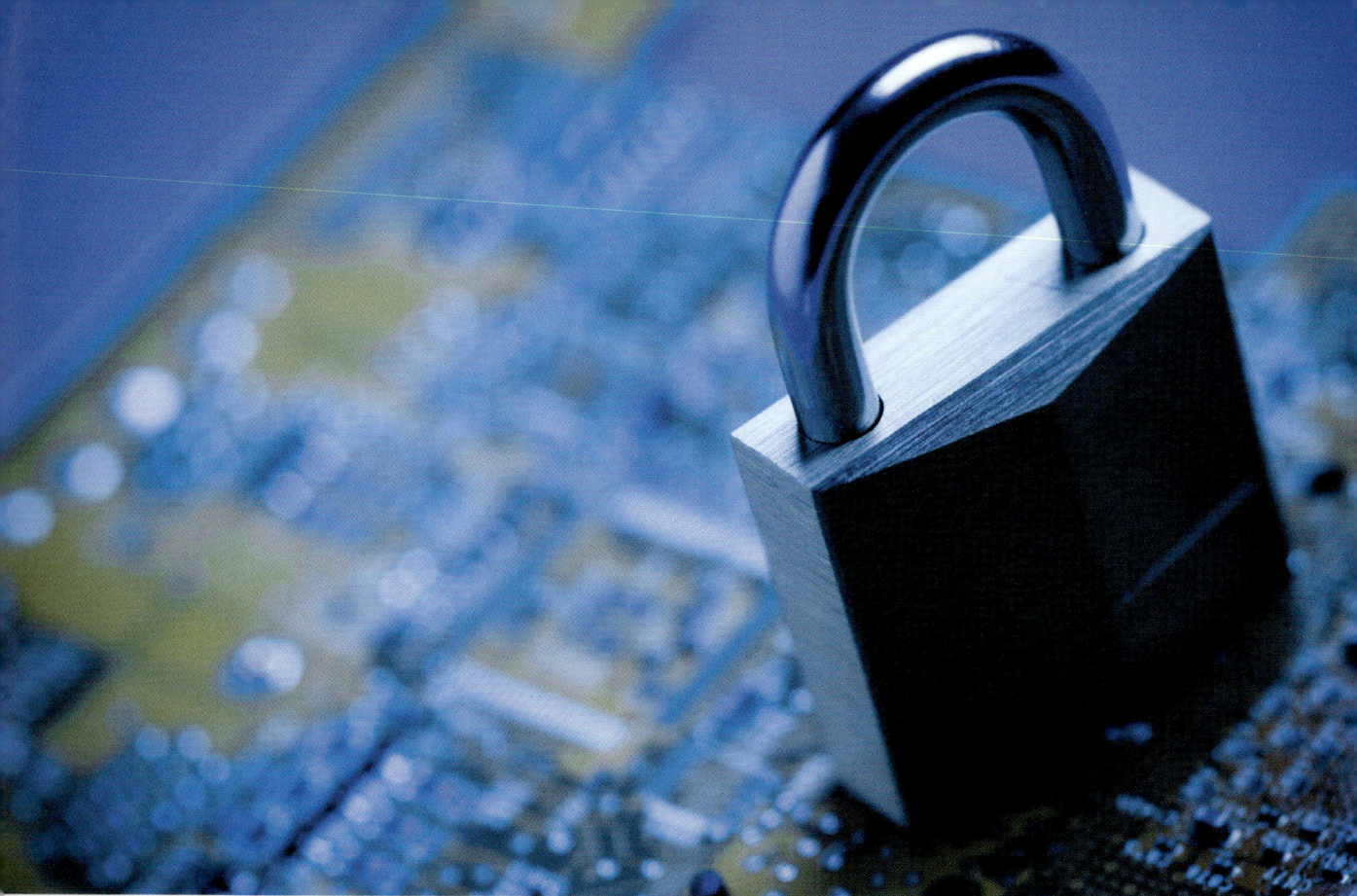

Figure 12.6 Protection. Downloaded over 1,000 times.

Protection

Creator	Marilyn Nieves (istockphoto.com/Mari)
Started	2004
Home	USA
Total portfolio	2,100
Total downloads	Over 40,000
About this photo	Mari says, "I used a padlock and a computer circuit board, two common household objects that when put together can make for a strong yet simple concept. Focus is sharply on the padlock, and the busy circuitry falls into the shallow depth of field, which allows for good copy space. This was captured with a Nikon D300 and two strobes."
Mari's tip	"Start with simple concepts. These can often be used in more ways than one, depending on the props used."

Find Your Photos in Use

One of the first things microstock contributors want to see (aside from increasing account balances) is where their downloaded photos end up being used. It is still very rewarding for me to find a new instance of one of my photo's incorporated into someone else's project. Since so much of microstock content ends up being used in online projects, it isn't that difficult to discover some of them for yourself. There's one major caveat: it can take quite a bit of time before you actually find anything. This shouldn't be a big surprise, but I don't want you to get the impression that this is an instantaneous process. It could easily be a year or more before you have enough work in circulation to start finding the places it has been used.

Over the years, I've had a few kind souls contact me to let me know they've used my work in their projects. I've even had a few folks send me samples. I've also had other contributors send me links to places where they happened to have spotted seeing one of my photos in action, and I've stumbled on a few myself (like that pet obituary ad I mentioned in Chapter 2). But such sightings are rare. To find more, you'll need to take matters into your own hands.

Google Google Google

This undisputed king of searches is the logical starting point for finding your work. There are a number of Google tools to help you discover your images in use. One of the first and most obvious is to do a few regular Google searches using combinations of:

- Your real name in quotes. For example, "Rob Sylvan." If you get a lot of hits on just your name, then also try adding in words like: photography, credits, copyright, and the individual names of the sites you are working with.

- Your username for each site (a good reason to have a single name across all sites). Some customers will add a credit line in their projects, and just as often they'll use your member name since it is often more visible at the point of purchase.

You're certainly not going to want to keep repeating those searches on a regular basis, but you can take advantage of another free service from Google, called Google Alerts (see **Figure 12.7** on the next page). Head over to www.google.com/alerts and use your most successful search configurations to create automated alerts that will be emailed to you at the frequency you choose.

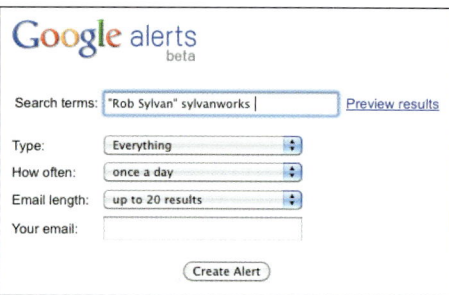

Figure 12.7 Setting up a Google Alert.

After setting up a few alerts, switch over to Google's Image Search (www.images.google.com) and again, enter the most successful search terms. I usually just start with my name, and then try other combinations. Online news agencies are some of the most likely customers to put your name as a credit with the photos they use. I've also had luck using the terms from the titles of my most successful photos (like the geese migration example from Chapter 11).

There's one last Google resource worth checking out before you go, and that's Google Books (www.books.google.com). Many book publishers and authors will include the name or username of the artist's work that was included in their books. I've done that with all of the stock photos I've used. Try a search on your real name and your username, and you might just find you've been published.

Reverse Image Search

Several years ago I learned of a website called TinEye that developed an image identification technology that allows you to take a starting image (like a photo from your portfolio) and search the Web to try to find other instances of that same image in other places. You can give it a test drive yourself over at www.tineye.com. It really is amazing, and it's free. TinEye is continually crawling the Web and indexing the images it finds, so this is not an exhaustive search of the entire Web (yet) but rather a search of all images TinEye had already found.

You can upload a photo from your desktop, or paste in a link to an image that is already online. But the easiest way is to install the browser plug-in (plug-ins exist for Firefox, Chrome, and Internet Explorer) that enables you to right-click an online photo from within your Web browser and initiate a search. If it finds any matches, it will return the matching thumbnails and links (**Figure 12.8**) for you to click through and investigate further. It can even find photos that have been cropped and changed pretty dramatically from the original. Remember, it takes time for your photos to be licensed, used online, and eventually indexed, so don't despair if you come up with empty results for a while.

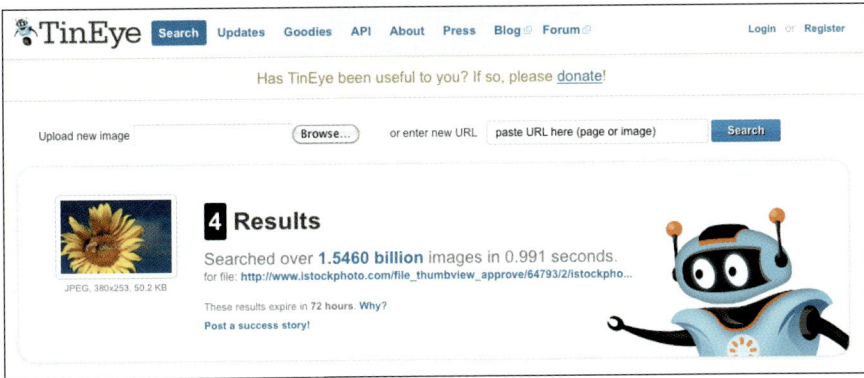

Figure 12.8 TinEye search results on one of my stock photos.

Move to the Next Level

The bulk of this book has been about building a solid foundation for getting started in shooting for microstock. I hope you will read the stories of my friends Nicole, who wrote the Foreword, and Rasmus, who wrote the Afterword, as well as all the tips from fellow contributors throughout the book, to get a sense of the bigger picture, and the notion that, like most things in life, the results you get out of the experience are in direct proportion to what you put in. This is not an easy and quick path to riches. It is a very accessible learning opportunity, and a way to grow and develop your craft while generating income along the way.

I've mentioned a few online resources in tips and notes throughout the book, but wanted to focus on a few that I really don't want you to miss. These are all resources I use frequently, are all lovingly maintained by other microstock contributors who are willing to share their experiences and expertise to provide these services to the rest of us, and, these are all free. From these, you will discover new resources, head down new paths, find new tools, and stay connected to everything you need to know beyond what this book can offer you:

- Microstock Diaries (www.microstockdiaries.com)

    This is the original blog about all the important happenings in the world of microstock. Run by a long-time contributor, Lee Torrens, it is a well-respected resource among contributors.

- Microstock Group (www.microstockgroup.com)

    This is the most popular, non-stock agency-affiliated, online forum for microstock contributors. Started and maintained by another long-time contributor,

Tyler Olsen, there's plenty of unbiased and unvarnished commentary about what the various stock sites are up to, sales trends, rejection woes, and what new tools and resources people have discovered. Don't take anything anyone says personally; use the forum search before asking a question, and you'll do just fine.

- Deepmeta (www.deepmeta.com)

   Although this tool is only useful for submitting photos to iStockphoto, it is such a better option than the Web interface offered by iStock itself (though that may change in the near future) so I am compelled to mention it. Deepmeta is completely free, and 100 percent developed and maintained by a fellow contributor, Franky De Meyer. He's done a great service for us all, and you'll be glad I told you about it.

- PicNiche (www.picniche.com)

   I mentioned PicNiche in the section on keywording, but I wanted to highlight it here because I think you'll find it incredibly useful. Developed by Rob Davies, another microstock contributor, it is a handy tool for providing some insight into subject matter supply and demand based on accumulated publicly available information from various stock sites. What I like most about what Rob has created, though, is the Contributor Toolbar for Firefox. The Toolbar puts links to various microstock forums, most popular content lists, blogs, and a really cool keywording tool all in one place.

- Myerson Photo Blog (www.myersonphoto.com/blog)

   This is the blog of fellow contributor Ethan Myerson (who also happened to be the Technical Editor of this book). Ethan's blog entries run the gamut from Photoshop tutorials to keywording tips (he is an image inspector and moderates the Keywording forum on iStockphoto, so he's a real resource in that area).

- Nicolesy Blog (www.nicolesyblog.com)

   Nicole shares a ton of information about her stock experience from photography tips, to processing advice, and a lot of really great stock photos. This is a great source of information and inspiration.

- Rasmus Rasmussen (www.rasmusrasmussen.com)

   I've been enjoying Rasmus' writing for many years. He's written articles on photography for iStockphoto and has even written his own microstock photographer's guide. He's a very down-to-earth guy with a wealth of wisdom to share.

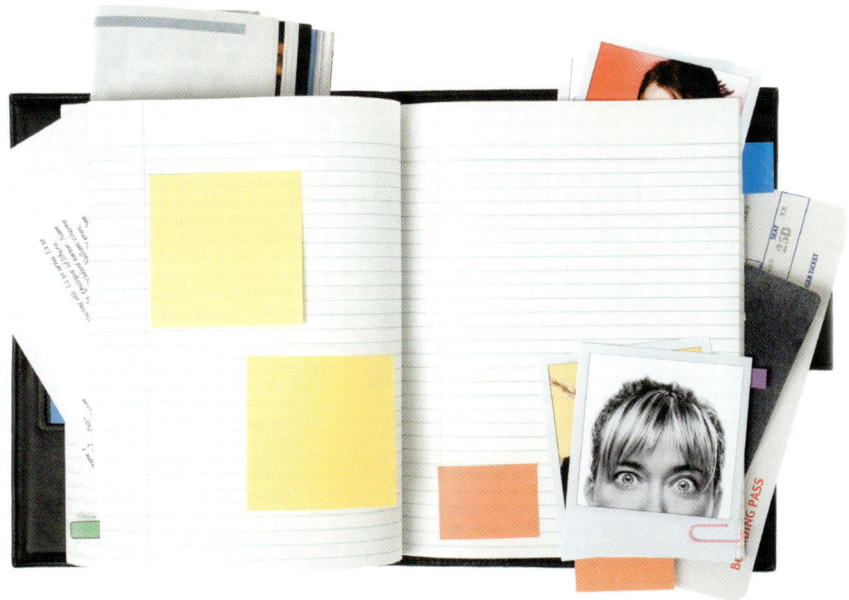

Figure 12.9 Planning a Trip. Downloaded over 1,000 times.

Planning a Trip

Creator	Claude Dagenais (istockphoto.com/twohumans)
Started	2006
Home	Canada
Total portfolio	1,593 images
Total downloads	Over 34,000
About this photo	Claude says, "Many of my beautiful people shoots, beautiful landscape, beautiful anything don't do as good as images that convey a strong concept. This was produced using two lights, one main light with a large softbox over the image, and one reflected on a foamcore under a Foba shooting table. We used a Canon EOS-1Ds Mark II and a EF 50mm f/2.5 lens."
Claude's tip	"Before investing in equipment, invest in yourself. Many times I was witness to photographers relying on equipment to create great imagery when the main ingredient for success in photography is knowledge and creativity. Participate in training activities beyond photography (such as creativity, theater, painting, and so on), read, experiment, and push yourself to go outside of your comfort zone. Have fun!

- Sean Locke Digital Imagery (www.seanlockedigitalimagery.wordpress.com)

  Sean is a stock-producing dynamo (I profiled him in Chapter 6). He just completely understands how to create clean useful stock, and works hard at doing it right. On top of that, he's an ubiquitous presence in a few microstock forums, and can be counted on for delivering no-nonsense advice. His blog is a great read and a great way to get a glimpse inside what has made him so successful.

- Yuri Arcurs (www.arcurs.com)

  Widely regarded as one of the most successful microstock contributors in terms of sheer volume of licenses sold, Yuri has accumulated a number of informative blog posts and contributor resources on his website.

I know there are more resources out there (and apologies if I missed your favorite), but this list should provide you with more than enough new information to chew on for a while. That said, there is one more resource I want to remind you to check out:

- Taking Stock (www.takingstockphoto.com)

  This is, of course, the website I built to support this book. Aside from giving you the opportunity to download all of the practice files for the lessons in the book, I provide additional tutorials, links to new resources, and an easy way for you to contact me if you have any questions about any of the material in this book. Don't be a stranger.

Parting Words

I sincerely hope this book has provided you with a solid foundation for deciding if this is the right path for you to follow, and more importantly, to get you started on the right foot. I have found that the people who focus first on the quality of their submissions, and then branch into diverse subject matter, before finally shifting to building up quantity tend to find greater success and satisfaction from the process. If there were any universal recipe for success, this is as close as it gets.

Are you familiar with the 80-20 rule? It can be applied to many things in life, but when applied to a microstock portfolio, it suggests that 80 percent of your earnings will come from 20 percent of your portfolio. In other words, you are bound to discover that your portfolio consists of a few really successful images (in terms of earnings) and a lot of much less successful content. It can be incredibly helpful for you to discover and monitor those high performers over time, so that when you get to the point where you are focusing on quantity, you consider creating new content that is similar but different enough that it doesn't directly compete with your top earners. For example, after seeing the success of my Christmas tree image I decided to create a few variations on the same snowy tree theme. My hope is that together, that offering can support a wider variety of customers without eating into the success of my top performer. So far it has turned out to be very positive, and they were all shots I enjoyed creating.

The point I am trying to make is that over time, just adding new content alone is not going to translate directly into an equal amount of income. Work smarter, not just harder, and follow your own interests and passions. Let the authenticity in your work be the engine of your success, and have fun!

Afterword

I am not the most successful microstock photographer in the world, not if you go by sales, in any case. But I would like to think that shooting and selling photos online has made me a successful person in many other ways. I was lucky enough to get in at the very birth of microstock. I signed up with iStockphoto in 2000, when there were fewer than 10,000 images in the collection. Today there are millions.

It was through microstock that I discovered my love of photography. I was working as a Web designer/developer, but in 2001 I bought my first point-and-shoot digital camera, and soon after, I left IT and went back to school to study photography full time. My interest was fueled not only by the pocket money I was making from sales, but also from the friendships I made. One of the first people I talked to was Rob, when he contacted me with a challenge: a race to reach the "bronze canister" status on iStock. Rob won that race, but I got a friend out of it, and though we did not meet (in person) until several years later, this still stands as a milestone for me.

Financially, microstock gave me the freedom to explore my newfound passion without taking a huge hit on my bank account. For a long time, I used it simply as a way to pay for my hobby and was happy enough with that. I learned what sells over time, but more importantly I learned what kind of photos I love taking (the two are not necessarily the same). It became part of my personal growth as an artist and a human being, and this is where I found true success—not through sales but through experience and connections made across the globe.

Making these personal connections is crucial in any venture, but I would have never in my wildest imagination guessed just how much microstock would bring me. I was living in Copenhagen, Denmark, and one day got a message from Bruce Livingstone, the founder and then CEO of iStockphoto. He was coming to my part of the world to attend a conference and wondered if I wanted to meet for a drink. We ended up spending a week together, which in turn led to my involvement behind the scenes at iStockphoto, as an image inspector and someone who got to help define some of the highest standards of an entire industry.

Eventually in 2005, Bruce invited me to attend a workshop in Seattle, a so-called iStockalypse. I went, thinking I would stay in the U.S. for two weeks and get a little vacation time in while I was at it. Little did I know that I would form the ultimate connection to another human being when I got there.

In Seattle, I met local food photographer Kelly Cline, who most graciously had offered to show me around town. And then magic happened. After the iStockalypse, I went down to California to visit some family, but every day I was on the phone with Kelly and when my vacation was about to end, she rented a car and drove down to meet me. I ended up missing my plane home, within three months we were married, and my two-week stay became two years, then three, four, and as I write this we have entered into our fifth year together. And I still haven't been back to Denmark. And all this because I was working on a website in 2000 and decided to check out this new thing I had just read about: microstock. Back then, it didn't have a name. It was just a new, democratic alternative to traditional stock photography—one that would change both the face of commercial imagery and my own life forever.

As you enter into the world of microstock, I urge you to keep your mind and heart open. Sure, there will be disappointments and setbacks along the way, as there is in anything worth pursuing, but with dedication and kindness, there is no limit to the success you might find.

If I am to give you a bit of "technical" advice, it would be to specialize in what you love. Don't try to guess what will sell, because you will never be as good as those who have mastered a niche chosen out of love for that particular genre or style of photography. Instead, find your own niche and become a master in your own right. Once you do, other people's work will matter less and success in many forms will find you.

In closing, Rob's initial challenge was a glimpse of things to come for me, and I am thrilled to have the honor of writing the afterword to his book. I hope you found his advice and openness as helpful as I have, and good luck in all of your microstock ventures.

—*Rasmus Rasmussen*

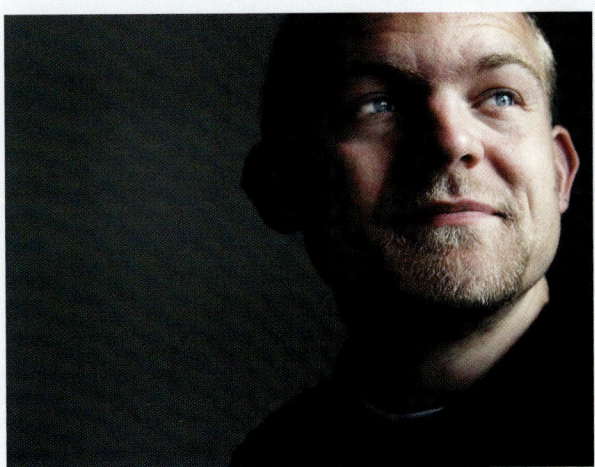

Rasmus Rasmussen	(istockphoto.com/theprint)
Started	2000
Total portfolio	1,222
Total downloads	Over 36,000

Great Expectations.
© Rasmus Rasmussen
(istockphoto.com/theprint)

Index

8 bits per channel, 110
16 bits per channel, 110, 111
80-20 rule, 218

A

Abuse photo, 37
"A" clamps, 68
Adobe
    Camera Raw, 65
    camera style profiles, 119
    Digital Negative format, 183
    Lightroom (*See* Lightroom)
    Photoshop (*See* Photoshop)
    Photoshop Elements (*See* Elements)
    RGB color space, 107, 110, 111, 206
advertising photos, 14, 20, 45, 61
airline magazines, 28
aluminum foil, 68, 69
Amazon, 104
American Society of Media Photographers, 53
Amount slider, Lightroom, 130, 133
annual-report photos, 14
apple photo, 39
application process, microstock site, 211
Apply During Import panel, Lightroom, 186
Arcurs, Yuri, 218
artifacts, 62, 155
artificial light, 67
assignment photography, 29
Association of Photoshop Professionals, National, 94, 98

B

Backblaze, 101
backgrounds, 40–41, 79, 85, 87, 93
backups, photo, 89, 99–101, 168, 180–181
backup software packages, 100, 181
Balderas, Christine, 22
balloons photo, 176
battery-powered hard drives, 180
beach photo, 22
bear photo, 115–116, 118, 123–124, 126, 129
Better Be Prompt! photo, 18–19
Bigstockphoto, 23, 24
billboards, 14, 28
binary digits, 109
bit depth, 109–110
bits, 109–110
black felt squares, 69
black foam core, 69
Blackmon, Mars, 56
Blacks slider, Lightroom, 127
Blake, Joshua, 78–79

blemishes, 151
blinkies, 77
blog photos, 14, 20
blogs, 138, 215, 216, 218
blown-out highlights, 128
Blu-Tack, 69
book covers, 45
Books, Google, 214
borders, 158
Boylan, Joey, 202
Boy Looking at Math Problem photo, 6–7
brightness levels, 109
Brightness slider, Lightroom, 127
brown bear photo. *See* bear photo
Bryukhanova, Anna, 92–93
bulk discounts, 21
Bunting, Fred, 106
Busy Warehouse photo, 61
bytes, 110

C

calibration, monitor, 103–104
Camera Calibration panel, Lightroom, 118, 119
camera manuals, 65
camera profiles, 118
Camera Raw, 65, 115
cameras, 56–60. *See also* digital cameras
camera settings, 64–67, 74–77, 83
camera sweet spots, 59, 60, 67
Canada Geese Migration photo, 27, 36
Canon cameras, 119
Canstockphoto, 23, 24
captions, 195–196
card readers, 180
catalogs, Lightroom, 183
CDs, as source of royalty-free content, 4, 23
cheesburger photo, 90
chef photo, 66
children, photographing, 176
chimping, 167
Christmas ornaments photo, 159
Christmas tree photo, 8–10, 161–163, 197–198
chromatic aberration, 142–146
ChronoSync, 100
CIELAB color space, 107
Clarity control, Lightroom, 129
Cline, Kelly, 90–91, 220
clip-art collections, 4, 23
clock photo, 18
Clone Stamp Tool, Lightroom, 153–154
clothespins, 68
Cole, Steve, 35
collections, smart, 192–193, 209

collection sets, Lightroom, 192–193
Collections panel, Lightroom, 189
color casts, 115, 121, 122
color management, 106
color noise, 136–137
color rendering, 115, 118
color space, 106–111, 206
color-styles setting, 65
color-to-grayscale conversions, 158
color values, 107–108
company logos, 49. *See also* logos
compass photo, 2–3
composition, cropping for, 146–151
compressed air, 68
computer monitors. *See* monitors
computers, 98–101
    backing up, 99–101
    desktop *vs.* laptop, 98
    for digital darkroom, 98–99
    how data is stored by, 110
    monitor considerations, 101 (*See also* monitors)
computer software. *See* software
consumer digital cameras, 5. *See also* digital cameras
contact information, 187
Container Terminal, Harbor photo, 182
content license, 44
contrast setting, 65
Contrast slider, Lightroom, 128, 138
contributor guidelines, 211
contributor profiles, 70
    Balderas, Christine, 22
    Blake, Joshua, 78–79
    Boylan, Joey, 202
    Bryukhanova, Anna, 92–93
    Cline, Kelly, 90–91
    Cole, Steve, 35
    Dagenais, Claude, 217
    Diederich, Diane, 7
    Dominick, Sharon, 19
    Fochesato, Giorgio, 12
    Gearhart, Rosemarie, 176
    Gearhart, Shawn, 159
    Goh, Li Kim, 149
    Gomez, Carole, 61
    Govorushchenko, Katja, 84–85
    Ivanovic, Zoran, 105
    Kwiatkowski, Arthur, 54
    Legg, Rich, 131
    Locke, Sean, 80–81
    Louie, Nancy, 72–73
    Lowe, Shaun, 102
    Mitic, Slobo, 117
    Nieves, Marilyn, 212
    Rohde, Amanda, 33
    Sanchez, Roberto A., 86–87
    Teunissen, Ivar, 51
    Thaysen, Arne, 182
    Trigg, Susan, 169
    Walls, Stephen, 66
Controlled Vocabulary Catalog, 199

conventions, photography-related, 46
copyright
    avoiding problems with, 49–55
    defined, 42
    embedding into metadata, 187
    and microstock licensing models, 17
    registration process, 53
copy space, 40–41
CPU chip photo, 98
.cr2 file extension, 63
Craig's List, 48
Crazy Paparazzi photo, 56–57
credit packages, 21
Crescendo Exhibition Poster, 34
Critique Request forum, iStockphoto, 170
cropping photos, 146–151

D

darkroom. *See* digital darkroom
data backup system, 99–101
Datacolor, 104
Davies, Rob, 216
Deepmeta, 216
De Meyer, Franky, 216
descriptions, photo, 195–196
desktop computers, 98–99, 101
Destination panel, Lightroom, 187
Detail slider, Lightroom, 132, 133, 138
Diederich, Diane, 7
digital artifacts. *See* artifacts
digital cameras, 4, 58–59, 74–77, 118
digital darkroom, 96–111
    choosing color space, 106–111
    hardware choices, 96–104
    purpose of, 96
    software choices, 104–106
digital editing, 113–139
    adjusting white balance, 121–124
    creating presets, 120–121
    dealing with noise, 135–138
    defined, 113
    making exposure adjustments, 126–130
    quality issues, 113–115
    setting defaults, 116–119
    sharpening for stock, 130–135
digital noise, 136. *See also* noise
digital photography, 70. *See also* digital cameras
digital-single-lens-reflex cameras, 58. *See also* DSLR cameras
digital zoom, 65
displays. *See* monitors
DNG format, 183
DNG Profile Editor, 119
doctors photo, 80
dog photos, 5, 16
Dominick, Sharon, 19
download statistics, 11–12
downsizing photos, 155–157
Dreamstime, 23, 194

Drobo, 100
dropbox.com, 173
DSLR cameras, 58, 59, 60, 63
dust, 140, 152

E

Echinacea photo, 132, 134, 135, 137
editing. *See* digital editing
Edit Metadata Presets dialog box, Lightroom, 187–188
editorial license, 20, 45–46
Elements
    and chromatic aberration, 144–145
    cloning and healing tools, 153–154
    cost of, 104
    creating reverse vignette in, 161–162
    downsizing photos in, 155–157
    trial version, 162
    using layer masks in, 145–146
    vs. other image editors, 142
emotions, 38
Epson photo viewer, 180
Evans, Mark, 34
EXIF metadata, 183. *See also* metadata
Export dialog box box, Lightroom, 206, 207
Export process, Lightroom, 205–207
exposure adjustment tools, 126–130
exposure levels, 115
exposure settings, 74–77, 94
external drives, 99, 100, 180
eyeglasses photo, 164–165

F

Facebook, 208
family photos, 29, 84
felt squares, 69
file formats, 62–64
File Handling panel, Lightroom, 186
file management, 179
File Settings panel, Lightroom, 206
fill light, 67
Fill Light control, Lightroom, 127
film grain, 136
filters, 158
Finishing Touch photo, 178–179
flagging photos, 190–191
flash photography, 67
Flickr, 207, 208
floral images, 105, 132
Flying Geese photo, 27, 36
foam core, 68, 69
Fochesato, Giorgio, 12
focus, 74, 77, 130
Folders panel, Lightroom, 189
food photos, 91, 220
forums, online, 24, 25, 94, 170, 215–216
Fotolia, 24
Fraser, Bruce, 106, 130, 133

fringe, purple, 142–146
Frying Pan photo, 31–34

G

gaffers tape, 68
Game Playing photo, 78
gamut, 106
gear, photography, 56–60, 67–69, 83
Gearhart, Rosemarie, 176
Gearhart, Shawn, 159
geese photo, 27, 36
Gentle Surf photo, 22
geometric distortion, 142
Getty Images, 24
Goh, Li Kim, 149
Gomez, Carole, 61
Google
    Alerts, 213–214
    Books, 214
    image search, 194, 213–214
Govorushchenko, Katja, 84–85
graphic designers, 31
graphics cards, 99
grayscale conversions, 158
grayscale tones, 109
Great Expectations photo, 221
Great Shot photo, 167
greeting cards, 45
Grid view, Lightroom, 189
Guests Strike Out photo, 16–17

H

hair, 140
Happy Woman photo, 39
hard drives, 99, 180
hardware, digital darkroom, 96–104
Hardy Waterlily photo, 105
Healthy Eating photo, 148
highlight clipping warning, 77, 126
highlights, blown-out, 128
hiker photo, 35
histograms, 74–76, 126
HoldTu, 69
horseshoes photo, 55
hot pixels, 140, 151

I

i1 Display 2, 104
Image Club Graphics, 23
image consumers, 26–28, 30–31
image copyright. *See* copyright
image-editing software, 104–106, 142. *See also* specific
    programs
image identification technology, 214
ImageIngester, 181
image inspectors, 165, 173, 220

image libraries, 24. *See also* microstock sites
image-processing, in-camera, 65–67
Image Search, Google, 214
image search, reverse, 214–215
Image Sizing panel, Lightroom, 206
Imaging USA, 46
Import dialog box, Lightroom, 184–185, 187
import process, Lightroom, 183–188
in-camera image processing, 65–67
in-flight magazines, 28
inspection workflow, 170–173
inspectors, photo, 165, 173
Internet
    forums, 24, 25, 94, 170, 215–216
    photo file formats, 62
interpolation, 65
ISO setting, 137, 155
iStockalypse, 220
iStockphoto
    application process for, 211
    approval standards, 5
    competing sites, 23, 24–25
    contributing to, 5–8, 9
    controlled vocabulary, 199
    Critique Request forum, 170
    download statistics, 10
    growth of, 220
    history of, 23–24
    how it works, 4, 5
    payment model, 21, 23
    permitted uses for content from, 44–45
    purchase by Getty Images, 24
    review process, 10–11
    sample model releases, 47
    sample property release, 52
    search mechanism for, 194–195, 199
    tool for submitting photos to, 216
Ivanovic, Zoran, 105

J

jogging photos, 53, 55
Jordan, Michael, 56
JPEG compression, 62, 65
JPEG format, 62–64, 110–111, 206
junk mail, 28
Justice Scale and Gavel photo, 42–43

K

keywording, 196–203
    forum, 216
    hardest aspect of, 199
    purpose of, 196
    resources/tutorials, 199
    time required for, 197
keyword lists, 199–201
Keyword Wizard, 200
Kid Having Good Time in Pool photo, 86

Kids Running with Balloons photo, 176
Kwiatkowski, Arthur, 54

L

Lane, Jordan, 196–197
laptop computers, 98–99, 101
layer masks, 145
LCD monitors, 101, 103. *See also* monitors
legal issues, 42–55
    copying work of others, 52–55
    editorial options, 45–46
    model releases, 47–48
    permitted uses, 44–45
    preventing, 49–52
Legg, Rich, 131
lens vignette, 142
license fees, 10, 42
licensing documents, 44–45
licensing models, 17–20
lighting, 67, 78, 87
light modifiers, 69
Lightroom
    adding metadata in, 195–196
    adding vignettes in, 160–161
    applying keywords in, 201–203
    Blacks slider, 127
    blog, 138
    Brightness slider, 127
    catalogs, 183
    and chromatic aberration, 142, 144
    Contrast slider, 128
    cost of, 104
    creating smart collections in, 192–193
    cropping photos in, 146–151
    Export process, 205–207
    Exposure control, 127
    Fill Light control, 127
    flagging photos in, 190–191
    importing into, 183–188
    memory-card backup function, 181
    metadata tools, 193–203
    noise-reduction tools, 135–138
    Painter Tool, 201–203
    and photo downsizing, 155
    post-processing adjustments in, 115
    Presence controls, 129–130
    Publish Services, 207–210
    purpose of, 106
    Recovery slider, 127, 128
    reviewing photos in, 189–193
    setting defaults in, 116–119
    Sharpening controls, 130
    Spot Removal tool, 151–152
    Synchronize Settings dialog box, 125
    training materials, 94
    trial version, 106, 138, 162
    tutorials, 138
    vs. other image editors, 106, 142, 179
    White Balance Selector tool, 123–124

Livingstone, Bruce, 23, 24, 220
Locke, Sean, 80–81, 218
logos, 49, 153–154, 158
lossless compression, 63
lossy compression, 62
Louie, Nancy, 72–73
Lowe, Shaun, 102
luminance, 155
luminance noise, 136–137
Luminance slider, Lightroom, 138

M

Mac
   backup software, 100
   computers, 98–99
Mad at Me photo, 166
magazine photos, 14, 20, 28, 45
Man Resting in the Alps photo, 12
marshmallow-toasting photo, 72
Masking slider, Lightroom, 132, 134
Math Problem photo, 6–7
Media Photographers, American Society of, 53
memory cards
   backing up, 168, 180
   formatting, 180, 181
   importing photos to Lightroom from, 184–188
   size considerations, 62, 63
metadata, 65, 179, 187–188, 193–203
Metadata panel, Lightroom, 195–196, 207
Metadata-Viewer Preset Builder, 196
micropayment stock photography, 8. *See also* microstock
microstock. *See also* stock photography
   blog, 215
   contributors (*See* microstock contributors)
   customers, 26–28, 30–31
   finding your niche in, 221
   getting feedback on, 10–11
   getting started in, 4–8, 19
   growth of, 8, 10
   history of, 23–25
   income potential, 4, 8–10
   licensing models, 20
   online community/resources, 8, 24, 25
   payment models, 21
   permitted uses for, 44–45
   pricing of, 20
   quality *vs.* quantity, 11–13
   resources, 215–218
   review process, 10–11
   role of image consumers in creating, 8
   thinking like consumer of, 30–31
   Web sites (*See* microstock sites)
microstock contributors
   cameras used by, 59
   featured, 70 (*See also* contributor profiles)
   and graphic design, 31
   independent forum for, 25
   interacting with other, 170
   and model releases, 48
   typical day job of, 48
Microstock Diaries, 25, 215
Microstock Group, 25, 215–216
microstock sites. *See also* specific sites
   application process for, 211
   avoiding rejection from, 140–142, 151, 157, 158–160
   choosing username for, 210–211
   contributor guidelines for, 211
   creating accounts on, 210
   dealing with rejection by, 173–175
   downloading free photos from, 168
   exporting photos for, 206–207
   file format required by, 63
   file-size considerations, 151, 155
   how they work, 8
   learning to use, 24–25
   licensing documents for, 44–45
   list of top, 24–25
   payment models used by, 21
   photo inspectors for, 165, 173, 220
   search features for, 194–195
   types of people who use, 26–28
Mitic, Slobo, 117
Model Mayhem, 48
model releases, 46, 47–48, 89
models
   communicating with, 82
   hiring, 48
   working with, 73, 79, 81, 85, 87, 93
monitor profiles, 103, 107
monitors
   calibrating, 103–104
   role of, in editing workflow, 101
   testing, 111
Mood for Love photo, 38
mother-and-daughter photo, 84
mother-and-son photo, 29
mountain photos, 12, 35
Mr. Muscle photo, 50–51
multicore processors, 99
Murphy, Chris, 106
Myerson, Ethan, 216
Myerson Photo Blog, 216

N

names, member, 210–211
National Association of Photoshop Professionals, 94, 98
.nef file extension, 63
negative space, 22
New Develop Preset dialog box, Lightroom, 120
newsletters, stock photography, 168
newspaper photos, 20, 45
Nicolesy Blog, 216
Nieves, Marilyn, 212
Nike commercials, 56

Nikon cameras, 119
noise, 114, 136–137, 140, 155
noise-reduction setting, camera, 65
noise-reduction tools, Lightroom, 135–138

O

Ocean Fury photo, 102
off-camera flash, 67
Olsen, Tyler, 216
One Minute to Midnight photo, 169
One Model Place, 48
online backup storage, 101
online forums, 24, 25, 94, 170, 215–216
organizing photos, 171, 189
Output Sharpening panel, Lightroom, 207
overexposed photos, 74–75
overfiltering, 157
overprocessing photos, 157–160
over-sharpening photos, 114

P

padlock photo, 212
Pain photo, 174
Painter Tool, Lightroom, 201–203
panoramas, 46
paparazzi photo, 56–57
paperwork, 89
parents photo, 29
pay-as-you-go payment model, 21
payment models, 21
PC-keyboard photo, 140–141
.pef file extension, 63
pen-input tablets, 154
Perfect Picture School of Photography, 94–95
permitted uses, 44–45
Peterson, Bryan, 94
Photo Blog, Myerson, 216
photo captions, 195–196
photo descriptions, 195–196
photo-editing tools, 104–106
Photographer photo, 70–71
photographers
  characteristics of avid, 2
  featured, 70 (*See also* contributor profiles)
  as microstock contributors, 8
photographer workflow. *See* workflow
photography
  blogs, 216
  tools of the trade, 56–69
  trade shows, 46
  training materials, 94–95
photography gear, 56–60, 67–69, 83
photo inspectors, 165, 173, 220
Photo Mechanic, 181
PhotoPlus Expo, 46

photos
  adding metadata to, 187, 193, 195–196 (*See also* metadata)
  avoiding rejection of, 140–142, 151, 157, 158–160
  backing up, 89, 99–101, 168, 180–181
  combining multiple, 106
  coming up with concepts for, 73, 79, 85, 87
  critically viewing, 165–166
  cropping for composition, 146–151
  darkening edges of, 160
  downsizing/upsizing, 155–157
  editing, 104–106 (*See also* digital editing; image-editing software)
  exporting for submission to microstock, 206–207
  fixing chromatic aberration in, 142–146
  flagging, 190–191
  helping people find, 193, 196–198
  organizing, 171, 189
  overprocessing, 157–160
  removing distracting elements from, 151–154
  reviewing, 152, 168
  reviewing in Lightroom, 189–193
  saving, 205, 207
  searching for your own, 213–214
  sharing with peers, 173
  sharpening, 130–135
  shooting, 82–94
  size considerations, 151, 155
  storing, 99, 180–181
photo-sharing model, 23
photo-sharing sites, 173, 207, 208
photo shoots, 82–94
Photoshop. *See also* Photoshop CS5
  Elements (*See* Elements)
  filters, 158
  training, 94
  trial version, 106
  tutorials, 216
  using Lightroom with, 104, 106
Photoshop CS5, 99, 104, 115, 142. *See also* Photoshop
Photoshop Professionals, National Association of, 94, 98
Photoshop User Magazine, 94, 95
Photoshop World, 46
photo titles, 194–196
PicNiche, 200, 216
pixels, 109–110, 154, 206
Planning a Trip photo, 217
point-and-shoot cameras, 58, 59, 60
Polester, The, 46
portable photo viewers, 180–181
postcards, 45
Post-Crop Vignetting, Lightroom, 160, 163
posters, 45
post-processing
  adjustments, 115
  errors, 113–114
post-production, 168
PPSOP, 94–95

practice files, 218
Presence controls, Lightroom, 129–130
presets, 120–121, 132, 187–188
pricing, size-based, 20
printer profiles, 107
promotional flyers, 14, 28, 45
property releases, 46, 52
ProPhoto RGB color space, 107, 108, 110
prosumer cameras, 59
Protection photo, 212
Publishing Manager dialog box box, Lightroom, 208
Publish Services, Lightroom, 207–210
purple fringe, 142–146
putty-like adhesive, 69
puzzle photo, 178–179

Q

Quick Develop panel, Lightroom, 120–121

R

Radius slider, Lightroom, 130
.raf file extension, 63
RAM, 99
Rasmussen, Rasmus, 216, 221
RAW conversion, 73
raw+JPEG mode, 63–64
raw mode, 63–64, 74, 110, 113
raw workflow, 113
Real Estate photo, 54
Real World Color Management, 106
Real World Sharpening with Adobe Photoshop, Camera Raw, and Lightroom, 133
Recovery slider, Lightroom, 127, 128
Red Apple photo, 39
Red Positive Tick photo, 171
reflective surfaces, 77
reflectors, 69
rejection, dealing with, 173–175
rejection notices, 114, 140, 151, 157, 158–160
Relax photo, 175
releases. *See* model releases; property releases
rendering styles, 118–119
Resize to Fit option, Lightroom, 206
reverse image search, 214–215
reverse vignettes, 161–162
RGB channels, 109
RGB color model, 106–107, 108, 110, 206
Riecks, David, 199
rights. *See* copyright
rights-managed license, 20
Rohde, Amanda, 33
royalty-free license, 20, 46, 49
royalty-free photos, 4, 23, 44. *See also* stock photography

S

sales statistics, 11–12
salmon photo, 115–116, 118, 123–124, 126, 129
Sanchez, Roberto A., 86–87
saturation, 114
Saturation control, Lightroom, 130
saving photos, 205, 207
Schewe, Jeff, 133
School of Photography, Perfect Picture, 94–95
scientific images, 197
scouting locations, 83
scratch disk, 99
seamless paper, 68, 69
Sean Locke Digital Imagery, 218
search engine optimization, 194–195
searches, Google, 213–214
self-portraits, 79
sensor spots, 140, 151, 152
SEO, 194–195
Set Default Develop Settings dialog box, Lightroom, 119
Sharpen For box, Lightroom, 207
Sharpening controls, Lightroom, 130
sharpening photos, 130–135
sharpening setting, 65, 114
sharp photos, 130
shooting, tethered, 180
shoot lists, 82, 88
shopping photo, 15
Short Superhero photo, 52
shutter speed, 155
Shutterstock, 23–24, 195, 211
signatures, 158
size-based pricing, 20
smart collections, Lightroom, 192–193, 209
Smugmug, 208
snoot, 69
software
 backup, 100, 181
 image-editing, 104–106, 142
 raw processing, 65
speedlight, 67, 69
Spot Removal tool, Lightroom, 151–152
Spyder3Pro, 104
sRGB color space, 107, 206
starfish photo, 38
statistics, views/sales, 11–12
Sticky Situation photo, 202
Sticky Tack, 69
stock photography, 14–21. *See also* microstock
 background for, 40–41
 building collection of, 30
 cameras used for, 59–60
 characteristics of good, 16–17
 communicating message via, 38
 deciding what to shoot, 30
 evolution of, 14
 ingredients of, 36–41
 keeping track of, 29–30
 legal issues, 42–55 (*See also* copyright)

licensing models, 17–20
newsletters, 168
origin of term, 14
payment models, 21
permitted uses for, 44–45
researching, 28–29, 33
shooting for, 26
thinking like consumer of, 30–31
users of, 14–16, 26–28
workflow (*See* workflow)
stock sites. *See* microstock sites
storage devices, 180–181
storing photos, 99
storyboards, 82
strobist.blogspot.com, 67
studio lights, 78
subscription payment model, 21, 23–24
sunlight, 67
superhero photo, 52
surf photo, 22
sweet spots, camera, 59, 60, 67
Synchronize Settings dialog box, Lightroom, 125

T

Taking Stock, 218
tape, gaffers, 68
tethered shooting, 180
textbook photos, 20
TFCD, 48
TFP, 48
Thaysen, Arne, 182
thumbnails, 172, 189
Time for CD, 48
Time for Portfolio, 48
Time for Prints, 48
TinEye, 214–215
titles, 194–196
Torrens, Lee, 25, 215
toy-house photo, 54
trademarks, 49
trade shows, 46
training materials, 30–31, 94
Trigg, Susan, 169
tripods, 67, 91
tutorials
    keywording, 199
    Lightroom, 138
    Photoshop, 216
    taking stock photos, 218
Two Generations photo, 117

U

underexposed photos, 75
Understanding Exposure, 94
Undo command, 119
upload pre-flight checklist, 171–173
upsizing photos, 155
urban photos, 73
US Copyright Office, 53
usernames, 210–211

V

Vibrance control, Lightroom, 129, 130
ViceVersa Pro, 100
view statistics, 11–12
vignette effects, 160–163
visual content, 4, 5, 8
vox.com, 173

W

Walls, Stephen, 66
warehouse photo, 61
waterlily photo, 105
watermarks, 158
WB controls, 121. *See also* white balance
Web banners, 14
Web images, 29, 45
white backgrounds, 39, 85, 87, 93
white balance, 115, 121–122
White Balance Selector tool, Lightroom, 123–124
white felt squares, 69
white foam core, 69
white seamless paper, 68, 69
Wide Eyes photo, 37, 38
Windows
    backup software, 100
    computers, 98–99
Wintery Decorations photo, 159
witnesses, model release, 48
workflow
    assessing/improving, 111
    changing nature of, 180
    defined, 179
    export, 205–206
    inspection, 170–173
    most important part of, 113
    post-production, 96
work-for-hire photos, 42
working spaces, 107

X

X-Rite, 104

Y

Young People in Movie Theater photo, 131

Z

Zeldman, Jeffrey, 23

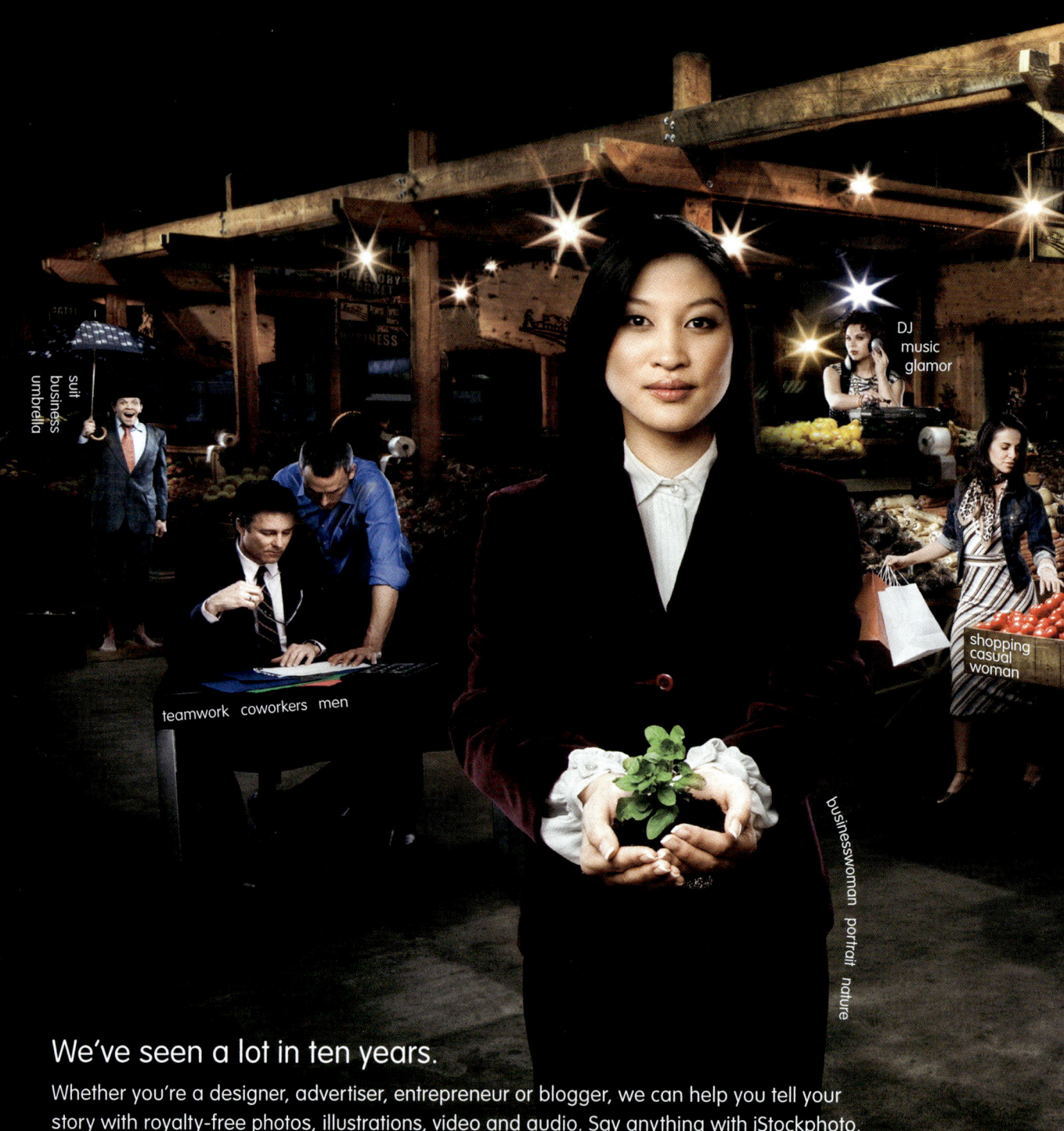

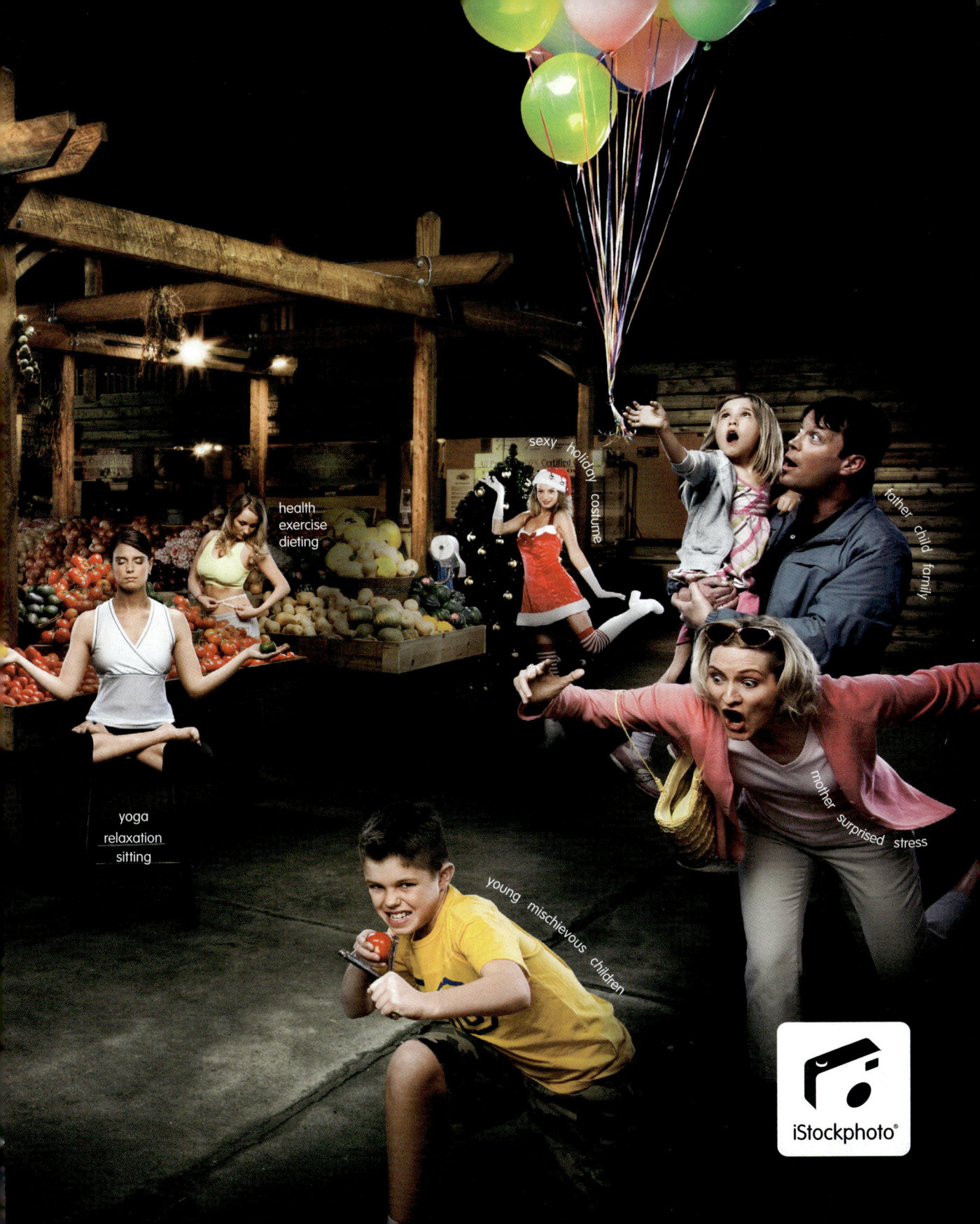

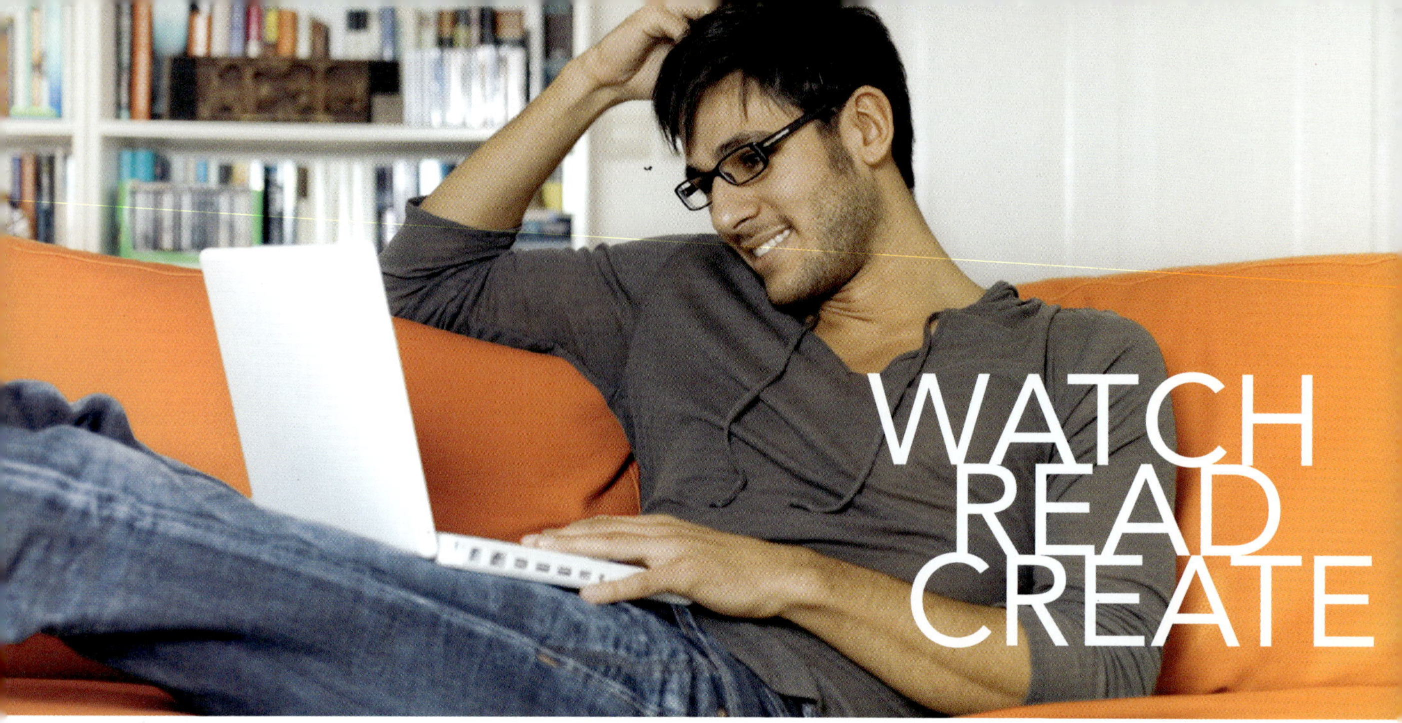

WATCH
READ
CREATE

Meet Creative Edge.

A new resource of unlimited books, videos and tutorials for creatives from the world's leading experts.

Creative Edge is your one stop for inspiration, answers to technical questions and ways to stay at the top of your game so you can focus on what you do best—being creative.

All for only $24.99 per month for access—any day any time you need it.

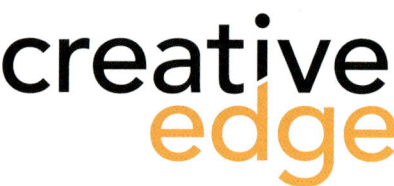

peachpit.com/creativeedge